CENTRAL TEXAS COLLEGE EDITION

COMPUTER AND INFORMATION SECURITY

Taken from:

Security: Computer Security Fundamentals
by Chuck Easttom

Security: Information Security Principles and Practices
by Mark Merkow and Jim Breithaupt

CENTRAL TEXAS COLLEGE

Taken from:

Security: Computer Security Fundamentals
by Chuck Easttom
Copyright © 2006 by Pearson Education, Inc.
Published by Prentice Hall
Upper Saddle River, New Jersey 07458

Security: Information Security Principles and Practices
by Mark Merkow and Jim Breithaupt
Copyright © 2006 by Pearson Education, Inc.
Published by Prentice Hall

Printed in the United States of America

6 7 8 9 V036 12 11 10

ISBN 0-536-21304-6

2006200104

AO

Please visit our web site at *www.pearsoncustom.com*

PEARSON CUSTOM PUBLISHING
75 Arlington Street, Suite 300, Boston, MA 02116
A Pearson Education Company

THE PATHWAY TO SUCCESS IN YOUR COLLEGE COURSES

Your journey through college can be winding, filled with detours and potholes, or it can be relatively straight and smooth. The information below will help you have a pleasant experience along the way.

Time Management

I am definitely going to take a course on time management . . . just as soon as I can work it into my schedule.
—*Louis E. Boone*

The time you spend preparing to study relates directly to a successful outcome. But time, or lack thereof, is a common complaint. How often do you comment that you don't have enough time to accomplish everything you wish to do?

How Do You Spend Your Time?

The first step in time management is to see how you currently spend your time. Have you ever taken the time to add up all of the hours you spend on your regular activities? Take a moment to write down everything you do during a seven-day period. These questions will help you consider all of the activities you do.

- You may spend 40 hours a week on your job, but what about commute time?

- You have to fuel your body. How many hours a week do you spend eating?

- Good grooming is essential. How many hours a week do you spend bathing and dressing?

- How much time do you give to your friends and family?

Remember, there are only 168 hours in a week. Is there any time left to sleep?

How Can I Make More Time?

You can't add hours to the day or days to the week, but if you learn to plan your time wisely, you should be able to make better use of the time you have. As an added bonus, you should feel less stress. Scheduling your time is a step in the right direction.

Develop schedules:

Long term

- Include fixed commitments only

- Include weekly obligations—job, classes, church, meetings, etc.

- Plan enough time for study—as a minimum, use two hours for every one hour in the classroom.

- Plan for weekly reviews—at least one hour each week for each class.

Intermediate

- One per week

- List major events and amount of work to be accomplished in each subject.

- Try to study at the same time every day.

- Make use of free hours between classes.

- Include non-study activities.

Short term

- Daily

- Use small note card you can carry with you.

- Write specifically what you need to accomplish that day.

- Mark out each item as it is completed.

Study Environment

Where you study and how you study is as important as how often you study.

- Identify a quiet place with a desk or table, a chair, and good lighting.

- Your bed might be inviting, but remember your goal is to stay awake and concentrate.

- Although music or some type of background noise might be ok, avoid the TV.

- It's too easy to get engrossed in a show rather than your course work.

- Watching CSI can be interesting, but it probably won't help you with your Introduction to Criminal Justice final exam.

- Make sure you have everything you need: your textbooks, notes, paper and pencil, and a clock.

- Why a clock? To help you manage your time.

- And, don't forget to take regular breaks.

Learning Styles

- If you are assembling a toy or using a new computer program, do you put instructions aside and refer to them only when you run into trouble?

- Do you have to see a name or address in writing in order to remember it?

- Do you enjoy audio books, or do you find your mind wandering as you listen?

Your answers to these questions relate to your preferred learning style, and like clothing, one learning style doesn't fit all. If you have access to the Internet, you can take a learning style inventory at *http://www.vark-learn.com/english/index.asp* and then view helpsheets at *http://www.vark-learn.com/english/page.asp?p=helpsheets* related to your preferred learning style.

Visual Learners

- learn through seeing

- need to see the teacher's body language and facial expression to fully understand the content of a lesson.

- tend to prefer sitting at the front of the classroom to avoid visual obstructions (e.g. people's heads).

- may think in pictures and learn best from visual displays including: diagrams, illustrated text books, overhead transparencies, videos, flip charts and hand-outs.

- During a lecture or classroom discussion, visual learners often prefer to take detailed notes to absorb the information.

If you are a visual learner, here are some suggestions just for you:

- use visual materials such as pictures, charts, maps, graphs, etc.

- have a clear view of your teachers when they are speaking so you can see their body language and facial expression

- use color to highlight important points in text

- take notes or ask your teacher to provide handouts

- illustrate your ideas as a picture or brainstorming bubble before writing them down

- write a story and illustrate it

- use multi-media (e.g. computers, videos, and filmstrips)

- study in a quiet place away from verbal disturbances

- read illustrated books

- visualize information as a picture to aid memorization

Aural Learners

- learn through listening

- learn best through verbal lectures, discussions, talking things through and listening to what others have to say.

- interpret the underlying meanings of speech through listening to tone of voice, pitch, speed and other nuances. Written information may have little meaning until it is heard.

- often benefit from reading text aloud and using a tape recorder.

If you are an aural learner, here are some suggestions just for you:

- participate in class discussions/debates
- make speeches and presentations
- use a tape recorder during lectures instead of taking notes
- read text out aloud
- create musical jingles to aid memorization
- create mnemonics to aid memorization
- discuss your ideas verbally
- dictate to someone while they write down your thoughts
- use verbal analogies, and story telling to demonstrate your point

Read/Write Learners

- learn through reading and writing
- learn best by reading and re-reading the textbook and their notes, writing and rewriting their notes, and in general, organizing items into lists.

Kinesthetic Learners

- learn through moving, doing, and touching
- learn best through a hands-on approach, actively exploring the physical world around them.
- may find it hard to sit still for long periods and may become distracted by their need for activity and exploration.

If you are a tactile/kinesthetic learner, here are some suggestions just for you:

- take frequent study breaks
- move around to learn new things (e.g. read while on an exercise bike, mold a piece of clay to learn a new concept)
- work at a standing position
- chew gum while studying
- use bright colors to highlight reading material
- dress up your work space with posters
- if you wish, listen to music while you study
- skim through reading material to get a rough idea what it is about before settling down to read it in detail.

Multimodal Learners

- don't have a single preferred learning style.
- learn best through combinations.

If you have multiple preferences, you are in the majority as somewhere between fifty and seventy percent of any population seems to fit into that group.

Reading Skills and Strategies

Good reading skills are essential to your success in your college-level classes. Here are a couple of reasons why:

- In high school, you may have been able to get good grades without reading much of the text. Now that you're in college, professors will expect you to read the textbook and they may test you on information not discussed in class but covered in the reading. In fact, many professors test on assigned readings as a check to make sure students are using their texts.

- The average freshman is assigned over 250 pages of reading each week, so clearly you're going to need to keep up with your reading assignments. If you do not read during week one, that means that you will need to read 500 pages the next week—just to stay caught up! If you choose not to read during the second week either . . . well, you can see how the work can just snowball.

Improving Your Reading Skills and Applying Reading Strategies

A good reader:

- seizes the main ideas.
- thinks about what the author is saying
- is active, not passive.
- concentrates on what is being read.
- remembers as much as possible.
- applies what is being read to personal experience.

Go to *http://www.how-to-study.com/Improving%20Reading%20Skills.htm* for more on reading skills.

SQ3R is one recommended method for improving your reading comprehension. The letters in the name stand for these five steps:

<u>S</u>urvey: Before you read, scan the titles, headings, pictures, and summaries. Consider using the heading and subheadings as an outline for notes as you read.

<u>Q</u>uestion: Ask yourself questions based on Step 1 and look for answers as you complete Step 3. For example, if a subheading is entitled "Basic Concepts of Reading," change it to read, "What are the Basic Concepts of Reading?"

<u>R</u>ead: Read and take notes.

<u>R</u>ecall: Without referring to the book or your notes, think about what you have read. See if your questions were answered. Could you explain the content to someone else? Try putting major concepts in your own words.

<u>R</u>eview: Look at your questions, answers, notes and book to see how well you did recall. Observe carefully the points stated incorrectly or omitted. Fix carefully in mind the logical sequence of the entire idea, concepts, or problem. Finish up with a mental picture of the WHOLE.

Another method is **PQR3,** which stands for

<u>P</u>review: Preview what you are going to read.

<u>Q</u>uestion: Question what you are going to learn after the preview.

<u>R</u>ead: Read the assignment.

<u>R</u>ecite: Stop every once in a while, look up from the book, and put in your own words what you have just read.

<u>R</u>eview: After you have finished, review the main points.

(Sounds similar to SQ3R, doesn't it?) Go to *http://www.how-to-study.com/pqr.htm* to learn more about this method.

There is even a related study method known as **M.U.R.D.E.R.**

<u>M</u>ood: Set a positive mood for yourself to study in.

<u>U</u>nderstand: Mark any information you don't understand in a particular unit and keep a focus on one unit or a manageable group of exercise.

<u>R</u>ecall: After studying the unit, stop and put what you have learned into your own words.

<u>D</u>igest: Go back to what you did not understand and reconsider the information. Contact external expert sources (e.g., other books or an instructor) if you still cannot understand it.

<u>E</u>xpand: ask three kinds of questions concerning the studied material:

- If I could speak to the author, what questions would I ask or what criticism would I offer?

- How could I apply this material to what I am interested in?

- How could I make this information interesting and understandable to other students?

<u>R</u>eview: Go over the material you've covered. Review what strategies helped you understand and/or retain information in the past and apply these to your current studies.

Check this system out at *http://www.studygs.net/murder.htm.*

Note Taking

Why take notes?

- It triggers basic lecturing processes and helps you to remember information.

- It helps you to concentrate in class.

- It helps you prepare for tests.   .

- Your notes are often a source of valuable clues for what information the instructor thinks most important (i.e., what will show up on the next test).

- Your notes often contain information that cannot be found elsewhere (i.e., in your textbook).

Evaluate your present note-taking system. Ask yourself:

- Did I use complete phrases or sentences that mean something to me later?

- Did I use any form at all?

- Are my notes clear or confusing?

- Did I capture main points and all subpoints?

- Did I streamline using abbreviations and shortcuts?

If you answered "no" to any of these questions, you may need to develop some new note-taking skills!

Guidelines for Taking Notes

- Concentrate on the lecture or on the reading material.

- Take notes consistently.

- Take notes selectively.

    - Do NOT try to write down every word.

    - Remember that the average lecturer speaks approximately 125-140 words per minute, and the average note-taker writes at a rate of about 25 words per minute.

- Translate ideas into your own words.

- Organize notes into some sort of logical form.

- Be brief. Write down only the major points and important information.

- Write legibly. Notes are useless if you cannot read them later!

- Don't be concerned with spelling and grammar.

There are many reasons for taking lecture notes.

- Making yourself take notes forces you to listen carefully and test your understanding of the material.

- When you are reviewing, notes provide a gauge to what is important in the text.

- Personal notes are usually easier to remember than the text.

- The writing down of important points helps you to remember then even before you have studied the material formally.

Instructors usually give clues to what is important to take down. Some of the more common clues are:

- Material written on the blackboard.

- Repetition

- Emphasis

  - Emphasis can be judged by tone of voice and gesture.

  - Emphasis can be judged by the amount of time the instructor spends on points and the number of examples he or she uses.

- Word signals (e.g. "There are **two points of view** on . . . " "The **third** reason is . . . " " In conclusion . . . ")

- Summaries given at the end of class.

- Reviews given at the beginning of class.

Each student should develop his or her own method of taking notes, but most students find the following suggestions helpful:

- Make your notes brief.

  - Never use a sentence where you can use a phrase. Never use a phrase where you can use a word.

  - Use abbreviations and symbols, but be consistent.

- Put most notes in your own words. However, the following should be noted exactly:

  - Formulas

  - Definitions

  - Specific facts

- Use outline form and/or a numbering system. Indention helps you distinguish major from minor points.

- Date your notes. Perhaps number the pages.

- If you miss a statement, write key words, skip a few spaces, and get the information later.

- Don't try to use every space on the page. Leave room for coordinating your notes with the text after the lecture. (You may want to list key terms in the margin or make a summary of the contents of the page.)

Here are some hints ("Do not's") regarding taking notes on classroom lectures that can save time for almost any student.

Do not plan to rewrite or type your notes later. To do so is to use a double amount of time; once to take the original notes a second to rewrite them. The advice is simple: DO IT RIGHT THE FIRST TIME!

Do not take notes in shorthand. Though shorthand is a valuable tool for a secretary, it is almost worthless for a student doing academic work. Here's why. Notes in shorthand cannot be studied in that form. They must first be transcribed. The act of transcribing notes takes an inordinate amount of time and energy but does not significantly contribute to their mastery. It is far better to have taken the notes originally in regular writing and then spend the time after that in direct study and **recitation** of the notes.

Do not record the lesson on a cassette tape or any other tape. The lecture on tape precludes flexibility. This statement can be better understood when seen in the light of a person who has taken his/her notes in regular writing. Immediately after taking the notes this person can study them in five minutes before the next class as s/he walks toward the next building, as s/he drinks his/her coffee, or whatever. Furthermore, this student, in looking over his/her notes, may decide that the notes contain only four worthwhile ideas which s/he can highlight, relegating the rest of the lecture to obscurity. Whereas the lecture on tape has to be listened to in its entirety including the worthwhile points as well as the "garbage," handwritten notes may be studied selectively. A student who takes the easy way out—recording the lecture on tape as he or she sits back doing nothing—will box him or herself into inflexibility.

Learning to make notes effectively will help you to improve your study and work habits and to remember important information. Often, students are deceived into thinking that because they **understand** everything that is said in class they will therefore remember it. This is dead wrong! Write it down.

As you make notes, you will develop skill in selecting important material and in discarding unimportant material. The secret to developing this skill is practice. Check your results constantly. Strive to improve. Notes enable you to retain important facts and data and to develop an accurate means of arranging necessary information.

Hints on Note Making

- Don't write down everything that you read or hear.

    - Be alert and attentive to the main points.

    - Concentrate on the "meat" of the subject and forget the trimmings.

- Notes should consist of key words or very short sentences. If a speaker gets sidetracked it is often possible to go back and add further information.

- Take accurate notes.

    - You should usually use your own words, but try not to change the meaning.

    - If you quote **directly** from an author, quote **correctly.**

- Think a minute about your material before you start making notes.

    - Don't take notes just to be taking notes!

    - Take notes that will be of real value to you when you look over them at a later date.

- Have a uniform system of punctuation and abbreviation that will make sense to you.

    - Use a skeleton outline and show importance by indenting.

    - Leave lots of white space for later additions.

- Omit descriptions and full explanations.

  - Keep your notes short and to the point.

  - Condense your material so you can grasp it rapidly.

- Don't worry about missing a point.

- Don't keep notes on oddly shaped pieces of paper.

  - Keep notes in order and in one place.

- Shortly after making your notes, go back and rework (not redo) your notes by adding extra points and spelling out unclear items.

  - Remember, we forget rapidly. Budget time for this vital step just as you do for the class itself.

- Review your notes regularly. This is the only way to achieve lasting memory.

These are only a few of the many methods for taking notes.

- the Cornell Method

- the Outline Method

- the Mapping Method (or Mindmapping)

- the Charting Method

- the Sentence Method

For details on these methods, go to h*ttp://www.sas.calpoly.edu/asc/ssl/notetaking .systems.html.* Also check out this resource about note taking: *http://www.how-to-study.com/Taking%20Notes%20in%20Class.htm*

Memory Techniques

We hope that the information on preparing to study has been helpful, but do you feel that your real problem is remembering? Don't worry. There are ways to help you build your memory skills too.

Acronym

- An *acronym* is defined as "a word formed from the initial letters of a name," such as PCS for permanent change of station or SOC for Servicemembers Opportunity Colleges, "or by combining initial letters or parts of a series of words," as radar for radio detecting and ranging.

- Can you think of other acronyms?

Mnemonic

- A *mnemonic* is defined as "a device, such as a formula or rhyme, used as an aid in remembering."

Examples

As a child, you might have determined the number of days in a given month

- by reciting the rhyme "Thirty days hath September, April, June, and November . . . ." or

- by using your knuckles ("peaks" have 31 days and "valleys" have 30, except February, of course).

If you have studied music, you might have used these techniques for remembering the names of the notes:

- FACE represents the names of the notes in the spaces on the staff.

- The first letters of the words in sentence "Every good boy does fine" represent the names of the notes on the lines on the staff.

A mnemonic used to recall the steps for simplifying algebraic expressions is "Please excuse my dear Aunt Sally."

- Perform operations within the innermost parentheses and work outward.

- Evaluate all exponential expressions.

- Perform multiplications and divisions as they occur, working from left to right.

- Perform additions and subtractions as they occur, working from left to right.

Use the sentence "My Very Educated Mother Just Served Us Nine Pizzas" to recall the order of the planets from the sun

- Mercury

- Venus

- Earth

- Mars

- Jupiter

- Neptune

- Pluto

Big Brown Rabbits Often Yield Great Big Vocal Groans When Gingerly Slapped for the color codes for resistors

- Black

- Brown

- Red

- Orange

- Yellow

- Green

- Blue

- Violet

- Gray

- White

- Gold

- Silver

Preparing For and Taking Tests

If you have practiced the strategies we have outlined in this orientation, you should be reviewing on a regular basis as you study rather than waiting to cram right before a test.

- Try to anticipate what is important and will be on the test, and use any review materials that are available, such as practice tests or review sheets.

- This doesn't mean that you don't need to study right before a test, but you shouldn't have to stay up all night to prepare for it, and you should feel more confident when you take the test.

Do You Suffer From Test Anxiety?

- Do you do great on homework assignments, but you dread test days?

- Do you forget everything you know when you sit down to take a test?

- Does it seem like what you studied has nothing to do with the test you are taking?

Once you are sitting in the hot spot with your pencil in hand, use the DETER strategy for taking tests as described at *http://www.how-to-study.com/A%20Strategy%20for%20Taking%20Tests.htm.*

Directions: Read and understand the test directions.

Examine: Examine the entire test to see what is required.

Time: Determine how much time to allow for each item.

Easiest: Answer the easiest items first.

Review: Allow time to review the test to check your answers for accuracy and completeness.

Again, practice makes perfect. There are several web sites for taking practice tests. Here are a few:

- *http://www.actstudent.org/testprep/index.html*

- *http://4tests.com/*

- *http://www.collegeboard.com/*

- *http://www.ets.org/*

Computer Basics

For many classes, you need to know the basics about using a computer and possibly even surfing the Internet in order to complete certain assignments. If you are taking a distance learning class, you MUST have some basic knowledge of computers and the Internet.

You must be able to

- prepare, save, and retrieve files

- send and receive emails with attachments

- deposit files in an electronic drop box

- locate and navigate web sites

- download software and plug ins

- participate in discussion boards.

A good resource for learning about these items is *http://www.learnthenet.com/english/index.html*.

- Once you have reached this site, note the "How To" list at the left side of the screen.

- If you are a novice, you might want to start with "How to Use this Site."

- Otherwise, start with "Master the Basics" and then work your way down the list.

You will find information ranging from making the connection to the Internet to building your own web site.

- Click on each underlined word or title to access the information.

- This information is also available as the "Animated Internet."

Jan's Illustrated Computer Literacy 101 at *http://www.jegsworks.com/Lessons/index.html* includes lessons on the topics listed on the next screens, and the approach is very detailed yet easy to understand. Even if you have never touched a mouse before, you should be able to follow along.

Do you want to learn about specific items; i.e., WindowsXP or MSWord2003?

- These are Microsoft products.

- You can go to *http://www.microsoft.com/* and find training on just about every product produced by Microsoft—even older versions.

The information above is just a teaser. We have included only a few websites because websites come and go. To learn more, check out the Internet and use a search engine, such as GOOGLE (*www.google.com*), to find sites on the topics we have referenced.

Table of Contents

Security Series Walk-Through

The Prentice Hall Security Series prepares students for careers in IT security by providing practical advice and hands-on training from industry experts. All of the books in this series are filled with real-world examples to help readers apply what they learn to the workplace. This walk-through highlights the key elements in this book created to help students along the way.

Chapter Objectives. These short-term, attainable goals outline what will be covered in the chapter text.

Chapter Objectives

After reading this chapter and completing the exercises, you will be able to do the following:

- Evaluate an organization's security policy.
- Create a basic security policy.
- Update a target system's patches.
- Shut down unnecessary ports.
- Scan a system for vulnerabilities.
- Activate port filtering in Windows 2000 or Windows XP.
- Use a port scanner.

Chapter Introduction. Each chapter begins with an explanation of why these topics are important and how the chapter fits into the overall organization of the book.

Introduction

As you learn more about computer security you will learn new techniques for securing a particular system. However it is critical to be able to assess a system's security. It is also chapter discusses the essential steps in assessing a system for vulnerabilities. It is also important to assess a system's security level prior to implementing any security measures. Information about the current state of affairs will help you appropriately address any vulnerabilities.

IN PRACTICE: Using NetCop

Let us begin with NetCop, since it is one of the easiest to use port scanners available. IT can be obtained from many sites. You can download NetCop at http://www.cotse.com/pscan.htm.

When you download NetCop you get a simple self-extracting executable that will install the program on your machine and will even put a shortcut in your program menu. When you launch NetCop, it has a very simple and intuitive screen.

You can type in a single IP address, or a range of IP addresses. That makes this tool particularly useful for network administrators that wish to check for open ports on their entire network. Four our purposes we will begin by scanning a single IP address, our own machine. You can either type your machines actual IP address, or simply the loop back address (127.0.0.1). When you type in a single IP address and click on scan now, you can see it checking each and every port. This is very methodical but also a bit slow.

You can, of course, stop the scan at any time you desire. These results are from a machine the author used specifically for this book. You would, of course, get different results on different machines.

You can see that NetCop gives you useful information about open ports. Before you choose to close any port, you should make sure that the port is not one that you actually need for system operations. The following websites list all well-known ports.

In Practice. Takes concepts from the book and shows how they are applied in the workplace.

FYI. Additional information on topics that go beyond the scope of the book.

FYI: The Microsoft Patch

Go to http://www.microsoft.com and on the left hand side of the website you will find a link under the sub heading Resources, entitled Windows Update. If you select that option and follow the very clear instructions you will be able to correct any and all Windows patch issues on a target machine.

7

twork is to probe the network. This means using for vulnerabilities. These tools are often the same tempting to breach your security, so it is critical n this section we will use three separate analysis other tools freely available on the Internet, and ver these three are the most commonly used. We r, NetBrute, and NetCop. Also this section will ions in this book. We will conduct the exercise d of the chapter. The reason for this is simply that tical aspects of applying these tools Additional f the chapter.

Caution

Security Audit

When conducting a security audit, it's critical that you document the specific steps taken during the audit, any flaws found, and what corrective actions where taken.

Caution. Critical, not to be forgotten information that is directly relevant to the surrounding text.

Test Your Skills

Each chapter ends with exercises designed to reinforce the chapter objectives.
Four types of evaluation follow each chapter.

Multiple Choice Questions. Test the
reader's understanding of the text.

Exercises. Brief, guided projects
designed around individual concepts
found in the chapter.

MULTIPLE CHOICE QUESTIONS

1. How does a JavaScript interpreter identify that a script is being used inside a
   web page?
   A. `<JavaScript>` tag
   B. `<SCRIPT>` tag
   C. `<JAVASCRIPT>` tag
   D. `<Script>` tag

2. Which of the following is NOT a valid language attribute for a web page script?
   A. JavaScript
   B. JavaScript1.2
   C. JavaScript1.3
   D. JavaScript1.4

3. Are JavaScripts and HTML tags case-sensitive?
   A. Both are case sensitive
   B. Both are case insensitive
   C. JavaScripts only are case sensitive
   D. HTML tags only are case sensitive

EXERCISES

Exercise 4.1: Patching the System

1. Locate a system running Windows 2000 or later. Your own personal computer
   would be the preferred system. You may find that public computer labs not

Projects. Longer, guided projects that
combine lessons from the chapter.

Case Study. A real-world scenario to
resolve using lessons learned in the chapter.

PROJECTS

Project 4.1: Personal Policy Password System

1. Analyze or develop a personal policy password system for your PC and online
   accounts.

   ```
   "<P>Welcome to Internet Banking</P>"
   "<P>Click NEXT to Continue...</P>"
   ```

2. Determine if your passwords are secure using the four basic password rules
   presented in this chapter. W

3. Write down if your passwords were secure and the steps that you will take to
   make them secure.

Case Study

Now that you have learned how to insert simple JavaScripts into web
pages, with calls to document.write Has the site used any of the features
you have learned about in this Lesson?

1. Import the appropriate Namespaces

2. Execute the Query/Instruction

   Using a web design package, or just notepad and your web browser,
   create a front page for an Internet banking that uses document.write to display text within the `<BODY>` section of the page. A link should be created
   to the login page, which will be examined in the next chapter.

   • The Computer Security Institute: http://www.gocsi.com/
   • The Computer Security Clearing House http://csrc.nist.gov/
   • The Computer Emergency Response Team http://www.cert.org/

This icon appears in the margin wherever
additional information or links to downloads
can be found at the series companion Web
site, **www.prenhall.com/security**

Part 1

Part 1 Preface

This section is designed as a gateway book: a general introduction to the field of information security. It explains how hackers target a system, obtain information, and use it to crack systems. Students will learn how to safeguard their systems, using passwords and network-scanning utilities. While it does explain security breaches in some detail, this book is not a cookbook for hackers. Explanations, definitions, and examples are designed to reinforce the importance of securing data, computers, and networks. They are always followed by the steps that should be taken to protect valuable information.

Finally, this book looks at security primarily from a Windows perspective. While the concepts covered apply to virtually any system, Windows was chosen because it is so widely used and has been a frequent target of attacks.

Audience

This book is a primer for students who want a solid introduction to the field. Although this book is introductory, the content assumes the readers are competent computer users -- meaning they have used a computer at work or at home, are comfortable with e-mail and Web browsers, and know what terms such as RAM and USB mean. Readers should have a basic understanding of PCs, but need not have taken formal computer courses.

People outside the typical computer science and computer information systems departments may also find this book useful, particularly law enforcement officers, criminal justice majors, and business majors.

Overview of the Book

Computer Security Fundamentals opens with an overview of cyber crime and security. Chapter 1, Introduction to Cyber Crime and Security, details just how serious cyber crime is and why learning how to protect systems from attack is so important. The chapter introduces some basics of computer security—types of threats, common attacks, terminology, and paradigms—and frames security efforts in a legal context. Finally, Chapter 1 describes some readily available security resources and directs students to explore these tools in the end of lesson exercises and projects.

Chapter 2, Networks and the Internet, reveals one of the most important elements of successful network security: a strong working knowledge of network operations. Some readers with more computer experience will be well-versed in the material presented here and may just need to skim the chapter as a refresher. However, readers with less experience will learn about the basic model of a network and how it works. Hands-on IPConfig, tracert, and ping exercises at the end of the chapter reinforce how understanding a network and its operations can help protect it.

Chapter 3, Assessing a System, highlights some of the tools hackers use to assess the vulnerability of a target system—and explains how network security managers can use these same tools to assess the safety of their systems so they never become targets. Several In Practice features walk students through some of the most popular port scanners and end-of-chapter exercises let students explore these tools further.

Chapters 4 and 5 delve into the specific types of attacks that hackers may launch. Chapter 4, Denial of Service Attacks, examines SYN flood, Smurf and Distributed Denial of Service attacks in particular. This chapter includes some real-world examples of Denial of Service attacks to demonstrate how damaging they can be and describes how best to protect against them. Chapter 5, Malware, describes viruses, Trojan horses, buffer overflow attacks, and spyware. Again, real-world examples are reviewed and specific tools for detecting and eradicating a malware problem are described and demonstrated including Norton and McAfee anti-virus software.

At this point in the book, readers will have been exposed to various threats to systems and some specific measures to prevent, detect, and eradicate these dangers. Chapter 6, Basics of Assessing and Securing a System, and Chapter 7, Encryption, shift away from specific attacks and defenses and take a more comprehensive look at computer security management. In Chapter 6, readers will learn some security fundamentals: probing for vulnerabilities, setting policies, evaluating consultants, securing individual workstations and servers, and safely surfing the Web. Chapter 7 introduces readers to encryption, covering the history of the field and modern cryptography methods. These chapters provide a wide angle lens view of the security management field, giving students enough information to at least 'ask the right questions' and preparing them for more in-depth study of the ideas in future coursework.

Chapters 8, 9 and 10 cover different types of crime perpetrated via the Internet. Chapter 8, Internet Fraud and Cyber Crime, discusses identity theft and cyber stalking, Chapter 9 explains industrial espionage in cyberspace, and Chapter 10 examines cyber terrorism and information warfare. Chapter 11, Cyber Detective, continues the vein of the three previous chapters, looking at how hackers exploit information on the Internet to perpetrate their crimes and contends that understanding these methods of exploitation are key to protecting against cyber crime. In each chapter, real-world examples show how the methods described in the first part of the book have been used to damage people and property, reinforcing the importance of network security.

Chapter 12, Computer Security Hardware and Software, turns to the more technical side of computer security, examining hardware and software, some of which was briefly mentioned in previous chapters. This chapter is intended to give readers a more detailed understanding of virus scanners, firewalls, intrusion detection systems, and anti-spyware. The practical information in this chapter will be particularly useful for students who will be moving forward into a career in computer security.

Finally, several appendices offer additional resources for instructors and students, including a list of links to useful Web sites, sample checklists, a glossary, and a list of references used in writing this book.

Conventions Used in This Book

To help you get the most from the text, we've used a few conventions throughout the book.

IN PRACTICE: About In Practice

These show readers how to take concepts from the book and apply them in the workplace.

FYI: About FYIs

These boxes offer additional information on topics that go beyond the scope of the book.

Caution

About Cautions

Cautions appear in the margins of the text. They flag critical, not-to-be forgotten information that is directly relevant to the surrounding text.

Snippets and blocks of code are boxed and numbered, and can be downloaded from the companion Web site (**www.prenhall.com/security**).

New key terms appear in ***bold italics***.

 This icon appears in the margin wherever more information can be found at the series companion Web site, **www.prenhall.com/security**.

Instructor and Student Resources

Instructor's Resource Center on CD-ROM

The Instructor's Resource Center on CD-ROM (IRC on CD) is distributed to instructors only and is an interactive library of assets and links. It includes:

- ■ Instructor's Manual. Provides instructional tips, an introduction to each chapter, teaching objectives, teaching suggestions, and answers to end-of-chapter questions and problems.

- ■ PowerPoint Slide Presentations. Provides a chapter-by-chapter review of the book content for use in the classroom.

- ■ Test Bank. This TestGen-compatible test bank file can be used with Prentice Hall's TestGen software (available as a free download at **www.prenhall.com/testgen**). TestGen is a test generator that lets you view and easily edit test bank questions, transfer them to tests, and print in a variety of formats suitable to your teaching situation. The program also offers many options for organizing and displaying test banks and tests. A built-in random number and text generator makes it ideal for creating multiple versions of tests that involve calculations and provides more possible test items than test bank questions. Powerful search and sort functions let you easily locate questions and arrange them in the order you prefer.

Companion Web Site

The Companion Web site (**www.prenhall.com/security**) is a Pearson learning tool that provides students and instructors with online support. Here you will find:

- ■ Interactive Study Guide, a Web-based interactive quiz designed to provide students with a convenient online mechanism for self-testing their comprehension of the book material.

- ■ Additional Web projects and resources to put into practice the concepts taught in each chapter.

- ■ Information on certification (from Appendix A), links to useful Web resources (from Appendix B) and sample policy and checklists (from Appendix C).

Chapter 1

Introduction to Cyber Crime and Security

Chapter Objectives

After reading this chapter and completing the exercises, you will be able to do the following:

- Identify the top threats to a computer network: intrusion, Denial of Service attacks, and malware.
- Assess the likelihood of an attack on your personal computer and network.
- Define key terms such as cracker, sneaker, firewall, and authentication.
- Compare and contrast perimeter and layered approaches to network security.
- Use online resources to secure your network.

Introduction

It's hard to find a facet of modern life that does not involve a computer system on some level. The following are just a few examples that illustrate this point.

- Financial transactions—including online banking, ATMs, and debit cards— are a pervasive part of modern commerce.
- Some retailers are using computerized automatic checkout.
- You may be taking this class online, or perhaps you registered for it online. You may have purchased this book online.
- There is even widespread discussion of eventually voting online.

Because so much of our business is transacted online, a great deal of personal information is stored in computers. Medical records, tax records, school records, and more are all stored in computer databases. Whether this level of technology in our daily lives is to our advantage or not is a question that is beyond the scope of this book. The fact is that our lives are inextricably intertwined with computer systems. This leads to several important questions:

- How is information safeguarded?
- What are the vulnerabilities to these systems?
- What steps are taken to ensure that these systems and data are safe?

FYI: Online Banking

A recent study found that 28% of U.S. consumers access their primary banking institution by phone, the Internet, or at branches at least three times per week (Online Banking Report). These consumers use online banking to view statements and checks, pay bills, check balances, and transfer funds.

Recent news stories do not offer encouraging answers to these questions. The media often gives a great deal of attention to dramatic virus attacks, hackers, and other interesting Internet phenomena. News of virus attacks, such as MyDoom, often become lead stories on national networks. Even the most technically naïve person cannot go more than a few weeks without hearing of some new virus or hacking incident, such as the dramatic attack in February 2003 when a hacker was able to get 5.6 million credit card numbers (CNN/Technology, 2003). Part of this article can be seen in Figure 1.1.

In spite of daily horror stories, however, many people (including some law enforcement professionals and trained computer professionals) lack an adequate understanding of the reality of these threats. Attention is often focused on the most dramatic computer security breaches (intrusions), which

FYI: Online Shopping

The U.S. Department of Commerce's reports show a rapid increase in online retail sales in just a few years. Since the year 2000, when sales were approximately $27.3 million, online sales increased by nearly 325% to approximately $88.2 million in 2004. At the time of this writing, sales for 2005 were projected to be approximately $109.4 million.

FIGURE 1.1 CNN report of a cyber attack.

do not necessarily give an accurate picture of the most plausible threat scenarios. Clearly, many people are aware of the attacks that can be executed against a target system. Unfortunately, they are often not familiar with the attack's mechanism, its actual danger level, or how to prevent it.

This chapter outlines current dangers, describes the most common types of attacks on your personal computer and network, teaches you how to speak the lingo of both hackers and security professionals, and outlines the broad strokes of what is necessary to secure your computer and your network. All of these topics are explored more fully in subsequent chapters.

How Seriously Should You Take Threats to Network Security?

The first step in understanding computer and network security is to formulate a realistic assessment of the threats to those systems. The general population tends to have two extreme attitudes about computer security. The first group assumes there is no real threat. Subscribers to this theory believe that there is little real danger to computer systems and that much of the negative news is simply unwarranted panic. They often think that taking only minimal security precautions should ensure the safety of their systems. The prevailing sentiment of these individuals is, "If our computer/organization has not been attacked so far, we must be secure." They tend to have a *reactive* approach to security. They will wait until after an incident occurs to address security issues—the proverbial "closing the barn door after the horse has already gotten out." If you are fortunate, the incident will have only minor impact on you or your organization and will serve as a much needed wakeup call. If you are unfortunate, then your organization may face serious and possible catastrophic consequences. For example there are organizations that did not have an effective network security system in place when the MyDoom virus attacked their systems. One of those companies estimated that lost productivity through downtime of the systems cost over $100,000.

The second extreme attitude toward the dangers to computer and network security is one that tends to overestimate the dangers. The people in this group are prone to assume that talented hackers exist in great numbers and all are imminent threats to your system. They may believe that any teenager with a laptop can traverse highly secure systems at will. This viewpoint has, unfortunately, been fostered by a number of movies that depict computer hacking in a somewhat glamorous light. Such a world view makes excellent movie plots, but it is simply unrealistic. The reality is that many people who call themselves hackers are less knowledgeable than they think. They have ascertained a few buzzwords from the Internet and are convinced of their own digital supremacy, but they are not able to affect any real compromises to even a moderately secure system.

Both extremes of attitudes regarding the dangers to computer systems are inaccurate. It is certainly true that there are people who have both the comprehension of computer systems and the skills to compromise the security of many, if not most, systems. However, it is also true that many who call themselves hackers are not as skilled as they claim. As with any field of human endeavor, the majority of hackers are, by definition, mediocre. Often, the people who most loudly declare their cyber prowess are usually those with the least actual skill. The truly talented hacker is no more common than the truly talented concert pianist. Consider how many people take piano lessons at some point in their lives; then consider how many of those ever truly become virtuosos. The same is true of computer hackers. Keep in mind that even those who do possess the requisite skill also need the motivation to expend the time and effort to compromise your system. This does not mean that unskilled hackers are no threat at all, but rather they are much less of a threat than administrators, and the hackers themselves, might think. Additionally, the greatest threat to any system is not hackers, but rather virus attacks and Denial of Service attacks. (These are discussed in more detail below.)

A more balanced view and, therefore, a better way to assess the threat level to your system is to weigh the attractiveness of your system to potential intruders against the security measures in place. One method of making this assessment is discussed in the following In Practice. More details on assessing system security will be given in Chapter 6.

IN PRACTICE: Assessing Your Own System

Unfortunately, assessing your system is not a science. There is no mathematical formula to apply. Therefore, I have developed a crude, but effective method you might use.

1. Start by giving a numerical weight to two areas of your system: profile and value. In other words, on a scale of 1 to 10, determine how high a profile your system might have for potential hackers. A little-known finance company might receive a 3, whereas a well-known government site or site of a popular company might receive a 9. Then give a similar numerical number to the value of the information your system holds. A system containing credit card information might receive a 7, sensitive nuclear research might receive a 10, and a home business Web site with no personal or credit card data might receive a 2.

2. Add these two numbers together to obtain a value between 2 and 20.

3. Now, rate your current security on a scale of 1 to 10. If you have a dedicated security staff, multiple firewalls, intrusion detection systems, antivirus software, anti-spyware, good security polices, and so on, you might receive an 8. A bare system would receive a 1.

4. Now, subtract the second number from the first. Your final number should be between −8 (indicating a highly secure system that has no valuable data and a low profile) to 18 (indicating a system with no security, but sensitive national security information and a high profile). The lower the number, the better position your system is in.

This method is clearly subjective, but it provides a working method for you to begin to assess your systems' security levels. More details on assessing a system can be found in Chapter 6.

Identifying Types of Threats

Most attacks can be categorized as one of three broad classes:

- **Malware.** Malware is a generic term for software that has a malicious purpose. It includes virus attacks, Trojan horses, and spyware. This is the most prevalent danger to your system.

- **Intrusions.** This group of attacks includes any attempt to gain unauthorized access to your system.

- **Denial of Service (DoS) attacks.** These are designed to prevent legitimate access to your system.

This section offers a broad description of each type of attack. Later chapters will involve greater detail with each specific attack, how it is accomplished, and how to avoid it.

Malware

Malware is a generic term for software that has a malicious purpose. This section discusses three types of malware: viruses, Trojan horses, and spyware. Trojan horses and viruses are the most widely encountered.

According to Symantec (makers of Norton AntiVirus and other software products), a *virus* is "a small program that replicates and hides itself inside other programs, usually without your knowledge" (Symantec, 2003). This is the definition used throughout this book. A computer virus is similar to a biological virus in that both replicate and spread. The most common method for spreading a virus is using the victim's e-mail account to spread the virus to everyone in their address book. Some viruses do not actually harm the system itself, but *all* of them cause network slowdowns or shutdowns due to the heavy network traffic caused by the virus replication.

The *Trojan horse* receives its name from an ancient tale. In this tale, the city of Troy was besieged for an extended period of time, but the attackers could not gain entrance. Therefore, they constructed a huge wooden horse and left it in front of the gates to Troy one night. The next morning, the residents of Troy saw the horse and assumed it to be a gift, consequently

FYI: The Bagle Virus

The Bagle virus was a mass-mailing virus. Some companies were flooded by this virus to the point that several servers went completely offline. This is just one example of a virus that has no malicious payload but, by its simple volume, crashes systems.

rolling the wooden horse into the city. Unbeknownst to them, several soldiers where hidden inside the horse. That evening, the soldiers left the horse, opened the city gates, and let their fellow attackers into the city. An electronic Trojan horse works in the same manner, appearing to be benign software but secretly downloading a virus or some other type of malware onto your computer from within. How Trojan horses operate in general is discussed in Chapter 9 and the basics of how to secure protection against them are covered in Chapter 4. Specific Trojan horses (specific attacks) are detailed in Chapter 5.

Another category of malware currently on the rise is spyware. *Spyware* is simply software that literally spies on what you do on your computer. Spyware can be as simple as a *cookie*—a text file that your browser creates and stores on your hard drive. Cookies are downloaded on to your machine by Web sites you visit. This text file is then used to recognize you when you return to the same site. That file can enable you to access pages more quickly and save you from having to enter your information multiple times on pages that you visit frequently. However, in order to do this, that file must be read by the Web site; this means that it can also be read by other Web sites. Any data that the file saves can be retrieved by any Web site, so your entire Internet browsing history can be tracked.

Another form of spyware, called a *key logger*, records all of your keystrokes. Some key loggers also take periodic screen shots of your computer. Data is then either stored for later retrieval by the person who installed the key logger or is sent immediately back via e-mail. This action can have a legitimate purpose, such as an employer who wants to track the computer activities of their employees, but it can also be used for illegal/unethical purposes. Spyware, including key loggers, are discussed in depth in Chapter 5, and anti-spyware software is discussed throughout this text.

Compromising System Security

We will now look at attacks that breach your system's security. This activity is commonly referred to as *hacking*, although that is not the term hackers themselves use. We will delve into appropriate terminology shortly; however, it should be noted at this point that *cracking* is the appropriate word for intruding onto a system without permission, usually with malevolent intent. Any attack that is designed to breach your security, either via some operating system flaw or any other means, can be classified as cracking. Simply put, hacking may or may not be for malevolent purposes. Cracking is hacking conducted for such malicious purposes.

Social engineering, which will be discussed in greater detail in Chapter 3, is a technique for breaching a system's security by exploiting human nature rather than technology. Social engineering uses standard con artist techniques to get users to offer up the information needed to gain access to a target system (Lemos, 2000). The way this method works is rather

FYI: Kevin Mitnick, A Social Engineer

Social engineering was the path that the famous hacker, Kevin Mitnick, most often used. Kevin Mitnick wrote a book on this subject titled *The Art of Deception: Controlling the Human Element of Security*. You may find this book to be a good resource for further information on social engineering. Mitnick, who now runs his own security company, is clearly one of the foremost experts on that topic.

simple. The perpetrator obtains preliminary information about a target organization and leverages it to gain additional information from the system's users.

Following is an example of social engineering in action. Armed with the name of a system administrator, you might call someone in the accounting department of a business and claim to be one of the company's technical support personnel. Mentioning the system administrator's name would help validate that claim, allowing you to ask questions in an attempt to ascertain more details about the system's specifications. A savvy intruder might even get the accounting person to say a username and password. As you can see, this method is based on how well the prospective intruder can manipulate people and actually has little to do with computer skills.

The growing popularity of wireless networks gives rise to new kinds of attacks. The most obvious and dangerous activity is *war-driving*. This type of attack is an offshoot of war-dialing. With *war-dialing*, a hacker sets up a computer to call phone numbers in sequence until another computer answers to try to gain entry to its system. War-driving, using much the same concept, is applied to locating vulnerable wireless networks. In this scenario, the hacker simply drives around trying to locate wireless networks (Poulsen, 2001). Many people forget that their wireless network signal often extends as much as 100 feet (thus, past walls). At the 2003 DefCon convention for hackers, there was a war-driving contest in which contestants drove around the city trying to locate as many vulnerable wireless networks as they could (DefCon II, 2003). While we will not discuss the mechanics of war-driving in this text, this kind of activity emphasizes the need for everyone, regardless of the size of their network, to be vigilant in their computer security.

Denial of Service Attacks

In addition to the various forms of malware and cracking attacks, there are attacks that prevent legitimate users from accessing their own systems. One such type of attack is called *Denial of Service (DoS)*. In this type of attack, the attacker does not actually access the system, but rather simply blocks access from legitimate users. One common way to prevent legitimate service is to flood the targeted system with so many false connection requests that the system cannot respond to legitimate requests. DoS is an extremely common attack, second only to malware.

Common Attacks on Your Network

Now that we have examined the three broad classes of attack, it is an appropriate time to ask: What are the most likely attacks, and what are your vulnerabilities? This section covers the basics of what threats are possible and which are most likely to cause you or your organization problems. Chapters 4 and 5 answer these questions in greater detail.

The most likely threat to individuals and large organizations is the computer virus. In the first nine days of September 2003, the F-Secure security information Web site listed 20 new viruses (F-Secure, 2003). This is a fairly common monthly statistic. In any given month, several new virus outbreaks will be documented. New viruses are constantly being created, and old ones are still out there. As of this writing, all the major antivirus software vendors have released protection for the SoBig virus; today alone I received 18 e-mails with that virus as an attachment. Therefore, even when a virus is known and there is protection against it, it can continue to thrive because many people do not update their protection or clean their systems regularly.

Following viruses, the most common attack is unauthorized usage of computer systems. Unauthorized usage includes everything from Denial of Service attacks to outright intrusion of your system. It also includes internal employees misusing system resources. A recent survey by the Computer

FYI: Misusing System Resources

This has become a somewhat controversial topic. What, exactly, constitutes misuse of system resources? This can range from using business software to produce items for personal use to misuse of the Internet. It is important to realize that your work computer, software, and Internet connection are the property of your employer. Every minute spent idly surfing the Web is a minute of lost productivity to the employer and, ultimately, lost revenue. Wasting time at work is, in effect, stealing. This might not be a popular opinion with many employees, but it is one that most employers would heartily agree with.

Security Institute of 223 computer professionals showed over $445 million in losses due to computer security breaches. In 75% of the cases, an Internet connection was the point of attack, while 33% of professionals cited the location as their internal systems. A rather astonishing 78% of those surveyed detected employee abuse of systems/Internet (Computer Security Institute, 2002). This statistic means that, in any organization, one of the chief dangers might be its own employees.

In addition to the negative effects of employees misusing system resources, you need to also consider the possibility of an outright attack by an employee. An "insider" attack can cause considerably more damage than your typical Internet-based attack because the employee has more familiarity with the organization as a whole.

Basic Security Terminology

The security and hacking terms in this section are merely an introduction to computer security terminology, but they are an excellent starting point to help you prepare for learning more about computer security. Additional terms will be introduced throughout the text and listed in the Glossary at the end of this book.

The world of computer security takes its vocabulary from both the professional security community and the hacker community. As we explore these terms, you will see that there is a great deal of overlap. However, most hacker terminology is concerned with the activity (phreaking) or the person performing the activity (sneaker). In contrast, security professionals' terminology describes defensive barrier devices, procedures, and policies. This is quite logical because hacking is an offensive activity centered around attackers and attack methodologies, whereas security is a defensive activity concerning itself with defensive barriers and procedures.

People

There are many titles used for those individuals who set their sites on breaching computer security systems. In this section we describe some of the most common names. These are the terms that we will use throughout this text.

Hackers You probably have heard the term *hacker* used in movies and news broadcasts. Most people use it to describe any person who breaks into a computer system. In the hacking community, however, a hacker is an expert on a particular system or systems who wants to learn more about the system. Hackers feel that looking at a system's flaws is the best way to learn about that system. For example, someone well-versed in the Linux operating system who works to understand that system by learning its weaknesses and flaws would be a hacker.

This process does indeed often mean seeing whether a flaw can be exploited to gain access to a system. This "exploiting" part of the process is where hackers differentiate themselves into three groups:

- *White hat hackers*, upon finding a vulnerability in a system, will report the vulnerability to the vendor of that system. For example, if they discovered some flaw in Red Hat Linuxtm, they would then e-mail the Red Hat company (probably anonymously) and explain exactly what the flaw is and how it was exploited.

- *Black hat hackers* are the people normally depicted in the media. Once they gain access to a system, their goal is to cause some type of harm. They might steal data, erase files, or deface Web sites. Black hat hackers are sometimes referred to as *crackers*.

- *Gray hat hackers* are typically law-abiding citizens, but in some cases will venture into illegal activities. They may do so for a wide variety of reasons. Commonly, gray hat hackers conduct illegal activities for reasons they feel are ethical, such as hacking into a system belonging to a corporation that the hacker feels is engaged in unethical activities. Note that this term is not found in many textbooks, but is very common in the hacking community itself.

Regardless of how hackers view themselves, intruding on any system without permission is illegal. This means that, technically speaking, all hackers, regardless of the color of the metaphorical hat they may wear, are in violation of the law. However, many people feel that white hat hackers actually perform a service by finding flaws and informing vendors before those flaws are exploited by less ethically inclined individuals.

Script Kiddies So what is the term for someone who calls themselves a hacker, but lacks the expertise? The most common term for this sort of person is *script kiddy* (Glossary of Hacker Terminology, 1993). The name comes from the fact that the Internet is full of utilities and scripts that one can download to perform some hacking tasks. Someone who downloads such a tool without really understanding the target system would be considered a script kiddy.

Ethical Hackers: Sneakers When and why would someone give permission to another party to hack his system? The most common answer is in order to assess their systems' vulnerabilities. This employee, commonly called a *sneaker*, legally breaks into a system in order to assess security deficiencies. In 1992, Robert Redford, Dan Aykroyd, and Sydney Poitier starred in a movie about this very subject. There are consultants who perform work of this type, and you can even find firms that specialize in this very activity as more and more companies are soliciting these services to assess their vulnerabilities.

Caution
Using Sneakers

It is amazing how few organizations employ sneakers to test their network defenses. While more employers are beginning to use these services, there are still a great many companies that do not. Perhaps your company uses internal employees or outside consultants to test its systems. Even so, it is my opinion that you also absolutely should have sneakers test your network defenses at least once per year. Although few organizations employ sneakers, it is crucial for your company to test its defenses by using actual hacking techniques.

Anyone hired to assess the vulnerabilities of a system should be both technically proficient and ethical. It is best to run a criminal background check and avoid those people with problem pasts. There are plenty of legitimate security professionals available who know and understand hacker skills, but have never committed security crimes. If you take the argument that hiring convicted hackers means hiring talented people to its logical conclusion, you would surmise that, obviously, the person in question is not as good a hacker as they would like to think because they where caught. Most importantly, giving a person with a criminal background access to your systems is on par with hiring a person with multiple DWI convictions to be your driver. In both cases, you are inviting problems and perhaps assuming significant civil liabilities.

Also, some review of their qualifications is clearly in order. Just as there are people who claim to be highly skilled hackers but are not, there are those who will claim to be skilled sneakers who lack the skills truly needed. You would not want to inadvertently hire a script kiddy who thinks she is a sneaker. Such a person might then pronounce your system to be sound, when in fact it was simply a lack of skills that prevented the script kiddy from successfully breaching your security. Later in this book we discuss the basics of assessing a target system. In that chapter, we also discuss the qualifications you should seek in any consultant you might hire for this purpose.

Security Devices

In addition to knowing the titles used for the people involved in breaching security, it would also be beneficial for you to start with a basic understanding of the security devices involved in stopping these individuals. You are probably familiar with some of these, and most of them will be discussed at much greater length in subsequent chapters.

Firewall The most basic security device is the *firewall*. A firewall is a barrier between a network and the outside world. Sometimes a firewall takes the form of a stand-alone server, sometimes a router, and sometimes software running on a machine. Whatever its physical form, a firewall filters traffic entering and exiting the network. Chapter 12 will discuss firewalls in greater depth.

Proxy Server A *proxy server* is often used with a firewall to hide the internal network's IP (Internet Protocol) address and present a single IP address (its own) to the outside world. (For those readers not familiar with IP addresses, this topic and other network concepts will be discussed thoroughly in Chapter 2.) A proxy server is a server that sits between a client application, such as a Web browser, and a real server. It intercepts all requests to the real server to see whether it can fulfill the requests itself. If not, it forwards the request to the real server. Proxy servers have two main purposes: to improve performance and filter requests (Webopedia, 2004).

Intrusion Detection System (IDS) Firewalls and proxy servers guard the perimeter, but they do not interfere with network traffic. These two safeguards are often augmented by an *Intrusion Detection System (IDS)*. An IDS simply monitors traffic, looking for suspicious activity that might indicate an attempted intrusion. For example, if you detect that some person has been scanning all the ports on your system to find out which ones are open, this might indicate that they are planning an attempt to breach your security. Chapters 3 and 12 discuss this in more detail.

Activities

The last set of terms that you need to be familiar with, before delving deeper into the topic of security, are the names given to the activities involved in either breaching security or preventing a security breach. Like the other terms defined in this introductory chapter, these terms will also be used throughout the text.

Phreaking One type of specialty hacking involves breaking into telephone systems. This sub-specialty of hacking is referred to as *phreaking*. The *New Hacker's Dictionary* actually defines phreaking as "The action of using mischievous and mostly illegal ways in order to not pay for some sort of telecommunications bill, order, transfer, or other service" (Raymond, 2003). Phreaking requires a rather significant knowledge of telecommunications, and many phreakers have some professional experience working for a phone company or other telecommunications business. This type of activity is often dependent upon specific technology required to compromise phone systems more than simply knowing certain techniques. For example, there are certain devices used to compromise phone systems. Phone systems are often dependent on frequencies. (If you have a touchtone phone, you will notice that, as you press the keys, each has a different frequency.) Machines that record and duplicate certain frequencies are often essential to phone phreaking.

Authentication In addition to the security devices discussed above, there are specific security activities. *Authentication* is the most basic security activity. It is merely the process of determining whether the credentials given by a user or another system (such as a username and password) are authorized to access the network resource in question. When you log in with your username and password, the system will attempt to authenticate that username and password. If authenticated, you will be granted access.

Auditing Another crucial safeguard is *auditing*, which is the process of reviewing logs, records, and procedures to determine whether these items meet standards. This activity will be mentioned in many places throughout this book and will be a definite focus in several chapters.

Network Security Paradigms

The approach you take toward security influences all subsequent security decisions and sets the tone for the entire organization's network security infrastructure. Network security paradigms can be classified by either the scope of security measures taken (perimeter, layered) or how proactive the system is.

Perimeter Security

In a *perimeter security approach*, the bulk of security efforts are focused on the perimeter of the network. This focus might include firewalls, proxy servers, password policies (*note:* password policies will be discussed throughout this book, but are given more thorough treatment in Chapter 6), or any technology or procedure to make unauthorized access of the network less likely. Little or no effort is put into securing the systems within the network. In this approach, the perimeter is secured, but the various systems within that perimeter are often vulnerable.

The perimeter approach is clearly flawed. So why do some companies use it? A small organization might use the perimeter approach if they have budget constraints or inexperienced network administrators. This method might be adequate for small organizations that do not store sensitive data, but it rarely works in a larger corporate setting.

Layered Security

A *layered security approach* is one in which not only is the perimeter secured, but individual systems within the network are also secured. All servers, workstations, routers, and hubs within the network are secure. One way to accomplish this is to divide the network into segments and secure each segment as if it were a separate network so that, if perimeter security is compromised, not all internal systems are affected. Layered security is the preferred method whenever possible.

Proactive Versus Reactive

You should also measure your security approach by how proactive and/or reactive it is. This is done by gauging how much of the system's security infrastructure and policies are dedicated to preventive measures as opposed to how much are devoted to simply responding to an attack after it has occurred. A passive security approach takes few or no steps to prevent an attack. A dynamic or proactive defense is one in which steps are taken to prevent attacks before they occur.

One example of a proactive defense is the use of an IDS, which works to detect attempts to circumvent security measures. These systems can tell a system administrator that an attempt to breach security has been made, even if that attempt is not successful. An IDS can also be used to detect various techniques that intruders use to assess a target system, thus alerting a network administrator to the potential for an attempted breach before the attempt is even initiated.

Hybrid Security Methods

In the real world, network security is usually a combination of approaches and not focused completely in one paradigm or another. The two categories also combine. One can have a network that is predominantly passive, but layered, or one that is primarily perimeter, but proactive. It can be helpful to consider approaches to computer security along a Cartesian coordinate system, with the x axis representing the level of passive–active approaches and the y axis depicting the range from perimeter to layered defense. This system is shown in Figure 1.2.

The most desirable hybrid approach is a layered paradigm that is dynamic, which would be located in the upper right-hand quadrant of the figure. In this system, there would be perimeter security as well as layered internal security. Adding intrusion detection would give the system a level of dynamic activity that would make a much more complete security solution.

FIGURE 1.2 A security approach guide.

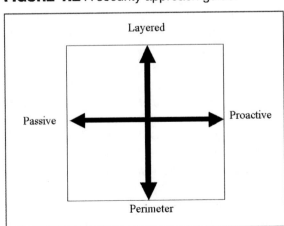

How Do Legal Issues Impact Network Security?

An increasing number of legal issues affect how one approaches computer security. If your organization is a publicly traded company, a government agency, or does business with either, there may be legal constraints regarding your network security. Even if your network is not legally bound to these security guidelines, it is useful to understand the various laws impacting computer security. You may choose to apply them to your own security standards.

One of the oldest pieces of legislation in the United States that affects computer security is the *Computer Security Act of 1987* (100th Congress, 1987). It requires government agencies to identify sensitive systems, conduct computer security training, and develop computer security plans. This law was a vague mandate ordering federal agencies in the United States to establish security measures, but it does not specify any standards.

This legislation established a legal mandate to enact specific standards, paving the way for future guidelines and regulations. It also helped define terms, such as what information is considered "sensitive." This quote is found in the legislation itself.

The term 'sensitive information' means any information, the loss, misuse, or unauthorized access to or modification of which could adversely affect the national interest or the conduct of Federal programs, or the privacy to which individuals are entitled under section 552a of title 5, United States Code (the Privacy Act), but which has not been specifically authorized under criteria established by an Executive order or an Act of Congress to be kept secret in the interest of national defense or foreign policy (100th Congress, 1987).

This definition should be kept in mind, for it is not just social security information or medical history that must be secured. When considering what information needs to be secure, simply ask the question: Would the unauthorized access or modification of this information adversely affect your organization? If the answer is yes, then you must consider that information sensitive and in need of security precautions.

Another more specific federal law that applied to mandated security for government systems is *OMB Circular A-130* (specifically, Appendix III). This document requires that federal agencies establish security programs containing specified elements. It also describes requirements for developing standards for computer systems and for records held by government agencies.

Most states have specific laws regarding computer security, such as legislation like the *Computer Crimes Act of Florida*, the *Computer Crime Act of Alabama,* and the *Computer Crimes Act of Oklahoma*. If you are responsible for network security, you might find yourself part of a criminal investigation. This could be an investigation into a hacking incident or employee misuse of computer resources. A list of computer crime laws

Caution

Privacy Laws

It is also critical to keep in mind that any law that governs privacy (such as the Health Insurance Portability and Accountability Act of 1996, HIPAA) also has a direct impact on computer security. If your system is compromised and, thus, data that is covered under any privacy statute is compromised, you may need to prove that you exercised due diligence in protecting that data. If it can be shown that you did not take proper precautions, you might be found civilly liable.

(organized by state) can be found at **www.alw.nih.gov/Security/FIRST/ papers/legal/statelaw.txt.** This government list is from the Advanced Laboratory Workstation (ALW), National Institutes for Health (NIH), and Center for Information Technology (CIT).

Online Security Resources

As you read this book and when you move out into the professional world, you will have frequent need for additional security resources. Appendix B includes a more complete list of resources, but this section highlights a few of the most important ones and those you may find useful now.

CERT

CERT (**www.cert.org**) stands for Computer Emergency Response Team. This group is sponsored by Carnegie-Mellon University. CERT was the first computer incident–response team and is still one of the most respected in the industry. Anyone interested in network security should visit the site routinely. On the Web site, shown in Figure 1.3, you will find a wealth of documentation including guidelines for security policies, cutting-edge security research, and more.

FIGURE 1.3 CERT Web site.

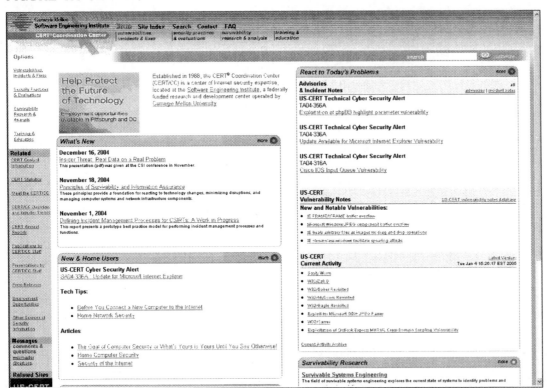

Microsoft Security Advisor

Because so many computers today run Microsoft operating systems, another good resource is the Microsoft Security Advisor Web site: **www. microsoft.com/security/default.mspx**. This site, shown in Figure 1.4, is a portal to all Microsoft security information, tools, and updates. If you use any Microsoft software, then it is advised that you visit this Web site regularly.

FIGURE 1.4 Microsoft Security Advisor Web site.

F-Secure

The F-Secure corporation maintains a Web site at **www.f-secure.com/** as shown in Figure 1.5. This site is, among other things, a repository for detailed information on virus outbreaks. Here you will not only find notifications about a particular virus, but you will also find detailed information about the virus. This information includes how the virus spreads; ways to recognize the virus; and, frequently, specific tools for cleaning an infected system of a particular virus.

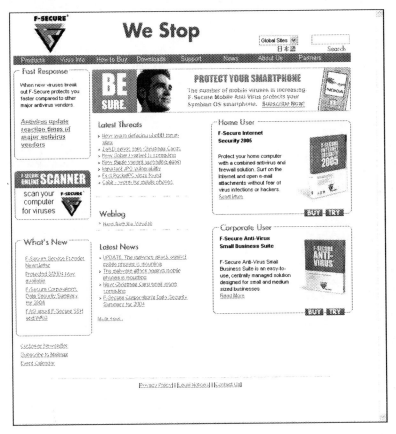

FIGURE 1.5 F-Secure Web site.

SANS Institute

The SANS Institute Web site (**www.sans.org/**) is a vast repository of security-related documentation. On this site, shown in Figure 1.6 on page 20, you will find detailed documentation on virtually every aspect of computer security you can imagine. The SANS Institute also sponsors a number of security research projects and publishes information about those projects on their Web site.

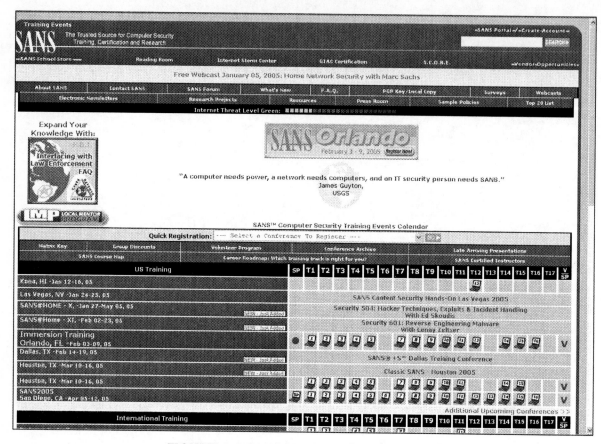

FIGURE 1.6 SANS Institute Web site.

Summary

Network security is a complex and constantly evolving field. Practitioners must stay on top of new threats and solutions and be proactive in assessing risk and protecting their networks. The first step to understanding network security is to become acquainted with the actual threats posed to a network. Without a realistic idea of what threats might affect your systems, you will be unable to effectively protect them. It is also critical that you acquire a basic understanding of the techniques used by both security professionals and those who would seek to compromise your network's security.

Test Your Skills

MULTIPLE CHOICE QUESTIONS

1. One extreme viewpoint about computer security is:

   A. the federal government will handle security.

   B. Microsoft will handle security.

   C. there are no imminent dangers to your system.

   D. there is no danger if you use Linux.

2. Before you can formulate a defense for a network, you will need:

   A. appropriate security certifications.

   B. a clear picture of the dangers to be defended against.

   C. to finish this textbook.

   D. the help of an outside consultant.

3. Which of the following is not one of the three major classes of threats?

   A. attempts to intrude on the system

   B. online auction fraud

   C. Denial of Service attacks

   D. a computer virus

4. A computer virus is any:

   A. program that is downloaded to your system without your permission.

   B. malicious program that self-replicates.

   C. program that causes harm to your system.

   D. program that can change your Windows registry.

5. Spyware is:

   A. any software that monitors your system.

   B. only software that logs keystrokes.

   C. any software used to gather intelligence.

   D. only software that monitors what Web sites you visit.

6. What is malware?

    A. software that has some malicious purpose

    B. software that is not functioning properly

    C. software that damages your system

    D. software that is not properly configured for your system

7. When a hacking technique uses persuasion and deception to get a person to provide information to help them compromise security, this is referred to as:

    A. social engineering.

    B. conning.

    C. human intel.

    D. soft hacking.

8. What is the most common threat on the Internet?

    A. auction fraud

    B. hackers

    C. computer viruses

    D. illegal software

9. According to a 2002 survey of 223 computer professionals prepared by the Computer Security Institute, which of the following was cited as an issue by more of the respondents?

    A. internal systems

    B. employee abuse

    C. routers

    D. Internet connection

10. What is the second most common attack on computer systems?

    A. Trojan horses

    B. unauthorized usage of the computer system

    C. illegal software

    D. sneakers

11. What is a sneaker?

    A. a person who hacks a system without being caught

    B. a person who hacks a system by faking a legitimate password

    C. a person who hacks a system to test its vulnerabilities

    D. a person who is an amateur hacker

12. What is the term for hacking a phone system?

    A. telco-hacking

    B. hacking

    C. cracking

    D. phreaking

13. An intrusion detection system is an example of:

    A. proactive security.

    B. perimeter security.

    C. hybrid security.

    D. good security practices.   .

14. Which of the following is the most basic security activity?

    A. authentication

    B. firewalls

    C. password protection

    D. auditing

15. The three approaches to security are:

    A. perimeter, layered, hybrid.

    B. high security, medium security, low security.

    C. internal, external, hybrid.

    D. perimeter, complete, none.

16. The most desirable approach to security is one that is:

    A. perimeter and dynamic.

    B. layered and dynamic.

    C. perimeter and static.

    D. layered and static.

17. The following type of privacy law affects computer security:

    A. any state privacy law.

    B. any privacy law applicable to your organization.

    C. any privacy law.

    D. any federal privacy law.

18. Which of the following is the best definition of "sensitive information?"

    A. any information that has impact on national security

    B. any information that is worth more than $1,000

    C. any information that, if accessed by unauthorized personnel, could damage your organization in any way

    D. any information that is protected by any privacy laws

19. The first computer incident–response team is affiliated with what university?

    A. Massachusetts Institute of Technology

    B. Carnegie-Mellon University

    C. Harvard University

    D. California Technical University

20. A major resource for detailed information on a computer virus is the:

    A. MIT Virus Library

    B. Microsoft Virus Library

    C. F-Secure Virus Library

    D. National Virus Repository

EXERCISES

Exercise 1.1: How Many Virus Attacks Have Occurred this Month?

1. Using a Web site resource, such as **www.f-secure.com**, look up recent computer virus outbreaks.

2. Write down how many virus outbreaks have occurred in the past seven days.

3. Write down how many outbreaks there have been in the past 30 days, 90 days, and one year.

4. Are virus attacks increasing in frequency?

Exercise 1.2: Learning About Cookies as Spyware

1. Perform some online research to get an idea of what kind of information cookies store. You might find the following Web sites helpful:

http://computercops.biz/article3911.html

www.ctc-solutions.co.uk/internet_security_2.html

www.howstuffworks.com/cookie1.htm

2. Write a brief essay explaining in what way cookies can invade privacy.

Exercise 1.3: Hacker Terminology

1. Use the *Hacker's Dictionary* at **www.hack.gr/jargon/** to define the following hacker terms:

alpha geek	grok
Red Book	wank

Exercise 1.4: Learning About the Law

1. Using the Web, journals, books, or other resources, find out whether your state or territory has any laws specific to computer security. You might find the following Web sites helpful:

   www.usdoj.gov/criminal/cybercrime/cclaws.html

   www.pbs.org/wgbh/pages/frontline/shows/hackers/blame/crime laws.html

   www.ncsl.org/programs/lis/cip/viruslaws.htm

   www.cybercrime.gov/

2. List three laws that you find, with a brief description of each. The list can be a simple one, noting the pertinent laws in your region. Describe each one with one or two sentences.

Exercise 1.5: Using Security Resources

1. Using one of the preferred Web resources listed in this chapter, find three policy or procedure documents from that resource that you think are important to your school or organization's security.

2. List the documents you selected.

3. Write a brief essay explaining why those particular documents are important to your organization's security.

PROJECTS

Project 1.1: Learning About a Virus

1. Using Web resources from Appendix B and sites such as **www. f-secure.com**, find a virus that has been released in the last six months.

2. Research how the virus spread and what damage it caused.

3. Write a brief (1/2–1 page) paper on this virus. Tell how the virus worked, how it spread, and any other essential information you can find.

Project 1.2: Considering the Law (a group project)

Write a description of a computer law that you would like to have passed, along with specifications as to its implementation, enforcement, and justification.

Project 1.3: Recommending Security

1. Using the Web, journals, or books, locate security recommendations from any reputable source, such as the SANS Institute. Any of the sites mentioned in the resources section of this chapter would be a good choice.

2. List five of those recommendations.

3. Explain why you agree or disagree with each one.

Case Study

Consider the job of a network administrator for a small, family-oriented video store. The store is not part of a chain of stores and has a very limited security budget. It has five machines for employees to use to check out movies and one server on which to keep centralized records. That server is in the manager's office. The administrator takes the following security precautions:

1. Each machine is upgraded to Windows XP, with the personal firewall turned on.

2. Antivirus software was installed on all machines.

3. A tape backup is added to the server, and tapes are kept in a locked file cabinet in the manager's office.

4. Internet access to employee machines is removed.

Now consider these questions:

1. What did these actions accomplish?

2. What additional actions might you recommend?

Chapter 2

Networks and the Internet

Chapter Objectives

After reading this chapter and completing the exercises, you will be able to do the following:

- Describe the OSI model of network communication.
- Explain the use of MAC addresses.
- Identify each of the major protocols used in network communication (for example, FTP and Telnet) and what use you can make of each.
- Understand the various connection methods and speeds used on networks.
- Compare and contrast a hub and switch.
- Identify what a router is and its use.
- Understand how data is transmitted over a network.
- Explain how the Internet works and the use of IP addresses and URLs.
- Use network utilities such as these: ping, IPConfig, and tracert.
- Explain the use of firewalls and proxy servers.

Introduction

To manage network security, you will need knowledge of how computer networks operate. Those readers who already have a strong working knowledge of network operations may choose to skim this chapter or perhaps give it a quick read as a review. For other readers new to computer networking, studying this chapter will give you a basic introduction to how networks and the Internet work. This understanding of networks and the Internet will be crucial to your comprehension of later topics presented in this book.

In this chapter, we will examine the basic model of a network and the underlying technologies that allow networks to communicate. This information will be the foundation on which all of the other materials in this course are built. In the exercises at the end of the chapter, you will be able to practice using some utilities such as IPConfig, tracert, and ping.

The OSI Model

Let's begin with the *OSI model* or Open Systems Interconnect model. This model is a description of how networks communicate. It describes the various protocols and activities, and it delineates how the protocols and activities relate to each other. This model is divided into seven layers, as shown in Table 2.1. It

TABLE 2.1 The OSI model.

Layer	Description	Protocols
Application	This layer interfaces directly to the application and performs common application services for the application processes.	None
Presentation	The presentation layer relieves the application layer of concern regarding syntactical differences in data representation within the end-user systems.	POP, SMTP, DNS, FTP, Telnet, ARP
Session	The session layer provides the mechanism for managing the dialogue between end-user application processes.	NetBIOS
Transport	This layer provides end-to-end communication control.	TCP
Network	This layer routes the information in the network.	IP, ICMP
Data Link	This layer describes the logical organization of data bits transmitted on a particular medium. Data Link is divided into two sublayers: the Media Access Control layer (MAC) and the Logical Link Control layer (LLC).	SLIP, PPP
Physical	This layer describes the physical properties of the various communications media, as well as the electrical properties and interpretation of the exchanged signals. In other words, the physical layer is the actual NIC, Ethernet cable, and so forth.	None

was originally developed by the International Standards Organization (ISO) in the 1980s.

Many networking students memorize this model. It is good to at least memorize the names of the seven layers and in general understand what they each do. From a security perspective, the more you understand about network communications, the more sophisticated your defense can be. The most important thing for you to understand is that this model describes a hierarchy of communication. One layer will only communicate with the layer directly above it or below it.

Network Basics

Getting two or more computers to communicate and transmit data is a process that is simple in concept, but complex in application. Consider all the factors involved. First, you will need to physically connect the computers. This connection requires either a cable that plugs into your computer or is accomplished by infrared light. The cable is then plugged either directly into another computer or is plugged into a router switch or a hub that will, in turn, connect to several other computers. (Routers and hubs are connective devices that will be explained in detail later in this chapter.)

There is a card in most modern computers called a ***Network Interface Card*** or simply a ***NIC***. If the connection is through a cable, the part of the NIC that is external to the computer has a connection slot that looks like a telephone jack, only slightly bigger. Of course, wireless networks, which are being used with greater frequency, also use a NIC but, rather than having a slot for a cable to connect to, the wireless network simply uses infrared signals to transmit to a nearby wireless router or hub.

Media Access Control (MAC) Addresses

MAC addresses are an interesting topic. (You might notice that MAC is also a sublayer of the data link layer of the OSI model.) A MAC address is a unique address for a NIC. Every NIC in the world has a unique address that

FYI: IP Address

An IP address is an identifier for a computer or device on a TCP/IP network. In these types of networks, messages are routed based on the IP address of the destination. The format of an IP address is a 32-bit numeric address written as four numbers separated by periods. Each number can be zero to 255. More information on IP addresses and TCP/IP will be given later in this chapter.

is represented by a six-byte hexadecimal number. There is a protocol that is used to convert IP addresses to MAC addresses. This protocol is the Address Resolution Protocol or ARP. Therefore, when you type in a Web address, the DNS (Domain Name Server) protocol is used to translate that into an IP address. The ARP protocol will then translate that IP address into a specific MAC address of an individual NIC.

DNS Servers

How does a URL get translated into an IP address? How does the computer know what IP goes with what URL? There are servers set up just to do this task. They are called *DNS servers*. *DNS* stands for *Domain Name Server* (or System or Service). DNS translates domain names (**www.example. com**) into IP addresses (198.203.167.9). Domain names are easy to remember because they are alphabetic, but the Internet is really based on IP addresses. Thus, every time you use a domain name, a DNS server must translate the name into the corresponding IP address. If you are on a corporate network, you probably have a DNS server on your network. If not, then your ISP has one. These servers maintain a table of IP-to-URL entries.

From time to time there are transfers of DNS data, called *zone transfers*, that allow one DNS server to send its changes to another. Across the Internet, there are root DNS servers that are maintained with centralized data for all registered URL/IP addresses. The DNS system is, in fact, its own network. If one DNS server does not know how to translate a particular domain name, it asks another one, and so on, until the correct IP address is returned.

Primary DNS is the name given to the server or service that holds the authoritative information for a domain. Actually, a DNS server (the computer/software) is not specifically "primary" or "secondary." A DNS server can be primary for one zone (domain) and secondary for another. By definition, a primary DNS server holds the master copy of the data for a zone, and secondary servers have copies of this data that they synchronize with the primary server through zone transfers at intervals or when prompted by the primary server.

The Physical Connection: Local Networks

As mentioned, cables are one of the ways that computers are connected to each other. The cable connection used with hard-wired NICs is an RJ 45 connection. (RJ is short for "Registered Jack," which is an international industry standard.) In contrast to the computer's RJ 45 jacks, standard telephone lines use RJ 11 jacks. The biggest difference between jacks involves the number of wires in the connector, also called the terminator. Phone lines have four wires, whereas RJ 45 connectors have eight. Figure 2.1 shows an example of an RJ 45 connector.

FIGURE 2.1 RJ 45 connector.

If you look on the back of most computers or the connection area of a laptop, you will probably find three ports that, at first glance, look like phone jacks. Two of the three ports are probably for a traditional modem and telephone and accept a standard RJ 11 jack. The other port is larger and accepts an RJ 45 jack. Not all computers come with a NIC, but most modern computers do. Additionally, many modern computers no longer contain an internal modem, in which case there would not be an RJ 11 jack.

This standard connector jack must be crimped on the end of the cable. The cable used in most networks today is a category 5 cable—or CAT-5, as it is commonly known. (Note that CAT-6 cable is becoming more prevalent with high-speed networks.) Table 2.2 summarizes the various categories of cable and their uses.

TABLE 2.2 Cable types and uses.

Category	Specifications	Uses
1	Low-speed analog (less than 1 MHz)	Telephone, doorbell
2	Analog line (less than 10 MHz)	Telephone
3	Up to 16 MHz or 10 Mbps (megabits per second)	Voice transmissions
4	Up to 20 MHz/16 Mbps	Data lines, Ethernet networks
5	100 MHz/100 Mbps	Most common type of network cable
6	250 MHz/1,000 Mbps	Very high-speed networks

The type of cable used in connecting computers is also often referred to as unshielded twisted pair cable (UTP). In UTP, the wires in the cable are in pairs, twisted together without any additional shielding. As you can see in Table 2.2, each subsequent category of cable is somewhat faster and more robust than the last. It should be noted that, although CAT-4 can be used for networks, it is almost never used for that purpose simply because it is slower, less reliable, and older technology. You will usually see CAT-5 cable and, increasingly, CAT-6.

Notice the speeds listed in Table 2.2, such as Mbps. This speed stands for megabits per second. Ultimately, everything in the computer is stored in a binary format using a 1 or a 0. These units are called bits. It takes eight bits, or one byte, to represent a single character such as a letter, number, or carriage return. It follows, then, that CAT-5 cable can transmit up to 100,000,000 bits per second. This is known as the bandwidth of the cable. Remember, though, that this is the maximum that can be transmitted "across the wire" at any given second. If multiple users are on a network and all of them are sending data, the traffic generated is going to quickly use up all of the bandwidth. Any pictures transmitted also use a great deal of bandwidth. Simple scanned-in photos can easily reach two megabytes (2 million bytes or 16 million bits) or much more. Streaming media, such as video, is perhaps the most demanding on bandwidth.

If you simply want to connect two computers to each other, you can have the cable go directly from one computer to the other. But what do you do if you wish to connect more than one computer? What if 100 computers need to be connected on a network? There are three devices that can help you accomplish this task: the hub, the switch, and the router. These devices each use CAT-5 or CAT-6 cable with RJ 45 connectors and are explained in the following sections.

FYI: Cable Speed

Category 6 cable is for the new gigabit Ethernet. CAT-5 cable works at speeds of up to 100 megabits per second (Mbps), whereas CAT-6 works at 1,000 Mbps. CAT-6 has been widely available for several years. However, for CAT-6 to truly function properly, you need hubs/switches (explained below) and NICs that also transmit at gigabit speeds. For this reason, the spread of gigabit Ethernet has been much slower than many analysts expected.

The Hub The simplest connection device is the *hub*. A hub is a small, box-shaped electronic device into which you can plug network cables. It will have four or more (commonly up to 24) RJ 45 jacks, each called a *port*. A hub can connect as many computers as it has ports. (For example, an eight-port hub can connect eight computers). You can also connect one hub to another; this strategy is referred to as "stacking" hubs. Hubs are quite inexpensive and simple to set up—just plug in the cable. However, hubs have a downside. If you send a packet from one computer to another, a copy of that packet is actually sent out from every port on the hub. (A packet is the unit of data transmission and will be examined later in this chapter.) All of these copies lead to a great deal of unnecessary network traffic. This occurs because the hub, being a very simple device, has no way of knowing where a packet is supposed to go. Therefore, it simply sends copies of the packet out of all of its ports.

In the context of the OSI model, a hub is a layer 1 device.

The Switch The next connection device option is the *switch*. A switch is basically an intelligent hub. However, a switch does not work in the same way as a hub. When a switch receives a packet, it will send that packet only out the port for the computer to which it needs to go. A switch builds a table based on MAC addresses and uses that to determine where a packet is being sent. How this determination is made is explained in the *Data Transmission* section below.

In the context of the OSI model, a switch is a layer 2 device.

The Router Finally, if you wish to connect two or more networks together, you use a *router*. A router is similar in concept to a hub or switch, as it does relay packets; yet, it is far more sophisticated. You can program most routers and control how they relay packets. The specifics of how you program the router are different from vendor to vendor. There are entire books written specifically on just programming routers. It is not possible to cover specific router programming techniques in this book; however, you should be aware that most routers are programmable, allowing you to change how they route traffic. Also, unlike using a hub or switch, the two networks connected by a router are still separate networks. In summary, the three basic connection devices are the hub, switch, and router, all of which connect category 5 or category 6 cable using RJ 45 connectors.

The Physical Connection: Internet

The explanation above covers the connections between computers on a local network, but what connection methods are used for the Internet? Your Internet service provider or the company for which you work probably use one of the fast Internet connections described in Table 2.3. This table summarizes the most common Internet connection types and their speeds.

TABLE 2.3 Internet connection types.

Connection Type	Speed	Details
DS0	64 kilobits per second	1/24 of a T1 line or one T1 channel
ISDN	128 kilobits per second	2 DS0 lines working together to provide a high-speed data connection
T1	1.54 megabits per second	24 DS0 lines working as one, with 23 carrying data and one carrying information about the other lines. This type of connection has become common for schools and businesses.
T3	43.2 megabits per second	672 DS0 lines working together. This method is the equivalent of 28 T1 lines.
OC3	155 megabits per second	All OC lines are optical and do not use traditional phone lines. OC3 lines are quite fast, very expensive, and are often found at telecommunications companies.
OC12	622 megabits per second	The equivalent of 336 T1 lines or 8064 phone lines.
OC48	2.5 gigabits per second	The equivalent of 4 OC12 lines.

It is common to find T1 connection lines in many locations. A cable modem can sometimes achieve speeds comparable to a T1 line. Note that cable modems were not listed in Table 2.3 simply because their actual speeds vary greatly depending on a variety of circumstances, including how many people in your immediate vicinity are using the same cable modem provider. You are not likely to encounter the OC lines unless you work in telecommunications.

Data Transmission

We have briefly seen the physical connection methods, but how is data actually transmitted? To transmit data, a packet is sent. The basic purpose of a cable is to transmit packets from one machine to another. It does not matter whether that packet is a part of a document, video, image, or just some internal signal from the computer. This fact begs the question: What, exactly, is a packet? As we discussed earlier, everything in a computer is ultimately stored as 1s and 0s, called bits, which are grouped into sets of eight, called a byte. A *packet*, also referred to as a *datagram*, is a certain number of bytes divided into a header and a body. The header is a 20-byte section at the beginning of the packet. The header tells you where the packet is coming from, where it is going, and more. The body contains the actual data, in binary format, that you wish to send. The aforementioned routers and switches work by reading the header portion of any packets that come to them. This process is how they determine where the packet should be sent.

Protocols   There are different types of network communications for different purposes. The different types of network communications are called *protocols*. A protocol is essentially an agreed-upon method of communication. In fact, this definition is exactly how the word "protocol" is used in standard, non-computer usage. Each protocol has a specific purpose and normally operates on a certain logical port. (Ports are discussed in more detail below.)

Some of the most significant protocols that are currently used include TCP, IP, UDP, and ICMP. *TCP* (*Transmission Control Protocol*) enables two host computers to establish a connection and exchange data. It guarantees the delivery of data in the proper order. *IP* (*Internet Protocol*) specifies the format of the packets and the addressing scheme. Most networks combine IP with the higher-level TCP to form the protocol suite known as *TCP/IP* (*Transmission Control Protocol/Internet Protocol*), which establishes a virtual connection between a destination and a source. IP by itself is something similar to the postal system. It allows you to address a package and drop it in the system, but there is no direct link between you and the recipient. TCP/IP, on the other hand, establishes a connection between two hosts so that they can send messages back and forth for a period of time (Webopedia, 2004).

UDP (*User Datagram Protocol*) is a connectionless protocol, meaning that it is a network protocol in which a host can send a message without establishing a connection with the recipient. UDP runs on top of IP networks (referred to as UDP/IP) and, unlike TCP/IP, it provides very few error recovery services. Instead, it offers a direct way to send and receive datagrams (packets) over an IP network. Its primary use is broadcasting messages over a network, but it does not guarantee the delivery of packets.

ICMP (*Internet Control Message Protocol*) is an extension of IP. It supports packets containing error, informational, and control messages. The ping command (explored later in this chapter), for example, uses ICMP to test an Internet connection.

Some of the most important and commonly used application-layer protocols are listed in Table 2.4.

Each of these protocols will be explained in more detail, as needed, in later chapters of this book. You should also note that this list is not complete. There are dozens of other protocols, but for now these will suffice. The most important thing for you to realize is that all communication on networks takes place via packets, and those packets are transmitted according to certain protocols depending on the type of communication that is occurring.

Ports You may be wondering what a port is. Do not confuse this type of port with the connection locations on the back of your computer such as a serial port, parallel port, or RJ-45 and RJ-11 ports (physical ports) we discussed earlier. A *port*, in networking terms, is a handle—a connection point. It is a numeric designation for a particular pathway of communications. All network communication, regardless of the port used, comes into your computer via the connection on your Network Interface Card.

The picture we have drawn of networks, to this point, is one of machines connected to each other via cables and perhaps to hubs/switches/routers. Networks transmit binary information in packets using certain protocols and ports.

How the Internet Works

Now that you have a basic idea of how computers communicate with each other over a network, it is time to discuss how the Internet works. The Internet is essentially just a large number of networks connected to each other. Therefore, the Internet works exactly the same way as your local network. It sends the same sort of data packets using the same protocols. These various networks are simply connected into main transmission lines called *backbones*. The points where backbones connect to each other are called *Network Access Points (NAP)*. When you log on to the Internet, you probably use an *Internet Service Provider (ISP)*. That ISP has a connection either to the Internet backbone or to yet another provider that has a backbone. Thus, logging on to the Internet is a process of connecting your computer to your ISP's network, which is, in turn, connected to one of the backbones on the Internet.

IP Addresses

With tens of thousands of networks and millions of individual computers communicating and sending data, a predictable problem arises. That problem is ensuring that the data packets go to the correct computer. This task is accomplished in much the same way as traditional letter mail is delivered to the right person: via an address. With network communications, this

TABLE 2.4 Application layer protocols.

Protocol	Purpose	Port
FTP (File Transfer Protocol)	For transferring files between computers	20, 21
tFTP (Trivial File Transfer Protocol)	A quicker, but less reliable, form of FTP	69
Telnet	Used to remotely log on to a system. You can then use a command prompt or shell to execute commands on that system. Popular with network administrators.	23
SMTP (Simple Mail Transfer Protocol)	Sends e-mail	25
WhoIS	Command that queries a target IP address for information	43
DNS (Domain Name Service)	Translates URLs into Web addresses	53
HTTP (Hypertext Transfer Protocol)	Displays Web pages	80
POP3 (Post Office Protocol Version 3)	Retrieves e-mail	110
NNTP (Network News Transfer Protocol)	Used for network news groups (usenet newsgroups). You can access these groups over the Web via **www.google.com** by selecting the "groups" tab.	119
NetBIOS	An older Microsoft protocol used for naming systems on a local network	137, 138, 139
IRC (Internet Relay Chat)	Used for chat rooms	194
ICMP (Internet Control Message Protocol)	These are simply packets that contain error messages, informational messages, and control messages.	No specific port

address is a special one, referred to as an IP address. An *IP address* is an address used to uniquely identify a device on an IP network. It is a unique number ID assigned to one host or interface in a network. The address consists of four 3-digit numbers separated by periods. (An example would be

107.22.98.198.) Each of the three-digit numbers must be between 0 and 255. This rule stems from the fact that IP addresses are actually four binary numbers; you just see them in decimal format. Recall that a byte is eight bits (1s and 0s), and an eight-bit binary number converted to decimal format will be between 0 and 255.

IN PRACTICE: Converting Binary Numbers

For those readers not familiar with converting binary numbers to decimal, there are several methods. We will discuss one of these methods here. You should be aware that the computer will do this for you in the case of IP addresses, but some readers may wish to know how this is done. While there are many methods, perhaps the simplest is:

divide repeatedly by 2,

using "remainders" rather than decimal places, until you get down to 1. For example, convert decimal 31 to binary:

$$31/2 = 15 \quad \text{Remainder 1}$$
$$15/2 = 7 \quad \text{Remainder 1}$$
$$7/2 \ = 3 \quad \text{Remainder 1}$$
$$3/2 \ = 1 \quad \text{Remainder 1}$$
$$1/2 \ = 0 \quad \text{Remainder 1}$$

Now read the remainders from bottom to top: the binary equivalent is 00011111. (Note that you complete the octet by filling in the leading spaces with "0"s to make an 8 bit numeral.)

While you can step through the math to convert a decimal number to a binary number, you may find it easier to use a converter. There are many converters available on the Internet that can be found by searching for the keywords "binary converter". Figures 2.2 and 2.3 show two examples of converters that are readily available.

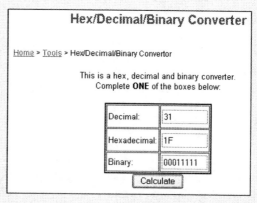

Hex/Decimal/Binary Converter

Home > Tools > Hex/Decimal/Binary Convertor

This is a hex, decimal and binary converter.
Complete **ONE** of the boxes below:

Decimal:	31
Hexadecimal:	1F
Binary:	00011111

Calculate

FIGURE 2.2 Example binary converter

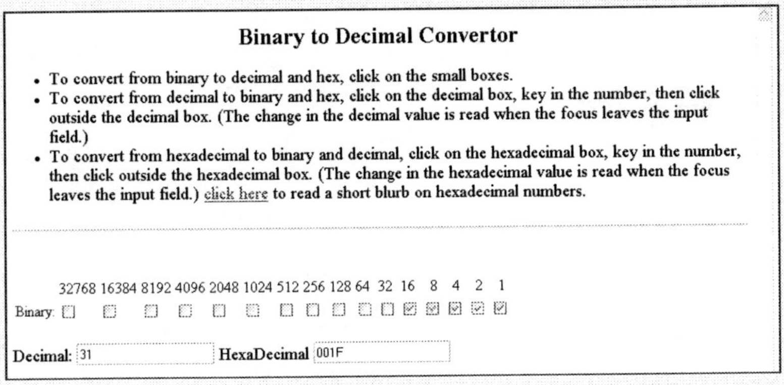

2

Binary to Decimal Convertor

- To convert from binary to decimal and hex, click on the small boxes.
- To convert from decimal to binary and hex, click on the decimal box, key in the number, then click outside the decimal box. (The change in the decimal value is read when the focus leaves the input field.)
- To convert from hexadecimal to binary and decimal, click on the hexadecimal box, key in the number, then click outside the hexadecimal box. (The change in the hexadecimal value is read when the focus leaves the input field.) click here to read a short blurb on hexadecimal numbers.

32768 16384 8192 4096 2048 1024 512 256 128 64 32 16 8 4 2 1

Binary: ☐ ☐ ☐ ☐ ☐ ☐ ☐ ☐ ☐ ☐ ☐ ☑ ☑ ☑ ☑ ☑

Decimal: 31   HexaDecimal 001F

FIGURE 2.3 Example binary converter

Public versus Private IP addresses come in two groups: public and private. Public IP addresses are for computers connected to the Internet. No two public IP address can be the same. However, a private IP address, such as one on a private company network, only has to be unique within that network. Within an isolated network, you can assign IP addresses at random as long as each one is unique. It does not matter whether other computers throughout the world have the same IP address because this computer is never connected to those other worldwide computers. However, connecting a private network to the Internet requires using registered IP addresses (called Internet addresses) to avoid duplicates. Often, network administrators use private IP addresses that begin with a 10, such as 10.102.230.17.

It should also be pointed out that an ISP will often buy a pool of public IP addresses and assign them to you when you log on. Therefore, an ISP might own 1,000 public IP addresses and have 10,000 customers. Because all 10,000 customers will not be online at the same time, the ISP simply assigns an IP address to a customer when he logs on, and the ISP unassigns the IP address when the customer logs off.

Classes The address of a computer tells you a great deal about that computer. The first byte (or first decimal number) in an address tells you to what class of network that machine belongs. Table 2.5 summarizes the five network classes.

The four numbers in an IP address are used in different ways to identify a particular network and host on that network. There are four regional Internet registries (ARIN, RIPE NCC, LACNIC, APNIC) that assign Internet addresses from the A, B, and C classes.

These five classes of networks will become more important later in this book (or should you decide to study networking on a deeper level). Observe Table 2.5 carefully, and you probably will discover that the IP range of

TABLE 2.5 Network classes.

Class	IP Range for the First Byte	Use
A	0–126	Extremely large networks. All Class A network IP addresses have been used and none are left.
B	128–191	Large corporate and government networks. All Class B network IP addresses have been used.
C	192–223	The most common group of IP addresses. Your ISP probably has a Class C address.
D	224–247	These are reserved for multicasting. *Note:* Multicasting is transmitting the same data to multiple (but not all) destinations.
E	248–255	Reserved for experimental use.

127 was not listed. This omission is because that range is reserved for testing. The IP address of 127.0.0.1 designates the machine you are on, regardless of that machine's assigned IP address. This address is often referred to as the ***loop back address***. That address will be used often in testing your machine and your NIC. We will examine its use a bit later in this chapter in the section on *Basic Network Utilities*.

Availablity of Addresses If you do the math, you will find that our current addressing method means there are a total of over 4.2 billion possible IP addresses. That seems like a very large number but, in reality, the number of unassigned Internet addresses is running out. You should not be concerned, however, as methods are already in place to extend the use of addresses. The new addressing system will be a classless scheme called CIDR (Classless Inter-Domain Routing), and it is tied to the replacement of IP V4 with IP V6.

The entire discussion of IP addresses up to this point is based on IP V4 (version 4.0), the current standard. IP V6 (version 6.0), however, is likely to be implemented in the future. Rather than 32-bit addresses (four 8-bit numbers), the IP V6 uses 128-bit addresses. IP V6 is configured for backward compatibility, which means that to use the new IP V6, there will fortunately not be a need to change every IP address in the world. Keep in mind that, when we discuss the packet structure of an IP packet, we are talking about both the IP V4 and IP V6 packets. In comparison to IP V4 packets, IP V6 packets have longer header segments and the header is structured a little differently.

2

With CIDR, a single IP address can be used to designate many different and unique IP addresses. In contrast to an IP address, a CIDR IP address ends with a slash followed by a number, called the *IP network prefix*. An example of a CIDR IP address is 156.201.10.10/12. The IP network prefix specifies how many addresses are covered by the CIDR address. Lower numbers specify more addresses. In addition to providing more addresses within organizations, CIDR addresses also reduce the size of routing tables.

Subnet A *subnet* is a portion of a network that shares a particular subnet address (a common address component). On a TCP/IP network, subnets are defined as all devices whose IP addresses have the same prefix. For example, all devices with an IP address that starts with 200.200.200. would be part of the same subnet. Dividing a network into subnets is useful for both security and performance reasons. Subnetting enables the network administrator to further divide the host part of the address into two or more subnets. In this case, a part of the host address is reserved to identify the particular subnet. IP networks are divided using a subnet mask.

Subnet Mask As we discussed earlier, an IP address is made up of 32 binary bits. These bits can be divided into two components: the network address and the host address. A *subnet mask* is a 32-bit combination used to describe which portion of an address refers to the subnet (network) and which part refers to the host. This mask is used to determine what subnet an IP address belongs to. For example, in the IP address 185.201.20.2 (assuming this is part of a Class B network), the first two numbers (185.201) represent the Class B network address, and the second two numbers (20.2) identify a particular host on this network.

Uniform Resource Locators

After you connect to your ISP you will, of course, want to visit some Web sites. You probably type names into your browser's address bar rather than IP addresses. For example, you might type in **www.chuckeasttom.com** to go my Web site. Your computer or your ISP must translate the name you typed (called a *Uniform Resource Locator (URL)*) into an IP address. The DNS protocol, mentioned in the Table 2.4, handles this translation process. You are typing in a name that makes sense to humans, but your computer is using a corresponding IP address to connect. If that address is found, your browser sends a packet (using the HTTP protocol) to port 80. If that target computer has software that listens and responds to such requests (like Web-server software such as Apache or Microsoft Internet Information Server), then the target computer will respond to your browser's request and communication will be established. This method is how Web pages are viewed.

If you have ever received an Error 404: File Not Found message, what you are seeing is that your browser received back a packet (from the Web server) with error code 404, denoting that the Web page you requested could not be found. There are a series of error messages that the Web server can send back to your Web browser, indicating different problems. Many of these problems can be handled by the browser itself and you never see the error message. All error messages in the 400 series are *client errors*. This term means that something is wrong on your side, not the Web server. Messages in the 500 series are *server errors*, which mean that there is a problem on the Web server. The 100-series messages are simply informational; 200-series messages indicate success (you usually do not see these, for the browser simply processes them); 300-series messages are re-directional, meaning the Web page you are seeking has moved and your browser is then directed to the new location.

E-mail works the same way as visiting Web sites. Your e-mail client (the software you use to manage your e-mail account) will seek out the address of your e-mail server. Your e-mail client will then use either POP3 to retrieve your incoming e-mail or SMTP to send your outgoing e-mail. Your e-mail server (probably at your ISP or company) will then try to resolve the address you are sending to. If you send something to a yahoo e-mail address, your e-mail server will translate that e-mail address into an IP address for the e-mail server at **yahoo.com**; your server will then send your e-mail there. Note that there are newer e-mail protocols available, but POP3 is still the most commonly used.

Many readers are probably familiar with chat rooms. A chat room, like the other methods of communication we have discussed, works with packets. You first find the address of the chat room and then you connect. The difference here is that your computer's chat software is constantly sending packets back and forth, which is unlike e-mail, which only sends and receives when you tell it to or on a predetermined time interval.

Remember that a packet has a header section. That header section contains your IP address and the destination IP address that you are going to, as well as other information. This packet structure will become an important concept for you to know in subsequent chapters.

Basic Network Utilities

Later in this book, you will use information and techniques that are based, in part, on certain techniques anyone can perform on her machine. There are network utilities that you can execute from a command prompt (Windows) or from a shell (Unix/Linux). Many readers are already familiar with Windows, so the text's discussion will execute the commands and discuss them from the Windows command-prompt perspective. However, it must be stressed that these utilities are available in all operating systems. In this section, you will read about IPConfig, ping, and tracert utilities.

IPConfig

When beginning to study networks, the first thing you will want to do is to get information about your own system. To accomplish this fact-finding mission, you will need to get to a command prompt. In Windows XP or Windows 2000, you can open the command prompt by performing the following steps:

1. Open the Start menu
2. Select Run.
3. In the dialog box that opens, type cmd and click OK.
4. Type **ipconfig**. (You could input the same command in Unix or Linux by typing in ifconfig once inside the shell.)
5. Press the Enter key. You should see something much like what is shown in Figure 2.4.

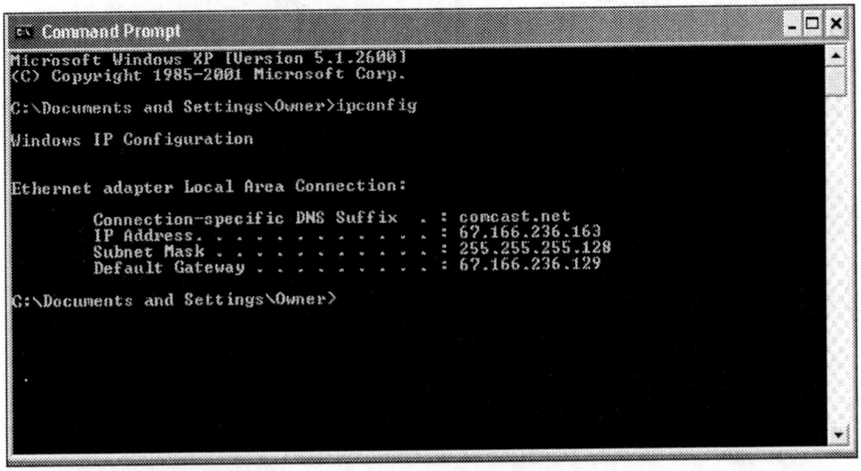

```
Command Prompt                                              _ □ X

Microsoft Windows XP [Version 5.1.2600]
(C) Copyright 1985-2001 Microsoft Corp.

C:\Documents and Settings\Owner>ipconfig

Windows IP Configuration

Ethernet adapter Local Area Connection:

        Connection-specific DNS Suffix  . : comcast.net
        IP Address. . . . . . . . . . . . : 67.166.236.163
        Subnet Mask . . . . . . . . . . . : 255.255.255.128
        Default Gateway . . . . . . . . . : 67.166.236.129

C:\Documents and Settings\Owner>
```

FIGURE 2.4 IPConfig.

This command gives you some information about your connection to a network (or to the Internet). Most importantly, you find out your own IP address. The command also has the IP address for your default gateway, which is your connection to the outside world. Running the *IPConfig* command is a first step in determining your system's network configuration. Most commands that this text will mention, including IPConfig, have a number of parameters, or flags, that can be passed to the commands to make the computer behave in a certain way. You can find out what these commands are by typing in the command, followed by a space, and then typing in hyphen question mark, -?. Figure 2.5 shows the results of this method for the IPConfig command.

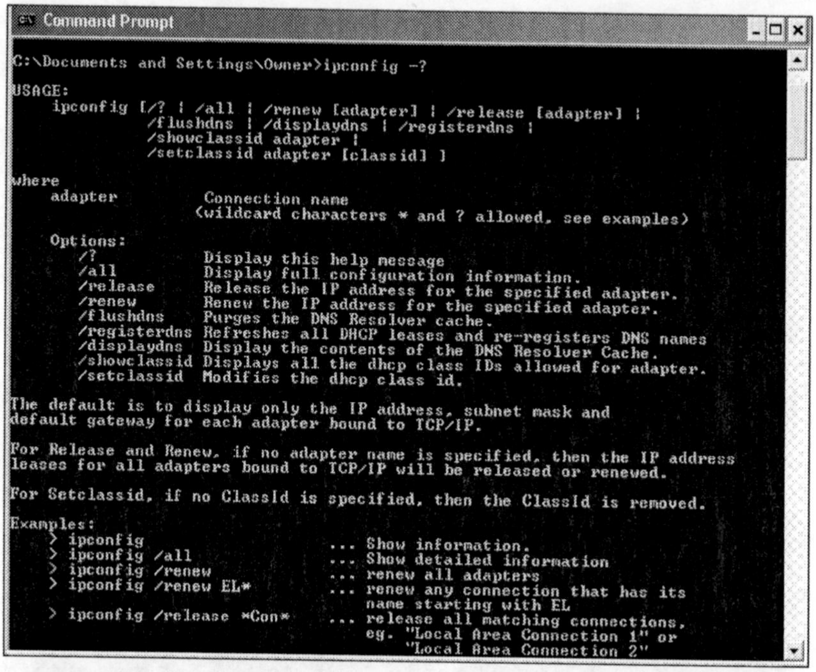

FIGURE 2.5 IPConfig help.

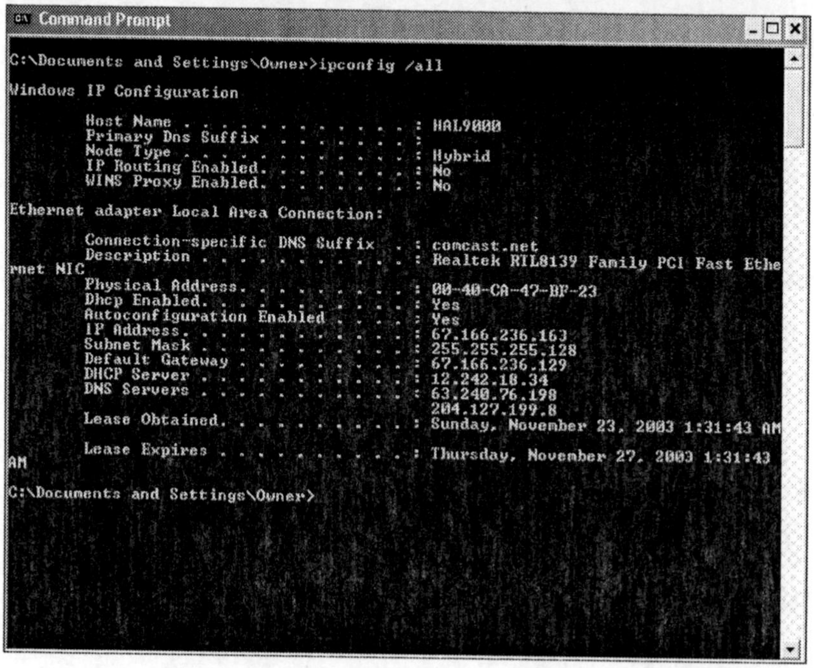

```
C:\Documents and Settings\Owner>ipconfig -?

USAGE:
    ipconfig [/? | /all | /renew [adapter] | /release [adapter] |
             /flushdns | /displaydns | /registerdns |
             /showclassid adapter |
             /setclassid adapter [classid] ]

where
    adapter            Connection name
                      (wildcard characters * and ? allowed, see examples)

    Options:
       /?              Display this help message
       /all            Display full configuration information.
       /release        Release the IP address for the specified adapter.
       /renew          Renew the IP address for the specified adapter.
       /flushdns       Purges the DNS Resolver cache.
       /registerdns    Refreshes all DHCP leases and re-registers DNS names
       /displaydns     Display the contents of the DNS Resolver Cache.
       /showclassid    Displays all the dhcp class IDs allowed for adapter.
       /setclassid     Modifies the dhcp class id.

The default is to display only the IP address, subnet mask and
default gateway for each adapter bound to TCP/IP.

For Release and Renew, if no adapter name is specified, then the IP address
leases for all adapters bound to TCP/IP will be released or renewed.

For Setclassid, if no ClassId is specified, then the ClassId is removed.

Examples:
    > ipconfig              ... Show information.
    > ipconfig /all         ... Show detailed information
    > ipconfig /renew       ... renew all adapters
    > ipconfig /renew EL*   ... renew any connection that has its
                                name starting with EL
    > ipconfig /release *Con*  ... release all matching connections,
                                eg. "Local Area Connection 1" or
                                    "Local Area Connection 2"
```

FIGURE 2.6
IPConfig/all.

```
C:\Documents and Settings\Owner>ipconfig /all

Windows IP Configuration

        Host Name . . . . . . . . . . . . : HAL9000
        Primary Dns Suffix  . . . . . . . :
        Node Type . . . . . . . . . . . . : Hybrid
        IP Routing Enabled. . . . . . . . : No
        WINS Proxy Enabled. . . . . . . . : No

Ethernet adapter Local Area Connection:

        Connection-specific DNS Suffix  . : comcast.net
        Description . . . . . . . . . . . : Realtek RTL8139 Family PCI Fast Ethe
rnet NIC
        Physical Address. . . . . . . . . : 00-40-CA-47-BF-23
        Dhcp Enabled. . . . . . . . . . . : Yes
        Autoconfiguration Enabled . . . . : Yes
        IP Address. . . . . . . . . . . . : 67.166.236.163
        Subnet Mask . . . . . . . . . . . : 255.255.255.128
        Default Gateway . . . . . . . . . : 67.166.236.129
        DHCP Server . . . . . . . . . . . : 12.242.18.34
        DNS Servers . . . . . . . . . . . : 63.240.76.198
                                            204.127.199.8
        Lease Obtained. . . . . . . . . . : Sunday, November 23, 2003 1:31:43 AM
        Lease Expires . . . . . . . . . . : Thursday, November 27, 2003 1:31:43
AM
C:\Documents and Settings\Owner>
```

As you can see in Figure 2.5, there are a number of options you might use to find out different details about your computer's configuration. The most commonly used method would probably be the IPConfig/all, shown in Figure 2.6. You can see that this option gives you much more information.

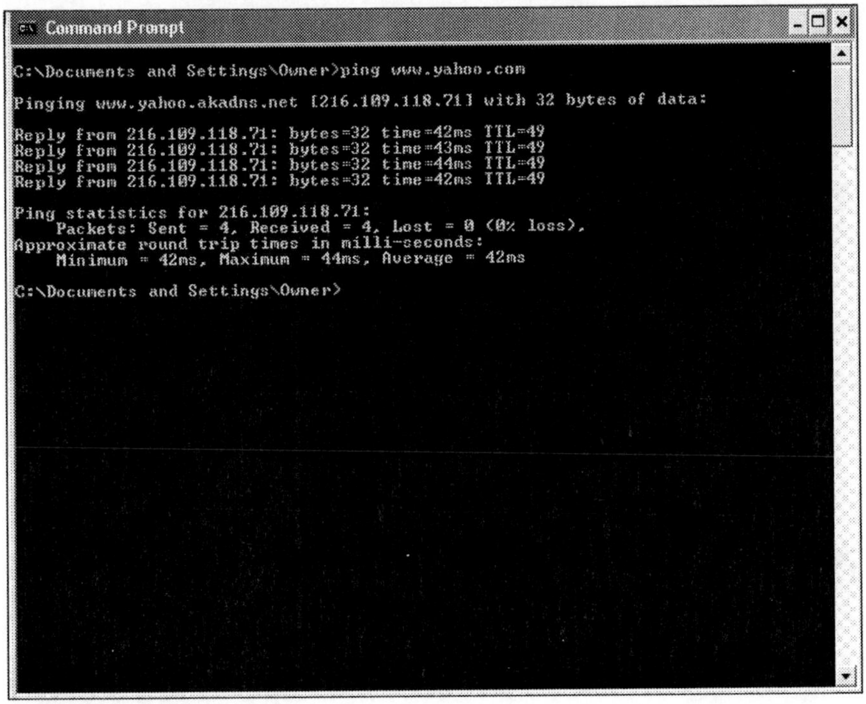

```
Command Prompt                                              _ □ ×

C:\Documents and Settings\Owner>ping www.yahoo.com

Pinging www.yahoo.akadns.net [216.109.118.71] with 32 bytes of data:

Reply from 216.109.118.71: bytes=32 time=42ms TTL=49
Reply from 216.109.118.71: bytes=32 time=43ms TTL=49
Reply from 216.109.118.71: bytes=32 time=44ms TTL=49
Reply from 216.109.118.71: bytes=32 time=42ms TTL=49

Ping statistics for 216.109.118.71:
    Packets: Sent = 4, Received = 4, Lost = 0 (0% loss),
Approximate round trip times in milli-seconds:
    Minimum = 42ms, Maximum = 44ms, Average = 42ms

C:\Documents and Settings\Owner>
```

FIGURE 2.7 Ping.

For example, IPConfig/all gives the name of your computer, when your computer obtained its IP address, and more.

Ping

Another commonly used command is *ping*. Ping is used to send a test packet, or echo packet, to a machine to find out whether the machine is reachable and how long the packet takes to reach the machine. This useful diagnostic tool can be employed in elementary hacking techniques (discussed in later chapters). In Figure 2.7, you see a ping command executed on **www.yahoo.com**.

This figure tells you that a 32-byte echo packet was sent to the destination and returned. The ttl item means "time to live." That time unit is how many intermediary steps, or hops, the packet should take to the destination before giving up. Remember that the Internet is a vast conglomerate of interconnected networks. Your packet probably will not go straight to its destination, but will have to take several hops to get there. As with IPConfig, you can type in ping -? to find out various ways you can refine your ping.

FIGURE 2.8 Tracert.

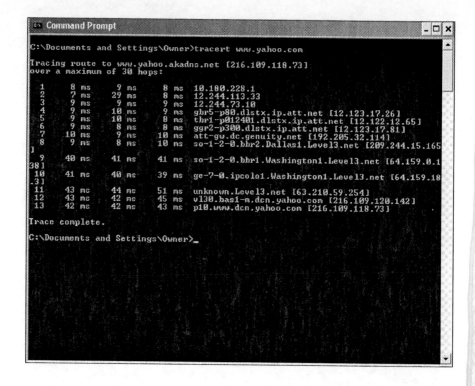

```
Command Prompt

C:\Documents and Settings\Owner>tracert www.yahoo.com

Tracing route to www.yahoo.akadns.net [216.109.118.73]
over a maximum of 30 hops:

  1     8 ms     9 ms     8 ms   10.180.228.1
  2     7 ms    29 ms     8 ms   12.244.113.33
  3     9 ms     9 ms     9 ms   12.244.73.10
  4     9 ms    10 ms     9 ms   gbr5-p80.dlstx.ip.att.net [12.123.17.26]
  5     9 ms    10 ms     8 ms   tbr1-p012401.dlstx.ip.att.net [12.122.12.65]
  6     9 ms     8 ms     8 ms   ggr2-p300.dlstx.ip.att.net [12.123.17.81]
  7    10 ms     9 ms    10 ms   att-gw.dc.genuity.net [192.205.32.114]
  8     9 ms     8 ms    10 ms   so-1-2-0.bbr2.Dallas1.Level3.net [209.244.15.165
]
  9    40 ms    41 ms    41 ms   so-1-2-0.bbr1.Washington1.Level3.net [64.159.0.1
38]
 10    41 ms    40 ms    39 ms   ge-7-0.ipcolo1.Washington1.Level3.net [64.159.18
.3]
 11    43 ms    44 ms    51 ms   unknown.Level3.net [63.210.59.254]
 12    43 ms    42 ms    45 ms   v130.bas1-m.dcn.yahoo.com [216.109.120.142]
 13    42 ms    42 ms    43 ms   p10.www.dcn.yahoo.com [216.109.118.73]

Trace complete.

C:\Documents and Settings\Owner>_
```

Tracert

The final command we will examine in this chapter is the *tracert*. This command is basically a "ping deluxe." Tracert not only tells you whether the packet got to its destination and how long it took, but also tells you all the intermediate hops it took to get there. This utility will prove very useful to you later in this book. Figure 2.8 illustrates a tracert to **www.yahoo.com**. (This same command can be executed in Linux or Unix, but there it is called "traceroute" rather than "tracert.")

With tracert, you can see (in milliseconds) the IP addresses of each intermediate step listed and how long it took to get to that step. Knowing the steps required to reach a destination can be very important, as you will find later in this book.

Certainly, there are other utilities that can be of use to you when working with network communications. However, the three we just examined are the core utilities. These three (IPConfig, ping, tracert) are absolutely essential to any network administrator, and you should commit them to memory.

Other Network Devices

There are other devices involved in networking that work to protect your computer from the outside world. Some of these devices were briefly mentioned in Chapter 1. We will now review a few of them in more detail. The two most common devices in this category are the firewall and the proxy server. A *firewall* is essentially a barrier between your network and the rest of the Internet. A personal computer (pc) can be used as a firewall or, in many cases, a special router can function as a firewall. Firewalls, which can be hardware, software, or a combination of both, use different techniques to protect your network, but the most common strategy is packet filtering. In a packet-filtering firewall, each incoming packet is examined. Only those packets that match the criteria you set are allowed through. (Commonly, only packets using certain types of protocols are allowed through.) Many operating systems, such as Windows XP and many Linux distributions, include basic packet-filtering software with the operating system.

The second common type of defensive device is a ***proxy server***. A proxy server will almost always be another computer. You might see the same machine used as both a proxy server and a firewall. A proxy server's purpose is quite simple: it hides your entire network from the outside world. People trying to investigate your network from the outside will see only the proxy server. They will not see the actual machines on your network. When packets go out of your network, their headers are changed so that the packets have the return address of the proxy server. Conversely, the only way you can access the outside world is via the proxy server. A proxy server combined with a firewall is basic network security. It would frankly be negligent to ever run a network that did not have a firewall and proxy server. In a later chapter, we will examine firewalls in more detail.

Summary

This chapter cannot make you a networking expert. However, you should now have a basic understanding of the structure of networks, how they work, and knowledge of network utilities and devices. You should also have an understanding of the Internet as a network. This material will be critical in later chapters. If you are new to this material, you should thoroughly study this chapter before continuing. In the exercises at the end of this chapter, you will be able to practice using IPConfig, tracert, and ping.

Test Your Skills

MULTIPLE CHOICE QUESTIONS

1. The TCP protocol operates at what layer of the OSI model?
   A. Transport
   B. Application
   C. Network
   D. DataLink

2. The layer of the OSI model that is divided into two sublayers is the:
   A. DataLink.
   B. Network.
   C. Presentation.
   D. Session.

3. A unique hexadecimal number that identifies your network card is called a:
   A. NIC address.
   B. MAC address.
   C. NIC ID.
   D. MAC ID.

4. What is a NIC?
   A. Network Interface Card
   B. Network Interaction Card
   C. Network Interface Connector
   D. Network Interaction Connector

5. A protocol that translates Web addresses into IP addresses is called:
   A. DNS.
   B. TFTP.
   C. DHCP.
   D. SMTP.

6. The connector used with network cables is called:
   A. RJ 11.
   B. RJ 85.
   C. RJ 12.
   D. RJ 45.

7. What type of cable do most networks use?

   A. net cable

   B. category 3 cable

   C. phone cable

   D. category 5 cable

8. The cable used in networks is also referred to as:

   A. unshielded twisted pair.

   B. shielded twisted pair.

   C. unshielded untwisted pair.

   D. shielded untwisted pair.

9. The simplest device for connecting computers is called a(n):

   A. NIC.

   B. interface.

   C. hub.

   D. router.

10. A device used to connect two or more networks together is a:

    A. switch.

    B. router.

    C. hub.

    D. NIC.

11. A T1 line sends data at what speed?

    A. 100 Mbps

    B. 1.54 Mbps

    C. 155 Mbps

    D. 56.6 Kbps

12. How big is a TCP packet header?

    A. The size is dependent on the data being sent.

    B. The size is always 20 bytes.

    C. The size is dependent on the protocol being used.

    D. The size is always 40 bytes.

13. What protocol is used to send e-mail, and on what port does it work?

    A. SMTP port 110

    B. POP3 port 25

    C. SMTP port 25

    D. POP3 port 110

14. What protocol is used for remotely logging on to a computer?

    A. Telnet

    B. HTTP

    C. DNS

    D. SMTP

15. What protocol is used for Web pages, and what port does it work on?

    A. HTTP port 21

    B. HTTP port 80

    C. DHCP port 80

    D. DHCP port 21

16. The point where the backbones of the Internet connect is called:

    A. connectors.

    B. routers.

    C. network access points.

    D. switches.

17. The IP address of 193.44.34.12 would be in what class?

    A. A

    B. B

    C. C

    D. D

18. The IP address of 127.0.0.1 always refers to your:

    A. nearest router.

    B. ISP.

    C. computer.

    D. nearest NAP.

19. Internet addresses in the form of **www.chuckeasttom.com** are called:

    A. user-friendly web addresses.

    B. iniform resource locators.

    C. user-accessible web addresses.

    D. uniform address identifiers.

20. The utility that gives you information about your machine's network configuration is:

    A. ping.

    B. IPConfig.

    C. tracert.

    D. MyConfig.

EXERCISES

Exercise 2.1: Using IPConfig

1. Open your command prompt or DOS prompt. (Go to Start > Run and type **cmd** ([DOS prompt in Windows 98]).

2. Type **ipconfig**.

3. Use the IPConfig to find out information about your computer.

4. Write down your computer's IP address, default gateway, and subnet mask.

Exercise 2.2: Using Tracert

1. Open your command prompt or DOS prompt.

2. Type **tracert www.chuckeasttom.com**.

3. Note what hops your computer takes to get to **www.chuckeasttom. com**.

4. Try the same process with **www.whitehouse.gov** and **www. prenhall.com**.

5. Did you notice that the first few hops are the same? Write down what hops are taken to reach each destination and what hops are the same. Then briefly describe why you think some of the intermediate steps are the same for different destinations.

Exercise 2.3: NSLOOKUP

The command NSLOOKUP is not mentioned in this chapter. Yet, if you are comfortable with ping, tracert, and IPConfig, this command will be easy to learn.

1. Go to the command prompt.

2. Type **nslookup www.chuckeasttom.com**.

3. Note that this command gives you the actual name of the server, as per the hosting company's naming conventions; its IP address; and any aliases under which that server operates.

Exercise 2.4: More About IPConfig

1. Open your command prompt or DOS prompt.

2. Use the -? flag on the IPConfig command to find out what other options you have with these commands. You should notice a number of options, including /all, /renew, and others.

3. Now try ipconfig/all. What do you see now that you didn't see when you simply used ipconfig in Exercise 2.1?

Exercise 2.5: More About Ping

1. Open your command prompt or DOS prompt.

2. Use the -? flag on the ping command and find out what other options you have with these commands. You should notice several additional options such as -w, -t, -n, and -i.

3. Try a simple ping of **www.chuckeasttom.com**.

4. Try the option ping -n 2 **www.chuckeasttom.com**, then try ping -n 7 **www. chuckeasttom.com**. What differences do you notice?

PROJECTS

Project 2.1: Learning About DNS

1. Using Web resources, look up the DNS protocol. You may find the following Web sites to be of help:

www.freesoft.org/CIE/Topics/75.htm

www.dns.net/dnsrd/docs/whatis.html

www.webfavor.com/tips/DNS.html

2. Look up these facts: Who invented this protocol? What is its purpose? How is it used?

3. Write a brief paper describing what the protocol does. Mention a bit of information about who invented it, when, and how it works.

Project 2.2: Learning About Your System

1. Find out whether your organization (for example, your school or business) uses switches, hubs, or both. Why does your group use these? You can find out by simply asking the network administrator or the help desk. Make sure you tell them that you are seeking this information for a class project.

2. Write a brief paper explaining your findings, including any changes you would make if you could. For example, if your organization uses only hubs, would you change that method? If so, why?

Project 2.3: Learning About NetStat

The NetStat command is used to display the status of network connections on either TCP, UDP, RAW, or UNIX. It displays network protocol statistics and information.

1. At the command prompt, type **netstat**. Notice the information it provides. You should be seeing any IP addresses or server names that are currently connected to your computer. (If you are using a home computer, you will need to log on to your Internet service provider in order to see anything.)

2. Now type **netstat -?** to see options with this command. You should see -a, -e, and others.

3. Now type **netstat -a** and note the information you see.

4. Finally, try **netstat -e**. What do you see now?

Caution

Stopping NetStat

Note that, with many versions of Windows, for the next steps you will need to use the control-break key combination to stop NetStat before starting it again with a new option.

▶ Case Study

You have been hired by the owner of a new technical writing business. Your task is to establish a network of computers for the six employees who will need to communicate with each other, share files, and also be able to access the Internet in order to send and receive e-mail and perform research. Eventually, they will also need to host a Web site for the company. Create an outline or detail in some other format exactly how you intend to set up the network. How they will connect to each other and to the Internet? What firewalls will be used?

Chapter | 3

Assessing a Target System

Chapter Objectives

After reading this chapter and completing the exercises, you will be able to do the following:

- Understand and be able to conduct basic system reconnaissance.
- Describe and use several port scanners.
- Understand how to derive useful information about a Web site from internic or the Netcraft Web site.
- Know how to locate information about a system or organization from Internet newsgroup postings.
- Understand the use of vulnerability scanners.
- Use port monitoring utilities.

Introduction

Ultimately, every hacker wishes to compromise a target system and gain access to that system. This goal is the same for any hacker, regardless of the hacker's "hat" (his or her ideology or motivation). Before a hacker can attempt to compromise a target system, he must know a great deal about the target system. There are a number of network utilities, Web sites, and programs that a hacker can use to find out about a target system. We will discuss these strategies in depth in this chapter. Learning these methods will help you for two reasons. First, you should know exactly what tools crackers have at their disposal to assess your system's vulnerabilities. Second, many security-savvy network administrators will frequently use these tools to assess their own systems. Another term for assessing your own system (or a client's) is *auditing*. When a hacker or cracker is examining a potential target system, this assessment is called *footprinting*. If you can find vulnerabilities, you have the chance to fix them before someone else exploits them.

Recall the discussion from Chapter 1 of the rather tedious process hackers have to use in order to enter a target system. The first stage of this process is learning about the system. It is important to know about the operating system, any software running on it, what security measures are in effect, and as much about the network as possible. This legwork is very similar to a robber "casing" a bank before attempting the crime. The thief needs to know all about alarm systems, work schedules, and guards. The same is true for a person planning to break into a computer system. The hacker's first step is to gather information about that system. To assess your own system, therefore, needs to be your first step also.

In this chapter, you will learn to use some common tools and techniques to assess a system. In the exercises at the end of this chapter, you will then have the chance to use tools, such as Netcop, NetBrute, Netcraft, tracert, and Netstat, to perform additional assessments.

FYI: Finding Utilities

You will find that some utilities will work only on some operating systems. In some cases, a utility might work in Windows 2000 but not Windows XP, or vice versa. For this reason, Appendix B is full of alternative sites to obtain similar utilities.

Basic Reconnaissance

On any system, you must first start finding out some general information. This task—commonly referred to as reconnaissance—is particularly easy with Web servers. A Web server, by definition, must communicate with Web clients. That activity means that a certain amount of information is easily accessible in the public domain. In the past, security managers had to use some rather arcane-looking commands from either a command prompt or a Linux/Unix shell to gather this information. But today, you can get the information in just a few simple steps by using some readily available utilities. These tools are used by both security managers as well as crackers.

The ways in which information is obtained by a cracker can vary greatly. Although there are many tools available, the ways listed below are the most likely initial reconnaissance methods used for Windows platforms:

- Nslookup

- Whois

- ARIN (This is available via any Internet browser client.)

- Web-based tools (Hundreds if not thousands of sites offer various reconnaissance tools.)

- Target Web site (The client's Web site often reveals too much information.)

- Social engineering (People are an organization's greatest asset as well as their greatest risk.)

In the following sections, we will explore a few of the many Web-based tools available for obtaining basic information on a target system.

Netcraft

The first stop on our journey is the Netcraft Web site. This Web site gathers information about Web servers—information that you can use in assessing a target system. It provides an online utility that will tell you what Web server software it is running, what operating system it is using, and other important and interesting information.

1. Open your browser and key **www.netcraft.com**.
2. Click the link titled "What's that site running," which is found on the left side of the page.
3. Key **www.chuckeasttom.com** into the "What's that site running?" text box.
4. Press Enter. As you see in Figure 3.1, you will find a great deal of important information.

You can see that the server is running the FreeBSD operating system, a Unix variant. You can also see the IP address of the machine. This step is your first in learning about the target system. In many cases, with other addresses, you would also find out what Web server the target system is running. You can then scan the Internet looking for any known flaws with either the operating system or the Web server software. This step gives you a starting place to find out about the system and what weaknesses you might be able to exploit. In this case, you would simply go to your favorite search engine (Google, Yahoo, Lycos, and so forth) and key in something such as "FreeBSD security flaws." You would be surprised how many Web sites will provide you with details on specific flaws in a system. Some sites even have step-by-step instructions on how to exploit these weaknesses.

The fact that this information is so readily available should be enough to alarm any system administrator. As software vendors become aware of flaws, they usually write corrections to their code, known as patches or updates. If you are not regularly updating your system's patches, then you are leaving your system open to attack.

Besides strengths and weaknesses of that software, sometimes just knowing the operating system and the Web server software is enough information in and of itself. For example, if a target system is running Windows

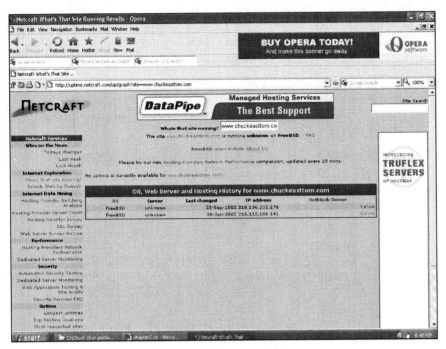

FIGURE 3.1 Running netcraft.com utilities.

NT 4.0, what would this fact tell a hacker? Because Microsoft has long ago released Windows 2000, Windows XP, and the Windows 2003 Server, the hacker can deduce that this target system does not frequently update its software. This could denote a company that is on a very tight budget or one that simply is not particularly computer-savvy. In either case, this lack of updating software means that this system probably does not employ the latest security devices and techniques.

Tracing the IP Address

The next piece of information you will want concerns the various connections between you and the target system. When you visit a Web site, the packets bouncing back and forth between you and the target site do not take a direct route from you to there. They usually bounce around the Internet, going through various Internet service providers and routers. The obvious way to obtain this information is to use the traceroute or tracert utility (discussed in Chapter 2). You can then write down the IP address of each step in the journey. However, this task can be very tedious. An easier process is offered through the Visualware Inc. Web site. Visualware offers some very interesting products, along with free online Web demos. These products automate network utilities, such as tracert and Whois, in a rich graphical interface. I find Visualware's product, VisualRoute, to be particularly useful and remarkably easy to employ.

IN PRACTICE: Using VisualRoute

To learn how this product works, we will use the online free demo of the product and perform a visual trace route on the Web site **www.chuckeasttom.com**. Note that, to try the demo, you must register your e-mail address. The Web site will only let you use the demo for a limited time.

1. Open your browser and enter **www.visualware.com**. You will see a Web page similar to that shown in Figure 3.2.

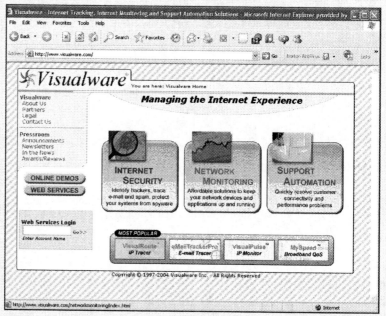

FIGURE 3.2 Visualware Web site.

2. Click the link to VisualRoute. You will see a Web page similar to that shown in Figure 3.3.

3. Click Live Demo on the left side of the page. This opens a page where you can select the starting location and enter your e-mail address in the Login/Quick Registration box, as shown in Figure 3.4.

4. Enter your e-mail address and click Go!. Within seconds (depending upon the speed of your Internet connection), you will receive an e-mail from Visualware Inc. with your login PIN number.

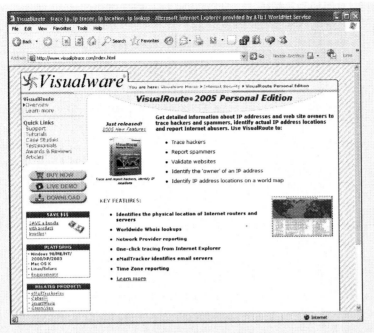

FIGURE 3.3 VisualRoute Web page.

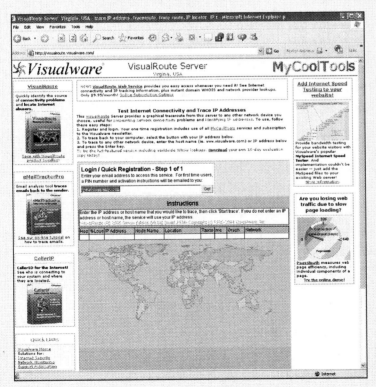

FIGURE 3.4 Live Demo login page.

CONTINUED ON NEXT PAGE

CONTINUED

5. Click the link within the e-mail or return to your browser and enter your PIN number. The VisualRoute Server page appears in your browser, as shown in Figure 3.5.

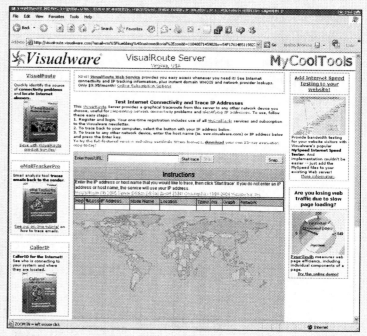

FIGURE 3.5 Visual Route Server page.

6. Enter **www.chuckeasttom.com** in the Enter Host/URL text box. You will actually be tracing the route from that location to the target, not from your location. With the full version, you will, of course, trace from your own location.

7. Click Start trace.

As a result, you can see a map of where the packet went around the world, as well as information on every single IP address it bounced through as shown in Figure 3.6.

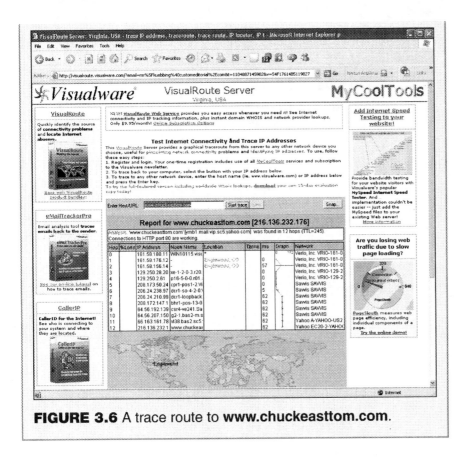

FIGURE 3.6 A trace route to **www.chuckeasttom.com**.

This information can be very useful. For example, let's say that you start a trace from different locations, and the trace always goes through the same IP address just before reaching the target. In that case, then, that IP is probably a router, gateway, or the target's ISP. With the full version of this product, you can do something even more interesting. You can double-click on any of the links and obtain a great deal of information about that IP address. You see, to register an IP on the Internet, you have to register a physical location, a person to contact (usually the network administrator), and other information. VisualRoute provides all of that information at the click of your mouse. The same information is available to you through **www.internic.net**, (see Figure 3.7) where you can look up any IP address.

Using IP Registration Information

The information gained with these utilities can be used in a variety of ways. For example, you can take the e-mail address of the administrator and do a Google "groups" search for that address. Google now provides a gateway,

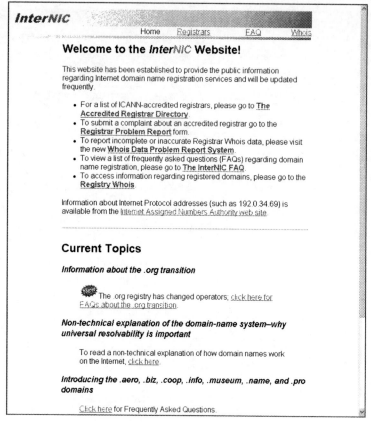

FIGURE 3.7 InterNIC Web page.

via its "groups" tab, to Usenet newsgroups. These groups are basically global bulletin boards where people can engage in discussions on a wide range of topics. Network administrators sometimes post questions in specific newsgroups hoping to get advice from their colleagues. If the network administrator of the target machine has posted, he or she may have given away more information about her network than is wise. In one case, a network administrator actually posted a link to a diagram showing his entire network, the servers, IP addresses, type of firewall, and so on. This information could have been easily exploited.

That is not to say that administrators must avoid using the Internet as an information source. That is certainly not the case. But when administrators do use newsgroups, they should not use their real name, their company's name, or any information that might facilitate tracking them back to their company. In this way, information that they discuss about their firm's network cannot readily be applied.

Social Engineering

One of the most common applications for using the information gained from reconnaissance work is social engineering, mentioned in Chapter 1. Social engineering is a non-technical way of intruding on a system. This can range from dumpster diving to trying to get employees to unwittingly compromise the system.

When *dumpster diving*, someone trying to obtain information will go through trash cans or dumpsters looking for garbage that contains information such as an IP address, password, or even a map of the network. This technique can be very messy, but also quite effective.

The most common tactic is to try to get an authorized user of a system to give you her password. This task may sound impossible, but it is actually quite easy. For example, if a hacker has discovered the name of the system administrator and knows that the company is rather large with a big Information Technology (IT) department, she can use this name to her advantage. Assume a scenario in which a hacker finds out that the network administrator for a certain firm is named Jane Smith. She can get Jane's office location, e-mail address, and phone number from internic or from using VisualRoute software. She can now call a remote office and speak to a secretary. The plan could work extremely well if that secretary (let's call him Eric) is new to the company. The hacker tells Eric that she is a new intern working for Jane Smith and that Jane has instructed her to check all the PCs to ensure that they have proper virus-scanning software. The hacker tells Eric that she cannot get on to his computer remotely without his username and password, so could Eric please give these to her? It is amazing how often the person will indeed give a username and password to a caller. With this information, the hacker does not need to use any technical skills at all. She can simply use Eric's legitimate username and password and log on to the target system.

Note that schemes such as this one are exactly why all employees in any organization need to be familiar with basic computer security. No matter how secure your system is or how much time and money you invest in security, it is all for naught if your employees are easily duped into compromising security.

There are entire volumes written on social engineering. As with all topics in this book, the goal is to acquaint you with the basics, not to make you a master of any of the topics. If you wish more information on this topic, the following links may be of interest to you:

- www.securityfocus.com/cgi-bin/sfonline/infocus.pl?id=1527
- cybercrimes.net/Property/Hacking/Social%20Engineering/SocialEngineering.html
- www.sans.org/rr/catindex.php?cat_id=51

Scanning

Once you have used VisualRoute or perhaps simply used the traceroute utility and manually looked up information on **www.internic.net**, you are now ready to move to the next phase in gathering information about a target system. This phase is completed by scanning.

The process of scanning can involve many tools and a variety of techniques. The basic goal of scanning is to identify security holes and vulnerabilities in a target host or network. Scanning is based in science, but is considered an art by many because a skilled attacker is patient and has a knack for knowing (usually based on experience) precisely where and how to scan target devices.

There are a number of utilities freely available on the Internet for performing scans. Some of the more common tools are:

- Nmap (Powerful tool available for Unix or Windows that finds ports and services available via IP)

- Hping2 (Powerful Unix-based tool used to gain important information about a network.)

- Netcat (Others have quoted this application as the "Swiss Army knife" of network utilities)

- Ping (Available on most every platform and operating system to test for IP connectivity)

- Traceroute (Maps out the hops of the network to the target device or system)

Of these, Nmap ("Network Mapper") is probably the best known and most flexible scanning tool available today. It uses IP packets in a novel way to determine what hosts are available on a network, what operating systems are running, and what firewalls are in use. It also provides options for fragmentation, use of decoy IP addresses, spoofing, stealth scans, and a number of other features. Nmap is the most widely used tool by both crackers and security professionals for the purpose of port scanning and operating system identification. Formerly, this was only a Unix-based utility, however, it has recently been extended for use with Windows systems. If you have access to or will be working on a Unix system or care to obtain the newer Windows-based Nmap, this is a utility with which you should certainly become familiar.

Network mapping is a process in which you discover information about the topology of the network. This can include gateways, routers, and servers. The first step is to "sweep" for a live system. To find live hosts, hackers ping them by sending ICMP packets. If a system is live, it will send an ICMP echo reply. ICMP messages can be blocked, so an alternative is to send a TCP or UDP packet to a port, such as 80 (http), that is frequently open, and live machines will send a SYN-ACK (acknowledgment) packet in response. Once the live system is known, utilities such traceroute or the others already discussed can provide additional information about the network by discovering the paths taken by packets to each host. This provides information about the routers and gateways in the network and the general layout of the network.

In the following sections, we will examine some methods for performing port scans. Fortunately, there are a number of utilities freely available on the Internet for doing port scanning. We will also discuss network mapping and vulnerability scanning.

3

FYI: Scanning Utilities

You can find a list of additional URLs for port scanning software in Appendix B of this book. You can also search the Internet using the keywords "port scanning."

Port Scanning

Once the IP address of a target system is known, the next step is *port scanning* and *network scanning*. Such scanning is the process of sending packets to each port on a target system to see what ports it has open (in the LISTEN state). A system has 65,535 port numbers, with one TCP port and one UDP port for each number. Each of these port numbers is a potential way to enter a system. Each port has an associated service that may be exploitable or contain vulnerabilities. Thus, viewing the ports tells you what sort of software is running. If someone has port 80 open, then he or she is probably running a Web server. If you see that all the default ports are open, that discovery probably indicates a network administrator who is not particularly security conscious and may have left all default settings on all of his or her systems. This deduction gives you valuable clues as to the kind of target you are examining. In the following sections, we will experiment with a few port scanning utilities.

IN PRACTICE: Using NetCop

We will start with NetCop, available as a free download from **www.cotse.com/pscan.htm**. (Note that this site lists other port scanners that we will work with as well.) When you download NetCop, you will get a simple, self-extracting executable that

CONTINUED ON NEXT PAGE

▸▸ CONTINUED

will install the program on your machine and will even put a shortcut in your program menu.

1. Launch NetCop. It has an intuitive screen, as shown in Figure 3.8.

Notice that the default, "Starting host," is the IP address reserved for your own machine.

2. Key in a single IP address and click Scan Now.

You will see Netcop checking each and every port. This activity is shown in Figure 3.9; it is a very methodical task and, hence, a bit slow. But the simplicity of this tool makes it particularly useful for network administrators who wish to check for open ports on their network.

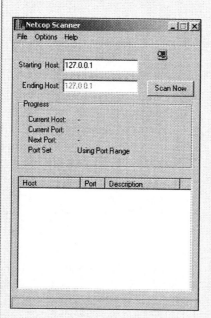

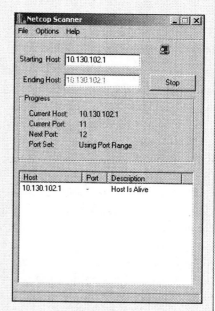

FIGURE 3.8 NetCop port scanner.

FIGURE 3.9 Scanning an IP address with NetCop.

You can, of course, stop the scan if you wish to do so; however, if you let the scan run through all of the ports, you will then see something similar to what is shown in Figure 3.10. Of course, different machines you examine will have different ports open.

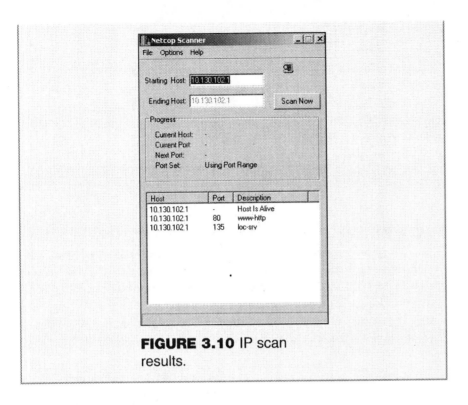

FIGURE 3.10 IP scan results.

Now that you have a tool for finding out what ports are open on a target machine, what can you do with that information? As we already mentioned, an open port can tell you a great deal about a system. Recall that, in Chapter 2, we briefly reviewed a number of well-known ports. That list was not exhaustive, but the list should give you an idea. The following Web sites list all well-known ports.

- www.networksorcery.com/enp/protocol/ip/ports00000.htm

- www.iana.org/assignments/port-numbers

- www.techadvice.com/tech/T/TCP_well_known_ports.htm

Using this information about well-known ports, you should be able to tell whether a system is using NetBIOS because such a system will have ports 137, 138, and 139 open. If a system is running an SQL server, then it may have port 118 open. This information can then be used by a hacker to begin to explore possible flaws or vulnerabilities in the service running on a given port number. Therefore, this information is quite important from a security perspective. If you are scanning your own machine and see ports that are open (ones that you do not use), then close them. All firewalls give you the option of blocking ports. That function is the most essential purpose of any firewall. A basic rule of thumb in security is that any port that you are not actively using should be blocked.

FYI: SQL Server

Generically, an SQL server is any database management system (DBMS) that can respond to queries from client machines formatted in the SQL language (Webopedia, 2004). When capitalized, the term SQL Server refers to the database management product from Microsoft: *SQL Server*. There are other SQL server programs available from other companies and each has a specific name, such as Sybase's *SQL Anywhere*.

NetBrute Some port scanners do more than simply scan for open ports. Some also give you additional information. One such product is NetBrute from RawLogic, located at **www.rawlogic.com/netbrute/**. This one is quite popular with both the security and hacker community. No computer security professionals should be without this item in their tool chest. This utility will give you open ports, as well as other vital information. Once you install and launch NetBrute, you will see a screen such as the one depicted in Figure 3.11.

FIGURE 3.11 NetBrute main screen.

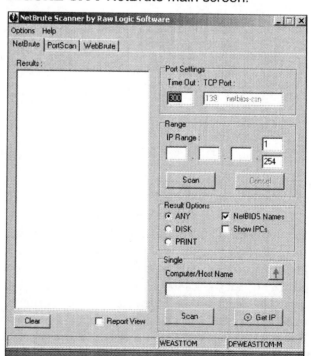

As you can see in the figure, there are three tabs. We will concentrate on the NetBrute tab first. You can elect to scan a range of IP addresses (perfect for network administrators assessing the vulnerability of their own systems), or you can choose to target an individual IP. When you are done, it will show you all the shared drives on that computer, as you see in Figure 3.12.

With the PortScan tab, you can find ports. It works exactly like the first tab except that, instead of giving you a list of shared folders/drives, it gives you a list of open ports. Thus, with NetBrute, you get a port scanner *and* a shared folder scanner. The WebBrute tab allows you to scan a target Web site and obtain information similar to what you would get from Netcraft. This scan gives you information such as the target system's operating system and Web server software. Shared folders and drives are important to security because they provide one possible way for a hacker to get into a system. If the hacker can gain access to that shared folder, she can use that area to upload a Trojan horse, virus, key logger, or other device.

Cerberus Internet Scanner Perhaps one of the most popular scanning utilities is the Cerberus Internet Scanner (a number of download locations are listed in Appendix B). This tool is remarkably simple to use and very informative. When you launch this tool, you will see a screen similar to the one shown in Figure 3.13.

FIGURE 3.12 Shared drives.

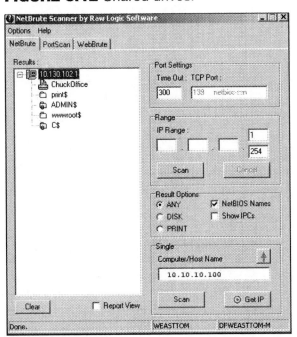

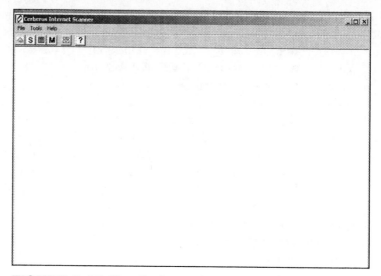

FIGURE 3.13 The Cerberus Internet Scanner.

From this screen, you can click the button on the far left that has an icon of a house, or you can go to "File" and select "Host." You then simply key in either the URL or the IP address of the machine that you wish to scan. Click either the button with the "S" on it or go to "File" and select "Start Scan." Cerberus will then scan that machine and give you back a wealth of information. You can see all the various categories of information that you receive from this scan in Figure 3.14.

FIGURE 3.14 Cerberus scan results.

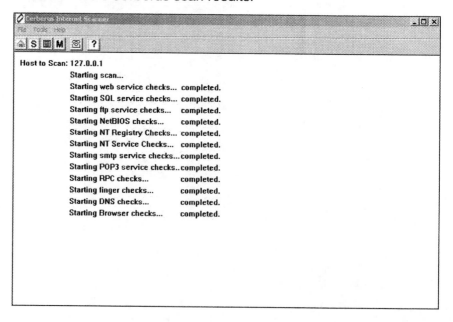

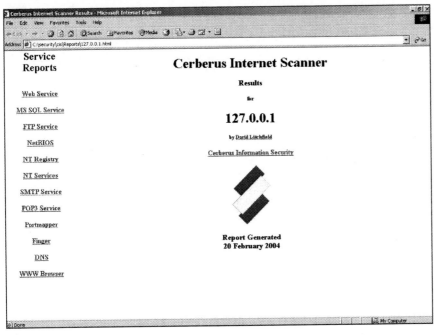

FIGURE 3.15 The Cerberus report.

Click on the third button to review the report. The report will launch a Hypertext Markup Language (html) document (thus the document is easy to save for future reference) with links to each category. (This document is shown in Figure 3.15.) Click on the category you wish to view.

One of the most interesting sections to review, particularly for a security administrator, is the NT Registry report. This report will examine the Windows Registry and inform you of any security flaws found there and how to correct them. This report is shown in Figure 3.16.

This list shows specific Windows Registry settings, why those settings are not particularly secure, and what you can do to secure them. For obvious reasons, this tool is very popular with hackers. Cerberus can provide a great map of all of a system's potential vulnerabilities including, but not limited to, shared drives, insecure registry settings, services running, and known flaws in the operating system.

All of these tools (and others we have not examined) have one thing in common: They provide information to anyone who wants it. Information is a powerful tool, but it is also a two-edged sword. Any information that a network administrator can use to secure his network, a cracker can also use to break into the network. It is imperative that all network administrators be comfortable with the various scanning tools that are available. It is a good idea to make a routine habit of scanning your own systems to search for vulnerabilities—and then close these vulnerabilities.

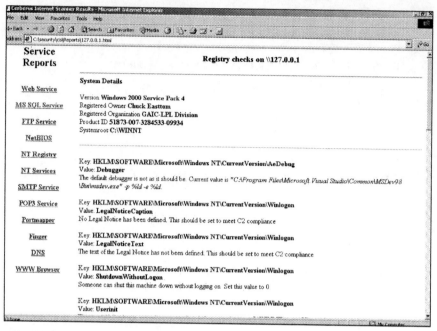

FIGURE 3.16 The NT Registry report.

FYI: Finding Utilities

There are other tools you can find for free on the Internet that will scan your computer. If you are interested in finding out more about these tools, then it is suggested that you consult the links in Appendix B. You might also consider simply using your favorite search engine to search for computer security utilities.

Port Scanner for Unix: SATAN One tool that has been popular with Unix administrators for years (as well as hackers) is SATAN. This tool is not some diabolical supernatural entity, but rather an acronym for Security Administrator Tool for Analyzing Networks. It can be downloaded for free from any number of Web sites. Many of those sites are listed at **www.fish. com/satan/mirrors.html** as shown in Figure 3.17. This tool is strictly for Unix and will not work in Windows. For that reason, we will not be discussing it here, but it is important that you be aware of it. If you intend to work with Unix or Linux, you should definitely get this utility.

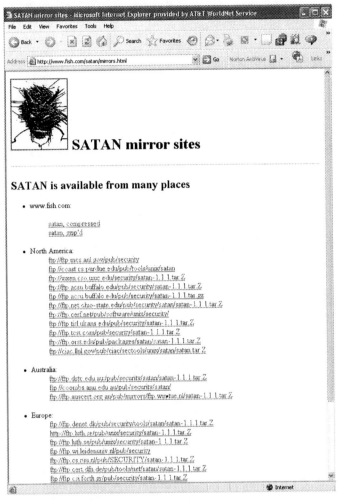

FIGURE 3.17 List of SATAN mirror sites.

Vulnerability Scanning

In addition to the utilities and scanners we have already discussed, another essential type of tool for any attacker or defender is the vulnerability scanner. A vulnerability scanner, or security scanner, will remotely audit a network and determine whether someone (or something, such as a worm) may break into it or misuse it in some way. These tools allow the attacker to connect to a target system and check for such vulnerabilities as configuration errors, default configuration settings that allow attackers access, and the most recently reported system vulnerabilities. As with port scanners, there are both commercial as well as free open-source versions of vulnerability scanners. We will discuss two vulnerability scanners here, but there are many others available.

SAINT SAINT is a network vulnerability assessment scanner that takes a preventative approach to securing computer networks. It scans a system and finds security weaknesses. It prioritizes critical vulnerabilities in the network and recommends safeguards for your data. SAINT can benefit you in several ways:

- Prioritized vulnerabilities let you focus your resources on the most critical security issues.

- Fast assessment results help you identify problems quickly.

- Highly configurable scans increase the efficiency of your network security program.

Nessus Nessus, or the "Nessus Project" as it is also known, is another extremely powerful network scanner. It is one of the most up-to-date and easy-to-use remote security scanners currently available. It is fast, reliable, and has a modular architecture that allows you to configure it to your needs. Nessus works on Unix-like systems (MacOS X, FreeBSD, Linux, Solaris, and more) and also has a Windows version called NeWT.

Additionally, Nessus includes a variety of plug-ins that can be enabled depending on the type of security checks you want to perform. These plug-ins work cooperatively with each test specifying what is needed to proceed with the test. For example, if a certain test requires a remote ftp server and a previous test showed that none exists, that test will not be performed. Not performing futile tests speeds up the scanning process. These plug-ins are updated daily and are available from the Nessus Web site.

The output from a Nessus scan of a system is incredibly detailed, and there are multiple formats available for the reports. These reports give information about security holes, warnings, and notes. Nessus does not attempt to fix any security holes that it finds. It simply reports them and gives suggestions on how to make the vulnerable system more secure.

FYI: All-In-One Reconnaissance

In addition to the number of different tools mentioned in this chapter, there are also several "all-in-one" reconnaissance tools. One such tool is Sam Spade, which can make performing initial site recon much easier on Windows. Sam Spade is a versatile network query tool with extra utilities built in to handle spam mail. It includes the typical utilities such as ping, traceroute, whois, and finger.

Port Monitoring and Managing

Using the tools we have already outlined in this chapter, you have access to a great deal of information about the ports in use on a system. There are, however, some additional tools that allow you to obtain more specific information about ports in use and their state, as well as about the flow of information in and out of those ports. Some of these tools also allow you to link a listening port to its application.

NetStat Live

One of the most popular protocol monitors is NetStat, which ships free with Microsoft Windows. A version of this, NetStat Live (NSL), which is freely available on the Internet, is a small, easy-to-use TCP/IP protocol monitor that can be used to see the exact throughput on both incoming and outgoing data whether you are using a modem, cable modem, DSL, or even a local network. It allows you see the speed at which your data goes from your computer to another computer on the Internet. It will even tell you how many other computers your data must go through to get to its destination. NSL also graphs the CPU usage of a system. This can be especially useful if, for example, you are experiencing slowed connection speeds. It can identify whether your computer is the reason for the slow down or if it is your Internet connection.

After you download and install the program, you simply run it. When the program launches, you will see a screen similar to Figure 3.18 (in this case, a distribution from AnalogX).

This display shows the last 60 seconds of data throughput. It displays the average datarate, the total amount of data sent since last reboot, and the maximum datarate. It tracks these for all incoming and outgoing messages. Figure 3.18 shows the default display window, but this window can be customized to show exactly what you want. To enable or disable a pane, simply right-click on the window, choose Statistics, and then place a check next to any statistics that you would like to see. Your choices are:

- Local Machine. The current machine name, IP address, and network interface being monitored

- Remote Machine. The remote machine, including average ping time and number of hops

- Incoming Data. Data on the incoming (download) channel

- Incoming Totals. Totals for the incoming data

- Outgoing Data. Data on the outgoing (upload) channel

- Outgoing Totals. Totals for the outgoing data

FIGURE 3.18
NetStat Live display.

- System Threads. Total number of threads currently running in the system

- CPU Usage. Graphs the CPU load

Notice that the Remote section has a machine listed and some information pertaining to it. You can easily change the server for which you are gathering information. Simply open your Web browser, go to a Web page, and copy the URL (including the http://) into the clipboard (by using Ctrl+C). When you return to viewing NSL, you will see that the server has been replaced with information on the site to which you browsed.

In addition to adjusting the display, NSL can also be configured to operate in several different ways from the Configure dialog box. To access the Configure options, right-click on the NSL display and choose Configure. You will see the Configure dialog box as shown in Figure 3.19.

From this dialog box, you can configure the program in many ways. Your configuration options are:

- Auto Minimize. If enabled, when NSL starts up, it will automatically show up in the system tray instead of as a window on the screen.

- Auto Start. If enabled, NSL will automatically run every time you reboot your machine. (This is good to use with the Auto Minimize option.)

- Always on Top. If enabled, the NSL dialog box will always be on top of other windows. This allows you to see the information no matter what else is on the screen.

- URL ClipCap. If enabled, NetStat will scan the Windows clipboard for URLs and, if it finds one, will automatically ping/traceroute it.

- Close Minimizes. If enabled, pressing the Close button does not actually close NSL, but rather minimizes it to the system tray.

- TCP/IP Interface. This drop-down list allows you to select from the TCP/IP interfaces currently available or to monitor All available interfaces. (If a specific interface cannot be found, it defaults back to All.)

FIGURE 3.19 NetStat Live Configure dialog box.

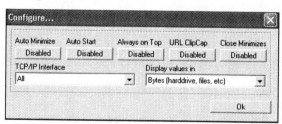

- Display values in. This drop-down list allows you to select whether or not the values are displayed in bits or bytes (the default).

NetStat Live tracks all network activity. This means that you can see how quickly data moves across the local network (as long as you are using TCP/IP) as well as to and from remote sites. Additionally, this means that, when used on a modem connection, you will see the actual throughput and not just what the dial-up networking adapter or modem says it is doing. This allows you to see exactly what kind of performance you are getting while you are browsing around Web pages.

Active Ports

Active Ports is another easy-to-use tool for Windows. This program enables you to monitor all open TCP and UDP ports on the local computer. Active Ports maps ports to the owning application so that you can watch which process has opened which port. It also displays a local and remote IP address for each connection and allows you to terminate the owning process. Active Ports can help you detect Trojan horses and other malicious programs. Figure 3.20 shows the Active Ports interface.

Like so many of these types of programs, Active Ports is available as a free download from many sites on the Internet.

Fport

Like Active Ports, fport reports all open TCP/IP and UDP ports and maps them to the owning application. Additionally, it maps those ports to running processes. Fport can be used to quickly identify unknown open ports and their associated applications.

FIGURE 3.20 Active Ports user interface.

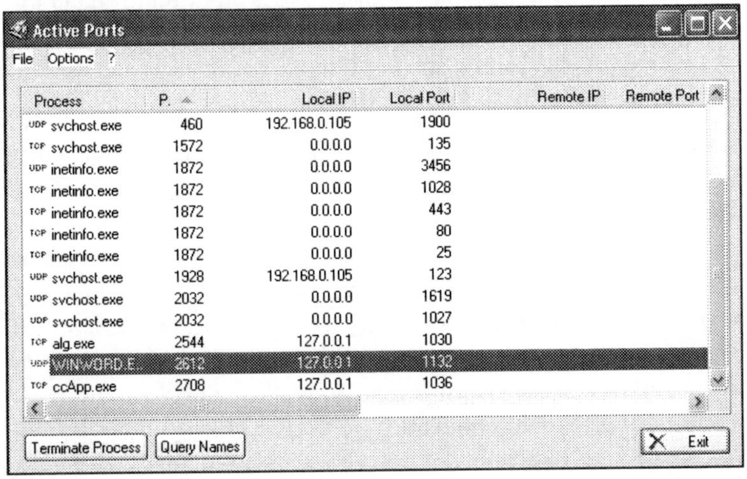

TCPView

TCPView is a Windows program that will show you detailed listings of all TCP and UDP endpoints on your system, including the remote address and the state of TCP connections. TCPView provides a conveniently presented subset of the Netstat program.

In-Depth Searches

Port scanners and other types of scanners can only tell you so much about a target system. At some point, you will probably have to take your investigation to a deeper level. For example, if you find out that a particular server is running IIS 5.0, that discovery probably means the company has Windows 2000. If you then uncover default shared folders and default registry settings, you know that the system is probably entirely set up with default settings. It is also less likely that this system is routinely patched and updated because a security-conscious administrator would not have left default settings in the first place. Your next step is to scan the Internet using various search engines (e.g., **www.yahoo.com**, **www.google.com**, **www.lycos.com**) to find out whether there are any known vulnerabilities with the target system and its configuration. There is a good chance that someone has actually documented the specific vulnerabilities and how these faults can be exploited. Once you have studied the potential vulnerabilities in a target system, you can take one of several actions, depending on your role in the investigation.

- If you are a system administrator, you must correct those vulnerabilities promptly.

- If you are a "sneaker" (or an "ethical" white hat hacker), you would document what you have found to then report to your client.

- If you are a cracker, you can use this information to select the most appropriate way to compromise the target system. However, be aware that such activities are illegal and can culminate in severe civil penalties, including as prison sentences.

Web searches and newsgroup searches (you can use Google's "groups" tab for this task) can also provide other interesting information about a site. You will often be able to find details about a company, such as its key personnel and ISP. There are several ways to use this information. For example, if you find that a company has a high turnover in its systems department (for example, you see the same job posted frequently, indicating rapid turnover), then it is less likely that the system is as secure as it should be. Or, if you see that one company is being bought out by another, this event might lead to some confusion in the two companies' IT departments as they try to merge. This information can help you identify other vulnerabilities in a target system.

Summary

Information is the key to compromising security. If someone can gain enough information about your systems and organization, then she has a much better chance of compromising the firm's security. It is imperative that you assess your own organization's vulnerabilities in this regard.

In this chapter, we have examined a variety of port scanners as well as vulnerability scanners. Having a port scanner and routinely examining your own system for vulnerabilities is a must for any security-conscious network administrator. These scanners are the same tools that hackers will use to assess your system; therefore, it is critical that you also use them.

Test Your Skills

MULTIPLE CHOICE QUESTIONS

1. When a hacker reviews a network's potential vulnerabilities, this assessment is referred to as:

   A. scanning.

   B. assessing.

   C. checking.

   D. footprinting.

2. To learn what operating system a Web server is running, what utility would you use?

   A. NetBrute

   B. NetCop

   C. www.netcraft.com

   D. www.netcheck.com

3. If you find a target Web server running Windows NT 4.0, what might this fact tell you about that system?

   A. It is a stable system that does not change often, and it is probably quite secure.

   B. The system, and possibly the administrator, have been around quite a long time and are therefore probably secure.

   C. The system is not updated frequently and may not be secure.

   D. The system is using an unproven version of Windows and therefore may not be secure.

4. Which of the following utilities will help you trace an IP address?

    A. tracert

    B. IPConfig

    C. NetCop

    D. NetBrute

5. If you trace to a destination IP from multiple-source IPs and if you see that the final few steps are always the same, what does this fact tell you?

    A. that there is an error in your trace

    B. that those final IPs could be the target's ISP or a router

    C. that those final IPs are within the target organization

    D. that those final IPs represent switches

6. What is the most common goal in social engineering?

    A. to get the phone number and e-mail address for the system administrator

    B. to get the username and password of an authorized user

    C. to get the open ports on a system

    D. to get the IP address of the e-mail server

7. What is port scanning?

    A. scanning a target to see what operating system it is running

    B. scanning a target to see what Web server it is running

    C. scanning a target to see what ports are open

    D. scanning a target to see what software is installed

8. Which of the following best describes the value of knowing what ports are open?

    A. It can reveal details about the operating system and software running.

    B. It can reveal details about the encryption of data transmission.

    C. It can reveal details about what Web server the firm is using.

    D. It can reveal details about system security.

9. If a scan determines that all default services are running, what might this finding indicate?

   A. that the system is set up with factory defaults and is therefore very secure

   B. that the system administrator is using a standard configuration

   C. that the system administrator is using a custom configuration

   D. that the system is set up with factory defaults and is therefore not very secure

10. What feature of NetCop makes it particularly useful?

    A. You can scan a single IP or multiple IPs.

    B. You can find out what ports are open.

    C. You can find out what operating system is running.

    D. You can scan multiple domains.

11. What application would you guess might be running on a Windows system that had port 118 open?

    A. Internet Information Server

    B. Windows XP

    C. Windows 2003

    D. SQL Server

12. What information do you get from the NetBrute tab of NetBrute?

    A. shared drives and folders on the target

    B. operating system on which the target is running

    C. open ports on the target

    D. Web server the target is using

13. Which scanner will give you information regarding Windows Registry settings?

    A. Cerberus Internet Scanner

    B. NetBrute

    C. NetCop

    D. Security Commander

14. Which of the following utilities gives you the most information?

    A. Cerberus Internet Scanner

    B. NetBrute

    C. NetCop

    D. Security Commander

Caution

**Scanning
and Intrusion
Detection**

In the following exercises and projects, if you use any of these port scanners on a machine that has an intrusion detection system, they will detect your port scan. For this reason, you are advised not to simply port scan random machines. You must have permission to scan a system.

15. What should a system administrator do about vulnerabilities that are found on their system?

    A. immediately correct them

    B. document them

    C. discuss the corrections with upper management

    D. change software to avoid them

EXERCISES

Exercise 3.1: Using NetCop

1. Use NetCop to scan a target machine (either your own or one that your instructor sets up for this purpose).

2. Identify any open ports, paying particular attention to open ports that your system does not require.

3. Shut down the services that use those ports.

Exercise 3.2: Using NetBrute

1. Use NetBrute to scan a target machine (either your own or one that your instructor sets up for this purpose).

2. Identify any open ports and shared drives.

3. If you have administrative rights in Windows, you can cause a shared drive or folder to no longer be shared.

Exercise 3.3: Using Netcraft

1. Use Netcraft to scan a Web site. You can use a Web site that your instructor designates, or you can select **www.chuckeasttom.com**.

2. Identify what operating system is employed and what Web server is running.

Exercise 3.4: Using Tracert and Netcraft

1. Use the tracert utility to trace any given IP address on the Internet. You can trace either the IP address or the URL (such as **www. prenticehall.com**).

2. Then use Netcraft to find information about the IP address just prior to your target.

3. Write a brief paper describing how that information might be useful to a hacker.

Exercise 3.5: Using Netstat

1. Use Netstat to determine the current statistics for the system you are using.

2. Use Ctrl+C to copy an URL from your browser window and establish that IP as the remote system.

3. Identify the speed at which data is moving across your local network as well as to the chosen remote IP address.

PROJECTS

Project 3.1: Using Cerberus Internet Scanner

1. Use Cerberus to scan a target machine that your instructor designates.

2. Note that Cerberus, in addition to port/service information, gives you information regarding insecure registry settings, shared drives, and even security flaws in database software.

3. Write a paper identifying all of the security flaws you find.

Project 3.2: Performing a Complete Scan of a System

1. Using all the utilities discussed in this chapter, scan a target system as designated by your instructor.

2. Note all deficiencies you find including open ports, insecure registry settings, shared folders, and so forth.

3. Write a paper discussing the different results you obtained from the different scanners. Did one scanner find flaws that another missed?

Project 3.3: Tracking Down Information

1. Gather information regarding a target's operating system and Web server. (You can use information derived from one of the previous exercises or projects.)

2. Then scan the Internet looking for known flaws in that version of that operating system. Simply using **www.google.com** or **www.yahoo.com** and searching for something such as "security flaws in Windows 98" should yield many results.

3. Write a brief paper on one of those flaws.

▶▶ Case Study

A network administrator named Juanita works for a small company that has a limited IT budget. Juanita has several years of network administration experience, but she is new to network security. To assess her system, she downloads NetCop and scans her system for open ports. She is able to identify several ports/services that are open that do not need to be, and she closes them. Given this scenario, consider the following questions:

- What did Juanita accomplish by closing the ports?

- What vulnerabilities might she have missed with this course of action?

- Considering what you have learned in this chapter, what further course of action would you recommend to Juanita?

Chapter | **4**

Denial of Service Attacks

Chapter Objectives

After reading this chapter and completing the exercises, you will be able to do the following:

- Understand how Denial of Service (DoS) attacks are accomplished.
- Know how certain DoS attacks work, such as SYN flood, Smurf, and DDoS.
- Take specific measures to protect against DoS attacks.
- Know how to defend against specific DoS attacks.

Introduction

By now you are aware, in a general way, of the dangers of the Internet and have also explored a few basic rules for protection on the Internet. In Chapter 3, you explored ways to investigate a target system and to learn a great deal about it. It is now time to become more specific about how attacks on systems are conducted. In this chapter, you will examine one category of attack that might be used to cause harm to a target computer system. This chapter will describe for you, in depth, the workings of the *Denial of Service (DoS)* attack. This threat is one of the most common attacks on the Internet, so it is prudent for you to understand how it works and how to defend yourself against it. Further, in the exercises at the end of the book, you will practice stopping a DoS. In information security, the old adage that "knowledge is power" is not only good advice, but also an axiom upon which to build your entire security outlook.

Overview

As was said in the introduction, one of the most common and simplest forms of attack on a system is a Denial of Service (DoS). This attack does not even attempt to intrude on your system or to obtain sensitive information; it simply aims to prevent legitimate users from accessing the system. This type of attack is fairly easy to execute. The basic concept requires a minimum of technical skill. It is based on the fact that any device has operational limits. For example, a truck can only carry a finite load or travel a finite distance. Computers are no different than any other machine; they, too, have limits. Any computer system, Web server, or network can only handle a finite load. A workload for a computer system may be defined by the number of simultaneous users, the size of files, the speed of data transmission, or the amount of data stored. If you exceed any of those limits, the excess load will stop the system from responding. For example, if you can flood a Web server with more requests than it can process, it will be overloaded and will no longer be able to respond to further requests (Webopedia, 2004). This reality underlies the DoS attack. Simply overload the system with requests, and it will no longer be able to respond to legitimate users attempting to access the Web server.

IN PRACTICE: Illustrating an Attack

One simple way to illustrate this attack, especially in a classroom setting, involves the use of the ping command discussed in Chapter 2.

1. Start a Web server service running on one machine (you can use Apache, IIS, or any Web server).
2. Ask several people to open their browsers and key the IP address of that machine in the address bar. They should then be viewing the default Web site for that Web server.

Now you can do a rather primitive DoS attack on the system. Recall from Chapter 2 that typing in ping /h will show you all the options for the ping command. The –l option changes the size of the packet you can send. Remember from Chapter 2 that a TCP packet can be only of a finite size. Thus, you are going to set these packets to be almost as large as you can send. The –w option determines how many milliseconds the ping utility will wait for a response from the target. You are going to use –0 so that the ping utility does not wait at all. Then the –t instructs the ping utility to keep sending packets until explicitly told to stop.

3. Open the command prompt in Windows 2000/XP (that is the DOS prompt in Windows 98 and the Shell in Unix/Linux).

4. Key **ping <address of target machine goes here>
   –l 65000 –w 0 –t**. You will then see something very much
   like what is shown in Figure 4.1. Note that, in the figure, I am
   pinging the loop-back address for my own machine. You will
   want to substitute the address of the machine on which you
   are running the Web server.

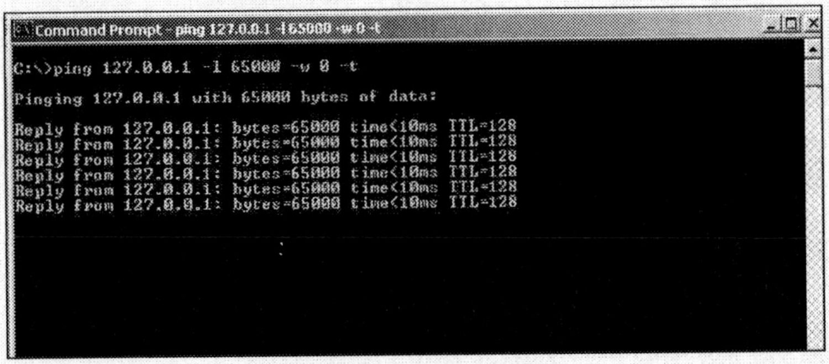

FIGURE 4.1 Ping from the command prompt.

What is happening at this point is that this single machine is
continually pinging away at the target machine. Of course, just
one machine in your classroom or lab that is simply pinging on
your Web server is not going to adversely affect the Web server.
However, you can now, one by one, get other machines in the
classroom pinging the server in the same way. After each batch of
three or four machines you add, try to go to the Web server's default Web page. After a certain threshold (certain number of machines pinging the server), it will stop responding to requests, and
you will no longer be able to see the Web page.

How many machines it will take to deny service depends on
the Web server you are using. In order to see this denial happen
with as few machines involved as possible, you could use a very
low-capacity PC as your Web server. For example, running an
Apache Web server on a simple Pentium III laptop running Windows 98, it can take about 15 machines simultaneously pinging
to cause a Web server to stop responding to legitimate requests.
This strategy is, of course, counter to what you would normally select for a Web server—no real Web server would be running on a
simple laptop with Windows 98. Likewise, actual DoS attacks use
much more sophisticated methods. This simple exercise, however,
should demonstrate for you the basic principle behind the DoS attack: Simply flood the target machine with so many packets that it
can no longer respond to legitimate requests.

Generally, the methods used for DoS attacks are significantly more sophisticated than the illustration. For example, a hacker might develop a small virus whose sole purpose is to initiate a ping flood against a predetermined target. Once the virus has spread, the various machines that are infected with that virus then begin their ping flood of the target system. This sort of DoS is easy to do, and it can be hard to stop. A DoS that is launched from several different machines is called a Distributed Denial of Service (DDoS).

Common Tools Used for DoS

As with any of the security issues discussed in this book, you will find that hackers have at their disposal a vast array of tools with which to work. The DoS arena is no different. While it is certainly well beyond the scope of this book to begin to categorize or discuss all of these tools, a brief introduction to just a few of them will prove useful. The two tools discussed here, TFN and Stacheldraht, are typical of the types of tools that someone wishing to perform a DoS attack would utilize.

TFN and TFN2K TFN, also known as Tribal Flood Network, and TFN2K are not viruses, but rather attack tools that can be used to perform a DDoS. TFN2K is a newer version of TFN that supports both Windows NT and Unix platforms (and can easily be ported to additional platforms). It has some features that make detection more difficult than its predecessor, including sending decoy information to avoid being traced. Experts at using TFN2K can use the resources of a number of agents to coordinate an attack against one or more targets. Additionally, TFN and TFN2K can perform various attacks such as UDP flood attacks, ICMP flood attacks, and TCP SYN flood attacks (all discussed later in this chapter).

TFN2K works on two fronts. First, there is a command-driven client on the master system. Second, there is a daemon process operating on an agent system. The attack works like this:

1. The master instructs its agents to attack a list of designated targets.

2. The agents respond by flooding the targets with a barrage of packets.

With this tool, multiple agents, coordinated by the master, can work together during the attack to disrupt access to the target. Additionally, there are a number of "safety" features for the attacker that significantly complicates development of effective and efficient countermeasures for TFN2K.

- Master-to-agent communications are encrypted and may be mixed with any number of decoy packets.

- Both master-to-agent communications and the attacks themselves can be sent via randomized TCP, UDP, and ICMP packets.

- The master can falsify its IP address (spoof).

Stacheldraht Stacheldraht, which is German for "barbed wire," is a DDoS attack tool that combines features of the Trinoo DDoS tool (another common tool) with the source code from the TFN DDoS attack tool. Like TFN2K, it adds encryption of communication between the attacker and the Stacheldraht masters. It also adds an automatic updating of the agents.

Stacheldraht can perform a variety of attacks including UDP flood, ICMP flood, TCP SYN flood, and Smurf attacks. It also detects and automatically enables source address forgery.

DoS Weaknesses

The weakness in any DoS attack, from the attacker's point of view, is that the flood of packets must be sustained. As soon as the packets stop sending, the target system is back up. A DoS/DDoS attack, however, is very often used in conjunction with another form of attack, such as disabling one side of a connection in TCP hijacking or preventing authentication or logging between servers.

If the hacker is using a distributed attack, as soon as the administrators or owners of the infected machines realize their machine is infected, they will take steps to remove the virus and thus stop the attack. If a hacker attempts to launch an attack from her own machine, she must be aware that each packet has the potential to be traced back to its source. This fact means that a single hacker using a DoS will almost certainly be caught by the authorities. For this reason, the DDoS is quickly becoming the most common type of DoS attack. The specifics of DDoS attacks will be discussed later in this chapter.

DoS Attacks

As you can see, the basic concept for perpetrating a DoS attack is not complicated. The real problem for the attacker is performing the attack without being caught. The next few sections of this chapter will examine some specific types of DoS attacks and look at specific case studies. This information should help you gain a deeper understanding of this particular Internet threat.

TCP SYN Flood Attack

One popular version of the DoS attack is the *SYN flood*. This particular attack depends on the hacker's knowledge of how connections are made to a server. When a session is initiated between the client and server in a network using the TCP protocol, a small buffer space in memory is set aside on the server to handle the "hand-shaking" exchange of messages that sets up the session. The session-establishing packets include a SYN field that identifies the sequence in the message exchange. An attacker can send a number of connection requests very rapidly and then fail to respond to the reply that is sent back by the server, or he can supply a spoofed (forged) IP address. In other words, he requests connections and then never follows through with the rest of the connection sequence. This process has the effect of leaving connections on the server half open, and the buffer memory allocated for them is reserved and not available to other applications. Although the packet in the buffer is dropped after a certain period of time (usually about three minutes) without a reply, the effect of many of these false connection requests is to make it difficult for legitimate requests for a session to get established.

There have been a number of well-known SYN flood attacks on Web servers. The reason for the popularity of this attack type is that any machine

---

FYI: Flood Attacks

In a **flood attack**, the attacker overwhelms a target system by sending a continuous flood of traffic designed to consume resources at the targeted server (CPU cycles, memory) and/or in the network (bandwidth, packet buffers). The goal of these attacks is to degrade service or completely shut down a site.

that engages in TCP communication is vulnerable to it—and all machines connected to the Internet engage in TCP communications. Such communication is obviously the entire reason for Web servers. There are, however, several methods and techniques you can implement to protect against these attacks. The basic defensive techniques are:

- SYN cookies
- RST cookies
- stack tweaking

Some of these methods require more technical sophistication than others. These methods will be discussed in general here. When you are entrusted with defending a system against these forms of attacks, you can select the methods most appropriate for your network environment and your level of expertise and examine it further at that time. The specifics of how to implement any of these methods will depend on the operating system that your Web server is using. You will need to consult your operating system's documentation, or appropriate Web sites, in order to find explicit instruction on how to implement methods.

SYN Cookies As the name *SYN cookies* suggests, this method uses cookies, not unlike the standard cookies used on many Web sites. With this method, the system does not immediately create a buffer space in memory for the hand-shaking process. Rather, it first sends a *SYNACK* (the acknowledgment signal that begins the hand-shaking process). The SYNACK contains a carefully constructed cookie, generated as a hash that contains the IP address, port number, and other information from the client machine requesting the connection. When the client responds with a normal ACK (acknowledgement), the information from that cookie will be included, which the server then verifies. Thus, the system does not fully allocate any memory until the third stage of the hand-shaking process as illustrated in Figure 4.2. This enables the system to continue to operate normally; typically, the only effect seen is the disabling of large windows. However, the cryptographic hashing used in SYN cookies is fairly resource intensive, so system administrators that expect a great deal of incoming connections may choose not to use this defensive technique.

FIGURE 4.2 Hand-shaking process.

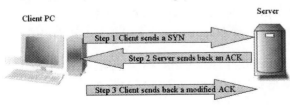

> ### FYI: Hashing
>
> A hash value is a number generated from a string of text. The hash is significantly smaller than the text itself and is generated by a formula in such a way that it is extremely unlikely that some other text will produce the same hash value. Hashing plays a role in security when it is used to ensure that transmitted messages have not been tampered with. To do this, the sending machine generates a hash of the message, encrypts it, and sends it with the message itself. The receiving machine then decrypts both the message and the hash, produces another hash from the received message, and compares the two hashes. If they are the same, there is a very high probability that the message was transmitted intact.

RST Cookies Another cookie method that is easier to implement than SYN cookies is the ***RST cookie***. In this method, the server sends a wrong SYNACK back to the client. The client should then generate an RST packet telling the server that something is wrong. Because the client sent back a packet notifying the server of the error, the server now knows the client request is legitimate and can now accept incoming connections from that client in the normal fashion. This method has two disadvantages. It might cause problems with Windows 95 machines and/or machines that are communicating from behind firewalls.

Stack Tweaking The method of ***stack tweaking*** involves altering the TCP stack on the server so that it will take less time to timeout when a SYN connection is left incomplete. Unfortunately, this protective method will just make executing a SYN flood against that target more difficult; to a determined hacker, the attack is still possible.

> ### FYI: Stack Tweaking
>
> The process of stack tweaking is often quite complicated, depending on the operating system. Some operating systems' documentation provides no help on this subject. For these reasons, this method is usually only used by very advanced network administrators and is not recommended unless you have a very solid knowledge of the operating system with which you are working.

Smurf IP Attack

The Smurf attack is a very popular version of the DoS attack. An ICMP (Internet Control Message Protocol) packet is sent out to the broadcast address of the network. Since it is broadcast, it responds by echoing the packet out to all hosts on the network, who then send it to the spoofed source address. Also, the spoofed source address can be anywhere on the Internet, not just on the local subnet. If the hacker can continually send such packets, she will cause the network itself to perform a DoS attack on one or more of its member servers. This attack is clever and rather simple. The only problem for the hacker is getting the packets started on the target network. This task can be accomplished via some software, such as a virus or Trojan horse, that will begin sending the packets.

In a Smurf attack, there are three people/systems involved: the attacker, the intermediary (who can also be a victim), and the victim. The attacker first sends an ICMP echo request packet to the intermediary's IP broadcast addresses. Since this is sent to the IP broadcast address, many of the machines on the intermediary's network will receive this request packet and will send an ICMP echo reply packet back. If all the machines on a network are responding to this request, the network becomes congested and there can be outages.

The attacker impacts the third party—the intended victim—by creating forged packets that contain the spoofed source address of the victim. Therefore, when all the machines on the intermediary's network start replying to the echo request, those replies will flood the victim's network. Thus, another network becomes congested and could become unusable.

The Smurf attack is an example of the creativity that some malicious parties can employ. It is sometimes viewed as the digital equivalent of the biological process in an auto-immune disorder. With such disorders, the immune system attacks the patient's own body. In a Smurf attack, the network performs a DoS attack on one of its own systems. This method's cleverness illustrates why it is important that you attempt to work creatively and in a forward-thinking manner if you are responsible for system security in your network. The perpetrators of computer attacks are inventive and always coming up with new techniques. If your defense is less creative and clever than the attackers' defense, then it is simply a matter of time before your system is compromised.

There are several ways to protect your system against this problem. One is to guard against Trojan horses. More will be said about the Trojan horse attack in later chapters; however, having policies prohibiting employees from downloading applications will help. Also, having adequate virus scanners can go a long way in protecting your system from a Trojan horse and, thus, a Smurf attack. It is also imperative that you use a proxy server, which was discussed in Chapter 2. If the internal IP addresses of your network are not known, then it is more difficult to target one in a

Smurf attack. Probably the best way to protect your system is to combine these defenses along with prohibiting directed broadcasts and patching the hosts to refuse to reply to any directed broadcasts.

UDP Flood Attack

UDP, as you will recall from Chapter 2, is a connectionless protocol that does not require any connection setup procedure prior to transferring data. In a *UDP flood attack*, the attacker sends a UDP packet to a random port on a target system. When the target system receives a UDP packet, it automatically determines what application is waiting on the destination port. In this case, since there is no application waiting on the port, the target system will generate an ICMP packet of "destination unreachable" and attempt to send it back to the forged source address. If enough UDP packets are delivered to ports on the target, the system will become overloaded trying to determine awaiting applications (which do not exist) and then generating and sending packets back.

ICMP Flood Attack

There are two basic types of *ICMP flood attacks*: floods and nukes. An ICMP flood is usually accomplished by broadcasting a large number of either pings or UDP packets. Like other flood attacks, the idea is to send so much data to the target system that it slows down. If it can be forced to slow down enough, the target will time out (not send replies fast enough) and be disconnected from the Internet. ICMP nukes exploit known bugs in specific operating systems. The attacker sends a packet of information that he knows the operating system on the target system cannot handle. In many cases, this will cause the target system to lock up completely.

The Ping of Death (PoD)

Recall from Chapter 2 that TCP packets are of limited size. In some cases, simply sending a packet that is too large can shut down a target machine.

FYI: Logic or Software Attacks

DoS attacks can also be of a logic or software type. In this type of attack a small number of malformed packets are sent to a target system. These packets are designed specifically to exploit known software bugs on the target system. Software attacks are relatively easy to counter. It is usually just a matter of installing a software patch that eliminates the vulnerabilities or adding specialized firewall rules to filter out the malformed packets before they reach the target system.

This action is referred to as the *Ping of Death (PoD)*. It works simply by overloading the target system. The hacker sends merely a single ping, but he does so with a very large packet and thus can shut down some machines.

This attack is quite similar to the classroom example discussed earlier in this chapter. The aim in both cases is to overload the target system and cause it to quit responding. PoD works to compromise systems that cannot deal with extremely large packet sizes. If successful, the server will actually shut down completely. It can, of course be rebooted.

The only real safeguard against PoD is to ensure that all operating systems and software are routinely patched. This attack relies on vulnerabilities in the way a particular operating system (or application) handles abnormally large TCP packets. When such vulnerabilities are discovered, it is customary for the vendor to release a patch. The possibility of PoD is one reason, among many, why you must keep patches updated on all of your systems.

Teardrop Attack

In a *teardrop attack*, the attacker sends a fragmented message. The two fragments overlap in ways that make it impossible to reassemble them properly without destroying the individual packet headers. Therefore, when the victim attempts to reconstruct the message, the message is destroyed. This causes the target system to halt or crash. There are a number of variations on the basic teardrop attack that are available such as TearDrop2, Boink, targa, Nestea Boink, NewTear, and SYNdrop.

Land Attack

A *land attack* is probably the simplest in concept. The attacker sends a forged packet with the same source IP address and destination IP address (the target's IP address). The method is to drive the target system "crazy" by having it attempt to send messages to and from itself. The victim system will often be confused and will crash or reboot.

Echo/Chargen Attack

The character generator (chargen) service was designed primarily for testing purposes. It simply generates a stream of characters. In an *echo/chargen attack*, this service is abused by attackers who exhaust the target system's resources. The attacker accomplishes this by creating a spoofed network session that appears to come from that local system's echo service and which is pointed at the chargen service to form a "loop." This session will cause huge amounts of data to be passed in an endless loop. This constant looping causes a heavy load to the system. Alternately, if the spoofed session is pointed at a system's echo service, it will cause heavy network traffic that slows down the target's network.

FYI: Man-in-the-Middle Attack

One form of attack, known as the man-in-the-middle attack, sometimes requires the use of a Denial of Service attack. In the man-in-the-middle attack, the attacker intercepts one side of an Internet conversation by using a packet sniffer at some point between the two end points. The attacker then pretends to be one end of the connection. For example the attacker might intercept traffic between a client PC and an e-commerce site. The attacker responds as if she were the intended server, therefore the client continues to send information that the attacker then retrieves. In some cases a Denial of Service is first used on the server the attacker wishes to impersonate to shut it down before the attacker attempts to 'hijack' the communication with clients.

The famous (or infamous, depending on your perspective) hacker Kevin Mitnick is alleged to have used this technique to gain passwords and login information that he later used to break into a number of major systems such as Digital Equipment Corporation (DEC), Santa Cruz Operation (SCO), and even the United States Defense Department.

Distributed Denial of Service (DDoS)

Another form of trickery is the *Distributed Denial of Service* attack (*DDoS*). As with all such denial attacks, it is accomplished by the hacker getting a number of machines to attack the target. However, this attack works a bit differently then other DoS attacks. Rather than getting computers to attack the target, one of the ways the hacker accomplishes a DDoS is to trick Internet routers into attacking a target. Another form of DDoS relies on compromised (zombie) hosts to simultaneously attack a given target with a large number of packets.

Recall from the discussion of ports in Chapter 2, that many of the routers on the Internet backbone communicate on port 179 (Gibson, 2002). This attack exploits that communication line and gets routers to attack a target system. What makes this attack particularly wicked is that it does not require the routers in question to be compromised in any way. Instead, the hacker sends a stream of packets to the various routers requesting a connection. The packets have been altered so that they appear to come from the target system's IP address. The routers respond by initiating connections with the target system. What occurs then is a flood of connections from multiple routers, all hitting the same target system. This flood has the effect of rendering the system unreachable.

Real-World Examples

A good deal of time has been spent discussing the basics of how various DoS attacks are conducted. By now, you should have a firm grasp of what a DoS attack is and have a basic understanding of how it works. It is now time to begin discussing specific, real-world, examples of such attacks. This section will take the theoretical knowledge you have gained and give you real-world examples of its application.

MyDoom

One of the most well publicized DoS attacks was the MyDoom attack. This threat was a classically distributed DoS attack. The virus/worm would e-mail itself to everyone in your address book and then, at a preset time, all infected machines would begin a coordinated attack on **www.sco.com** (Delio, 2004). Estimates put the number of infected machines between 500,000 and 1 million. This attack was successful and promptly shut down the SCO Web site. It should be noted that well before the day that the DoS attack was actually executed, network administrators and home users were well aware of what MyDoom would do. There were also several tools available free of charge on the Internet for removing the virus/worm. However, it appears that many people did not take the steps necessary to clean their machines of this virus/worm.

What makes this attack so interesting is that it is clearly an example of domestic cyber terrorism (although it is certain that the creators of My-Doom would probably see it differently). (Cyber terrorism will be discussed further in Chapter 10.) For those readers who do not know the story, it will be examined here briefly. Santa Cruz Operations (SCO) makes a version of the Unix operating system. Like most Unix versions, their version is copyright protected. Several months before this attack, SCO began accusing certain Linux distributions of containing segments of SCO Unix code. SCO sent demand letters to many Linux users demanding license fees. Many

---

FYI: Virus or Worm?

Definitions of the terms virus and worm are widely debated among the experts. And, depending upon the definition, what some would call a virus, others would call a worm. One general distinction that is accepted by many is that worms do not require direct human interaction to propagate, whereas viruses do. If you accept this definition, then both MyDoom and Slammer are worms. To avoid confusion on this issue, however, the term "virus/worm" will be used.

people in the Linux community viewed this request as simply an attempt to undermine the growing popularity of Linux, an open-source operating system. SCO went even further and filed suit against major companies that were distributing Linux (SCO./Linux, 2003). This claim by SCO seemed unfounded to many legal and technology analysts. It was also viewed with great suspicion because SCO had close ties to Microsoft, which had been trying desperately to stop the growing popularity of Linux.

Many analysts feel that the MyDoom virus/worm was created by some individual (or group of individuals) who felt that the Santa Cruz Operations tactics were unacceptable. The hackers wished to cause economic harm to SCO and damage its public image. This probable motive makes this case clearly one of domestic economic terrorism: One group attacks the technological assets of another group based on an ideological difference. Prior to this virus/worm, there were numerous Web site defacements and other small-scale attacks that were part of ideological conflicts. However, this virus/worm was the first such attack to be so widespread and successful. This incident began a new trend in information warfare. As technology becomes less expensive and the tactics more readily available, you can expect to see an increase in this sort of attack in the coming years.

Slammer

Another virus/worm responsible for DoS attacks was the Slammer virus/worm. Some experts rate Slammer as the fastest-spreading virus/ worm to ever hit the Internet (Moore, 2004). This virus/worm achieved its DoS simply by spreading so fast that it clogged up networks. It began spreading on January 25th, 2003. It would scan a network for any computers running the Microsoft SQL Server Desktop Engine. It then used a flaw in that application to infect the target machine. It would continually scan every computer connected to the infected machine, seeking one with Microsoft SQL Server Desktop Engine. At its peak, it performed millions of scans per second. This activity resulted in a tremendous number of packets going across infected networks. That flood of scanning packets brought many systems down.

This particular attack was interesting for two reasons. First, what defines this virus as also being a worm, is its method of propagation. It was able to spread without anyone downloading it or opening an attachment on an e-mail. Instead, it would randomly scan IP addresses, looking for any machine it could infect. This method meant that it spread much faster than many other virus/worm attacks had previously. The second interesting fact about this attack was that it was totally preventable. Microsoft had released a patch for this flaw weeks before the attack took place. This story should illustrate the critical need to frequently update your machine's software. You must make certain that you have all the latest patches installed on your machine.

How to Defend Against DoS Attacks

There is no guaranteed way to prevent all DoS attacks, just as there is no sure way to prevent any hacking attack. However, there are steps you can take to minimize the danger. Some methodologies, such as SYN cookies and RST cookies, have already been mentioned. In this section, a few of the steps you can take to make your system less susceptible to a DoS attack will be examined.

One of the first things for you to consider is how these attacks are perpetrated. They may be executed via ICMP packets that are used to send error messages on the Internet or are sent by the ping and traceroute utilities. If you have a firewall (and you absolutely should have one), then simply configuring it to refuse ICMP packets from outside your network will be a major step in protecting your network from DoS attacks. Since DoS/DDoS attacks can be executed via a wide variety of protocols, you can also configure your firewall to disallow any incoming traffic at all, regardless of what protocol or port it occurs on. This step may seem radical, but it is certainly a secure one.

It is also possible to detect some threats from certain DoS tools, such as TFN2K, by using information tools like NetStat. Many of these tools can be configured to look for the SYN_RECEIVED state, which could indicate a SYN flood attack.

FYI: Blocking ICMP Packets

There are very few legitimate reasons (and, some would argue, no good reasons) for an ICMP packet from outside your network to enter your network. Thus, blocking such packets is very often used as one part of the strategy to defend against DoS attacks.

If your network is large enough to have internal routers, then you can configure those routers to disallow any traffic that does not originate with your network. In that way, should packets make it past your firewall, they will not be propagated throughout the network. You should also consider disabling directed IP broadcasts on all routers. This strategy will prevent the router from sending broadcast packets to all machines on the network, thus stopping many DoS attacks. Additionally, you can install a filter on the router to verify that external packets actually have external IP addresses and that internal IPs have internal IP addresses.

Because many distributed DoS attacks depend on "unwitting" computers being used as launch points, one way to reduce such attacks is to protect your computer against virus attacks and Trojan horses. This problem will be discussed in more detail in a later chapter, but for now, it is important that you remember three things:

- Always use virus-scanning software and keep it updated.

- Always keep operating system and software patches updated.

- Have an organizational policy stating that employees cannot download anything onto their machines unless the download has been cleared by the IT staff.

As previously stated, none of these steps will make your network totally secure from either being the victim of a DoS attack or being the launch point for one, but they will help reduce the chances of either occurring. A good resource for this topic is the SANS Institute Web site, at **www.sans.org/dosstep/**. This site, shown in Figure 4.3, has some good tips on how to prevent DoS attacks.

FIGURE 4.3 SANS steps to defeat DoS attacks.

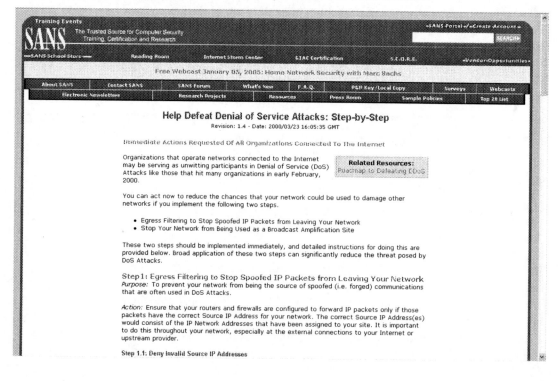

Summary

DoS attacks are among the most common attacks on the Internet. They are easy to perform, do not require a great deal of sophistication on the part of the perpetrator, and can have devastating effects on the target system. Only virus attacks are more common. (And, in some cases, the virus can be the source of the DoS attack.) In the exercises, you will practice stopping a DoS.

4

Test Your Skills

MULTIPLE CHOICE QUESTIONS

1. What is one of the most common and simplest attacks on a system?
   A. Denial of Service
   B. Buffer overflow
   C. Session hacking
   D. Password cracking

2. Which of the following is not a valid way to define a computer's workload?
   A. Number of simultaneous users
   B. Storage capacity
   C. Maximum voltage
   D. Speed of network connection

3. What do you call a DoS launched from several machines simultaneously?
   A. Wide-area attack.
   B. Smurf attack
   C. SYN flood
   D. DDoS attack

4. Leaving a connection half open is referred to as a:
   A. Smurf attack.
   B. Partial attack.
   C. SYN flood attack.
   D. DDoS attack.

5. What is the basic mechanism behind a DoS attack?

   A. Computers don't handle TCP packets well.

   B. Computers can only handle a finite load.

   C. Computers cannot handle large volumes of TCP traffic.

   D. Computers cannot handle large loads.

6. What is the most significant weakness in a DoS attack from the attacker's viewpoint?

   A. The attack is often unsuccessful.

   B. The attack is difficult to execute.

   C. The attack is easy to stop.

   D. The attack must be sustained.

7. What is the most common class of DoS attacks?

   A. Distributed Denial of Service

   B. Smurf attacks

   C. SYN floods

   D. Ping of Death

8. What are three methods for protecting against SYN flood attacks?

   A. SYN cookies, RST cookies, and stack tweaking

   B. SYN cookies, DoS cookies, and stack tweaking

   C. DoS cookies, RST cookies, and stack deletion

   D. DoS cookies, SYN cookies, and stack deletion

9. Which attack mentioned in this chapter causes a network to perform a DoS on one of its own servers?

   A. SYN flood

   B. Ping of Death

   C. Smurf attack

   D. DDoS

10. A defense that depends on a hash encryption being sent back to the requesting client is called:

    A. Stack tweaking

    B. RST cookies

    C. SYN cookies

    D. Hash tweaking

11. What type of defense depends on sending the client an incorrect SYNACK?

    A. Stack tweaking

    B. RST cookies

    C. SYN cookies

    D. Hash tweaking

12. What type of defense depends on changing the server so that unfinished hand-shaking times out sooner?

    A. Stack tweaking

    B. RST cookies

    C. SYN cookies

    D. Hash tweaking

13. What type of attack is dependent on sending packets too large for the server to handle?

    A. Ping of Death

    B. Smurf attack

    C. Slammer attack

    D. DDoS

14. What type of attack uses Internet routers to perform a DoS on the target?

    A. Ping of Death

    B. Smurf attack

    C. Slammer attack

    D. DDoS

15. Which of the following is an example of a DDoS attack?

    A. MyDoom virus

    B. Bagle virus

    C. DoS virus

    D. Smurf virus

16. How can securing internal routers help protect against DoS attacks?

    A. Attacks cannot occur if your internal router is secured.

    B. Because attacks originate outside your network, securing internal routers cannot help protect you against DoS.

    C. Securing the router will only stop router-based DoS attacks.

    D. It will prevent an attack from propagating across network segments.

17. What can you do to your internal network routers to help defend against DoS attacks?

    A. Disallow all traffic that is not encrypted

    B. Disallow all traffic that comes from outside the network

    C. Disallow all traffic that comes from inside the network

    D. Disallow all traffic that comes from untrusted sources

18. Which of the following was rated by many experts to be the fastest growing virus on the Internet?

    A. MyDoom virus

    B. Bagle virus

    C. Slammer virus

    D. Smurf virus

19. What can you do with your firewall to defend against DoS attacks?

    A. Block all incoming traffic

    B. Block all incoming TCP packets

    C. Block all incoming traffic on port 80

    D. Block all incoming ICMP packets

20. Why will protecting against Trojan horse attacks reduce DoS attacks?

   A. Because many DoS attacks are conducted using a Trojan horse to get an unsuspecting machine to execute the DoS.

   B. Because if you can stop a Trojan horse attack, you will also stop DoS attacks.

   C. Because a Trojan horse will often open ports allowing a DoS attack.

   D. Because a Trojan horse attacks in much the same way as a DoS attack.

EXERCISES

Exercise 4.1: Executing a DoS

Exercise 4.1 is best done in a laboratory setting where there are several machines available for this purpose.

1. Set up one machine (preferably a machine with very limited capacity) to run a small Web server. (You can download Apache for free for either Windows or Linux from **www.apache.org/**)

2. Use the ping utility with various other computers to attempt to perform a simple DoS on that Web server. This attempt is accomplished by getting other machines to begin a continuous ping of that target machine using the previously mentioned ping command of 'ping–l 65000 –w0 –t <insert target address here>.

3. You should add only one to three lab machines to the "attack" at a time (start with one, add on a few more, and then a few more).

4. As you add more machines, time how long it takes for another machine to bring up the home page of the target server. Also note the threshold (when that server quits responding completely).

Exercise 4.2: Stopping SYN Flood Attacks

Note that this exercise is advanced. Some students may wish to work in groups.

1. Search the Web or your operating system's documentation for instructions on implementing either the RST cookie or the SYN cookie.

2. Follow those implementation instructions on either your own machine or on a machine designated by your instructor. The following Web sites might be of help to you in this matter.

Linux:

www.liquifried.com/docs/security/scookies.html

www.linuxjournal.com/article.php?sid=3554

Windows:

cr.yp.to/syncookies.html

www.securityfocus.com/infocus/1729

Both Linux and Windows:

www.securiteam.com/tools/6D00K0K01O.html

Exercise 4.3: Using Firewall Settings

This exercise is only for students with access to a lab firewall.

1. Use your firewall's documentation to see how to block ICMP packets.

2. Set your firewall to block those packets.

Exercise 4.4: Using Router Settings

This exercise is only for students with access to a lab router.

1. Use your router's documentation to see how to block all traffic not originating on your own network.

2. Set your router to block that traffic.

PROJECTS

Project 4.1: Employing Alternative Defenses

1. Using the Web or another research tool, search for alternative means of defending against either general DoS attacks or a specific type of DoS attack. This means can be any defense other than the ones already mentioned in this chapter.

2. Write a brief paper concerning this defense technique.

Project 4.2: Defending Against Specific Denial of Service Attacks

1. Using the Web or other tools, find a DoS attack that has occurred in the last six months. You might find some resources at **www. f-secure.com**.

2. Note how that attack was conducted.

3. Write a brief explanation of how one might have defended against that specific attack.

Project 4.3: Hardening the TCP Stack Against DoS

Note that this project requires access to a lab machine. It is also a long project, requiring some research time on the part of the students.

1. Using manuals, vendor documentation, and other resources, find one method for altering TCP communications to help prevent DoS attacks. You may find the following Web sites helpful:

   support.microsoft.com/default.aspx?scid=kb;en-us;315669

   moat.nlanr.net/Software/TCPtune/

   www.anzio.com/support/whitepapers/tuning.htm

2. Using this information, implement one of these methods on your lab computer.

Case Study

Runa Singh is the network administrator in charge of network security for a medium-sized company. The firm already has a firewall, its network is divided into multiple segments separated by routers, and it has updated virus scanners on all machines. Runa wants to take extra precautions to prevent DoS attacks. She takes the following actions:

- She adjusts her firewall so that no incoming ICMP packets are allowed.

- She changes the Web server so that it uses SYN cookies.

Now consider the following questions:

- Are there problems with any of her precautions? If so, what are the problems?

- What additional steps would you recommend to Runa?

Chapter | 5

Malware

Chapter Objectives

After reading this chapter and completing the exercises, you will be able to do the following:

- Understand viruses (worms) and how they propagate, including the Sobig and Sasser types.
- Have a working knowledge of several specific virus outbreaks.
- Understand how virus scanners operate.
- Understand what a Trojan horse is and how it operates.
- Have a working knowledge of several specific Trojan horse attacks.
- Grasp the concept behind the buffer overflow attack.
- Have a better understanding of spyware and how it enters a system.
- Defend against each of these attacks through sound practices, anti-virus software, and anti-spyware software.

Introduction

In Chapter 4, we examined the Denial of Service attack. It is a very common attack and one that can easily be perpetrated. In this chapter, you will continue your examination of security threats by learning about several other types of attacks. First, you will learn about virus outbreaks. Our discussion will focus on crucial information about how and why virus attacks work, including their deployment through Trojan horses. This chapter is not a "how to create your own virus" tutorial, but rather an introduction to the concepts underlying these attacks as well as an examination of some specific case studies.

This chapter will also explore buffer overflow attacks, spyware, and several other forms of malware. Each of these brings a unique approach to an attack, and each needs to be considered when defending a system. Your ability to defend against such attacks will be enhanced by expanding your knowledge of how they work. In the exercises at the end of the chapter, you will have the opportunity to research preventative methods for viruses and to try out antivirus methods from McAffee and Norton.

Viruses

By definition, a computer *virus* is a program that self-replicates. Generally, a virus will also have some other unpleasant function, but the self-replication and rapid spread are the hallmarks of a virus. Often this growth, in and of itself, can be a problem for an infected network. The last chapter discussed the Slammer virus and the effects of its rapid, high-volume scanning. Any rapidly spreading virus can reduce the functionality and responsiveness of a network. Simply by exceeding the traffic load that a network was designed to carry, the network may be rendered temporarily non-functional.

How a Virus Spreads

A virus will usually spread primarily in one of two ways. The first is to simply scan your computer for connections to a network, then copy itself to other machines on the network to which your computer has access. This is actually the most efficient way for a virus to spread. However, this method requires more programming skill than other methods. The more common method is to read your e-mail address book and e-mail itself to everyone in your address book. Programming this is a trivial task, which explains why it is so common.

The latter method is, by far, the most common method for virus propagation, and Microsoft Outlook may be the one e-mail program most often hit with such virus attacks. The reason is not so much a security flaw in Outlook as it is the ease of working with Outlook. All Microsoft Office products are made so that a legitimate programmer who is writing software for a business can access many of the application's internal objects and thereby easily create applications that integrate the applications within the Microsoft Office suite. For example, a programmer could write an application that would access a Word document, import an Excel spreadsheet, and then use Outlook to automatically e-mail the resulting document to interested parties. Microsoft has done a good job of making this process very easy, for it usually takes a minimum amount of programming to accomplish these tasks. Using Outlook, it takes less than five lines of code to reference Outlook and send out an e-mail. This means a program can literally cause Outlook itself to send e-mails, unbeknownst to the user. There are numerous code examples on the Internet that show exactly how to do this, free for the taking. For this reason, it does not take a very skilled programmer to be able to access your Outlook address book and automatically send e-mails. Essentially, the ease of programming Outlook is why there are so many virus attacks that target Outlook.

While the overwhelming majority of virus attacks spread by attaching themselves to the victim's existing e-mail software, some recent virus outbreaks have used other methods for propagation, such as their own internal e-mail engine. Another virus propagation method is to simply copy itself across a network. Virus outbreaks that spread via multiple routes are becoming more common.

The method of delivering a payload can be rather simplistic and rely more on end-user negligence than on the skill of the virus writer. Enticing users to go to Web sites or open files they should not is a common method for delivering a virus and one that requires no programming skill at all. Regardless of the way a virus arrives at your doorstep, once it is on your system, it will attempt to spread and, in many cases, will also attempt to cause some harm to your system. Once a virus is on your system, it can do anything that any legitimate program can do. That means it could potentially delete files, change system settings, or cause other harm.

Recent Virus Examples

The threat from virus attacks cannot be overstated. While there are many Web pages that give virus information, in my opinion, there are only a handful of Web pages that consistently give the latest, most reliable, most detailed information on virus outbreaks. Any security professional will want to consult these sites on a regular basis. You can read more about any virus, past or current, at the following Web sites:

- www.f-secure.com/virus-info/virus-news/
- www.cert.org/nav/index_red.html
- securityresponse.symantec.com/
- vil.nai.com/vil/

The sections below will look at a few recent virus outbreaks and review how they operated and what they did.

The Sobig Virus The virus that received the most media attention and perhaps caused the most harm in 2003 was clearly the Sobig virus. The first interesting thing about this virus was how it spread. It spread utilizing a multi-modal approach to spreading. This means that it used more than one mechanism to spread and infect new machines. It would copy itself to any shared drives on your network *and* it would e-mail itself out to everyone in your address book. For these reasons, this virus was particularly virulent.

FYI: Virulent Virus

The term ***virulent*** means essentially the same thing in reference to a computer virus as it does to a biological virus. It is a measure of how rapidly the infection spreads and how easily it infects new targets.

In the case of Sobig, if one person on a network was unfortunate enough to open an e-mail containing the virus, not only would his machine be infected, but so would every shared drive on that network to which this person had access. However, Sobig, like most e-mail-distributed virus attacks, had tell-tale signs in the e-mail subject or title that could be used to identify the e-mail as one infected by a virus. The e-mail would have some enticing title such as "here is the sample" or "the document" to encourage you to be curious enough to open the attached file. The virus would then copy itself into the Windows system directory.

This particular virus spread so far and infected so many networks that the multiple copying of the virus alone was enough to bring some networks to a standstill. This virus did not destroy files or damage the system, but it generated a great deal of traffic that bogged down the networks infected by it. The virus itself was of moderate sophistication. Once it was out, however, many variants began to spring up, further complicating the situation. One of the effects of some variants of Sobig was to download a file from the Internet that would then cause printing problems. Some network printers would just start printing junk. The Sobig.E variant would even write to the Windows registry, causing itself to be in the computer startup (F-Secure, 2003). These complex characteristics indicate that the creator knew how to access the Windows registry, access shared drives, alter the Windows startup, and access Outlook.

This brings up the issue of virus variants and how they occur. In the case of a biological virus, mutations in the genetic code cause new virus strains to appear, and the pressures of natural selection allow some of these strains to evolve into entirely new species of viruses. Obviously, the biological method is not what occurs with a computer virus. With a computer virus, what occurs is that some intrepid programmer with malicious intent will get a copy of a virus (perhaps her own machine becomes infected) and will then reverse-engineer it. Since many virus attacks are in the form of a script attached to an e-mail, unlike traditionally compiled programs, the source code of these attacks is readily readable and alterable. The programmer in question then simply takes the original virus code and introduces some change, then re-releases the variant. Frequently, the people who are caught for virus creation are actually the developers of the variants who lacked the skill of the original virus writer and therefore were easily caught.

The Mimail Virus The Mimail virus did not receive as much media attention as Sobig, but it had its intriguing characteristics. This virus not only collected e-mail addresses from your address book, but also from other documents on your machine (Gudmundsson, 2004). Thus, if you had a Word document on your hard drive and an e-mail address was in that document, Mimail would find it. This strategy meant that Mimail would spread farther than many other viruses. Mimail had its own built-in e-mail engine, so it did not have to "piggy back" off your e-mail client. It could spread regardless of what e-mail software you used.

These two variations from most virus attacks made Mimail interesting to people who study computer viruses. There are a variety of techniques that allow one to programmatically open and process files on your computer; however, most virus attacks do not employ them. The scanning of the document for e-mail addresses indicates a certain level of skill and creativity on the part of the virus writer. In this author's opinion, Mimail was not the work of an amateur, but rather a person with professional-level programming skill.

The Bagle Virus Another virus that spread rapidly in the fourth quarter of 2003 was the Bagle virus. The e-mail it sent claimed to be from your system administrator. It would tell you that your e-mail account had been infected by a virus and that you should open the attached file to get instructions. Once you opened the attached file, your system was infected. This virus was particularly interesting for several reasons. To begin with, it spread both through e-mail and copying itself to shared folders. Secondly, it could also scan files on your PC looking for e-mail addresses. Finally, it would disable processes used by antivirus scanners. In biological terms, this virus took out your computers "immune system." The disabling of virus scanners is a new twist that indicates at least moderate programming skills on the part of the virus creator.

A Non-Virus Virus Another new type of virus has been gaining popularity in the past few years, and that is the "non-virus virus" or, put simply, a hoax. Rather than actually writing a virus, a hacker sends an e-mail to every address he has. The e-mail claims to be from some well known antivirus center and warns of a new virus that is circulating. The e-mail instructs people to delete some file from their computer to get rid of the virus. The file, however, is not really a virus but part of a computer's system. The jd-bgmgr.exe virus hoax used this scheme (Vmyths.com, 2002). It encouraged the reader to delete a file that was actually needed by the system. Surprisingly, a number of people followed this advice and not only deleted the file, but promptly e-mailed their friends and colleagues to warn them to delete the file from their machines.

FYI: The Morris Internet Worm

The Morris worm was one of the first computer worms ever to be distributed over the Internet. And it was certainly the first to gain any significant media attention.

Robert Tappan Morris, Jr., then a student at Cornell University, wrote this worm and launched it from an MIT system on November 2, 1988. Morris did not actually intend to cause any damage with the worm. Instead, he wanted the worm to reveal bugs in the programs it exploited in order to spread. However, bugs in the code allowed an individual computer to be infected multiple times, and the worm became a menace. Each additional 'infection' spawned a new process on the infected computer. At a certain point the high number of processes running on an infected machine slowed down the computer to the point of being unusable. At least 6,000 Unix machines were infected with this worm.

Morris was convicted of violating the 1986 Computer Fraud and Abuse Act and was sentenced to a $10,000 fine, three years probation, and 400 hours of community service. But perhaps the greatest impact of this worm was that it led to the creation of the Computer Emergency Response Team (CERT).

5

Rules for Avoiding Viruses

You should notice a common theme with all virus attacks (except the hoax), which is that they want you to open some type of attachment. The most common way for a virus to spread is as an e-mail attachment. This realization leads to some simple rules that will drastically reduce the odds of becoming infected with a virus.

- Use a virus scanner. McAffee and Norton (explored in the exercises at the end of this chapter) are the two most widely accepted and used virus scanners. Each costs about $30 per year to keep your virus scanner updated. Do it.

- If you are not sure about an attachment, do not open it.

- You might even exchange a code word with friends and colleagues. Tell them that if they wish to send you an attachment, they should put the code word in the title of the message. Without seeing the code word, you will not open any attachment.

- Do not believe "security alerts" that are sent to you. Microsoft does not send out alerts in this manner. Check the Microsoft Web site regularly, as well as one of the antivirus Web sites previously mentioned.

These rules will not make your system 100% virus proof, but they will go a long way toward protecting your system.

Trojan Horses

Recall from earlier chapters that a *Trojan horse* is a term for a program that looks benign but actually has a malicious purpose. You might receive or download a program that appears to be a harmless business utility or game. More likely, the Trojan horse is just a script attached to a benign-looking e-mail. When you run the program or open the attachment, it does something else other than or in addition to what you thought it would. It might:

- Download harmful software from a Web site.

- Install a key logger or other spyware on your machine.

- Delete files.

- Open a backdoor for a hacker to use.

It is common to find combination virus plus Trojan horse attacks. In those scenarios, the Trojan horse spreads like a virus. The MyDoom virus opened a port on your machine that a later virus, doomjuice, would exploit, thus making MyDoom a combination virus and Trojan horse.

A Trojan horse could also be crafted especially for an individual. If a hacker wished to spy on a certain individual, such as the company accountant, she could craft a program specifically to attract that person's attention. For example, if she knew the accountant was an avid golfer, she could write a program that computed handicap and listed best golf courses. She would post that program on a free Web server. She would then e-mail a number of people, including the accountant, telling them about the free software. The software, once installed, could check the name of the currently logged-on person. If the logged-on name matched the accountant's name, the software could then go out, unknown to the user, and download a key logger or other monitoring application. If the software did not damage files or replicate itself, then it would probably go undetected for quite a long time.

FYI: Virus or Worm?

As noted in the previous chapter, there is disagreement among the experts as to the distinction between a virus and a worm. Some experts would call MyDoom (as well as Sasser, which will be discussed later) a worm because it spread without human intervention. For the purpose of this text, these malware will be referred to as viruses.

Such a program could be within the skill set of virtually any moderately competent programmer. This is one reason that many organizations have rules against downloading ANY software onto company machines. I am unaware of any actual incident of a Trojan horse being custom-tailored in this fashion. However, it is important to remember that those creating virus attacks tend to be innovative people.

Another scenario to consider is one that would be quite devastating. Without divulging programming details, the basic premise will be outlined here to illustrate the grave dangers of Trojan horses. Imagine a small application that displays a series of unflattering pictures of Osama Bin Laden. This application would probably be popular with many people in the United States, particularly people in the military, intelligence community, or defense-related industries. Now assume that this application simply sits dormant on the machine for a period of time. It need not replicate like a virus because the computer user will probably send it to many of his associates. On a certain date and time, the software connects to any drive it can, including network drives, and begins deleting all files. If such a Trojan horse were released "in the wild," within 30 days it would probably be shipped to thousands, perhaps millions, of people. Imagine the devastation when thousands of computers begin deleting files and folders.

This scenario is mentioned precisely to frighten you a little. Computer users, including professionals who should know better, routinely download all sorts of things from the Internet, such as amusing flash videos and cute games. Every time an employee downloads something of this nature, there is the chance of downloading a Trojan horse. One need not be a statistician to realize that if employees continue that practice long enough, they will eventually download a Trojan horse onto a company machine. If so, hopefully the virus will not be as vicious as the theoretical one just outlined here.

The Buffer Overflow Attack

You have become knowledgeable about a number of ways to attack a target system: Denial of Service, virus, and Trojan horse. While these attacks are probably the most common, they are not the only methods. Another method of attacking a system is called a ***buffer overflow*** (or buffer overrun) attack. A buffer overflow attack happens when one tries to put more data in a buffer than it was designed to hold (searchSecurity.com, 2004a). Any program that communicates with the Internet or a private network must take in some data. This data is stored, at least temporarily, in a space in memory called a *buffer*. If the programmer who wrote the application was careful, when you try to place too much information into a buffer, that information is then either simply truncated or outright rejected. Given the number of applications that might be running on a target system and the number of buffers in each application, the chances of having at least one buffer that was not written properly are significant enough to cause any prudent person some concern.

Someone who is moderately skilled in programming can write a program that purposefully writes more into the buffer than it can hold. For example, if the buffer can hold 1024 bytes of data and you try to fill it with 2048 bytes, the extra 1024 bytes is then simply loaded into memory. If that extra data is actually a malicious program, then it has just been loaded into memory and is thus now running on the target system. Or, perhaps the perpetrator simply wants to flood the target machine's memory, thus overwriting other items that are currently in memory and causing them to crash. Either way, the buffer overflow is a very serious attack.

Fortunately, buffer overflow attacks are a bit harder to execute than a DoS or simple Microsoft Outlook script virus. To create a buffer overflow attack, you must have a good working knowledge of some programming language (C or C++ is often chosen) and understand the target operating system/application well enough to know whether it has a buffer overflow weakness and how that weakness might be exploited.

The Sasser Virus/Buffer Overflow

It should be interesting to note that, while writing this book, several major new virus outbreaks took place—most notably, the Sasser virus. Sasser is a combination attack in that the virus (or worm) spreads by exploiting a buffer overrun.

The Sasser virus spreads by exploiting a known flaw in a Windows system program. Sasser copies itself to the Windows directory as avserve.exe and creates a registry key to load itself at startup. In that way, once your machine is infected, you will start the virus every time you start the machine. This virus scans random IP addresses, listening on successive TCP ports starting at 1068 for exploitable systems—that is, systems that have not been patched to fix this flaw. When one is found, the worm exploits the vulnerable system by overflowing a buffer in LSASS.EXE, which is a file that is part of the Windows operating system. That executable is a built-in system file and is part of Windows. Sasser also acts as an FTP server on TCP port 5554, and it creates a remote shell on TCP port 9996. Next, Sasser creates an FTP script named cmd.ftp on the remote host and executes that script. This FTP script instructs the target victim to download and execute the worm from the infected host. The infected host accepts this FTP traffic on TCP port 5554. The computer also creates a file named win.log on the C: drive. This file contains the IP address of the localhost. Copies of the virus are created in the Windows System directory as #_up.exe. Examples are shown here:

- c:\WINDOWS\system32\12553_up.exe
- c:\WINDOWS\system32\17923_up.exe
- c:\WINDOWS\system32\29679_up.exe

A side effect of this virus is that it causes your machine to reboot. A machine that is repeatedly rebooting without any other known cause may well be infected with the Sasser virus.

This is another case in which the infection can easily be prevented by several means. First, if you update your systems on a regular basis, your systems should not be vulnerable to this flaw. Secondly, if your network's routers or firewall block traffic on the ports mentioned (9996 and 5554), you will then prevent most of Sasser's damage. Your firewall should only allow in traffic on specified ports; all other ports should be shut down. In short, if you as the network administrator are aware of security issues and are taking prudent steps to protect the network, your network will be safe. The fact that so many networks were affected by this virus should indicate that not enough administrators are properly trained in computer security.

Spyware

In Chapter 1, *spyware* was mentioned as one of the threats to computer security. Using spyware, however, requires a great deal more technical knowledge on the part of the perpetrator than some other forms of malware. The perpetrator must be able to develop spyware for the particular situation or customize existing spyware for his needs. He must then be able to get the spyware on the target machine.

Spyware can be as simple as a cookie used by a Web site to record a few brief facts about your visit to that Web site, or spyware could be of a more insidious type, such as a key logger. Recall from Chapter 1 that key loggers are programs that record every keystroke you make on your keyboard; this spyware then logs your keystrokes to the spy's file. The most common use of a key logger is to capture usernames and passwords. However, this method can capture every username and password you enter and every document you type, as well as anything else you might type. This data can be stored in a small file hidden on your machine for later extraction or sent out in TCP packets to some predetermined address. In some cases, the software is even set to wait until after hours to upload this data to some server or to use your own e-mail software to send the data to an anonymous e-mail address. There are also some key loggers that take periodic screen shots from your machine, revealing anything that is open on your computer. Whatever the specific mode of operation, spyware is software that literally spies on your activities on a particular computer.

Legal Uses of Spyware

There are some perfectly legal uses for spyware. Some employers have embraced such spyware as a means of monitoring employee use of company technology. Many companies have elected to monitor phone, e-mail, or Web traffic within the organization. Keep in mind that the computer, network, and phone systems are the property of the company or organization, not of the employee. These technologies are supposedly only used for work purposes; therefore, company monitoring might not constitute any invasion of privacy. While courts have upheld this monitoring as a company's right, it is critical to consult an attorney before initiating this level of employee monitoring as well as to consider the potential negative impact on employee morale.

Parents can also elect to use this type of software on their home computer to monitor the activities of their children on the Internet. The goal is usually a laudable one—protecting their children from online predators. Yet, as with employees in a company, the practice may illicit a strong negative reaction from the parties being spied upon—namely, their children. Parents have to weigh the risk to their children versus what might be viewed as a breach of trust.

How Is Spyware Delivered to a Target System?

Clearly, spyware programs can track all activity on a computer, and that information can be retrieved by another party via a number of different methods. The real question is this: How does spyware get onto a computer system in the first place? The most common method is a Trojan horse. It is also possible that, when you visit a certain Web site, spyware may download in the background while you are simply perusing the Web site. Of course, if an employer (or parent) is installing the spyware, it can then be installed non-covertly in the same way that organization would install any other application.

Obtaining Spyware Software

Given the many other utilities and tools that have been mentioned as available from the Internet, you probably will not be surprised to learn that you can obtain many spyware products for free, or at very low cost, on the Internet. You can check the Counterexploitation (**www.cexx.org**) Web site, shown in Figure 5.1, for a lengthy list of known spyware products circulating on the Internet and for information about methods one can use to remove them. The Spyware Guide Web site (SpywareGuide, 2004) (**www. spywareguide.com**) lists spyware that you can get right off the Internet should you feel some compelling reason to spy on someone's computer activities. Figure 5.2 (on page 120) shows the categories of malware that are available from this site. Several key logger applications are listed on this site, as shown in Figure 5.3 (on page 120). These applications include well-known key loggers such as **Absolute Keylogger**, **Tiny Keylogger**, and **TypO**. Most can be downloaded for free or for a nominal charge from the Internet.

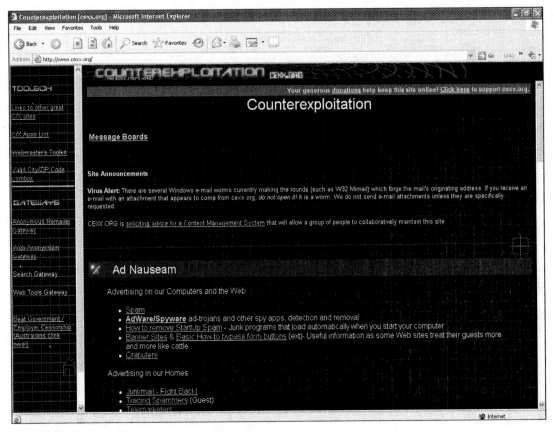

FIGURE 5.1 Counterexploitation Web site.

Some well-known Trojan horses are also listed at this site (as shown in Figure 5.4, on page 121), such as the 2nd Thought application that downloads to a person's personal computer (PC) and then blasts it with advertisements. This particular piece of spyware is one that downloads to your PC when you visit certain Web sites. It is benign in that it causes no direct harm to your system or files, nor does it gather sensitive information from your PC. However, it is incredibly annoying as it inundates your machine with unwanted ads. This sort of software is often referred to as *adware*. Frequently, these ads cannot be stopped by normal protective pop-up blockers because the pop-up windows are not generated by a Web site that you visit, but rather by some rogue software running on your machine. Pop-up blockers only work to stop sites you visit from opening new windows. Web sites use well-known scripting techniques to cause your browser to open a window, and pop-up blockers recognize these techniques and prevent the ad window from opening. However, if the adware launches a new browser instance, it bypasses the pop-up blocker's function.

FIGURE 5.2
Malware categories at
the Spyware Guide
Web site.

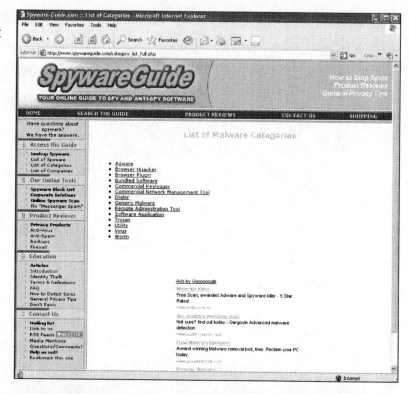

FIGURE 5.3 List of
key loggers available
through the Spyware
Guide Web site.

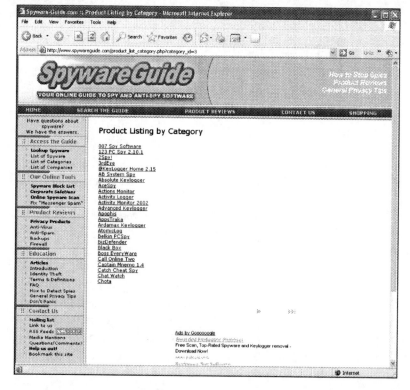

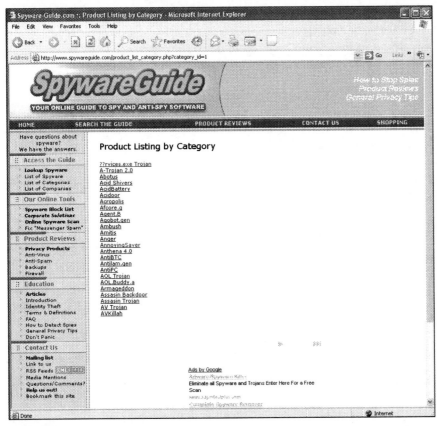

FIGURE 5.4 Trojan horses available at the Spyware Guide Web site.

Other Forms of Malware

In this and preceding chapters, the most prominent forms of malware have been discussed. There are, however, many other forms of attack. It is beyond the scope of this book to explore each of these, but you should be aware of the existence of these other forms of malware. Simply being aware can go a long way toward enabling you to defend your system efficiently. This section will touch upon just a few other forms of malware. You should reference the Web sites discussed in the end of chapter exercises and projects often so that you can stay up-to-date with all current forms of attack and defenses.

Rootkit

A rootkit is a collection of tools that a hacker uses to mask her intrusion and obtain administrator-level access to a computer or computer network. The intruder installs a rootkit on a computer after first obtaining user-level access, either by exploiting a known vulnerability or cracking a password. The rootkit then collects user IDs and passwords to other machines on the network, thus giving the hacker root or privileged access.

A rootkit may consist of utilities that also:

- monitor traffic and keystrokes

- create a "backdoor" into the system for the hacker's use

- alter log files

- attack other machines on the network

- alter existing system tools to circumvent detection

The presence of a rootkit on a network was first documented in the early 1990s. At that time, Sun and Linux operating systems were the primary targets for a hacker looking to install a rootkit. Today, rootkits are available for a number of operating systems and are increasingly difficult to detect on any network (searchSecurity.com, 2004b).

Malicious Web-Based Code

A malicious Web-based code, also known as a Web-based mobile code, simply refers to a code that is portable to all operating systems or platforms such as HTTP, Java, and so on. The "malicious" part implies that is it a virus, worm, Trojan horse, or some other form of malware. Simply put, the malicious code does not care what the operating system may be or what browser is in use. It infects them all blindly (Yakabovicz, 2003).

Where do these codes come from, and how are they spread? The first generation of the Internet was mostly indexed text files. However, as the Internet has grown into a graphical, multimedia user experience, programmers have created scripting languages and new application technologies to enable a more interactive experience. As with any new technology, programs written with scripting languages run the gamut from useful to poorly crafted to outright dangerous.

Technologies such as Java and ActiveX enable these buggy or untrustworthy programs to move to and execute on user workstations. (Other technologies that can enable malicious code are executables, JavaScript, Visual Basic Script, and plug-ins.) The Web acts to increase the mobility of code without differentiating between program quality, integrity, or reliability. Using available tools, it is quite simple to "drag and drop" code into documents that are subsequently placed on Web servers and made available to employees throughout the organization or individuals across the Internet. If this code is maliciously programmed or just improperly tested, it can cause serious damage.

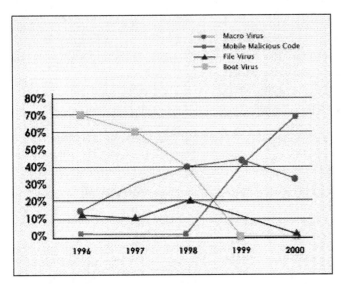

FIGURE 5.5 Growth of mobile malicious code.

Not surprisingly, hackers have used these very useful tools to steal, alter, and erase data files as well as gain unauthorized access to corporate networks. A malicious code attack can penetrate corporate networks and systems from a variety of access points including Web sites, HTML content in e-mail messages, or corporate intranets. Figure 5.5 shows the rapid growth of mobile malicious code in recent years versus viruses.

Today, with over 200 million Internet users, new malicious code attacks can spread almost instantly through corporations. The majority of damage caused by malicious code happens in the first hours after a first-strike attack occurs—before there is time for countermeasures. The costs of network downtime or theft of IP make malicious code a top priority (finjan software, 2004).

Detecting and Eliminating Viruses and Spyware

Antivirus Software

In this chapter and throughout this book, the need for running virus-scanning software has been discussed. It is prudent at this point to provide you with some details on how virus scanners work and information on the major virus-scanning software packages. This information should help you better understand how a virus scanner might help protect your system and help you make intelligent decisions regarding the purchase and deployment of some antivirus solution.

A virus scanner can work in one of two ways. The first is to look for a signature (or pattern) that matches a known virus. This is why it is important to keep your virus software updated so that you have the most recent list of signatures with which to work.

The other way in which a virus scanner might check a given PC is to look at the behavior of an executable. If that program behaves in a way consistent with virus activity, the virus scanner may flag it as a virus. Such activity could include:

- attempting to copy itself

- attempting to access the address book of the system's e-mail program

- attempting to change registry settings in Windows

Figure 5.6 shows the Norton AntiVirus software in action. You can see that the virus definitions are up-to-date, that the virus scanning is enabled, auto-protection is enabled, and the Internet worm protection is enabled as well. The other popular virus scanners have many of the same features.

Anti-Spyware Software

Fortunately, just as there are many different spyware applications available, there are likewise many different software applications on the market that are designed specifically to detect and remove spyware. These applications are also usually available at extremely low cost. You can often get a free trial

FIGURE 5.6 Norton AntiVirus interface.

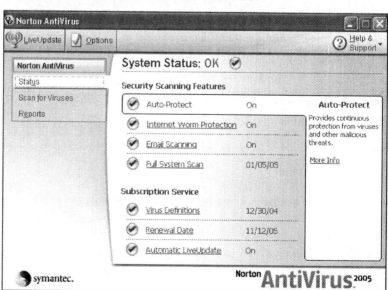

version to use for a limited time so you can make a more intelligent purchasing decision. Of course, the most prudent course of action you can take to avoid getting spyware on your machine is to never download anything from the Internet that does not come from a very well-known and trusted Web site. However, in an organizational environment, you cannot simply rely on your employees to do the right thing. It is prudent as the company's computer security expert to take steps yourself to prevent the employees from compromising your system security.

Some of the better known and more widely used anti-spyware applications include Spy Sweeper from **www.webroot.com**, Spy Killer from **www.spykiller.com**, Zero Spyware Removal from **www.zerospyware. com**, and Spector Pro from **www.spectorsoft.com**. All of these applications can be obtained for anywhere from $20 to $50, and many offer a free trial version.

Figure 5.7 shows the items found by running the WebRoot Spy Sweeper software on a system. These items can be selected for quarantine and removal.

Figure 5.8 shows the summary results after all of the items found have been quarantined. Note that the number of files scanned, the number of items removed, the date the full sweep was performed, as well as additional information is all detailed on this summary page. Each of the anti-spyware applications would provide similar results and each contain similar options for sweeping a system.

FIGURE 5.7 Items recommended for removal by Spy Sweeper.

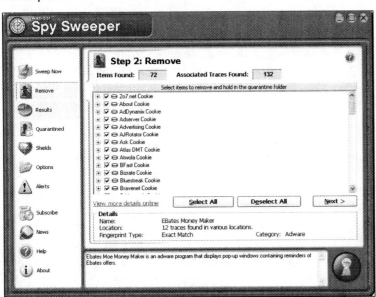

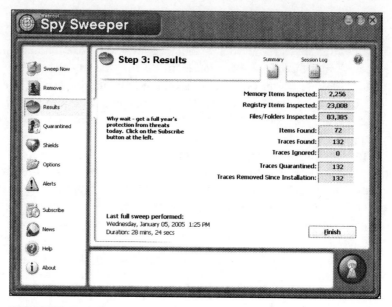

FIGURE 5.8 Summary results of a system sweep.

Summary

Clearly, there are a number of ways to attack a target system: by Denial of Service, virus/worm, Trojan horse, buffer overflow attacks, and spyware. Each type of attack comes in many distinct variations. It should be obvious by this point that securing your system is absolutely critical. In the upcoming exercises, you will try out the antivirus programs by Norton and McAffee. There are so many ways for a hacker to attack a system that securing your system can be a rather complex task. Chapter 6 will deal with specific methods whereby you can secure your system.

Another theme that is driven home throughout this chapter is that many, if not most, attacks are preventable. The exercises ahead will give you practice in figuring out how to prevent the Sasser and Sobig virus. In most cases, prompt and regular patching of the system, use of antivirus tools, and blocking unneeded ports would prevent the attack. The fact that so many systems do get infected is an indication of the very real problem of network professionals who are not skilled in computer security.

Test Your Skills

MULTIPLE CHOICE QUESTIONS

1. Which of the following is the best definition of virus?

    A. program that causes harm on your computer

    B. program used in a DoS attack

    C. program that slows down networks

    D. program that self-replicates

2. What is the most common damage caused by virus attacks?

    A. slowing down networks by the virus traffic

    B. deleting files

    C. changing the Windows registry

    D. corrupting the operating system

3. What is the most common way for a virus to spread?

    A. by copying to shared folders

    B. by e-mail attachment

    C. by FTP

    D. by downloading from a Web site

4. Which of the following is the primary reason that Microsoft Outlook is so often a target for virus attacks?

    A. Many hackers dislike Microsoft.

    B. Outlook copies virus files faster.

    C. It is easy to write programs that access Outlook's inner mechanisms.

    D. Outlook is more common than other e-mail systems.

5. Which of the following virus attacks used a multi-modal approach?

    A. Slammer virus

    B. Mimail virus

    C. Sobig virus

    D. Bagle virus

6. What factor about the Sobig virus made it most intriguing to security experts?

   A. It spread in multiple ways.

   B. It deleted critical system files.

   C. It was difficult to protect against.

   D. It was very sophisticated.

7. What was most interesting to security experts about the Mimail virus?

   A. It spread more rapidly than other virus attacks.

   B. It spread in multiple ways.

   C. It grabbed e-mail addresses from documents on the hard drive.

   D. It deleted critical system files.

8. Which of the following reasons most likely made the Bagle virus spread so rapidly?

   A. The e-mail containing it claimed to be from the system administrator.

   B. It copied itself across the network.

   C. It was a sophisticated virus.

   D. It was particularly virulent.

9. What made the Bagle virus so dangerous?

   A. It changed Windows registry settings.

   B. It disabled antivirus software.

   C. It deleted key system files.

   D. It corrupted the operating system.

10. Which of the following is a way that any person can use to protect against virus attacks?

    A. set up a firewall

    B. use encrypted transmissions

    C. use secure e-mail software

    D. never open unknown e-mail attachments

11. Which of the following is the safest way to send and receive attachments?

    A. use a code word indicating the attachment is legitimate

    B. only send spreadsheet attachments

C. use encryption

D. use virus scanners before opening attachments

12. Which of the following is true regarding e-mailed security alerts?

 A. You must follow them.

 B. Most companies do not send alerts via e-mail.

 C. You can trust attachments on security alerts.

 D. Most companies send alerts via e-mail.

13. Which of the following is something a Trojan horse might do?

 A. open a back door for malicious software

 B. change your memory configuration

 C. change ports on your computer

 D. alter your IP address

14. What is a buffer overflow attack?

 A. overflowing a port with too many packets

 B. putting more e-mail in an e-mail system than it can hold

 C. overflowing the system

 D. putting more data in a buffer than it can hold

15. What virus exploited buffer overflows?

 A. Sobig virus

 B. Mimail virus

 C. Sasser virus

 D. Bagle virus

16. What can you do with a firewall to help protect against virus attacks?

 A. There is nothing you can do on the firewall to stop virus attacks

 B. Shut down all unneeded ports

 C. Close all incoming ports

 D. None of the above

17. A key logger is what type of malware?

 A. virus

 B. buffer overflow

 C. Trojan horse

 D. spyware

18. Which of the following is a step that all computer users should take to protect against virus attacks?

    A. purchase and configure a firewall

    B. shut down all incoming ports

    C. use non-standard e-mail clients

    D. install and use antivirus software

19. What is the primary way a virus scanner works?

    A. by comparing files against a list of known virus profiles

    B. by blocking files that copy themselves

    C. by blocking all unknown files

    D. by looking at files for virus-like behavior

20. What other way can a virus scanner work?

    A. by comparing files against a list of known virus profiles

    B. by blocking files that copy themselves

    C. by blocking all unknown files

    D. by looking at files for virus-like behavior

EXERCISES

Exercise 5.1: Using Norton Anti-Virus

1. Go to the Norton antivirus Web site (**www.symantec.com/ downloads**) and download the trial version of their software.

2. Install and run their software.

3. Carefully study the application, noting features that you like and dislike.

Exercise 5.2: Using McAffee Anti-virus

1. Go to the Mcaffee antivirus Web site (**us.mcafee.com/root/ package.asp?pkgid=100&cid=9901**) anddownload the trial version of their software.

2. Install and run their software.

3. Carefully study the application, noting features you like and dislike.

Exercise 5.3: Preventing Sasser

1. Using resources on the Web or in journals, carefully research the Sasser virus. You may find that **www.f-secure.com** or Symantec's virus information center at **www.sarc.com/avcenter/** are helpful in this exercise.

2. Write a brief essay about how it spread, what damage it caused, and what steps could be taken to prevent it.

Exercise 5.4: Preventing Sobig

1. Using resources on the Web or in journals, carefully research the Sobig virus. You may find that **www.f-secure.com** or Symantec's virus information center at **www.sarc.com/avcenter/** are helpful in this exercise.

2. Write a brief essay about how it spread, what damage it caused, and what steps could be taken to prevent it.

Exercise 5.5: Learning about Current Virus Attacks

1. Using resources on the Web or in journals, find a virus that has been spreading in the last 90 days. You may find that **www.f-secure. com** or Symantec's virus information center at **www.sarc.com/ avcenter/** are helpful in this exercise.

2. Write a brief essay about how it spread, what damage it caused, and what steps could be taken to prevent it.

Exercise 5.6: Using Anti-Spyware Software

1. Go to Spy Sweeper Web site (**www.webroot.com/downloads**) and download the trial version of the software.

2. Install and run the Spy Sweeper software.

3. Carefully study the application, exploring the options and noting features that you like and dislike.

4. Repeat this process to download and explore Adaware software (which is available from a variety of Web sites).

5. Assess which of these two anti-spyware applications would work best for your computer system.

PROJECTS

Project 5.1: Antivirus Policies

This activity can also work as a group project.

Considering what you have learned in this chapter and in previous chapters, as well as using outside resources, write an antivirus policy for a small business or school. Your policy should include technical recommendations as well as procedural guidelines. You may choose to consult existing antivirus policy guidelines that you find on the Web to give you some ideas. The following Web sites may be of some help to you in this project:

- www.sans.org/resources/policies/Anti-virus_Guidelines.pdf
- irmc.state.nc.us/documents/approvals/1_VirusPolicy.pdf

However, you should not simply copy their antivirus policies. Rather, you should come up with your own.

Project 5.2: The Worst Virus Attacks

Using resources on the Web, books, or journals, find a virus outbreak that you consider to have been the worst in history. Write a brief paper describing this attack, and explain why you think it is the worst. Was it widely spread? How quickly did it spread? What damage did it do?

Project 5.3: Why Write a Virus?

A number of hypotheses have been formed regarding why people write a virus. These hypotheses range from the frankly conspiratorial to the academically psychological. Taking whatever position you feel is most likely, write a paper explaining why you think people take the time and effort to write a virus.

Case **Study**

Chiao Chien manages IT security for a school. Given the wide range of people who use the school's computers, it is difficult for Chien to prevent virus attacks. Chien has a reasonably good budget and has installed antivirus software on every machine. He also has a firewall that has all unneeded ports blocked, and there is a school policy prohibiting the downloading of any software from the Web. Consider the following questions:

- How secure do you think Chien's network is from virus attacks?

- What areas has Chien not secured?

- What recommendations would you make to Chien?

5

Chapter | 6

Basics of Assessing and Securing a System

Chapter Objectives

After reading this chapter and completing the exercises, you will be able to do the following:

- Probe a system for vulnerabilities.
- Understand how policies are set.
- Evaluate potential security consultants.
- Properly set security on an individual workstation.
- Properly secure a server.
- Establish general guidelines for network security.
- Safely surf the Web.

Introduction

At this point, it should be clear that it is necessary to assess any system periodically for vulnerabilities. The first part of this chapter will discuss the essential steps that you should follow in assessing a system for vulnerabilities. The purpose of this chapter is to get someone who is new to computer security to begin thinking about these issues. This chapter is not meant to be a comprehensive treatment of the subject, nor a substitute for getting an expert consultant. In fact, many of the topics, such as disaster recovery and policies, have had entire volumes written on them. However, it should give you a basic blueprint you can follow. Specific details will depend on your particular environment, budget, skills, and security needs.

In this book, you have thus far examined a number of threats to individual computers and networks. You have discussed specific defenses against each of these dangers. However, you have not yet looked at a comprehensive approach to security. In the second part of this chapter, you will learn many of the security procedures that can be implemented to provide your environment with more secure computing. Note that this chapter is about overall procedures that you need to perform in securing a system rather than specific step-by-step techniques.

Basics of Assessing a System

Disaster recovery, access rights, and appropriate policies are topics that are often overlooked by those new to security. To keep it simple and easy to remember, the stages of assessing a system's security can be separated into the "six p's":

- Patch
- Ports
- Protect
- Policies
- Probe
- Physical

Patch

The first rule of computer security is to check patches. This is true for networks, home computers, laptops—literally any computer. This means that the operating system, database management systems, development tools, Internet browsers, and so forth are all checked for patches. In a Microsoft

---

FYI: Patching and Applications

Whenever there is a patch to an operating system or application, there is also documentation (sometimes in a Read Me file, sometimes at the download site) that indicates what the patch is fixing. This documentation also lists any known adverse interactions with other applications. Therefore, you should always read this documentation before you install a patch. In most cases, the problems are minimal and often involve obscure situations. But it is always good to check first to make sure that a service or application upon which you are dependent is not adversely impacted.

environment, this should be easy, as the Microsoft Web site has a utility that will scan your system for any required patches to the browser, operating system, or Office products. It is a very basic tenet of security to ensure that all patches are up to date. This should be one of the first tasks when assessing a system.

Once you have ensured that all patches are up to date, the next step is to set up a system to ensure that they are kept up to date. One simple method is to initiate a periodic patch review where, at a scheduled time, all machines are checked for patches. There are also automated solutions that will patch all systems in your organization. It is imperative that all machines be patched, not just the servers.

Ports

As you learned in Chapter 2, all communication takes place via some port. Any port you do not explicitly need should be shut down. This means that those unused services on servers and individual workstations should be shut down. Both Windows XP and Linux have built-in port-filtering capability. Windows 2000 Professional also has port-filtering capability. Shutting down a service in Windows and port filtering are both discussed in more detail below.

You should also shut down any unused router ports in your network. If your network is part of a larger wide area network (WAN), then it is likely you have a router connecting you to that WAN. Every open port is a possible avenue of entry for a virus or intruder. Therefore, every port you can close is one less opportunity for such attacks to affect your system.

Caution

**Don't Know—
Don't Touch**

Caution should be taken when shutting down services so you do not inadvertently shut down a service that you need. It is always a good idea to check with your operating system documentation. The rule of thumb is that if you are not sure, don't touch it.

IN PRACTICE: Shutting Down a Service in Windows

For an individual machine that is not running firewall software, you do not directly close ports; instead, you shut down the service using that port. For example, if you do not use an FTP service but you see that port is on, chances are that you unknowingly have an

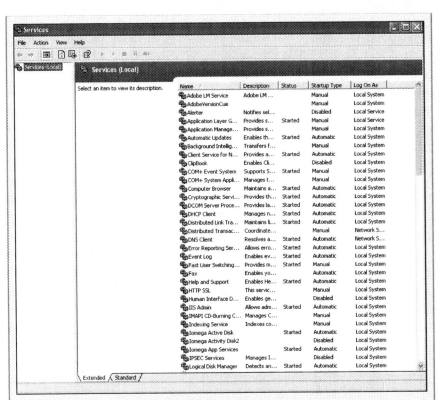

FIGURE 6.1 Services.

FTP service running on that machine. In Windows 2000 or Windows XP, if you have administrative privileges, the following three steps can be taken to shut down an unneeded service.

1. Go to Start, select Settings (in Windows 2000 only), and choose Control Panel. Double-click Administrative Tools.

2. Double-click Services. You should see a window similar to the one shown in Figure 6.1.

   The window in Figure 6.1 shows all services installed on your machine, whether they are running or not. Notice that the window also displays information about whether a service is running, whether it starts up automatically, and so forth. In Windows XP, more information can be seen by selecting an individual service. When you double-click on an individual service in either Windows 2000 or Windows XP, you see a dialog box similar to Figure 6.2 that describes the details about that service.

▶▶ CONTINUED ON NEXT PAGE

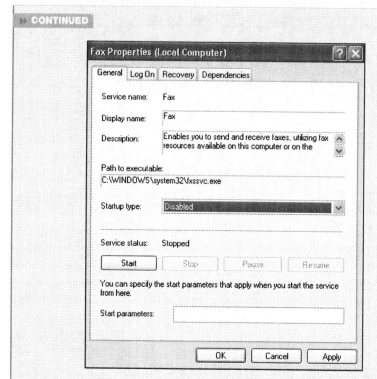

FIGURE 6.2 Disabled services.

In the example shown in Figure 6.1, you see a fax service on a machine that does not require it. To illustrate the procedure, this service is going to be disabled. Before you turn off any service, however, you need to check whether other services depend on the one you are about to shut off. If other services depend on the one you want to turn off and you proceed to turn it off, you will cause the other services to fail.

3. Click on the Dependencies tab. In our case, the fax service has no dependencies.

4. Click the General tab.

5. Change the Startup type to Disabled.

6. Click the Stop button in the Service status section, if necessary. Your dialog box should look similar to Figure 6.2. The fax service is now shut down.

7. Click OK to accept the edits made and close the Properties dialog box. Close the Services dialog box and the Administrative Tools dialog box.

Caution

Dependencies

Always check dependencies before shutting down a service. If other services depend on that service, you will then be causing them to malfunction by shutting it down.

Shutting down unneeded ports and services is an essential and very basic part of computer security. As mentioned above, every port open (and every service running) is a possible avenue for a hacker or virus to get to your machine. Therefore, the rule is: If you don't need it, shut it down and block it. NetCop, which was discussed in Chapter 3, is a tool that allows you to detect running ports. It is easy to use and effective, but is not the only tool available. In fact, there are many such tools, some of which are listed in Appendix B of this book. Or, you can simply conduct a Web search for *port scanner* to find a number of options, many of which are free.

IN PRACTICE: Port Filtering in Windows

Windows 2000 and Windows XP also have port-filtering services available. (Note that port filtering cannot be applied to adapters on an interface-by-interface basis. Anything you set will be applied universally to all adapters.)

1. Go to the Control Panel and double-click Network Connections. You will see a window similar to Figure 6.3.

FIGURE 6.3 Network connections.

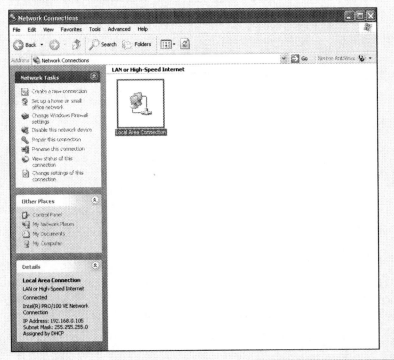

▶▶ CONTINUED ON NEXT PAGE

2. Right-click Local Area Connection and select Properties. You will see a dialog box similar to Figure 6.4.

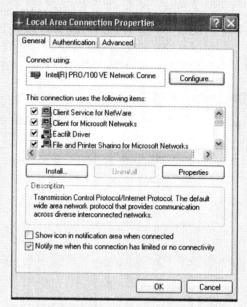

FIGURE 6.4 TCP/IP properties.

3. Scroll down, if necessary, select Internet Protocol (TCP/IP), and then click Properties.

4. In the Internet Protocol (TCP/IP) Properties dialog box, click Advanced. You will see a dialog box with four tabs.

5. Select the Options tab as shown in Figure 6.5. (In addition to the filtering option shown, you may also have a security option. The security option is rather simple. You simply choose whether to use IPSec or not. Because the topic of IPSec is beyond the scope of this chapter, just leave that set to the default setting.)

6. Select TCP/IP filtering and then click Properties. The TCP/IP Filtering dialog box, shown in Figure 6.6, allows you to choose whether to allow all packets or only packets communicating on certain ports. You can choose to allow all traffic or only traffic on ports or protocols that you set.

7. Make your selections and then click OK three times to close the dialog box, accepting your changes.

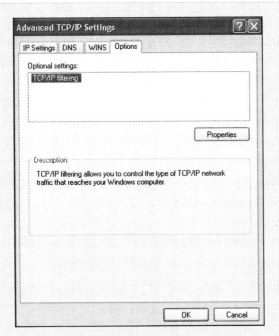

FIGURE 6.5 Options tab.

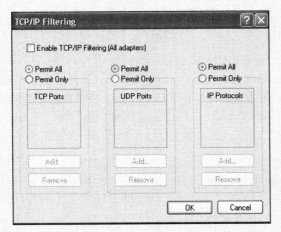

FIGURE 6.6 Filtering ports and protocols.

8. Click Close in the Local Area Connections Properties dialog box to accept any changes made.
9. Close the Network Connections window.

It is best for you to first make a list of all software that you are running. Then, look up the ports and protocols that you will need for that software and allow only those. It is important to keep in mind that these are ports for incoming traffic. If your machine is not used as a database server, Web server, or other type of server and if your machine is a stand-alone one, you can (and should) close all ports. Workstations on networks may need some ports open for network utilities.

Protect

The next phase of assessing a system's security is to ensure that all reasonable protective software and devices are employed. This means, at a minimum, a firewall between your network and the outside world. Firewalls were discussed in Chapter 2. You should also consider using an intrusion detection system (IDS) on that firewall and any Web servers. An IDS is considered non-essential by some security experts; you can certainly have a secure network without one. However, they are the only way to know of impending attacks, and there are free, open source IDSs available. For that reason, most experts highly recommend them. The firewall and IDS will provide basic security to your network's perimeter, but you also need virus scanning. Each and every machine, including servers, must have a virus scanner that is updated regularly. The point has already been made that a virus infection is the greatest threat to most networks. As also previously discussed, it is probably prudent to consider anti-spyware software on all of your systems. This will prevent users of your network from inadvertently running spyware on the network.

Finally, a proxy server, also discussed in Chapter 2, is a very good idea. It not only masks your internal IP addresses, but most proxy servers allow you to discover what Web sites users visit and put on filters for certain sites. Many security experts consider a proxy server to be as essential as a firewall.

IN PRACTICE: Finding a Firewall

When selecting a firewall to use, you have a number of options. You can purchase a very inexpensive router-based firewall for your high speed Internet connection. You can get a router that is separate from your DSL or cable router. Or you can get one that includes the functions of your cable or DSL router with the firewall. The Web sites listed below should be helpful to you in finding more information on these options and determining which will best suit your needs.

- Linksys: **www.linksys.com/products/product.asp?prid=20& grid=5**
- Home PC Firewall Guide: **www.firewallguide.com/**

- Broadband Guide: **www.firewallguide.com/broadband.htm**

In addition to the information on the firewall options available, you can also find many free or very inexpensive firewall packages on the Internet. Following is a list of some of the more popular firewalls available via the Internet.

- Firestarter: This is a free packet filtering application for Linux available at **www.fs-security.com**. This software is installed a Linux machine designed to be used as your network firewall.
- Norton Personal Firewall: This product is inexpensive and is available for multiple operating systems. A free trial download is available from **www.symantec.com**.
- McAffee Personal Firewall: This product is similar in price and basic function to Norton Personal Firewall. You can find out more about this product at **us.mcafee.com**.
- Outpost Firewall: This product is designed for the home or small office user. It has both a free version and an enhanced commercial version. You can find out more about this product at **www.agnitum.com/products/outpost/**.

For medium-sized or larger networks, with more flexible budgets, you might consider the options listed below.

- The company Teros offers an application gateway specifically tailored for Web servers. This solution is relatively inexpensive and can be ideal for companies whose primary function is to provide Web sites or Web services. Information is available at **www.teros.com/products/appliances/gateway/index.shtml**.
- The Firebox, from Watchguard Technologies (**www.watchguard.com/products/fireboxx.asp**), is an application gateway firewall that is router-based. It is relatively easy to setup and configure and is appropriate for medium sized networks.

And finally, for Linux users, you might consider the Wolverine product. Wolverine is a robust commercial firewall solution for Linux available from **www.coyotelinux.com**. Wolverine provides stateful packet inspection, built in VPN capabilities (VPNs will be discussed in detail in Chapter 7), several encryption methods (AES, DES, and more), and offers a Web-based administration utility. It is also very inexpensive. This is an excellent solution for any network using Linux.

Policies

It is absolutely essential that any organization have clearly written policies on computer security—and that those policies be strongly enforced by management. Those policies should cover acceptable use of organizational computers, the Internet, e-mail, and any other aspect of the system. Policies should prohibit the installation of any software on the systems. Only IT personnel should install software and only after they have verified its safety.

Policies should also advise users against opening unknown and/or unexpected attachments. Something that I recommend is for people within an organization or department use a codeword. If that codeword does not appear in the body of the e-mail (or in the subject line), then they do not open the attachment. Most virus attacks spread via e-mail attachments. The subject line and body of such e-mail messages are generated automatically by the virus itself. If all of your legitimate attachments have a codeword in the subject line, it is highly unlikely that this word would be in the subject line of an e-mail sent by a virus. This alone could prevent your users from inadvertently opening a virus.

Polices should also be in place that clearly delineate who has access to what data, how backups are performed, and what to do to recover data in the case of a disaster (commonly called a disaster recovery plan). Data access must be limited to only those personnel with an actual need to access the data. For example, not everyone in the human resources department needs access to disciplinary files on all employees. Does your organization have a plan for what to do if a fire destroys your servers with all their data? Where do you get new machines? Who gets them? Is there an offsite copy of the data backup? All of these questions must be addressed in a disaster recovery plan.

There should be a policy regarding passwords: acceptable minimum length, lifetime of a password, password history, and passwords to be avoided, such as any word that has a direct connection to the user. For example, a user who is a big fan of the Dallas Cowboys should not use a password that has any relation to that sports team. Also, passwords that relate to personal data, such as spouse's birthday, children's names, or pet's names, are poor choices. A password policy could also include recommendations or restrictions on a password.

Additionally, a password should not be kept for long periods of time. A 90- or 180-day password replacement schedule is good for most situations. This is referred to as *password age*. (This, of course, must be weighed against the user's access to sensitive information or data. A company financial officer might change her password weekly; a nuclear arms engineer might change his password daily; and a mail clerk might need to change her password on a much less frequent basis.) You can set many systems (including Windows) to force the user to get a new password after a certain period of time. You should also make sure the person does not merely reuse old

FYI: Good Passwords

A good password is at least eight (preferably 15) characters long; contains letters, numbers, and characters; and combines upper- and lowercase. A good general practice is to select a word that has no personal meaning to you, a random sequence of numbers, and then various case letters and characters to further disguise the password. For example, you might use something such as $TrEe785. That password would be virtually impossible for anyone to guess and difficult for password-cracking software to break. It would, however, also be difficult to remember. For this reason, many people in the information security field are recommending the use of **pass phrases** instead of passwords. These create longer passwords that are even more difficult to break. An example would be: *My telephone # is 555-555-1234.* This is a 30-character password containing uppercase, lowercase, numbers, and special characters. It is also much easier to remember than $TrEe785.

6

passwords, referred to as **password history** and also referred to in some operating systems as uniqueness. A good rule of thumb is a history depth of five—meaning that the person cannot reuse any of their previous five passwords. Additionally, you may need to implement a minimum password age to prevent users from immediately changing their password five times to return to their current password. Generally, a minimum of one day is recommended.

FYI: How Extensive Should Policies Be?

This question frequently arises: How extensive should policies be? Should they be a few brief pages or a lengthy manual? Various computer security experts will have differing opinions. My opinion is that the policies should be lengthy enough to cover your organizational needs, but not so lengthy as to be unwieldy. In short, overly long policy manuals are likely to be left unread by employees and hence not be followed. If you absolutely must have a long policy manual, then create a few brief sub-manuals for specific employee groups so as to increase the chances of the policies being read and followed. It is probably a good idea to have new hires briefed on security polices by someone from the IT Security department.

Finally, policies should include specific instructions on what to do in case of an employee termination. It is imperative that all of that person's login accounts be immediately disabled and any physical access they have to any part of the system be immediately discontinued. Unfortunately, many organizations fail to address this properly and give an opportunity to a disgruntled former employee to inflict retribution on his or her former employer.

Probe

An important step in assessing any network is to probe the network. In Chapter 3, several tools were mentioned that are freely available from the Internet that can be used to scan your network. Microsoft also has its own security analyzer tool that can scan one or a range of IP addresses. This tool is available from **support.microsoft.com/default.aspx?scid=kb%3Ben-us%3Bq320454**, or you can simply do a Web search in any search engine for it. A general recommendation is that any security assessment be comprised of at least three separate analysis tools to assess the network. For example, on a Microsoft network, you should use the Cerberus Internet Scanner, the Microsoft Security Analyzer, and one other tool, such as Net-Cop or SATAN.

The key is to periodically probe your own network for security flaws. This should be a regularly scheduled event—perhaps once a quarter. At a minimum, a complete audit of your security should be completed once per year. That would, of course, include probing your ports. However, a true security audit would also include a review of your security policies, your patching system, any security logs you maintain, personnel files of those in secure positions, and so forth.

Physical

Lastly, you cannot ignore physical security. The most robustly secure computer that is left sitting unattended in an unlocked room is not at all secure. You must have some policy or procedure governing the locking of rooms with computers as well as the handling of laptops, PDAs, and other mobile computer devices. Servers must be in a locked and secure room with as few people as is reasonably possible having access to them. Backup tapes should be stored in a fireproof safe. Documents and old backup tapes should be destroyed before disposal (e.g., by melting tapes, magnetizing hard disks, breaking CDs).

Physical access to routers and hubs should also be tightly controlled. Having the most hi-tech, professional information security on the planet but leaving your server in an unlocked room to which everyone has access is a recipe for disaster. One of the most common mistakes in the arena of physical security is co-locating a router or switch in a janitorial closet. This means that, in addition to your own security personnel and network administrators, the entire cleaning staff has access to your router or switch, and any one of them could leave the door unlocked for an extended period of time.

There are some basic rules you should follow regarding physical security:

- Server Rooms: The room where servers are kept should be the most fire-resistant room in your building. It should have a strong door with a strong lock, such as a deadbolt. Only those personnel who actually have a need to go in the room should have a key. You might also consider a server room log wherein each person logs in when they enter or exit the room. There are actually electronic locks that record who enters a room, when they enter, and when they leave. Consult local security vendors in your area for more details on price and availability.

- Workstations: All workstations should have an engraved identifying mark. You should also routinely inventory them. It is usually physically impossible to secure them as well as you secure servers, but you can take a few steps to improve their security.

- Miscellaneous equipment: Projectors, CD burners, laptops, and so forth should be kept under lock and key. Any employee that wishes to use one should be required to sign it out, and it should be checked to see that it is in proper working condition and that all parts are present when it is returned.

Securing Computer Systems

In this section, you will examine various security specifics for an individual workstation, a server, and a network. You should be aware, however, that you do not need to reinvent the wheel. A number of very reputable organizations have put together step-by-step guides, or security templates, that you can use in your network setting. These can be modified to fit your particular organization, or they can be used as a starting point for you in forming your own security strategy.

- The National Security Agency has a Web site with a number of specific network security guides: **www.nsa.gov/snac/**

- The Center for Internet Security offers a number of security guides and benchmarks: **www.cisecurity.com/**

- The SANS institute has a number of sample policies you can download and modify or use: **www.sans.org/resources/policies/**

There are also templates that can be applied to many operating systems and applications (such as Microsoft Windows and Microsoft Exchange) that will implement certain security precautions. These templates can be found for many products and then simply installed on the appropriate machine. Some security professionals prefer to handle the details of security themselves, but many administrators find these templates to be useful—and they can be invaluable for the beginner.

- Windows 2000 templates:
  web.ukonline.co.uk/cook/sectemplate.htm

- MS Exchange templates:
  www.microsoft.com/exchange/default.mspx

- A collection of Windows templates:
  www.networkcert.net/security/templates.htm

The use of these templates will at least give you a baseline of security on the applications to which they are applied.

Securing an Individual Workstation

There are a number of steps that any prudent individual can take to make their individual computer secure. These steps should be taken for both home computers and workstations on a network. In the former case, securing the individual computer is the only security option available. In the

---

FYI: Hardening a System

The process of securing a computer system against hackers, malware, and other intruders is sometimes referred to as **hardening** a system. You may see the terms "server hardening" or "router hardening" commonly used.

latter case, securing the individual computers as well as the perimeter allows for a layered approach to security. While some network administrators simply secure the perimeter via a firewall and/or proxy server, it is generally believed that you should also secure each and every machine in your organization. This is particularly vital in protecting against virus attacks and some of the Distributed Denial of Service attacks that you learned about in Chapter 4.

The first step with an individual computer is to ensure that all patches are appropriately applied. Microsoft's Web site has utilities that will scan your machine for needed patches for both Windows and Microsoft Office. It is critical that you do this on a regular basis—once per quarter as a minimum. You should also check your other software vendors to see whether they have some similar mechanism to update patches for their products. It is amazing how many virus outbreaks have been widespread despite patches being available to secure the flaws they exploited. Too many people simply do not ensure that patches are applied regularly. For a home computer, this is the most critical step in your security strategy and will protect you from a number of attacks designed to exploit security flaws. For a networked workstation, this is still a vital piece of the overall security strategy and cannot be ignored.

The second step in securing an individual computer is restricting the ability to install programs or alter the machine configuration. In a network environment, this would mean that most users do not have permissions to install software or change any system settings. Only network administrators and designated support staff should have that ability. In a home environment, this would mean that only a responsible party or parties (such as the parents) have access rights to install software.

One of the reasons for this particular precaution is to prevent users from accidentally installing a Trojan horse or other malware on their machine. If a person is prevented from installing any software, then there is no chance of inadvertently installing improper software such as a Trojan horse, adware, or other malware. Blocking users from altering the machine's configuration also prevents them from changing system security settings. Novice users may hear of some way to change some setting and will do so, not realizing the security risks they are exposing their system to.

A perfect example in which a novice might adversely alter security settings involves the Windows messenger service. This is not used for chat rooms or instant messaging, as many novices incorrectly assume. It is instead used for network administrators to send a broadcast message to all people on a network. Unfortunately, some adware programs also use that service to circumvent pop-up blockers and inundate you with ads. Thus, a security-conscious person might disable that service. You would not want an inexperienced person to turn it back on by thinking it is needed for instant messaging.

It is absolutely critical in any network environment that limits be placed on what the average user can do to a machine's configuration. Without such limits, even well-meaning employees could eventually compromise security. This particular step is often met with some resistance from the organization. If you are in charge of a system's security, it is your job to educate the decision makers as to why this step is so critical.

The next step has been discussed previously in this book. Each and every computer must have antivirus and anti-spyware software. You must also set it to routinely automatically update its virus definitions. Updated, running antivirus software is an integral part of any security solution. The two-pronged approach of anti-spyware and antivirus software should be a major component in your individual computer security strategy. Some analysts feel that anti-spyware is a nice extra, but not a critical component. Others contend that spyware is a rapidly growing problem and will probably eventually equal or surpass the dangers of virus attacks.

Of course, if your operating system has a built-in firewall, it is a good idea to configure it and have it turned on. Windows XP and Linux both come with built-in firewall features. Turn them on and configure them properly. The only significant problem you may encounter in implementing this step is that most networks require a certain amount of traffic between key servers (such as the DNS server) and individual computers. When you configure your firewall, make certain you are allowing appropriate traffic through. If you are at home, you can simply block all incoming traffic. If you are on a network, you must identify what traffic you need to allow.

Passwords and physical security, as discussed earlier in this chapter, are a critical part of computer security. You must ensure that all users utilize passwords that are at least eight characters long and consist of a combination of letters, numbers, and characters. In general, make sure that your password policy is complete and that all employees follow it. This will ensure that your physical security system is sound.

Following these guidelines will not make your computer totally impervious to danger, but these guidelines will make your workstation as secure as it reasonably can be. Remember that, even in a network environment, it is critical to also secure each individual computer as well as the perimeter.

Securing a Server

The core of any network lies in its servers. This includes database servers, Web servers, DNS servers, file and print servers, and so on. These computers provide the resources for the rest of the network. Generally, your most critical data will be stored on these machines. This means that these computers are an especially attractive target for intruders and securing them is of paramount importance.

Caution

Completely Secure?

You should not be lulled into a false sense of security by employing these methods. The very best security will always be attentive and security-conscious computer users. The only totally secure computer is one that is not connected to any network or the Internet and never has any software installed on it. Unfortunately, that is also a useless computer.

Essentially, to secure a server, you should apply the steps you would to any workstation and then add additional steps. There will not be a user on that machine routinely typing documents or using spreadsheets, so extra-tight restrictions are unlikely to cause the same difficulties for end users that they might on a workstation.

To begin with, you must follow the same steps you would for a workstation. Each and every server should have its software routinely patched. It should also have virus-scanning software and perhaps anti-spyware as well. It is critical that access to these machines, both via logging on and physical access, be limited to only those people with a clear need. There are, however, additional steps you should take with a server that you might not take with a standard workstation.

Most operating systems for servers (e.g., Windows 2000 Server edition, Linux) have the ability to log a variety of activities. These activities would include failed logon attempts, software installation, and other activities. You should make sure that logging is turned on and that all actions that might pose any security risk are logged. You then must make certain that those logs are checked on a periodic basis.

Remember that the data on a server is more valuable than the actual machine. For this reason, data must be backed up on a regular basis. A daily backup is usually preferred but, in some cases, a weekly backup might be adequate. The backup tapes should be kept in a secure offsite location (such as a bank safety deposit box) or in a fireproof safe. It is critical that you limit access to those backup tapes just as you would limit access to the servers themselves.

With any computer, you should shut down any service you do not need. However, with a server, you may wish to take the extra step of uninstalling any software or operating system components you do not need, meaning that anything not required for the server to function should be removed. But think carefully about this before proceeding. Clearly, games and office suites are not needed for a server. However, a browser might be necessary to update patches.

There is another step that should be taken with servers that is not necessary with workstations. Most server operating systems have built-in accounts. For example, Windows has built-in administrator, guest, and power user accounts. Any hacker who wants to try and guess passwords will begin by trying to guess the passwords that go with these standard users. In fact, there are utilities on the Web that will do this automatically for the would-be intruder. First, you should create your own accounts with names that do not reflect their level of permission. For example, disable the administrator account and create an account called basic_user. Set up basic_user as the administrator account, with appropriate permissions. (Of course, only give that username and password to those people you want to have administrator privileges.) If you do this, a

Caution

Windows Registry

A note of caution should be made: If you are not comfortable and experienced with the Windows registry, you should not make any changes. You can change things that can severely impact your computer's operation.

FYI: Handling Old Backup Media

Unfortunately, many network administrators simply throw old backup media in the trash. If a person with malicious intent retrieves this discarded media, they could restore it to their own machine. This could give them access to your older data without breaking in to your system or could give them very valuable clues as to your current security practices, depending on what is found on that media. Old media (e.g., tapes, CDs, hard disks) should be thoroughly destroyed. For a CD, this means physically breaking it. For a tape, this means partially or completely melting it. Hard disks should be magnetized with a powerful magnet.

hacker would not immediately guess that this account is the one that they want to crack. Remember, hackers ultimately want administrative privileges on a target system; concealing which accounts have those privileges is a vital step in preventing the hacker from breaching your security.

There are a variety of registry settings in any version of Windows that can be altered to increase your security. If you use a scanning tool, such as Cerberus, it returns a report stating the weaknesses in your registry settings. What items in the registry settings might cause a security problem? A few items that are commonly examined include:

- Logon: If your registry is set so that the logon screen shows the last user's name, you have done half of the hacker's work for her. Since she now has a username, she only needs to guess the password.

- Default Shares: Certain drives/folders are shared by default. Leaving them shared like this presents a security hazard.

These are just a few of the potential problems in the Windows registry. A tool such as Cerberus will not only tell you what the problems are, but will make recommendations for corrections. To edit your registry, go to Start, select Run, and then key regedit. This will start the registry editor.

Securing a Network

Obviously, the first step in securing a network is to secure all computers that take part in that network, including all workstations and servers. However, this is just one part of network security. By now it should be clear that using a firewall and proxy server are also critical elements in network security. Chapter 12 will provide more details on these devices. For now, it is important to realize that you need to have them. Most experts also recommend using an IDS. There are a number of such systems available—some are even free. These systems can detect things, such as port scanning, which might indicate that a person is preparing to attempt a breach of your security perimeter.

If your network is at all large, then you might consider partitioning it into smaller segments with a firewall-enabled router between segments. In this way, if one segment is compromised, the entire network will not be compromised. In this system, you might consider putting your most important servers (database, file) on a secure segment.

Since Web servers must be exposed to the outside world and are the most common point of attack, it then makes sense to separate them from the rest of the network. Many network administrators will put a second firewall between the Web server and the rest of the network. This means that, if a hacker exploits a flaw in your Web server and gains access to it, then he will not have access to your entire network. This brings up the issue of what should be on your Web server. The answer is: only what you need to post Web pages. No data, documents, or other information should be stored on that server, and certainly no extraneous software. The operating system and Web server software are all that are required. You may add a few other items (such as an IDS) if your situation requires it. Any other software running on that server is a potential security risk.

You must also have policies that guide users in how to use the system, as we discussed earlier in this chapter. The most robust security in the world will not be of much use if a careless user inadvertently compromises your security. Keep in mind that you must have policies in place that guide users in what is considered appropriate use of the system and what is not.

Just as you take steps to harden your servers (e.g., patching the operating system, shutting down unneeded services), you should also harden your router. The specifics of what needs to be done will be contingent on your particular router manufacturer and model, but a few general rules should be followed:

- Use good passwords: All routers are configurable. They can be programmed. Therefore, you must obey the same password policies on a router that you would use on any server including minimum password length and complexity, age of password, and password history. If your router allows you to encrypt the password (as Cisco and other vendors do), then do it.

- Use logging: Most routers allow for logging. You should turn this on and monitor it just as you would monitor server logs.

- Security Rules: Some basic router security rules should also be followed:

- Do not answer to Address Resolution Protocol (ARP) requests for hosts that are not on the user local area network (LAN).
- If no applications on your network use a given port, that port should be also shut down on the router.
- Packets not originating from inside your LAN should not be forwarded.

These rules are simply a beginning. You will need to consult your vendor's documentation for additional recommendations. You must absolutely pay as much attention to securing your router as you do to securing your servers. The following links might be helpful:

- Router security: **www.mavetju.org/networking/security.php**

- Cisco router hardening: **www.sans.org/rr/whitepapers/firewalls/ 794.php**

Safe Web Surfing

People like to surf the Web. It is one of the most common activities that people engage in on a computer. There are privacy and security settings within your browser software. Utilizing these tools is the first step to safe Web surfing. You should not even consider Web surfing without first setting the appropriate privacy and security settings for your browser.

Obviously, antivirus and anti-spyware software play a role in safe Web surfing. In fact, using the Internet without those two pieces of software is simply reckless. Likewise, you should not reveal any personal information online. That, too, is a critical part of Web surfing.

Are there other things you can do to surf the Web safely? Yes, there are. To begin with, the World Wide Web (WWW) is much like any city—there are good neighborhoods and bad neighborhoods. Some Web sites, often referred to as warez sites, offer the ability to download illegal copies of commercial software. In addition to the fact that this is both illegal and unethical, it should be noted that these sites are famous for virus infections. Visiting those sites is an open invitation to getting a virus or Trojan horse. Similarly, you should be extremely cautious in your use of bulletin boards and chat rooms. These sites can be magnets for potential hackers and other individuals whose intention it is to do you harm. In short, you should follow the same advice on the Web as you do in an unknown city: stick to the well-lit, populated, major streets.

You should also be wary of downloading anything from the Internet. Unless it comes from a well-known and reliable source, simply do not download it. It is often tempting to download free music, games, and so on. However, anytime you download anything from the Internet, there is a chance of downloading a virus or a Trojan horse.

Getting Professional Help

You may decide that you need outside help to set up and test your system's security. This option is one that most security professionals would highly recommend if at all possible, particularly if you are new to security. It can be extremely helpful to get a professional consultant to assist you in setting up your initial security strategy and policies and perhaps do a periodic audit of your security. As mentioned in Chapter 1, there are a number of people who claim to be hackers who are not. Frankly, there are also a number of self-proclaimed security experts who simply do not have the requisite skills. The question here is: How do you determine whether an individual is qualified? Following are some guidelines to consider in making this decision.

Experience is the most important factor when looking for a security professional. You want someone with a minimum of five years of IT experience, with two years related to security. Often, this will be a network administrator or programmer who has moved into security. Note that this is a minimum level of experience. More experience is always better. It is certainly possible that someone with less experience might have the requisite skill, but it is unlikely. Everyone needs a place to start, but you do not want your systems to be the place where someone is learning.

The quality of the person's experience is as important as the length of experience. Ask details about the person's experience. For example, exactly what role did she play in computer security? Did she simply set up policies, or did she actually do hands-on security work? What was the result? Was her system free from virus infections and hacker breaches or not? Can you contact her references? In short, simply because a person states that she was responsible for information security on her resume is not enough. You need to find out exactly what she did and what the results were.

Another important aspect of a security professional is education. Remember that computer security is a very broad subject. One needs an understanding of networks, protocols, programming, and more. It is entirely possible for a person with no formal education to have these skills, but it is less likely than if they had a formal education. Generally, these skills will most likely be found in a person with experience and a degree in a computer- or math-related field. That may sound somewhat intellectually snobbish, but it is a fact. There are many people in IT who are self-taught, such as people with history degrees that are network administrators or psychology majors that are now programmers. However, the more areas a person focuses in, the harder it is to obtain mastery. This is not to say that a person cannot be a security professional without a computer science, math, or engineering degree. The point is simply that this is one factor you should consider. If someone has an unrelated degree but meets or exceeds all other qualifications, you might still consider them. Some colleges are beginning

6

Caution

Free from Intrusion?

No matter how good a security system is most will eventually fail. When considering the qualifications of a security professional, you may start by asking: *Was your system free from virus infections and breaches?* It would not be surprising, nor necessary disqualifying, if the answer to this question was *No.* You would just need to follow up that question with: *How often was your system infected with a virus or breeched by a hacker?*

to offer security-specific curriculum, and a few even offer security degrees. Clearly, specific training in computer security would be the most preferable security background.

Certifications have become very controversial in the IT profession. Some people swear by them. You can easily find many job advertisements that demand certain certifications, such as the CNE (Certified Novel Engineer) or MCSE (Microsoft Certified Systems Engineer). On the other hand, you would have no problem finding some IT professionals who denigrate certifications and consider them utterly worthless. A more reasonable position is somewhat between the two extremes. A certification can be a good indicator of a candidate's knowledge of a specific product. For example, if you want someone to secure your Microsoft network, looking at people that are Microsoft-certified is not a bad idea. You should balance that, however, by keeping in mind that it is entirely possible for someone with a good memory to use the various study guides available on the Internet and pass a test they don't actually understand. That is where experience comes in. A certification coupled with appropriate experience is a good indicator of skill.

In addition to the certifications for network administrators, there are a number of security-related certifications. Some have more credibility than others. The Security+ exam from CompTIA and the CIW Security Analyst are both conceptual exams. This means that they test a candidate's knowledge of security concepts and not their ability to actually implement any security solution. This means that, by themselves, they may not indicate the skill level you need. But if, for example, you are securing a network using Novell, a candidate who is a CNE and has CIW Security Analyst or Security+ might be a good person to consider.

Microsoft also now offers a security track to their MCSE certification. If you have a Microsoft network you wish to secure, it might be a good idea to consider this. However, the most respected security certification is the CISSP (Certified Information Systems Security Professional). This test is a grueling six-hour exam and can only be taken if you first verify three years of security-related experience. CISSP holders are also required to submit a

---

FYI: Computer Security Education and Certifications

More detailed information on computer security education (both academic and corporate training) as well as professional certifications can be found in Appendix A. This appendix also contains useful information to consider should you need to hire a security professional.

recommendation from another CISSP or an officer of their company and to take continuing education credits to maintain the certification. This is probably the most respected security-related certification.

With all of that being said, you should never hire a person based solely on certifications. Those certifications should simply be one element that you consider.

Finally, you should consider personal background. A security consultant or full-time employee will, by definition, have access to confidential information. Any legitimate security professional will not mind giving you:

- References
- Permission to check their credit history
- Permission to check their criminal background

Anyone who seems reluctant to provide any of these items should be avoided. Therefore, an ideal security consultant might be a person with five or more years of experience, a degree in a computer-related discipline, a certification in your organization's operating systems as well as one of the major security certifications, and a completely clean background, with references. As a rule, you simply cannot be too careful in hiring a security consultant.

Unless you have a highly trained security expert on staff, you should consider bringing in a security consultant to assess your system at least once. In our current legal environment, liability for security breaches is still being hotly debated. Companies are being sued for failing to practice due diligence in computer security. It is simply a wise move, both from a computer industry perspective as well as from a legal perspective, to do everything reasonable to ensure the security of your systems.

Summary

This chapter has outlined some basic items to look for in any security assessment. You should periodically assess your network/system for security vulnerabilities. A general recommendation would be a quarterly assessment for non-critical/low-security sites and perhaps as frequently as a weekly assessment for high-security sites. In any case, what are outlined in this chapter are the basics of assessing the security of a network, and they should give you a start toward securing your own network.

Safe computing is a matter of securing your computer, your network, and your servers and using common sense on the Web. It is important to rigorously apply security practices and standards to all computers, whether they are home computers or part of an organizational network.

Test Your Skills

MULTIPLE CHOICE QUESTIONS

1. What are the six p's of security?

   A. patch, ports, personnel, privacy, protect, policies

   B. ports, patch, protect, probe, policies, physical

   C. physical, privacy, patch, ports, probe, protect

   D. ports, patch, probe, physical, privacy, policies

2. What is the most basic rule of computer security?

   A. Keep systems patched.

   B. Always use an IDS.

   C. Install a firewall.

   D. Always use anti-spyware.

3. How might you ensure that system patches are kept up to date?

   A. Use an automated patching system.

   B. Patch anytime you receive a vendor notification of a new patch.

   C. Patch whenever a new threat is announced.

   D. Use periodic scheduled patching.

4. What is the rule about ports?

   A. Block all incoming ports.

   B. Block ICMP packets.

   C. Block all unused ports.

   D. Block all non-standard ports.

5. Which of the following is a good reason to check dependencies before shutting down a service?

   A. to determine whether you will need to shut down other services as well

   B. to determine whether shutting down this service will affect other services

   C. to find out what this service does

   D. to find out whether this service is critical to system operations

6. If your machine is not used as a server and is not on a local network, what packet-filtering strategy should you use?

   A. Block all ports except 80.

   B. Do not block any ports.

   C. Block all ports.

   D. Do not block well-known ports.

7. Which of the following is the least essential device for protecting your network?

   A. firewall

   B. virus scanners on all machines

   C. IDS system

   D. proxy server

8. What is the rule of thumb on data access?

   A. Data must be available to the widest range of people possible.

   B. Only administrators and supervisors should access sensitive data.

   C. Only those with a need for the specific data should have access.

   D. All employees should have access to any data used in their department.

9. What is password age?

   A. how long a user has had a password

   B. the length the password history

   C. a reference to the sophistication (maturity) of the password

   D. a reference to a password's length

10. What is the minimum frequency for system probing and audits?

   A. once per month

   B. once per year

   C. every other year

   D. every other month

11. An audit should check what areas?

    A. System patching, review polices, check personnel records of all managers, and probe for flaws

    B. Only probe for flaws

    C. System patches, probe for flaws, check logs, and review policies

    D. Check all machines for illicit software, complete system virus scan, and review of firewall polices

12. Which of the following is true of the room in which the server is located?

    A. It should be in the most fire-resistant room in the building.

    B. It should have a strong lock with a strong door.

    C. It should be accessible only to those who have a need for access.

    D. All of the above

13. What would be most important to block end users from doing on their own machine?

    A. Running programs other than those installed by the IT staff

    B. Surfing the Web and using chat rooms

    C. Changing their screen saver and using chat rooms

    D. Installing software or changing system settings

14. What is the preferred method for storing back ups?

    A. Near the server for quick restore if needed

    B. Offsite in a secure location

    C. In the IT manager's office for security

    D. At the home of one of the IT staff

15. Which of the following is a step you would definitely take with any server, but might not be required for a workstation?

    A. Uninstall all unneeded programs/software.

    B. Shut down unneeded services.

    C. Turn off the screen saver.

    D. Block all Internet access.

16. Which of the following is a step you might take for large networks, but not for smaller networks?

    A. Use an IDS.

    B. Segment the network with firewalls between the segments.

    C. Use antivirus software on all machines on the network.

    D. Do criminal background checks for network administrators.

17. Which of the following is a common way to establish security between a Web server and a network?

    A. Block all traffic between the Web server and the network.

    B. Place virus scanning between the network and the Web server.

    C. Put a firewall between the Web server and the network.

    D. Do not connect your network to the Web server.

18. What is the rule on downloading from the Internet?

    A. Do not ever download anything.

    B. Only download if the download is free of charge.

    C. Only download from well-known, reputable sites.

    D. Never download executables. Only download graphics.

19. Which of the following certifications is the most prestigious?

    A. CISSP

    B. PE

    C. MCSA

    D. Security+

20. Which of the following set of credentials would be best for a security consultant?

    A. Ten years' IT experience, one year in security, CIW Security analyst, MBA

    B. Eight years' IT experience, three years in security, CISSP, BS in computer science

    C. Eleven years' IT experience, three years in security, MCSE and CISSP, MS in information systems

    D. Ten years' experience as a hacker and cracker, MCSE/CIW/ and Security +, Ph.D. in computer science

EXERCISES

Exercise 6.1: Patching Systems

1. Using a lab system, find and apply all operating system patches.

2. Check with all vendors of software installed on that machine and apply patches for those applications as well (if available).

3. Note the time taken to fully patch a machine. Consider how long it would take to patch a 100-machine network.

4. Write an essay that answers the following questions: Are there ways you could speed the process of patching a 100-machine network? How might you approach such a task?

Exercise 6.2: Learning About Policies

1. Using the resources given or other resources, find at least one sample security policy document.

2. Analyze that document.

3. Write a brief essay giving your opinion of that policy. Did it miss items? Did it include items you had not thought of?

Exercise 6.3: Learning About Disaster Recovery

1. Using the resources given, or other resources, find at least one sample disaster recovery plan.

2. Analyze that document.

3. Write a brief essay giving your opinion of that disaster recovery plan. Also note any changes you would recommend to that policy.

Exercise 6.4: Learning About Audits

1. Using the resources given or other resources, find at least one sample security audit plan.

2. Analyze that document.

3. Write a brief essay giving your opinion of that plan. Do you feel the audit plan is adequate? What changes might you recommend?

FYI: Helpful Resources

For Exercises 6.2, 6.3, and 6.4, you may find the following resources helpful:

- **www.cert.org/**
- **www.sans.org/**
- **csrc.nist.gov/fasp/**
- **www.information-security-policies-and-standards.com/**

Exercise 6.5: Securing Your Computer

Using either your home computer or a lab computer, follow the guidelines given in this chapter to secure that computer. Those steps should include:

- Scan for all patches and install them.

- Shut down all unneeded services.

- Install anti-virus software. (A demo version can be used for this exercise.)

- Install anti-spyware software. (A demo version can be used for this exercise.)

- Set appropriate password permissions.

Exercise 6.6: Secure Passwords

1. Using the Web or other resources, find out why longer passwords are harder to break.

2. Also find out what other things you should do to make a password harder to crack.

3. Write a brief essay describing what makes a perfect password.

Exercise 6.7: Securing a Server

Note: This exercise is for those students with access to a lab server.

Using the guidelines discussed in this chapter, secure a lab server. The steps taken should include:

- Scan for all patches and install them.

- Shut down all unneeded services.

- Remove unneeded software.

- Install anti-virus software. (A demo version can be used for this exercise.)

- Install anti-spyware software. (A demo version can be used for this exercise.)

- Set appropriate password permissions.

- Enable logging of any security violations. (Consult your operating system documentation for instructions.)

Exercise 6.8: Backups

Using the Web and other resources as a guide, develop a backup plan for a Web server. The plan should cover how frequently to back up and where to store the backup media.

Exercise 6.9: User Accounts

Note: This exercise is best done with a lab computer, not a machine actually in use.

1. Locate user accounts. (In Windows 2000 or Windows XP, this is done by going to Start > Control Panel > Administrative Tools > Computer Management and looking for Groups and Users.)

2. Disable all default accounts (Guest, Administrator).

PROJECTS

Project 6.1: Writing and Executing an Audit Plan

With the knowledge you have gained while studying six chapters of this text and in examining security policies in the preceding exercises, it is now time to devise your own audit plan. This plan should detail all the steps in an audit.

Note: The second part of this project is contingent upon getting permission from some organization to allow you to audit their security. It is also ideal for a group project.

Taking the audit plan you wrote, audit a network. This audit can be conducted for any sort of organization, but you should make your first audit one with a small network (less than 100 users).

Project 6.2: Forming a Disaster Recovery Plan

Using the knowledge you have gained thus far, create an IT disaster recovery plan for an organization. You may use a fictitious organization, but a real organization would be better.

Project 6.3: Writing a Security Policy Document

Note: This project is designed as a group project.

It is now time to bring all you have learned thus far together. Write a complete set of security policies for an organization. Again, you may use a fictitious company, but real organizations are better. This set of policies must cover user access, password policies, frequency of audits (both internal and external), minimum security requirements, guidelines for Web surfing, and so on.

Project 6.4: Secure Web Servers

Using the information in this chapter as well as other resources, come up with a strategy specifically for securing a Web server. This strategy should include the security of the server itself as well as securing the network from the server.

Project 6.5: Adding Your Own Guidelines

Note: This project is ideal for a group project.

This chapter has outlined some general procedures for security. Write an essay detailing your own additional guidelines. These can be guidelines for individual computers, servers, networks, or any combination thereof.

6

▶▶ Case Study

Juan Garcia is the network administrator for a small company that also maintains its own Web server. He has taken the following precautions:

- All computers are patched, have antivirus software, and have unneeded services shut down.

- The network has a firewall with proxy server and IDS.

- The organization has a policy requiring passwords of ten characters in length, and they must be changed every 90 days.

Has Juan done enough to secure the network? What other actions would you recommend he take?

Chapter 7

Encryption

Chapter Objectives

After reading this chapter and completing the exercises, you will be able to do the following:

- Explain the basics of encryption.
- Discuss modern cryptography methods.
- Select appropriate cryptography for your organization.
- Understand the function and protocols of VPNs.

Introduction

There are many aspects of computer and information security. *Encryption*, the process of scrambling a message or other information so that it cannot be easily read, is one of the most critical parts to the security puzzle. If you have the best firewall, very tight security policies, hardened operating systems, virus scanners, intrusion detection software, anti-spyware, and every other computer security angle covered but send your data in raw, plain text, then you simply are not secure.

In this chapter, you will obtain what can be termed a "manager's understanding" of *cryptography*—the art of writing in or deciphering secret code. It is important to understand that this chapter will not make you a cryptographer. In fact, reading several volumes on encryption would not accomplish that lofty goal. Rather, this chapter is designed to give you a basic overview of what encryption is, some idea of how it works, and enough information so that you can make intelligent decisions about what sorts of encryption to incorporate in your organization. You will learn the basic history of encryption, the fundamental concepts, and, once you have completed the exercises at the end of the chapter, enough knowledge to at least be able to ask the right questions.

Cryptography Basics

The aim of cryptography is not to hide the existence of a message, but rather to hide its meaning—the process known as encryption. To make a message unintelligible, it is scrambled according to a particular algorithm, which is agreed upon beforehand between the sender and the intended recipient. Thus, the recipient can reverse the scrambling protocol and make the message comprehensible (Singh, 2001). This reversal of the scrambling is referred to as *decryption*. The advantage of using encryption/decryption is that, without knowing the scrambling protocol, the message is difficult to re-create.

There are two basic types of cryptography: *transposition* and *substitution*. Transposition involves simply rearranging the letters of a message, as is done in an anagram. Substitution, the type on which we will focus in this text, involves, at its root, replacing each letter in the alphabet with a different letter (or number).

Within the substitution branch of cryptography, there are two basic forms of encryption:

- Single key encryption / Symmetric key encryption
- Public key encryption / Asymmetric key encryption

We will discuss these two forms of encryption, along with a few popular examples, later in this chapter. But first, let's take a brief look at the history of encryption.

History of Encryption

The idea of encryption is probably as old as written communication. The basic concept is actually fairly simple. Messages must be changed in such a way that the message cannot be easily read by an enemy, but they can be easily decoded by the intended recipient. In this section, you will examine a few historical methods of encryption. It should be noted that these are very old methods, and they cannot be used for secure communication today. The methods discussed in this section would be easily cracked, even by an amateur. However, they are wonderful for conveying the concept of encryption without having to incorporate a great deal of math, which is required of the more complex encryption methods.

If you are interested in learning more about the history of cryptography than what we touch upon here, you may wish to read one of the many books written on the subject. Or, you might consult the following Web sites which are shown in Figure 7.1 and Figure 7.2:

- The Stanford University History of Cryptography Web site: **www-cs-education.stanford.edu/classes/sophomore-college/ projects-97/cryptography/history.html**

- A Brief History of Cryptography from Cybercrimes.net: **www.cybercrimes.net/Cryptography/Articles/Hebert.html**

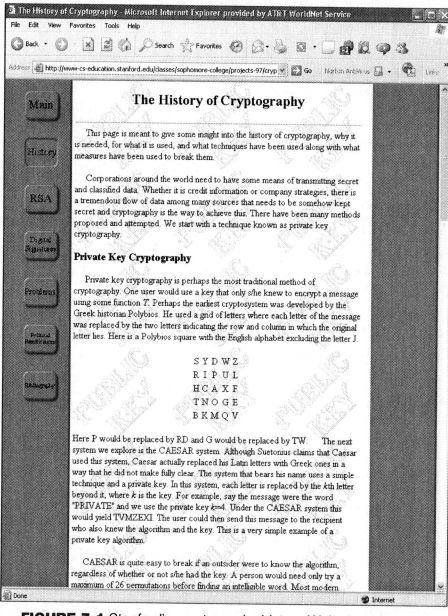

FIGURE 7.1 Stanford's cryptography history Web site.

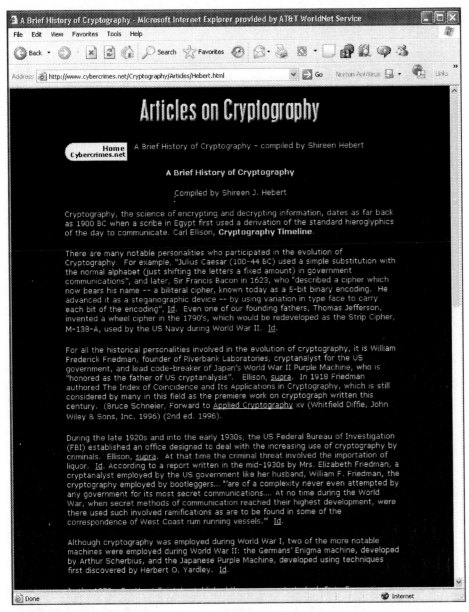

FIGURE 7.2 Hebert's cryptography history Web site.

Understanding the simple methods described here and other methods listed on the aforementioned Web sites should give you a sense of how cryptography works as well as what is involved in encrypting a message. Regardless of whether you go on to study modern, sophisticated encryption methods, it is important for you to have some basic idea of how encryption works at a conceptual level. Having a basic grasp of how encryption works, in principle, will make you better able to understand the concepts of any encryption method you encounter in the real world.

The Caesar Cipher

One of the oldest encryption methods is the *Caesar cipher*. This method is purported to have been used by the ancient roman Caesars—thus the name. It is actually quite simple to do. You choose some number by which to shift each letter of a text. For example, if the text is:

```
A cat
```

And you choose to shift by two letters, then the message becomes:

```
C ecv
```

Or, if you choose to shift by three letters, it becomes:

```
D fdw
```

You can choose any shifting pattern you wish. You can shift either to the right or left by any number of spaces you like. Because this is a very simple method to understand, it makes a good place to start our study of encryption. It is, however, extremely easy to crack. You see, any language has a certain letter and word frequency, meaning that some letters are used more frequently than others (Security in Computing, 1988). In the English language, the most common single-letter word is *a*. The most common three-letter word is *the*. Those two rules alone could help you decrypt a Caesar cipher. For example, if you saw a string of seemingly nonsense letters and noticed that a three-letter word was frequently repeated in the message, you might easily surmise that this word was *the*—and the odds are highly in favor of this being correct. Furthermore, if you frequently noticed a single-letter word in the text, it is most likely the letter *a*. You now have found the substitution scheme for *a, t, h,* and *e*. You can now either translate all of those letters in the message and attempt to surmise the rest or simply analyze the substitute letters used for *a, t, h,* and *e* and derive the substitution cipher that was used for this message. Decrypting a message of this type does not even require a computer. It could be done in less than ten minutes using pen and paper by someone with no background in cryptography.

The substitution scheme you choose (e.g., +2, +1) is referred to as a *substitution alphabet* (i.e., b substitutes for a, u substitutes for t). Thus, the Caesar cipher is also referred to as a *mono-alphabet substitution* method, meaning that it uses a single substitution for the encryption.

The Caesar cipher, however, is not useless. Since most programming languages have some function to convert a character or number to its ASCII code, a programmer can write a simple function that loops through text converting each character to its ASCII code, then either adding or subtracting the appropriate number. Again, it must be stressed that this is not a secure method of encrypting messages, but an interesting exercise to begin introducing you to the basic concepts of encryption.

7

IN PRACTICE: Converting to ASCII Code

ASCII (American Standard Code for Information Interchange) is a standard code for every letter (upper- and lowercase), number, and key on your keyboard. It was proposed by ANSI (www.ansi.org) in 1963, and finalized in 1968. ASCII's purpose was to establish compatibility between the various types of data processing equipment. All key strokes can be converted to a numeric ASCII code.

ASCII, pronounced "ask-key," is the common code for microcomputer equipment. The standard ASCII character set consists of 128 decimal numbers ranging from zero through 127 assigned to letters, numbers, punctuation marks, and the most common special characters. The Extended ASCII Character Set also consists of 128 decimal numbers and ranges from 128 through 255 representing additional special, mathematical, graphic, and foreign characters. For example the capital A is ASCII code 65 and the return key is ASCII code 13.

As we discussed in Chapter 2, decimal numbers can be converted to binary numbers. So, as you can probably guess, there are binary equivalents (as well as hexadecimal equivalents) to each of these decimal values. Like the ASCII decimal values, there

CONTINUED ON NEXT PAGE

>> CONTINUED

TABLE 7.1 ASCII decimal values.

Decimal	Value	Decimal	Value
000	NUL (Null char.)	030	RS (Request to Send)(Record Separator)
001	SOH (Start of Header)	031	US (Unit Separator)
002	STX (Start of Text)	032	SP (Space)
003	ETX (End of Text)	033	! (exclamation mark)
004	EOT (End of Transmission)	034	" (double quote)
005	ENQ (Enquiry)	035	# (number sign)
006	ACK (Acknowledgment)	036	$ (dollar sign)
007	BEL (Bell)	037	% (percent)
008	BS (Backspace)	038	& (ampersand)
009	HT (Horizontal Tab)	039	' (single quote)
010	LF (Line Feed)	040	((left/opening parenthesis)
011	VT (Vertical Tab)	041	) (right/closing parenthesis)
012	FF (Form Feed)	042	* (asterisk)
013	CR (Carriage Return)	043	+ (plus)
014	SO (Shift Out)	044	, (comma)
015	SI (Shift In)	045	- (minus or dash)
016	DLE (Data Link Escape)	046	. (dot)
017	DC1 (XON) (Device Control 1)	047	/ (forward slash)
018	DC2 (Device Control 2)	048	0
019	DC3 (XOFF) (Device Control 3)	049	1
020	DC4 (Device Control 4)	050	2
021	NAK (Negative Acknowledgement)	051	3
		052	4
022	SYN (Synchronous Idle)	053	5
023	ETB (End of Trans. Block)	054	6
024	CAN (Cancel)	055	7
025	EM (End of Medium)	056	8
026	SUB (Substitute)	057	9
027	ESC (Escape)	058	: (colon)
028	FS (File Separator)	059	; (semi-colon)
029	GS (Group Separator)	060	< (less than)

table continued

Decimal	Value	Decimal	Value
061	= (equal sign)	096	`
062	> (greater than)	097	a
063	? (question mark)	098	b
064	@ (AT symbol)	099	c
065	A	100	d
066	B	101	e
067	C	102	f
068	D	103	g
069	E	104	h
070	F	105	i
071	G	106	j
072	H	107	k
073	I	108	l
074	J	109	m
075	K	110	n
076	L	111	o
077	M	112	p
078	N	113	q
079	O	114	r
080	P	115	s
081	Q	116	t
082	R	117	u
083	S	118	v
084	T	119	w
085	U	120	x
086	V	121	y
087	W	122	z
088	X	123	{ (left/opening brace)
089	Y	124	| (vertical bar)
090	Z	125	} (right/closing brace)
091	[(left/opening bracket)	126	~ (tilde)
092	\ (back slash)	127	DEL (delete)
093	] (right/closing bracket)		
094	^ (caret/cirumflex)		
095	_ (underscore)		

7

CONTINUED ON NEXT PAGE

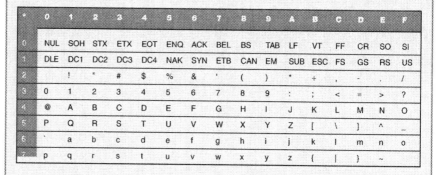

▶ CONTINUED

are tables available for determining either the binary or hexadecimal values. Table 7.2 is an example of a table for determining hexadecimal values.

TABLE 7.2 ASCII hexadecimal values.

*	0	1	2	3	4	5	6	7	8	9	A	B	C	D	E	F
0	NUL	SOH	STX	ETX	EOT	ENQ	ACK	BEL	BS	TAB	LF	VT	FF	CR	SO	SI
1	DLE	DC1	DC2	DC3	DC4	NAK	SYN	ETB	CAN	EM	SUB	ESC	FS	GS	RS	US
2		!	"	#	$	%	&	'	(	)	*	+	,	-	.	/
3	0	1	2	3	4	5	6	7	8	9	:	;	<	=	>	?
4	@	A	B	C	D	E	F	G	H	I	J	K	L	M	N	O
5	P	Q	R	S	T	U	V	W	X	Y	Z	[	\	]	^	_
6	`	a	b	c	d	e	f	g	h	i	j	k	l	m	n	o
7	p	q	r	s	t	u	v	w	x	y	z	{	|	}	~	

Like the conversion to binary numbers that we discussed in Chapter 2, there are many readily available converters that can make determining the ASCII equivalencies much easier than searching through tables. A simple search of the Internet will turn up many such converters. Figure 7.3 is an example of a converter found at **www.cplusplus.com/doc/papers/ascii.html**. This particular converter, given any one value, will generate the other three. In this illustration, the uppercase A was entered and the decimal, hexadecimal, and binary ("oct.") numbers were all generated.

FIGURE 7.3 ASCII converter.

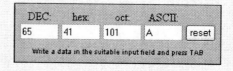

Multi-Alphabet Substitution

Eventually, a slight improvement on the Caesar cipher was developed, called **_multi-alphabet substitution_**. In this scheme, you select multiple numbers by which to shift letters (i.e., multiple substitution alphabets). For example, if you select three substitution alphabets ($+2$, -2, $+3$), then

A CAT

becomes

C ADV

Notice that the fourth letter starts over with another +2, and you can see that the first A was transformed to C and the second A was transformed to D. This makes it more difficult to decipher the underlying text. While this is harder to decrypt than a Caesar cipher, it is not overly difficult. It can be done with simple pen and paper and a bit of effort. It can be cracked very quickly with a computer. In fact, no one would use such a method today to send any truly secure message, for this type of encryption is considered very weak.

Binary Operations

Various operations on *binary numbers* (numbers made of only zeroes and ones) are well known to programmers and programming students. But for those readers not familiar with them, a brief explanation follows. When working with binary numbers, there are three operations not found in normal math: AND, OR, and XOR operations. Each is illustrated below.

AND

To perform the AND operation, you take two binary numbers and compare them one place at a time. If both numbers have a one in both places, then the resultant number is a one. If not, then the resultant number is a zero, as you see here:

1 1 0 1

1 0 0 1

---

1 0 0 1

OR

The OR operation checks to see whether there is a one in either or both numbers in a given place. If so, then the resultant number is one. If not, the resultant number is zero, as you see here:

1 1 0 1

1 0 0 1

---

1 1 0 1

XOR

The XOR operation impacts your study of encryption the most. It checks to see whether there is a one in a number in a given place, but *not* in both numbers at that place. If it is in one number but not the other, then the resultant number is one. If not, the resultant number is zero, as you see here:

```
1  1  0  1

1  0  0  1
_____

0  1  0  0
```

XORing has a very interesting property in that it is reversible. If you XOR the resultant number with the second number, you get back the first number. And, if you XOR the resultant number with the first number, you get the second number.

```
0  1  0  0

1  0  0  1
_____

1  1  0  1
```

Binary encryption using the XOR operation opens the door for some rather simple encryption. Take any message and convert it to binary numbers and then XOR that with some key. Converting a message to a binary number is really a simple two-step process. First, convert a message to its ASCII code, then convert those codes to binary numbers. Each letter/number will generate an eight-bit binary number. Then you can use a random string of binary numbers of any given length as the key. Simply XOR your message with the key to get the encrypted text, then XOR it with the key again to retrieve the original message. This method is easy to use and great for computer science students; however, it does not work well for truly secure communications because the underlying letter and word frequency remains. This exposes valuable clues that even an amateur cryptographer can use to decrypt the message. Yet, it does provide a valuable introduction to the concept of *single-key encryption*, which will be discussed in more detail in the next section. While simply XORing the text is not the method typically employed, single-key encryption methods are widely used today. For example, you could simply include a multi-alphabet substitution that was then XORed with some random bit stream—variations of which do exist in a few actual encryption methods currently used.

Modern Methods

Modern cryptography methods, as well as computers, make decryption a rather advanced science. Therefore, encryption must be equally sophisticated in order to have a chance of success.

What you have seen so far regarding encryption is simply for educational purposes. As has been noted several times, you would not have a truly secure system if you implemented any of the previously mentioned encryption schemes. You may feel that this has been overstated in this text. However, it is critical that you have an accurate view of what encryption methods do and do not work. It is now time to discuss a few methods that are actually in use today.

Single-Key (Symmetric) Encryption

Basically, single-key encryption means that the same key is used to both encrypt and decrypt a message. This is also referred to as symmetric key encryption.

Blowfish Blowfish is a symmetric block cipher. This means that it uses a single key to both encrypt and decrypt the message and works on "blocks" of the message at a time. It uses a variable-length key ranging from 32 to 448 bits (MyCrypto.net, 2004). This flexibility in key size allows you to use it in various situations. Blowfish was designed in 1993 by Bruce Schneier. It has been analyzed extensively by the cryptography community and has gained wide acceptance. It is also a non-commercial (i.e., free of charge) product, thus making it attractive to budget-conscious organizations.

Data Encryption Standard *Data Encryption Standard*, or *DES* as it is often called, was developed by IBM in the early 1970s. DES uses a symmetric key system. The DES uses short keys and relies on complex procedures to protect its information. The actual DES algorithm is quite complex and beyond the scope of this text. The basic concept, however, is as follows: (Federal Information Processing Standards, 1993)

FYI: Block Ciphers and Stream Ciphers

When applying a key to plain text to encrypt it and produce the cipher text, you must also choose how to apply the key and the algorithm. In a block cipher, the key is applied to blocks (often 64 bits in size) at a time. This differs from a stream cipher that encrypts one bit at a time.

1. Data is divided into 64-bit blocks, and those blocks are then transposed.

2. Transposed data is then manipulated by 16 separate steps of encryption involving substitutions, bit-shifting, and logical operations using a 56-bit key.

3. Data is then further scrambled using a swapping algorithm.

4. Data is finally transposed one last time.

One advantage that DES offers is efficiency. Some implementations of DES offer data throughput rates on the order of hundreds of megabytes per second. In plain English, what this means is that it can encrypt a great deal of data very quickly. You might assume that 16 steps would cause encryption to be quite slow; however, that is not the case using modern computer equipment. The problem with DES is the same problem that all symmetric key algorithms have: How do you transmit the key without risking it becoming compromised? This issue led to the development of public key encryption.

Public Key (Asymmetric) Encryption

Public key encryption is essentially the opposite of single-key encryption. With any public key encryption algorithm, one key is used to encrypt a message (called the public key) and another is used to decrypt the message (called the private key). You can freely distribute your public key so that anyone can encrypt a message to send to you, but only you have the private key and only you can decrypt the message. The actual mathematics behind the creation and application of the keys is a bit complex and beyond the scope of this book. It should be pointed out, however, that many public key algorithms are dependent, to some extent, on large prime numbers, factoring, and number theory.

Many commonly used algorithms, such as PGP, use public key encryption. It is very easy to implement since the public key can be freely distributed to anyone and sometimes even put on a Web site for download.

Public key encryption is fast becoming the most widely used type of encryption because there are no issues to deal with concerning distribution of the keys. With symmetric key encryption, you must get a copy of the key to every person to whom you wish to send your encrypted messages. If that key were lost or copied, someone else might be able to decrypt all of your messages. With public key encryption, you can freely distribute your public key to the entire world, yet only you can decrypt messages encrypted with that public key.

PGP *PGP*, a public key system, stands for *Pretty Good Privacy*. It is a widely used system that is considered very secure by most experts (International PGP, 2004). There are several software implementations available as

Caution

Encryption Strength

Federal law prohibits the exportation of encryption beyond a certain strength. Currently, that exact limit is being contested in various court cases. It is recommended that you consult current federal guidelines before implementing encryption in your organization.

7

FYI: "Old" Encryption

PGP is more than ten years old. Some readers might wonder whether it is old and outdated. Cryptography is unlike other technological endeavors in this regard—older is better. It is usually unwise to use the "latest thing" in encryption for the simple reason that it is unproven. An older encryption method, provided it has not yet been broken, is usually a better choice because it has been subjected to years of examination by experts and to cracking attempts by both experts and less honorably motivated individuals. This is sometimes hard for computer professionals to understand since the newest technology is often preferred in the computer business.

---

freeware for most desktop operating systems. There are PGP plug-ins for Netscape Messenger, MSN Messenger, and many other popular communications software packages (McCune, 2004). A simple Yahoo or Google search for *PGP* will help you find many of these software products.

PGP was invented by Phil Zimmermann (Zimmermann, 2004). Before creating PGP, Mr. Zimmermann had been a software engineer for 20 years and had experience with existing forms of cryptography. A great deal of controversy surrounded the birth of PGP because it was created without an easy means for government intrusion and its encryption was considered too strong for export. This caused Mr. Zimmermann to be the target of a three-year government investigation. However, those legal matters are now resolved and PGP is one of the most widely used encryption methods available.

The important things to know about PGP are that it is:

- A public key encryption
- Considered quite secure
- Available free of charge

These facts make it well worth your time to investigate PGP as a possible solution for your organization's encryption needs.

RSA The *RSA* method is a very widely used encryption algorithm. You cannot discuss cryptography without at least some discussion of RSA. This is a public key method developed in 1977 by three mathematicians, Ron Rivest, Adi Shamir, and Len Adlema. The name RSA is derived from the first letter of each mathematician's last name (Burnett and Paine, 2001). This text will not delve too deeply into the mathematics; however, for those who are curious, the following paragraphs will give you a brief description of the essential math.

To start, two large prime numbers are selected and then multiplied together:

```
n = p*q.
```

You then let

```
f(n) = (p - 1) (q - 1), and e>1
```

such that

```
greatest common denominator (e, f(n)) = 1
```

Here e will have a large probability of being co-prime to $f(n)$, if n is large enough and e will be part of the encryption key. You solve the equation for d. (The actual equation is based on linear algebra and is not really critical for this discussion. You can reference details in the RSA Security's *Official Guide to Cryptography* if desired, or you can do a Web search and find details on several Web sites.) The pair of integers (e, n) is the public key, and (d, n) form the private key. Encryption of M can be accomplished by an equation using these integers for the keys. This method has become very popular.

Legitimate versus Fraudulent Encryption Methods

The encryption methods discussed above are just a few of the more widely used modern encryption methods. Dozens of other methods are released to the public for free or are patented and sold for profit every year. However, it is important to realize that this particular area of the computer industry is replete with frauds and charlatans. One need only scan any search engine searching for *encryption* to find a plethora of advertisements for the latest and greatest "unbreakable" encryption. If you are not knowledgeable about encryption, how do you separate legitimate encryption methods from frauds?

Matt Curtin has a Web site titled *Snake Oil Warning Signs* (Curtin, 1998) (**www.interhack.net/people/cmcurtin/snake-oil-faq.html**) that does a very good job of listing specific warning signs and also explaining some of the basics of cryptography. If you have an interest in cryptography, you should definitely visit his Web site and bookmark it for future reference. Below is a list of warning signs. You will notice that it is similar to Curtin's, with just a few differences.

- **Unbreakable:** Anyone with experience in cryptography knows that there is no such thing as an unbreakable code. There are codes that have not yet been broken. There are codes that are very hard to break. But when someone claims that their method is "completely unbreakable," you should be suspicious.

- **Certified:** Guess what? There is no recognized certification process for encryption methods. Therefore, any "certification" the company has is totally worthless.

- **Inexperienced people:** A company is marketing a new encryption method. What is the experience of the people working with it? Does the cryptographer have a background in math, encryption, or algorithms? If not, has he submitted their method to experts in peer-reviewed journals? Or, is he at least willing to disclose how their method works so that it can be fairly judged? Recall that PGP's inventor had decades of software engineering and encryption experience.

Some experts claim that you should only use widely known methods, such as Blowfish and PGP, although it is certainly possible to use less well-known, or even new, encryption methods and have a very secure system. Consider the fact that today's widely used methods were once new and untested. However, if you are using a less well-known method, you need to take extra precautions to ensure that you are not being misled.

Virtual Private Networks

A *VPN* is a *virtual private network*. This is essentially a way to use the Internet to create a virtual connection between a remote user or site and a central location. The packets sent back and forth over this connection are encrypted, thus making it private. The VPN must emulate a direct network connection.

There are three different protocols that are used to create VPN's. They are:

- Point to Point Tunneling Protocol (PPTP)

- Layer 2 Tunneling Protocol (L2TP)

- Internet Protocol Security (IPSec)

These are each discussed in more depth in the following sections.

PPTP

Point-to-Point Tunneling Protocol (PPTP) is the oldest of the three protocols used in VPNs. It was originally designed as a secure extension to Point-to-Point Protocol (PPP). The Point-to-Point Tunneling Protocol was originally proposed as a standard in 1996 by the PPTP Forum—a group of companies that included Ascend Communications, ECI Telematics, Microsoft, 3Com, and U.S. Robotics. It adds the features of encrypting packets and authenticating users to the older PPP protocol. PPTP works at the data link layer of the OSI model (discussed in Chapter 2).

PPTP offers two different methods of authenticating the user: Extensible Authentication Protocol (EAP) and Challenge Handshake Authentication Protocol (CHAP). EAP was actually designed specifically for PPTP and is not proprietary. CHAP is a three-way process whereby the client sends a code to the server, the server authenticates it, and then the server responds to the client. CHAP also periodically re-authenticates a remote client, even after the connection is established.

PPTP uses Microsoft Point-to-Point Encryption (MPPE) to encrypt packets. MPPE is actually a version of DES. DES is still useful for many situations; however, newer versions of DES, such as DES 3, have been released.

L2TP

Layer 2 Tunneling Protocol (L2TP) was explicitly designed as an enhancement to PPTP. Like PPTP, it works at the data link layer of the OSI model. It has several improvements to PPTP. First, it offers more and varied methods for authentication—PPTP offers two, whereas L2TP offers five. In addition to CHAP and EAP, L2TP offers PAP, SPAP, and MS-CHAP.

- **PAP:** Password Authentication Protocol is the simplest form of authentication and the least secure. Usernames and passwords are sent unencrypted, in plain text.

- **SPAP:** Shiva Password Authentication Protocol is an extension to PAP that does encrypt the username and password that is sent over the Internet.

- **MS-CHAP** is a Microsoft-specific extension to CHAP.

In addition to more authentication protocols available for use, L2TP offers other enhancements. PPTP will only work over standard IP networks, whereas L2TP will work over X.25 networks (a common protocol in phone systems) and ATM (asynchronous transfer mode, a high-speed networking technology) systems. L2TP also uses IPSec for its encryption.

IPSEC

IPSec is short for *Internet Protocol Security*. It is the latest of the three VPN protocols. One of the differences between IPSec and the other two methods is that it encrypts not only the packet data (recall the discussion of packets in Chapter 2), but also the header information. It also has protection against unauthorized retransmission of packets. This is important because one trick that a hacker can use is to simply grab the first packet from a transmission and use it to get their own transmissions to go through. Essentially, the first packet (or packets) has to contain the login data. If you simply re-send that packet (even if you cannot crack its encryption), you will be sending a valid logon and password that can then be followed with additional packets. Preventing unauthorized retransmission of packets prevents this from happening.

Summary

A basic element of computer security is encryption. Sending sensitive data that is not encrypted is simply foolish. This chapter provided the basic information on how cryptography works. The most important thing to remember is that, ultimately, it is not your computer or your network that will be compromised, but rather your data. Encrypting the data when transmitting it is an integral part of any security plan.

In the exercises at the end of this chapter, you will practice using different cipher methods and learn more about a number of encryption methods.

7

Test Your Skills

MULTIPLE CHOICE QUESTIONS

1. Which of the following most accurately defines encryption?

   A. changing a message so it can only be easily read by the intended recipient

   B. using complex mathematics to conceal a message

   C. changing a message using complex mathematics

   D. applying keys to a message to conceal it

2. Which of the following is the oldest encryption method discussed in this text?

   A. PGP

   B. multi-alphabet encryption

   C. Caesar cipher

   D. cryptic cipher

3. What is the main problem with simple substitution?

    A. It does not use complex mathematics.

    B. It is easily broken with modern computers.

    C. It is too simple.

    D. It maintains letter and word frequency.

4. Which of the following is an encryption method using two or more different shifts?

    A. Caesar cipher

    B. multi-alphabet encryption

    C. DES

    D. PGP

5. Which binary mathematical operation can be used for a simple encryption method?

    A. bit shift

    B. OR

    C. XOR

    D. bit swap

6. Why is binary mathematical encryption not secure?

    A. It does not change letter or word frequency.

    B. It leaves the message intact.

    C. It is too simple.

    D. The mathematics of it is flawed.

7. Which of the following is most true regarding binary operations and encryption?

    A. They are completely useless.

    B. They can form a part of viable encryption methods.

    C. They are only useful as a teaching method.

    D. They can provide secure encryption.

8. What is PGP?

    A. Pretty Good Privacy, a public key encryption method

    B. Pretty Good Protection, a public key encryption method

    C. Pretty Good Privacy, a symmetric key encryption method

    D. Pretty Good Protection, a symmetric key encryption method

9. Which of the following methods is available as an add-in for most e-mail clients?

   A. DES

   B. RSA

   C. Caesar cipher

   D. PGP

10. Which of the following is a symmetric key system using 64-bit blocks?

   A. RSA

   B. DES

   C. PGP

   D. Blowfish

11. What advantage does a symmetric key system using 64-bit blocks have?

   A. It is fast.

   B. It is unbreakable.

   C. It uses asymmetric keys.

   D. It is complex.

12. What size key does a DES system use?

   A. 64 bit

   B. 128 bit

   C. 56 bit

   D. 256 bit

13. What type of encryption uses different keys to encrypt and decrypt the message?

   A. private key

   B. public key

   C. symmetric

   D. secure

14. Which of the following methods uses a variable-length symmetric key?

   A. Blowfish

   B. Caesar

   C. DES

   D. RSA

7

15. What should you be most careful of when looking for an encryption method to use?

    A. complexity of the algorithm

    B. veracity of the vendor's claims

    C. speed of the algorithm

    D. how long the algorithm has been around

16. Which of the following is most likely to be true of an encryption method that is advertised as unbreakable?

    A. It is probably suitable for military use.

    B. It may be too expensive for your organization.

    C. It is likely to be exaggerated.

    D. It is probably one you want to use.

17. Which of the following is most true regarding certified encryption methods?

    A. These are the only methods you should use.

    B. It depends on the level of certification.

    C. It depends on the source of the certification.

    D. There is no such thing as certified encryption.

18. Which of the following is most true regarding new encryption methods?

    A. Never use them until they have been proven.

    B. You can use them, but you must be cautious.

    C. Only use them if they are certified.

    D. Only use them if they are rated unbreakable.

19. Which of the following is the oldest protocol used by VPN?

    A. PPTP

    B. L2TP

    C. IPSec

    D. SPAP

20. Which of the following is used by PPTP to encrypt packets?

    A. Microsoft Point-to-Point Encryption

    B. Layer 2 Tunneling Protocol

    C. Extensible Authentication Protocol

    D. Challenge Handshake Authentication Protocol

EXERCISES

Exercise 7.1: Using the Caesar Cipher

Note: This exercise is well suited for group or classroom exercises.

1. Write a sentence in normal text.

2. Use a Caesar cipher of your own design to encrypt it.

3. Pass it to another person in your group or class.

4. Time how long it takes that person to break the encryption.

5. (Optional) Compute the mean time for the class to break Caesar ciphers.

Exercise 7.2: Using Multi-Alphabet Ciphers

Note: This exercise also works well for group settings and is best used in conjunction with the preceding exercise.

1. Write a sentence in normal text.

2. Use a multi-alphabet cipher of your own design to encrypt it.

3. Pass it to another person in your group or class.

4. Time how long it takes that person to break the encryption.

5. (Optional) Compute the mean time for the class to break these, and compare that to the mean time required to break the Caesar ciphers.

Exercise 7.3: Using PGP

1. Download a PGP attachment for your favorite e-mail client. Doing a Web search for PGP and your e-mail client (i.e., PGP and Outlook or PGP and Euodora) should locate both modules and instructions.

2. Install and configure the PGP module.

3. Send encrypted messages to and from a classmate.

Exercise 7.4: Finding Good Encryption Solutions

1. Scan the Web for various commercial encryption algorithms.

2. Find one that you feel may be "snake oil."

3. Write a brief paper explaining your opinion.

Exercise 7.5: Learn More about VPN

1. Using the Web, journals, books, or other resources, find out more about VPN.

2. Write a brief essay describing how VPN could increase the security of your transmissions.

PROJECTS

Project 7.1: RSA Encryption

Using the Web or other resources, write a brief paper about RSA, its history, methodology, and where it is used. Students with a sufficient math background may choose to delve more deeply into the RSA algorithm's mathematical basis.

Project 7.2: Programming Caesar Cipher

Note: This project is for those students with some programming background.

Write a simple program in any language you prefer (or your instructor dictates) that can perform a Caesar cipher. In this chapter, you not only saw how this cipher works, but were also given some ideas on how to use ASCII codes to make this work in any standard programming language.

Project 7.3: Other Encryption Methods

Write a brief essay describing any encryption method not already mentioned in this chapter. In this paper, describe the history and origin of that algorithm. You should also provide some comparisons with other well-known algorithms.

▶▶ Case **Study**

Jane Doe is responsible for selecting an encryption method that is suitable for her company, which sells insurance. The data they send is sensitive, but is not military or classified in nature. Jane is looking at a variety of methods. She ultimately selects a commercial implementation of RSA. Was this the best choice? Why or why not?

Chapter | 8

Internet Fraud
and Cyber Crime

Chapter Objectives

After reading this chapter and completing the exercises, you will be able to do the following:

- Explain the methods used in Internet investment scams and auction frauds, such as pump and dump and bid siphoning.
- Take specific steps to avoid fraud on the Internet.
- Know specific steps to avoid identity theft.
- Understand cyber stalking and relevant laws.
- Know some legal aspects that apply to computer crimes.
- Configure a Web browser's privacy settings.

Introduction

In every new frontier, a criminal element is bound to emerge. In times past, the high seas gave rise to pirates and America's Wild West produced gangs of outlaws. The Internet is no different than any other frontier; it has its share of outlaws. Besides hacking and virus creation, which where both mentioned earlier in this book, there are other dangers. Fraud is one of the most common dangers of the Internet. Fraud has been a part of life for as long as civilization has existed. In past centuries, "snake oil" salespeople roamed the country selling fake cures and elixirs. As more people use the Internet as a conduit for commerce, there arises a greater opportunity for fraud. In fact, many experts would consider fraud to be the most prevalent danger on the Internet.

There are multiple reasons for the popularity of Internet fraud among con artists. First, committing an Internet fraud does not require the technical expertise that hacking and virus creation require. Secondly, there are a great number of people engaging in various forms of online commerce, and this large amount of business creates a great many opportunities for fraud.

There are many avenues for fraud on the Internet. This chapter will explore what the various major types of fraud are, what the law says, and what you can do to protect yourself. Chapter exercises will give you a chance to try out setting browsers for privacy and using anti-spy methods. This chapter is not particularly technical simply because most Internet fraud does not rely on in-depth technological expertise. Internet fraud merely uses the computer as a venue for many of the same fraud schemes that have been perpetrated throughout history.

Internet Fraud

There are a variety of ways that a fraud can be perpetrated via the Internet. The Securities and Exchange Commission lists several types of Internet fraud on their Web site (U.S. Securities and Exchange Commission, 2001). Figure 8.1 shows part of the list from this Web site. This chapter briefly discusses each of the types listed, as well as others. However, it is not possible for this text to cover every variation of each fraud scheme that has been used on the Internet. Such an undertaking would not only fill an entire book, but possibly also several volumes. What this text can do is cover the more common scams and then extrapolate from these to form some general principles that you can apply. These should enable you to avoid most fraudulent schemes.

FYI: Investment Offers

Investment offers are nothing new. Some stockbrokers make their living by "cold calling," the process of simply calling people (perhaps from the phone book) and trying to get them to invest in a specific stock. This practice is employed by some legitimate firms, but it is also a favorite con game for perpetrators of fraud. The Internet has allowed investment offers, both genuine and fraudulent, to be more easily disseminated to the general public. Most readers are probably familiar with investment offers flooding their inbox on a daily basis. Some of these e-mail notifications entice you to become directly involved with a particular investment plan, while other e-mails offer seemingly unbiased information from investors, free of charge. Unfortunately, much of this advice is not as unbiased as it might appear to be. While legitimate online newsletters can help investors gather valuable information, keep in mind that some online newsletters are fraudulent.

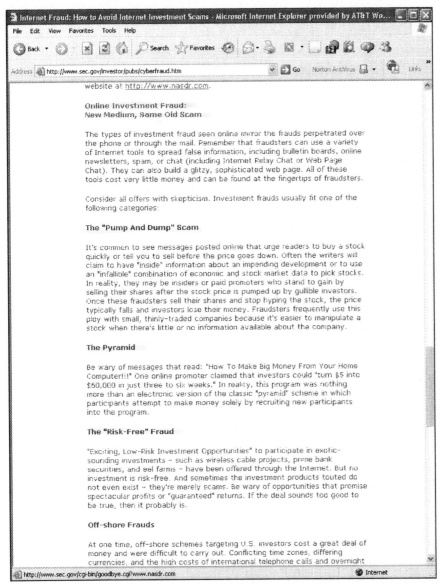

FIGURE 8.1 List of Internet frauds at the SEC Web site.

Fraudulent Investment Offers

One of the more common investment offer schemes involves sending out an e-mail suggesting that you can make an outrageous sum of money with a very minimal investment. Perhaps the most famous of these schemes has been the Nigerian Fraud. In this scenario, an e-mail is sent to a number of random e-mail addresses. Each one contains a message purporting to be from a relative of some deceased Nigerian doctor or government official. The deceased person will be someone you would associate with significant social standing, thus increasing the likelihood that you would view the offer more favorably. The offer goes like this: A person has a sum of money he wishes to transfer out of his country and, for security reasons, he cannot use normal channels. He wishes to use your bank account to "park" the funds temporarily. If you will allow him access to your account, you will receive a hefty fee. If you agree to this arrangement, you will receive, via normal mail, a variety of very official-looking documents, enough to convince most casual observers that the arrangement is legitimate. You will then be asked to advance some money to cover items such as taxes and wire fees. Should you actually send any money, you will have lost the money you advanced and will never hear from these individuals again. The U.S. Secret Service has issued a bulletin detailing this particular fraud scheme (U.S. Secret Service, 2002).

Now consider this investment scam, and variations of it, from a logical point of view. If you had large sums of money you needed to transfer, would you send it to a person you had never met in a foreign country? Wouldn't you be worried that the recipient would cash out her account and take the next plane to Rio? If a person needs to transfer money internationally, why not just transfer the money to an account in the Bahamas? Or, cash out the account and send it via Federal Express or United Parcel Service to a storage facility in the United States? The point is that there are many ways a person could get money out of a country without trusting a stranger he has never met. That fact alone should indicate to you that this offer is simply not legitimate. This concept is the first general principle you should derive concerning fraud. In any offer, consider the point of view of the person offering it. Does it sound as if he is taking an inordinately large risk? Does the deal seem oddly biased in your favor? Put yourself in his position. Would you engage in the deal if you where in his position? If not, then this factor is a sign that the deal might not be what it seems.

FYI: Allowing Active Code

Any time you allow active code to run on your browser there is a risk that you may be opening the door to a Trojan horse or virus. Active code includes Active X components, Java Script, and other scripting languages. These items are often used by Web designers to add multimedia to a Web site. If you simply block all active code you will find that you cannot view some Web pages. On the other hand if you allow all active code, you will be endangering your system. The best route to take is to set your browser to prompt you for permission before executing any Active X or script code.

FYI: Prosecuting Cyber Crime

As mentioned in this chapter, many countries are developing specific laws to counteract cyber crime. One of the greatest challenges to prosecution of computer crime, however, is the difficulty of determining jurisdiction. This is especially true with the international usage of the Internet.

Fraudulent Investment Advice

Such fraudulent investment offer schemes are not the only investment pitfall on the Internet. Some companies pay the people who write online newsletters to recommend their stocks. While this activity is not actually illegal, U.S. federal securities laws do require the newsletters to disclose that they where paid to proffer this advice. Such laws are in place because, when the writers are recommending any product, their opinion might be swayed by the fact that compensation is being provided to them for that opinion. Despite the laws, many online investment newsletters do not disclose that they are actually being paid to recommend certain stocks. This situation means that the "unbiased" stock advice you are getting could actually be quite biased. Rather than getting the advice of an unbiased expert, you may be getting a paid advertisement. This pitfall is one of the most common traps of online investment advice and is more common than the blatant investment offer frauds.

Sometimes these online stock bulletins can be part of a wider scheme, often called a *pump and dump*. A classic pump and dump is rather simple. The con artist takes a stock that is virtually worthless and purchases large amounts of the stock. She then artificially inflates ("pumps") its value in one or more ways (Fraud Bureau, 1999). One common method is to begin circulating rumors on various Internet bulletin boards and chat rooms that the stock is about to go up significantly. The trickster often suggests that the company has some new innovative product due out in the next few weeks. Another method is to simply push the stock on as many people as possible. The more people vying to buy a stock, the higher its price will rise. If both methods are combined, it is possible to take a worthless stock and temporarily double or triple its value. The perpetrator of the fraud has already purchased large volumes of the stock, at a very low price, before executing this scheme. When the stock goes as high as she thinks it can, she then "dumps" her stock and takes the money. In a short time, and certainly by the time the companies' next quarterly earnings report is released, the stock returns to its real value. This sort of scheme has been very popular in the past several decades. One should always be wary of such "insider" information. If a person is aware that Company X is about to release an innovative new product that will drive her stock value up, why would she share that information with total strangers?

The U.S. Securities and Exchange Commission (2000) lists several tips for avoiding such scams.

■ **Consider the source.** If you are not well versed in the market, make sure you accept advice only from well-known and reputable stock analysts.

■ **Independently verify claims.** Do not simply accept someone else's word about anything.

■ **Research.** Read up on the company, the claims about the company, its stock history, and so forth.

■ **Beware of high-pressure tactics.** Legitimate stock traders do not pressure customers into buying. They help customers pick stocks that customers want. If you are being pressured, that is an indication of potential problems.

■ **Be skeptical.** A healthy dose of skepticism can save you a lot of money. Or, as the saying goes, "If it's too good to be true, it probably isn't true."

The truth is that these types of fraud depend on the greed of the victim. It is not my intent to blame victims of fraud, but it is important to realize that, if you allow avarice to do your thinking for you, you are a prime candidate to be a victim of fraud. Your 401K or IRA may not earn you exorbitant wealth overnight, but they are steady and relatively safe (no investment is completely safe). If you are seeking ways to make large sums of money with minimal time and effort, then you are an ideal target for perpetrators of fraud.

Auction Frauds

Online auctions, such as eBay, can be a wonderful way to find merchandise at very good prices. Many people routinely use such auctions to purchase goods. However, any auction site can be fraught with peril. Will you actually get the merchandise you ordered? Will it be "as advertised?" Most online auctions are legitimate and most auction Web sites take precautions to limit fraud on their Web site, but problems still occur. In fact, the U.S. Federal Trade Commission (FTC) lists the following four categories of online auction fraud (U.S. Federal Trade Commission, 2004):

■ Failure to send the merchandise

■ Sending something of lesser value than advertised

■ Failure to deliver in a timely manner

■ Failure to disclose all relevant information about a product or terms of the sale

IN PRACTICE: Handling Online Investments

Practically speaking, the recommended way to handle online investments is to only participate in them if you initiated the discussion with a reputable broker. This rule would mean you would never respond to (or participate in) any investment offer that was sent to you via e-mail, online ads, and so forth. You would only participate in investments that you initiated with well-known brokers. Usually, such brokers are from traditional investment firms with long-standing reputations that now simply offer their services online.

The first category, failure to deliver the merchandise, is the most clear-cut case of fraud and is fairly simple. Once you have paid for an item, no item arrives. The seller simply keeps your money. In organized fraud, the seller will simultaneously advertise several items for sale, collect money on all the auctions, and then disappear. If he has planned this well, the entire process was done with fake identification, using a rented mailbox and anonymous e-mail service. The person then walks away with the proceeds of the scam.

The second category of fraud, delivering an item of lesser value than the one advertised, can become a gray area. In some cases, it is outright fraud. The seller advertises something about the product that simply is not true. For example, the seller might advertise a signed copy of the first printing of a famous author's book, but then instead ships you a fourth printing with either no autograph or one that is unverified. However, in other cases of this type of problem, it can simply be that the seller is overzealous or frankly mistaken. The seller might claim his baseball was signed by a famous athlete, but not be aware himself that the autograph is a fraud.

This problem is closely related to the fourth item on the FTC list, failure to disclose all relevant facts about the item. For example, a book might be an authentic first printing and autographed, but be in such poor physical condition as to render it worthless. This fact may or may not be mentioned in advance by the seller. Failure to be forthcoming with all relevant facts about a particular item might be the result of outright fraud or simply the seller's ignorance.

The FTC also lists failure to deliver the product on time as a form of fraud. It is unclear whether this is considered fraud in many cases or merely woefully inadequate customer service.

The FTC also lists three other areas of bidding fraud that are growing in popularity on the Internet (U.S. Federal Trade Commission, 2004):

FYI: Phishing

Phishing is a growing problem that is plaguing Internet users. Phishing is the process of sending e-mails that claim to be from some legitimate source in an attempt to get the receiver to divulge sensitive data—in essence, electronic social engineering. This might include an e-mail that claims to be from your credit card company and is requesting your account details. If you do provide the information, it may be used to make purchases with your account or as part of an identity theft scam.

In 2003, there was a widespread phishing scam in which users were sent e-mails purporting to be from eBay claiming that the user's account was about to be suspended unless he clicked on the provided link and updated the credit card information. When users clicked on the link, they were taken to a spoofed site that was meant to look like eBay. All the information they entered was taken by the criminals perpetrating the scam.

- *Shill bidding,* whereby fraudulent sellers (or their "shills") bid on the seller's items to drive up the price.

- *Bid shielding,* whereby fraudulent buyers submit very high bids to discourage other bidders from competing for the same item. The fake buyers then retract their bids so that people they know can get the item at a lower price.

- *Bid siphoning,* whereby con artists lure bidders off legitimate auction sites by offering to sell the "same" item at a lower price. Their intent is to trick consumers into sending money without proffering the item. By going off-site, buyers lose any protections the original site may provide such as insurance, feedback forms, or guarantees.

All of these tactics have a common aim: to subvert the normal auction process. The normal auction process is an ideal blend of capitalism and democracy. Everyone has an equal chance to obtain the product in question if they are willing to outbid the other shoppers. The buyers themselves set the price of the product based on the value they perceive the product to have. Auctions are an excellent vehicle for commerce; however, unscrupulous individuals will always attempt to subvert the process for their own goals.

Shill Bidding *Shill bidding* is probably the most common of these three auction frauds. It is not very complex. If the perpetrator is selling an item at an auction site, she will also create several fake identities. She will use these fake identities to bid on the item and thus drive up the price. It is very difficult to detect whether such a scheme is in operation. However, a simple rule of thumb on auctions is to decide what your maximum price is before you start bidding. Then, under no circumstances, do you exceed that price by even one penny.

Bid Shielding   While shill bidding may be difficult to combat, *bid shielding* can be addressed fairly easily by the proprietors of the auction site. Many major auction sites, such as eBay, have taken steps to prevent bid shielding. The most obvious is to revoke bidding privileges for bidders who back out after they have won an auction. If a person puts in a very high bid to keep others away and then at the last moment retracts his bid, he might lose his ability to return to that auction site.

Bid Siphoning   *Bid siphoning* is a less common practice. In this scheme, the perpetrator places a legitimate item up for bid on an auction site. Yet, in the ad for that item, she provides links to sites that are not part of the auction site. The unwary buyer who follows these links might find himself on an alternative site that is a "setup" to perpetrate some sort of fraud.

Identity Theft

Identity theft is a growing problem—and a very troubling one. The concept is rather simple, although the process can be complex and the consequences for the victim can be quite severe. The idea is simply for one person to take on the identity of another. This con game is usually attempted to make purchases. However, identity theft can be done for other reasons, such as obtaining credit cards or even driver's licenses in the victim's name.

If the perpetrator obtains a credit card in someone else's name, he can then purchase products. The victim of this fraud is left with debts she was not aware of and did not authorize.

Getting a driver's license in the victim's name might be an attempt to shield the perpetrator from the consequences of his own poor driving record. For example, a person may have a very bad driving record and possibly have warrants out for immediate arrest. Should the person be stopped by law enforcement officers, he can then show the fake license. When the police officer checks the license, it is legitimate and has no outstanding warrants. However, the ticket the criminal receives will be going on your driving record because it is your information on the driver's license. It is also unlikely that the perpetrator of that fraud will actually pay the ticket, so at some point you—whose identity was stolen—will receive notification that your license has been revoked for failure to pay a ticket. Unless you can then prove, with witnesses, that you were not at the location at the time the ticket was given, you may have no recourse but to pay the ticket in order to re-establish your driving privileges.

The U.S. Department of Justice defines identity theft in this manner (U.S. Department of Justice, 2000):

> *"Identity theft* and *identity fraud* are terms used to refer to all types of crime in which someone wrongfully obtains and uses another person's personal data in some way that involves fraud or deception, typically for economic gain."

The advent of the Internet has made the process of stealing a person's identity even easier than previously. Many states now have court and motor vehicle records online. In some states, a person's social security number is used for the driver's license number. Therefore, if a criminal obtains a person's social security number, she can look up that person's driving record, perhaps get a duplicate of the person's license, find out about any court records concerning that person, and, on some Web sites, even run the person's credit history. Using the Internet as an investigative tool will be examined later in this book. Like any tool, it can be used for benign or malevolent purposes. The same tools you can use to do a background check on a prospective employee can be used to find out enough information to forge someone else's identity.

IN PRACTICE: Credit Card Security

There is a new method for conducting identity theft using a handheld scanner. A ring of criminals in the Dallas-Fort Worth area were working with waiters in restaurants. When the waiter took a patron's credit or debit card to pay for the meal, the waiter used a small handheld device (kept hidden in a pocket) to scan the patron's credit card information. The waiter gave this information to the identity theft ring, which could either make online purchases or use that information to produce fake credit cards with the patron's name and account data. This fraud is a new twist on identity theft. The only way to avoid this sort of danger is to never use your credit or debit card unless it is going to be processed right there in front of you. Do not let someone take your card out of your sight to process it.

Most people trust a waiter or waitress with important credit card information without even giving it a thought. But many of those same people are leery of using their credit card numbers online. In truth, if the site uses encryption and your Web protocol has changed to https: you are just as safe on the Web as if you watched the credit card processed in front of you at the restaurant.

Cyber Stalking

Stalking in general has received a great deal of attention in the past few years. The primary reason for this awareness is that stalking has often been a prelude to violent acts, including sexual assault and homicide. For this reason, many states have passed a variety of anti-stalking laws. However, this stalking problem has recently been expanded into cyberspace. What is *cyber stalking*? It is using the Internet to harass another person or, as the U.S. Department of Justice puts it (U.S. Department of Justice, 2003):

> "Although there is no universally accepted definition of *cyber stalking*, the term is used in this report to refer to the use of the Internet, e-mail, or other electronic communications devices to stalk another person. Stalking generally involves harassing or threatening behavior that an individual engages in repeatedly, such as following a person, appearing at a person's home or place of business, making harassing phone calls, leaving written messages or objects, or vandalizing a person's property. Most stalking laws require that the perpetrator make a credible threat of violence against the victim; others include threats against the victim's immediate family; and still others require only that the alleged stalker's course of conduct constitute an implied threat. While some conduct involving annoying or menacing behavior might fall short of illegal stalking, such behavior may be a prelude to stalking and violence and should be treated seriously."

If someone uses the Internet to harass, threaten, or intimidate another person, then the perpetrator is guilty of cyber stalking. The most obvious example is the sending of threatening e-mail. The guidelines on what is considered "threatening" can vary a great deal from jurisdiction to jurisdiction. But a good rule of thumb is that, if the e-mail's content would be considered threatening in normal speech, then it will probably be considered a threat if sent electronically. *Black's Law Dictionary* (2000) defines *harassment* as:

> "A course of conduct directed at a specific person that causes substantial emotional distress in such person and serves no legitimate purpose."

> "Words, gestures, and actions that tend to annoy, alarm, and abuse (verbally) another person."

Other examples of cyber stalking are less clear. If you request that someone quit e-mailing you, yet he continues to do so, is that a crime? Unfortunately, there is no clear answer on that issue. The truth is that it may or may not be considered a crime depending on such factors as the content of the e-mails, the frequency, and the prior relationship between you and the

8

sender, as well as your jurisdiction. Usually, law enforcement officials will need some credible threat of harm in order to pursue harassment complaints. In simple terms, this situation means that if you are in an anonymous chat room and someone utters some obscenity, that act probably will not be considered harassment. However, if you receive specific threats via e-mail, those threats would probably be considered harassment.

The following three cases from a 1999 report by the Department of Justice illustrate episodes of cyber stalking (U.S. Department of Justice, 2003). Examining the facts in these cases might help you get an idea of what legally constitutes cyber stalking.

- In the first successful prosecution under California's new cyber stalking law, prosecutors in the Los Angeles District Attorney's Office obtained a guilty plea from a 50-year-old former security guard who used the Internet to solicit the rape of a woman who rejected his romantic advances. The defendant terrorized his 28-year-old victim by impersonating her in various Internet chat rooms and online bulletin boards, where he posted, along with her telephone number and address, messages that she fantasized being raped. On at least six occasions, sometimes in the middle of the night, men knocked on the woman's door saying they wanted to rape her. The former security guard pleaded guilty in April 1999 to one count of stalking and three counts of solicitation of sexual assault. He faces up to six years in prison.

- A local prosecutor's office in Massachusetts charged a man who, using anonymous re-mailers (a computer service which privatizes your e-mail), allegedly engaged in a systematic pattern of harassment of a co-worker that culminated in an attempt to extort sexual favors from the victim under threat of disclosing past sexual activities to the victim's new husband.

- An honors graduate from the University of San Diego terrorized five female university students over the Internet for more than a year. The victims received hundreds of violent and threatening e-mails, sometimes receiving four or five messages a day. The graduate student, who has entered a guilty plea and faces up to six years in prison, told police he committed the crimes because he thought the women were laughing at him and causing others to ridicule him. In fact, the victims had never met him.

The entire 1999 report, of which these three cases were a small part, is available at the Department of Justice Web site (**www.usdoj.gov/criminal/ cybercrime/cyberstalking.htm**). A portion of this report is shown in Figure 8.2.

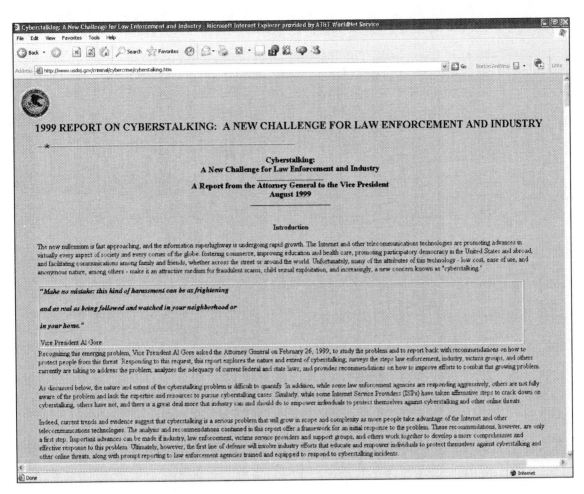

FIGURE 8.2 A 1999 report from the Attorney General to the Vice

Clearly, using the Internet to harass people is just as serious a crime as harassing them in person. This problem has even extended to workplace issues. For example, court cases have upheld that unwanted e-mail pornography can be construed as sexual harassment. If an employee complains about unwanted e-mail, the employer has a duty to at least attempt to ameliorate the situation. This attempt can be as simple as installing a very inexpensive spam blocker (software that tries to limit or eradicate unwanted e-mail). However, if the employer takes no steps whatsoever to correct the problem, that reticence may be seen by a court as contributing to a hostile work environment.

Laws Concerning Cyber Crime

Over the past several years, various legislatures (in the United States and other countries) have passed laws defining "Internet fraud" and stated the proscribed punishments. In many cases, existing laws against fraud and harassment are applicable to the Internet as well; however, some legislators felt that cyber crime warranted its own distinct legislation.

Identity theft has been the subject of various state and federal laws. Most states now have laws against identity theft (National Conference of State Legislatures, 2004). This crime is also covered by federal law. In 1998, the federal government passed 18 U.S.C. 1028, also known as "The Identity Theft and Assumption Deterrence Act of 1998" (U.S. Federal Trade Commission, 1998). This law made identity theft a federal crime. Throughout the United States, federal law now covers identity theft and, in many states, identity theft is also covered by state law.

Many states specifically prohibit cyber stalking; in general, existing anti-stalking laws can be applied to the Internet. In 2001, a California man was convicted of cyber stalking under existing anti-stalking statutes (California Youth Authority, 2000). Other countries also have existing anti-stalking laws that can be applied to cyber stalking as well. Canada has had a comprehensive anti-stalking law since 1993.

One nation that has decided to crack down hard on cyber criminals is Romania. Some experts have described Romanian cyber crime law as the strictest in the world (Romanian Information Technology Initiative, 2002). However, what is most interesting about Romanian law is how specific it is. The crafters of this legislation went to some effort to very specifically define all terms used in the legislation. This specificity is very important in order to avoid defendants finding loopholes in laws. Unfortunately, the Romanian government only took such measures after media sources around the world identified their country as a "Citadel for Cyber Crime." The country's reactive approach to cyber crime is probably not the best solution.

Susan Brenner, a renowned cyber crime scholar and a Professor of Law at the University of Dayton School of Law, has an entire Web site devoted to cyber crime. This site (**www.cybercrimes.net**), shown in Figure 8.3, has some rather extensive links on cyber crime, cyber stalking, and other Internet-based crimes. As the twenty-first century moves forward, one can expect to see more law schools with courses dedicated to cyber crime. An interesting phenomenon has begun in the past few years: the emergence of attorneys who specialize in cyber crime cases. The fact that lawyers specialize in this area of law is a strong indicator that Internet crime is becoming a growing problem in modern society.

FIGURE 8.3 Brenner's cyber crime Web site.

Protecting Yourself against Cyber Crime

Now that you know about various frauds that are prevalent on the Internet and have looked at the relevant laws, you might be wondering what you can do to protect yourself. There are several steps you can take to minimize the chances of being the victim of Internet crime. There are also some clear guidelines on how you should handle the situation if should you become a victim.

Protecting Against Investment Fraud

To protect yourself against investment fraud, follow these guidelines:

- Only invest with well-known, reputable brokers.

- If it sounds too good to be true, then avoid it.

- Ask yourself why this person is informing you of this great investment deal. Why would a complete stranger decide to share some incredible investment opportunity with you?

- Remember that even legitimate investment involves risk, so never invest money that you cannot afford to lose.

Protecting Against Auction Fraud

Dealing with auction fraud involves a different set of precautions. Here are four good ideas.

- Only use reputable auction sites. The most well-known site is eBay, but any widely known, reputable site will be a safer gamble. Such auction sites tend to take precautions to prevent fraud and abuse.

- If it sounds too good to be true, do not bid.

- Some sites actually allow you to read feedback that other buyers have provided on a given seller. Read the feedback and only work with reputable sellers.

- When possible, use a separate credit card with a low limit for online auctions. In that way, your liability is limited should your credit card be compromised. Using your debit card is simply inviting trouble.

Online auctions can be a very good way to obtain valuable merchandise at low prices. However, one must exercise some degree of caution when using these services.

Protecting Against Identity Theft

When the issue is identity theft, your steps are clear:

- Do not provide your personal information to anyone if it is not absolutely necessary. This rule means that, when communicating on the Internet with anyone you do not personally know, do not reveal anything about yourself—not your age, occupation, or real name. Reveal nothing.

- Destroy documents that have personal information on them. If you simply throw away bank statements and credit card bills, then someone rummaging through your trash can get a great deal of personal data. You can obtain a paper shredder from an office supply store or many retail department stores for less than $20. Shred these documents before disposing of them. This rule may not seem related to computer security, but information gathered through nontechnical means can be used in conjunction with the Internet to perpetrate identity theft.

- Check your credit frequently. Many Web sites, including **www. qspace.com**, allow you to check your credit and even get your beacon score for a nominal fee. It is good practice to check your credit twice per year. If you see any items you did not authorize, that is a clear indication that you might be a victim of identity theft.

- If your state has online driving records, then check yours once per year. If you see driving infractions that you did not commit, this evidence is a clear sign that your identity is being used by someone else. Chapter 11 will explore, in detail, how to obtain such records online, often for less than $5.

Another part of protecting your identity is protecting your privacy in general. That task means preventing others from gaining information about you that you do not explicitly provide them. That preventative method includes keeping Web sites from gathering information about you without your knowledge. Many Web sites store information about you and your visit to their site in small files called cookies. These cookie files are stored on your machine. The problem with cookies is that any Web site can read any cookie on your machine, even ones that the Web site you are currently visiting did not create. Thus, if you visit one Web site and it stores items, such as your name, the site you visited, and the time you where there, then another Web site could potentially read that cookie and know where you have been on the Internet. One of the best ways to stop cookies you do not want is anti-spyware software. You can also change your Internet settings to help reduce exposures to your privacy.

IN PRACTICE: Securing Browser Settings for Microsoft Internet Explorer

1. Open Microsoft Internet Explorer.
2. Select Tools on the menu bar, and then select Internet Options. You will see a screen much like the one shown in Figure 8.4.

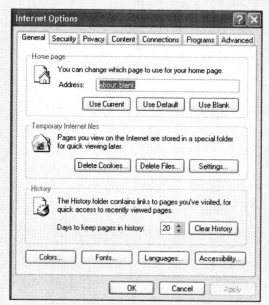

FIGURE 8.4 Internet Explorer options.

3. Select the Privacy tab. You will see the screen shown in Figure 8.5.

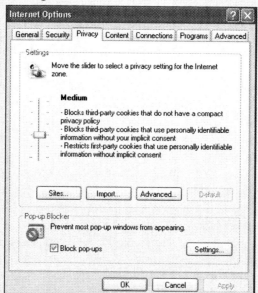

FIGURE 8.5 Internet Explorer privacy options.

4. Notice the sliding bar on the left that lets you select various levels of general protection against cookies. Select medium high as your level.

5. Note the Advanced button in the lower half of the screen. This button allows you to block or allow individual Web sites from creating cookies on your computer's hard drive. Altering cookie settings on your machine is just one part of protecting your privacy, but it is an important part.

6. Click OK to close the Advanced Privacy Settings dialog box if necessary and then click OK to close the Internet Options dialog box.

IN PRACTICE: Securing Browser Settings for Netscape Navigator

1. Open Netscape Navigator.
2. Select Edit on the menu bar and then select Preferences. You will see the screen shown in Figure 8.6.

FIGURE 8.6 Netscape preferences.

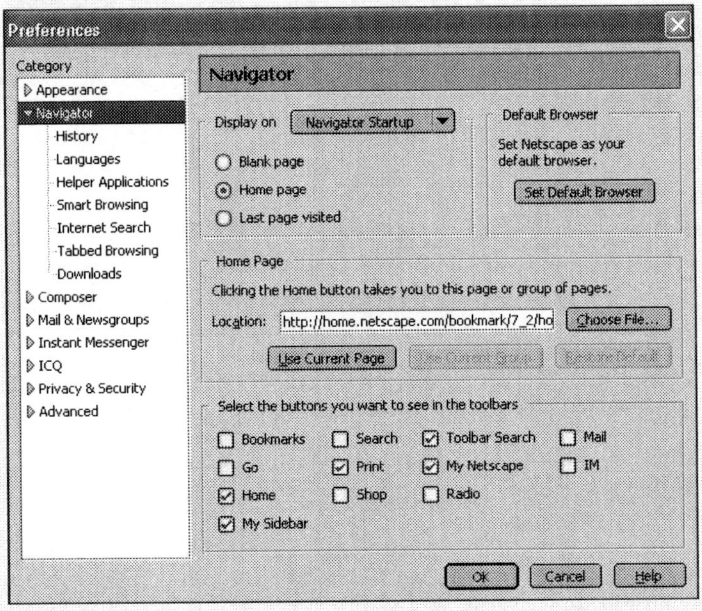

CONTINUED ON NEXT PAGE

▶ CONTINUED

3. Notice the Privacy and Security option near the bottom of the Category panel. Double-click on that option. It will expand, giving you several options.

4. Select cookies from the expanded options. The panel on the right side of the dialog box will appear as shown in Figure 8.7.

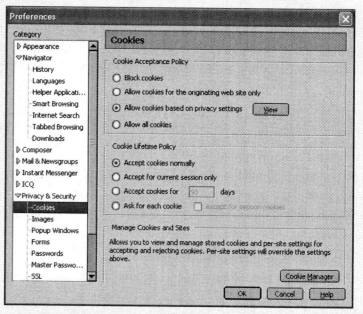

FIGURE 8.7 Netscape cookie settings.

You can use the Cookie Manager button to access a dialog box that lets you choose how to handle cookies as well as delete all cookies currently on your hard drive. If you use Netscape, it is recommended that you periodically visit this screen and delete all cookies on your computer. It is a good idea to limit the life of cookies to ten days or less. That limit significantly reduces the likelihood of another site getting much data about your Internet travels.

5. Click on the View button in order to fine-tune your settings. The Privacy Settings dialog box is shown in Figure 8.8.

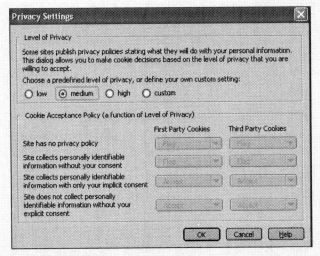

FIGURE 8.8 Netscape Privacy Settings.

You should select high security or custom. If you select custom, you can then choose specifically how to handle first-party and third-party cookies. It is safest to only allow first-party cookies. Third-party cookies are notorious for behaving in ways that violate user privacy. These simple steps can go a long way toward helping to secure your privacy.

Protecting Against Cyber Stalking

Protecting yourself from online harassment also has its own guidelines:

- If you use chat rooms, discussion boards, and so forth, do not use your real name. Set up a separate e-mail account with an anonymous service, such as Yahoo or Hotmail. Use that account and a fake name online. This strategy makes it very hard for an online stalker to trace a path back to you personally.

FYI: Netscape Navigator

It is important that anyone in the security business be familiar with alternative software and not simply be familiar with one vendor in a given product line. If you do not have Netscape Navigator, it can be downloaded for free from **channels.netscape.com/ns/ browsers/default.jsp.**

- If you are the victim of online harassment, keep all of the e-mails in both digital and printed format. Use some of the investigative techniques that will be explored later in Chapter 11 to try and identify the perpetrator. If you are successful, you can then take the e-mails and information on the perpetrator to law enforcement officials.

- Do not, in any case, ignore cyber stalking. According to the Working to Halt Online Abuse Web site (2004) (**www.haltabuse.org**) shown in Figure 8.9, 19% of cyber stalking cases escalate to stalking in the real world.

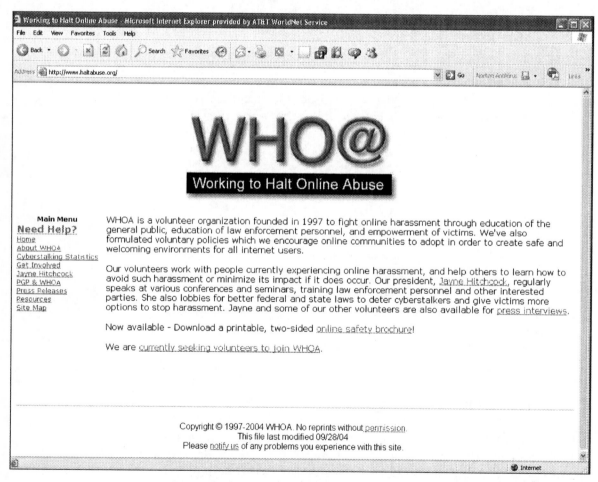

FIGURE 8.9 Home page of the Working to Halt Online Abuse Web site.

Summary

Clearly, fraud and identity theft are very real and growing problems. It is not the intent of this chapter or this book to make you frightened about using the Internet. Millions of people routinely use the Internet for entertainment, commerce, and informational purposes. You simply need to exercise some caution when using the Internet.

In our modern age of instant access to information and online purchasing, it is critical that all people take steps to protect themselves against this problem. Individuals must work to protect their privacy using steps outlined in this chapter. In the exercises at the end of this chapter, you will have a chance to try out various protection methods.

Test Your Skills

MULTIPLE CHOICE QUESTIONS

1. A common Internet investment fraud is known as the:

   A. Nigerian Fraud

   B. Manhattan Fraud

   C. pump and dump

   D. bait and switch

2. What is the most likely problem with unsolicited investment advice?

   A. You might not earn as much as claimed.

   B. The advice might not be truly unbiased.

   C. The advice might not be from a legitimate firm.

   D. You might lose money.

3. Artificially inflating a stock in order to sell it at a higher value is referred to as:

   A. bait and switch

   B. the Nigerian Fraud

   C. pump and dump

   D. the Wall Street Fraud

8

4. What are the four categories of auction fraud?

    A. failure to send, failure to disclose, sending to wrong address, failure to deliver in a timely manner

    B. failure to send, failure to disclose, sending something of lesser value, failure to deliver in a timely manner

    C. failure to disclose, sending something of greater value, failure to send, failure to deliver in a timely manner

    D. failure to disclose, sending something of lesser value, failure to send, sending something of greater value

5. A seller bidding on her own item to drive up the price is referred to as:

    A. bid siphoning

    B. bid shielding

    C. shill bidding

    D. ghost bidding

6. Submitting a fake but very high bid to deter other bidders is referred to as:

    A. bid siphoning

    B. bid shielding

    C. shill bidding

    D. ghost bidding

7. Identity theft is most often attempted in order to accomplish what goal?

    A. make illegal purchases

    B. discredit the victim

    C. avoid criminal prosecution

    D. invade privacy

8. According to the U.S. Department of Justice, identity theft is generally motivated by:

    A. malicious intent

    B. personal hostility toward the victim

    C. economic gain

    D. thrill-seeking

9. Why is cyber stalking a serious crime?

   A. It is frightening to the victim.

   B. It can be a prelude to violent crime.

   C. It is using interstate communication.

   D. It can be a prelude to identity theft.

10. What is cyber stalking?

    A. any use of the Internet to send or post threats

    B. any use of electronic communications to stalk a person

    C. only use of e-mail to send threats

    D. only use of e-mail to stalk a person

11. What will law enforcement officials usually require of the victim in order to pursue harassment allegations?

    A. verifiable threat of death or serious injury

    B. credible threat of death or serious injury

    C. verifiable threat of harm

    D. credible threat of harm

12. What must exist in order for cyber stalking to be illegal in a state or territory?

    A. specific laws against cyber stalking in that state or territory

    B. specific laws against cyber stalking in that nation

    C. nothing; existing stalking laws can apply

    D. nothing; existing international cyber stalking laws apply

13. What is the top rule for avoiding Internet fraud?

    A. If it seems too good to be true, it probably is.

    B. Never use your bank account numbers.

    C. Only work with people who have verifiable e-mail addresses.

    D. Do not invest in foreign deals.

14. Which of the following is not one of the Security and Exchange Commission's tips for avoiding investment fraud?

    A. Do not invest online.

    B. Consider the source of the offer.

    C. Always be skeptical.

    D. Always research the investment.

8

15. Which of the following is not an efficient method of protecting yourself from auction fraud?

    A. Only use auctions for inexpensive items.

    B. Only use reputable auction sites.

    C. Only work with well-rated sellers.

    D. Only bid on items that seem realistic.

16. What is the first step in protecting yourself from identity theft?

    A. Never provide any personal data about yourself unless absolutely necessary.

    B. Routinely check your records for signs of identity theft.

    C. Never use your real name on the Internet.

    D. Routinely check for spyware on your computer.

17. Why is it useful to have a separate credit card dedicated to online purchases?

    A. If the credit card number is used illegally, you will limit your financial liability.

    B. You can keep better track of your auction activities.

    C. If you are defrauded, you can possibly get the credit card company to handle the problem.

    D. You can easily cancel that single card if you need to do so.

18. What can you do on your local computer to protect your privacy?

    A. install a virus scanner

    B. install a firewall

    C. set your browser's security settings

    D. set your computer's filter settings

19. What percentage of cyber stalking cases escalates to real-world violence?

    A. less than 1%

    B. 25%

    C. 90% or more

    D. approximately 19%

20. What is the top way to protect yourself from cyber stalking?

    A. Do not use your real identity online.

    B. Always use a firewall.

    C. Always use a virus scanner.

    D. Do not give out e-mail addresses.

EXERCISES

Exercise 8.1: Setting Web Browser Privacy in Internet Explorer

This exercise gives you practice in setting Web browser privacy. You may also want to review the description in the chapter of this process where you can see detail and screen images.

1. Select Tools from the menu bar in Internet Explorer.

2. Choose Internet Options.

3. Select the Privacy tab.

4. Click the Advanced button.

5. Set your browser to accept first-party cookies; to prompt for third-party cookies; and to accept session cookies.

6. Click OK twice to close the dialog boxes. Close the browser.

Exercise 8.2: Setting Web Browser Privacy in Netscape Navigator

This exercise provides practice in setting the Web browser privacy options in Netscape Navigator. You may also want to review the description in the chapter of this process where you can see detail and screen images.

1. Select Edit from the menu bar in Netscape Navigator

2. Choose Preferences.

3. Double-click Privacy and Security—the second option from the bottom—to expand the list of options beneath it.

4. Select Cookies.

5. Choose *Allow cookies for originating web site only.*

6. Choose *Accept cookies for* and then limit cookie lifetime to two days. This limit means that any cookie on your machine will be deleted after two days.

   (Note that Internet Explorer does not provide a mechanism for setting the lifetime of a cookie.)

7. Click OK to close the Preferences dialog box. Close the browser.

Exercise 8.3: Using an Alternative Web Browser

1. Download the Mozilla browser from **www.mozilla.org**.

Caution

Appropriate Chat Room Behavior

The purpose of this exercise is merely to show you how easy it is for someone to learn about another person from his online activities. In no case would you consider using this information to invade another person's privacy or to harass or embarrass another person.

FYI: Settings in Mozilla

You should note that the newer versions of Mozilla (specifically Firefox) do not have menus like Netscape. To alter your settings in this browser or others, you may have to use the Help system to learn more or explore the options available.

2. Locate the settings for cookies and privacy in this browser. Use Help if necessary.

3. Set your Mozilla browser's cookie settings identical to how you set your Navigator settings.

4. Exit the settings dialog boxes.

5. Open the browser and then enter an URL for a Web site.

6. Answer these questions: Do you see any messages about cookies being set? Do you notice any other differences?

7. Close the browser.

Exercise 8.4: Tracking in a Chat Room

The purpose of this exercise is to grasp how easy it is to obtain personal information about someone from his online activities.

1. Enter any chat room. If you are not familiar with chat rooms or have not used them before, any of the following Web sites would make a good starting point for you:

    chat.yahoo.com/?myHome

    www.aol.com/community/chat/allchats.html

    www.javachatrooms.net/

    www.chathouse.com/

2. Note those people who use their real names.

3. Note those people who reveal personal details.

4. Compile as much information as you can about those posting in the chat room.

Exercise 8.5: Using Anti-Spyware

You should be aware that there are many products on the Web that help you to prevent spyware and cookies from being installed on your computer. One of the easiest to use is Spy Sweeper, which is available at **www.Webroot.com**.

1. Download and install the evaluation version of Spy Sweeper. (Complete instructions are available on the Web.)

2. Scan your computer for spyware and cookies. This review may take several minutes

3. Note what is found on your machine.

4. Delete the spyware and cookies.

PROJECTS

Project 8.1: Finding out About Cyber Stalking and the Law

1. Using the Web or other resources, find out what your state, country, or province's laws are regarding cyber stalking.

2. Write a brief essay describing those laws and what they mean. You may select to do a quick summary of several laws or a more in-depth examination of one law. If you choose the former, list the laws and write a brief paragraph explaining what they cover. If you choose the latter option, discuss the law's authors, why it was written, and possible ramifications of the law.

Project 8.2: Looking for Auction Fraud

Go to any auction site and try to identify whether there are any sellers you feel might be fraudulent. Write a brief essay explaining what indicated to you that the seller may not be dealing honestly.

Project 8.3: Examining Cyber Stalking Case Studies

1. Using the Web, find a case of cyber stalking not mentioned in this chapter. You may find some of the following Web sites helpful:

   www.safetyed.org/help/stalking/

   www.cyber-stalking.net/

   www.technomom.com/harassed/index.shtml

2. Write a brief essay discussing the case you chose. Mention the steps that you think might have helped avoid or ameliorate the situation.

▶▶ Case **Study**

Consider the case of an intrepid identity thief named Jane. Her victim is John. Jane encounters John online in a chat room. John is using his real first name, but only his last initial. However, over a series of online conversations, he does reveal personal details about his life (marital status, children, occupation, region he lives in, and so forth). Eventually, Jane offers John some piece of information (i.e., an investment tip) as a trick to get John's e-mail address. Once she gets his e-mail address, an e-mail exchange begins outside of the chat room, wherein Jane purports to give John her real name, thus encouraging John to do the same. Of course, she uses "Mary" as a fictitious name. Jane now has John's real name, city, marital status, occupation, and so on, and John really knows nothing about Jane.

Jane has a number of options she can try, but she begins by using the phone book or the Web to get John's home address and phone number. She can then use this information to obtain John's social security number in a variety of ways. The most straightforward would be to go through John's trash while he was at work. However, if John works in a large company, Jane can just call (or enlist someone to call), claiming to be John's wife or another close relative and wanting to verify personnel data. If Jane is clever enough, she may come away with John's social security number. It is then a trivial matter (as we will see in Chapter 11) to get John's credit report and receive credit cards in his name.

From this scenario, consider the following questions:

1. What reasonable steps could John have taken to protect his identity in the chat room?

2. What steps should any employer take to prevent being unwittingly complicit in identity theft?

Chapter 9

Industrial Espionage in Cyberspace

Chapter Objectives

After reading this chapter and completing the exercises, you will be able to do the following:

- Know what is meant by industrial espionage.
- Understand the low-technology methods used to attempt industrial espionage.
- Be aware of how spyware is used in espionage.
- Know how to protect a system from espionage.

Introduction

When you hear the word *espionage*, perhaps you conjure up a number of exciting and glamorous images. Perhaps you have visions of a well-dressed man who drinks martinis, shaken but not stirred, traveling to glamorous locations with equally glamorous travel companions. Or perhaps you envision some exciting covert operation with high-speed car chases and guns blazing in far-away exotic lands. Contrary to popular media portrayals, espionage is often much less exciting than those visions. The ultimate goal of espionage is to obtain information that would not otherwise be made available. Generally, espionage is best done with as little fanfare as possible. Blazing gun battles and glamorous locations tend to be the antithesis of intelligence gathering. Rather, information is the goal. If possible, it is best to obtain that information without the target organization even realizing that its information has been compromised.

Many people assume that such spying is only engaged in by governments, intelligence agencies, and nefarious international organizations, such as Al Queda. While those entities do indeed engage in espionage, they are certainly not the only organizations that do so. The aforementioned organizations desire to acquire information for political and military goals. However, economic goals are also dependent on accurate and often sensitive data. With billions of dollars at stake, private companies can become engaged in industrial espionage as either a target or a perpetrator. What company would not like to know exactly what its competitor is doing? In fact, corporate or economic espionage is on the rise.

Corporate or economic espionage is a growing problem, but it can be difficult to accurately assess just how great a problem it is. Companies that perpetrate corporate espionage do not share the fact that they do it, for obvious reasons. Companies that are victims of such espionage often do not wish to reveal that fact, either. Revealing that their security was compromised could have a negative impact on their stock value. It is also possible, in certain cases, that such a breach of security might open the company to liability claims from customers whose data may have been compromised. For these reasons, companies often are hesitant to disclose any industrial espionage activities. Because you will want to protect yourself and your company, it is important that you learn about espionage methods and protections. In the exercises at the end of this chapter, you will run anti-spyware, key loggers, and screen capture software so you are aware of how they work and, hence, will be cognizant of the risks they pose.

What Is Industrial Espionage?

Industrial espionage is simply the use of spying techniques to find out key information that is of economic value. Such data might include details on a competitor's new project, a list of a competitor's clients, research data, or any information that might give the spying organization an economic advantage. While the rationale for corporate espionage is different from military espionage, corporate techniques are often the same as those methods employed by intelligence agencies and can include electronic monitoring, photocopying files, or compromising a member of the target organization. Not only does economic espionage use the same techniques as intelligence agencies, but it often also uses the same people. There have been a number of incidents in which former intelligence agents are found working in corporate espionage. When such individuals bring their skills and training to the world of corporate espionage, the situation becomes much more difficult for computer security experts.

IN PRACTICE: Leaving with Sensitive Data

While various computer experts and government agencies attempt to estimate the impact and spread of corporate espionage, its very nature makes accurate estimates impossible. Not only do the perpetrators not wish to disclose their crimes, but often the victims will not disclose the event, either. However, anecdotal evidence would suggest that the most common form of espionage is simply an employee who quits, takes a job with another firm, and leaves with sensitive data. In many cases, these employees choose data that is readily available within the company and, as such, the data is considered a "gray area" as to its confidentiality. For example, a salesperson may leave with a printout of contacts and customers so that he can solicit them on behalf of the next employer. It is critical that you have a very well-worded non-disclosure and non-compete agreement with all employees. It is best to solicit the services of an employment attorney to draw up this agreement. Additionally, you might consider limiting an employee's access to data prior to terminating their employment. You should also conduct exit interviews and consider confiscating items such as company phone books which may at first seem insignificant but which could contain data useful to another company.

9

Information as an Asset

Many people are used to viewing tangible objects as assets, but have difficulty appreciating how mere information can be a real asset. Companies spend billions of dollars every year on research and development. The discovered information is worth at least the amount of resources taken to derive the information, plus the economic gain produced by the information. For example, if a company spends $200,000 researching a process that will in turn generate $1 million in revenue, then that data is worth at least $1.2 million. You can think of this economic gain as a simple equation:

```
VI (value of information) = C (cost to produce)
              + VG (value gained)
```

While some people are not yet fully cognizant of the concept, data does indeed represent a valuable asset. When we speak of the "information age" or our "information-based economy," it is important to realize that these terms are not just buzzwords. Information is a real commodity. It is as much an economic asset as any other item in the company's possession. In fact, it is most often the case that the data residing on a company's computer is worth far more than the hardware and software of the computer system itself. It is certainly the case that the data is much more difficult to replace than the computer hardware and software.

To help you truly appreciate the concept of information as a commodity, consider the process of earning a college degree. You spend four years sitting in various classrooms. You pay a significant amount of money for the privilege of sitting in a room and listening to someone speak at length on some topic. At the end of the four years, the only tangible product you receive is a single piece of paper. Surely you can get a piece of paper for far less cost and with much less effort. What you actually paid for was the information you received. The same is true of the value of many professions. Doctors, attorneys, engineers, consultants, managers, and so forth all are consulted for their expert information. Information itself is the valuable commodity.

The data stored in computer systems has a high value for two reasons. First, there is a great deal of time and effort that goes into creating and analyzing the data. If you spend six months with a team of five people gathering and analyzing information, then that information is worth at least an amount equal to the salaries and benefits of those people for that length of time. Second, data often has intrinsic value, apart from the time and effort spent acquiring those facts. If the facts are about a proprietary process, invention, or algorithm, its value is obvious. However, any data that might provide a competitive edge is inherently valuable. For example, insurance companies frequently employ teams of statisticians and actuaries who use the latest technology to try to predict the risks associated with any given group of potential insureds. The resulting statistical information might be quite valuable to a competing insurance company. Even a customer contact list has a certain inherent value.

Thus, as you work in the computer security field, always keep in mind that any data that might have economic value is an asset to your organization and that such data provides an attractive target for any competitors who may not have ethical inhibitions against using espionage. If your company management thinks that this threat is not real, then they are very much mistaken. Any company is a potential victim of corporate espionage. You should take steps to protect your valuable information—and the first critical step in this process is asset identification.

Asset identification is the process of listing the assets that you believe support your organization. This list should include things that impact direct day-to-day operations as well as those that are tied to your company's services or products. The CERT Web site (**www.cert.org/archive/ pdf/tutorial-workbook.pdf**) offers a very useful worksheet that you can use to itemize the assets in your organization. This workbook also offers a number of other useful worksheets for assuring information security

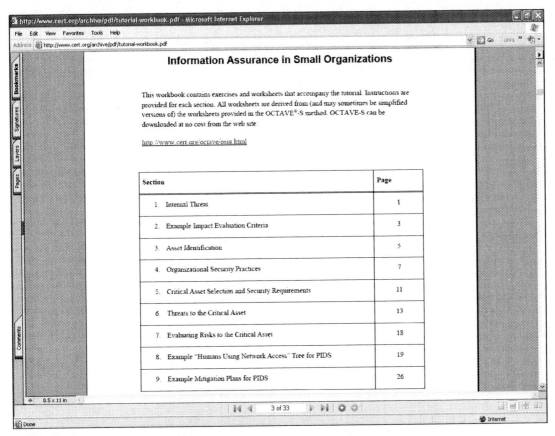

FIGURE 9.1 Table of contents from the CERT Information Assurance on Small Organizations Workbook.

within your organization. As the table of contents in Figure 9.1 shows, this workbook is also a tutorial that steps you through all the information security considerations.

Table 9–1 is a variation on the worksheet provided by CERT. Armed with this table and based on your knowledge and experience with the company, you can complete your asset identification following the steps outlined below.

1. In the first column of the table, list the information assets. You should list the types of information used by people in your company—the information people need to do their jobs. Examples are product designs, software programs, system designs, documentation, customer orders, and personnel data.

2. For each entry in the *Information* column, fill in the names of the systems on which the information resides. In each case, ask yourself which systems people need to perform their jobs.

TABLE 9.1 Asset Identification Worksheet

Information	Systems	Services and Applications	Other Assets

3. For each entry in the *Information* column, fill in the names of the related applications and services. In each case, ask yourself what applications or services are needed for individuals to perform their jobs.

4. In the last column, list any other assets that may or may not be directly related to the other three columns. Examples are databases with customer information, systems used in production, word processors used to produce documentation, compilers used by programmers, and human resources systems.

Once you complete the proceeding steps and fill out the Asset Identification worksheet, you will have a good understanding of the critical assets for your organization. With this information, you will know how best to devote your defensive efforts. Some specific protective steps will be examined later in this chapter.

How Does Espionage Occur?

There are two ways that espionage can occur. An easy, low-technology avenue would be for current or former employees to simply take the data or for someone to use social engineering methods (discussed in Chapter 3) to extract data from unsuspecting company employees. The second, more technology-oriented method is for the individuals to use spyware, which includes the use of cookies and key loggers.

Low-Tech Industrial Espionage

Corporate espionage can occur without the benefit of computers or the Internet. Disgruntled former (or current) employees can copy sensitive documents, divulge corporate strategies and plans, or perhaps reveal sensitive information. In fact, whether the method used is technological or not, disgruntled employees are the single greatest security risk to any organization. A corporate spy need not hack into a system in order to obtain sensitive and confidential information if an employee is willing to simply hand over the information. Just as with military and political espionage, the motives for the employee to divulge the information vary. Some engage in such acts for obvious financial gains. Others may elect to reveal company secrets merely because they are angry over some injustice (real or imagined). Whatever the motive, any organization has to be cognizant of the fact that it has any number of employees who may be unhappy with some situation and have the potential to divulge confidential information.

Certainly one can obtain information without the benefit of modern technology; however, computer technology (and various computer-related tactics) can certainly assist in corporate espionage, even if only in a peripheral manner. Some incidents of industrial espionage are conducted with technology that requires little skill on the part of the perpetrator as illustrated in Figures 9.2 and 9.3. This technology can include using Universal

FIGURE 9.2 Low-tech espionage is easy.

FIGURE 9.3 Low-tech espionage is portable.

Serial Bus (USB) flash drives, CD ROMs, or other portable media to take information out of the organization. Even disgruntled employees who wish to undermine the company or make a profit for themselves will find it easier to burn a wealth of data onto a compact disk (CD) and carry that out in their coat pocket rather than attempting to photocopy thousands of documents and smuggle them out. And the new USB flash drives, smaller than your average key chain, are a dream come true for corporate spies. These drives can plug into any USB port and store 256 megabytes or more of data.

While information can be taken from your company without overt hacking of the system, you should keep in mind that if your system is insecure, it is entirely possible that an outside party would compromise your system and obtain that information without an employee as an accomplice. In addition to these methods, there are other low-tech, or virtually "no-tech," methods used to extract information. Social engineering, which was discussed at great length in Chapter 3, is the process of talking a person into giving up information she otherwise would not divulge. This technique can be applied to industrial espionage in a number of ways.

The first and most obvious use of social engineering in industrial espionage is in direct conversation in which the perpetrator attempts to get the targeted employee to reveal sensitive data. As illustrated in Figure 9.4,

FIGURE 9.4 Social engineering used as low-tech espionage.

employees will often inadvertently divulge information to a supplier, vendor or salesperson without thinking the information is important or that it could be given to anyone. A more interesting way of using social engineering would be via e-mail. In very large organizations, one cannot know every member. This loophole allows the clever industrial spy to send an e-mail message claiming to come from some other department and perhaps simply asking for sensitive data. A corporate spy might, for example, forge an e-mail to appear to be coming from the legal office of the target company, requesting an executive summary of some research project.

Computer security expert Andrew Briney (Briney, 2003) places people as the number one issue in computer security.

Spyware Used in Industrial Espionage

Clearly, any software that can monitor activities on a computer can be used in industrial espionage. *Security IT World,* an online e-zine, featured an article in their October 2003 issue that dealt with the fact that monitoring a computer is an easy thing to do in the 21st century. One method to accomplish monitoring is via spyware, which we discussed in detail in Chapter 5. Clearly, software or hardware that logs key strokes or takes screen shots would be most advantageous to the industrial spy.

The application of this type of software to espionage is obvious. A spy could get screen shots of sensitive documents, capture logon information for databases, or in fact capture a sensitive document as it is being typed. Any of these methods would give a spy unfettered access to all data that is processed on a machine that contains spyware.

Protecting Against Industrial Espionage

By now, you are aware that there are many ways that your organization's valuable information assets can be compromised. The question thus becomes: What steps can you take to alleviate the danger? Note that I said "alleviate" the danger. There is nothing you can do to make any system, any information, or any person totally secure. Totally unbreakable security is simply a myth. The best you can do is work to achieve a level of security that makes the effort required to get information more costly than the value of the information.

One obvious protection is to employ anti-spyware software. This software, coupled with other security measures such as firewalls and intrusion-detection software (both examined in Chapter 6), should drastically reduce the chance that an outside party will compromise your organization's data. Furthermore, implementing organizational policies (also discussed in Chapter 6) that help guide employees on safely using computer and Internet resources will make your system relatively secure. If you add to your protection arsenal the strategy of encrypting all transmissions, your system will be as secure as you can reasonably make it. (Chapter 7 is devoted to encryption.) However, all of these techniques (firewalls, company policies, anti-spyware, encryption, and so forth) will only help in cases in which the employee is not the spy. What do you do to ameliorate the danger of employees intentionally stealing or compromising information? Actually, there are several courses of action any organization can take to lesson risks due to internal espionage. Here are 11 steps you can use:

1. Always use all reasonable network security: firewalls, intrusion-detection software, anti-spyware, patching and updating the operating system, and proper usage policies.

2. Give the personnel of the company access to only the data that they absolutely need to perform their jobs. Use a "need-to-know" approach. One does not want to stifle discussion or exchange of ideas, but sensitive data must be treated with great care.

3. If possible, set up a system for those employees with access to the most sensitive data in which there is a rotation and/or a separation of duties. In this way, no one employee has access and control over all critical data at one time.

4. Limit the number of portable storage media in the organization (such as CD burners, zip disks, and flash drives) and control access to these media. Log every use of such media and what was stored. Some organizations have even prohibited cell phones because many phones allow the user to photograph items and send the pictures electronically.

5. Do not allow employees to take documents/media home. Bringing materials home may indicate a very dedicated employee working on her own time or a corporate spy copying important documents and information.

6. Shred documents and melt old disks/tape backups/CDs. A resourceful spy can often find a great deal of information in the garbage.

7. Do employee background checks. You must be able to trust your employees, and you can only do this with a thorough background check. Do not rely on "gut feelings." Give particular attention to information technology (IT) personnel who will, by the nature of their jobs, have a greater access to a wider variety of data. This scrutiny is most important with positions such as database administrators, network administrators, and network security specialists.

8. When any employee leaves the company, scan their PC carefully. Look for signs that inappropriate data was kept on that machine. If you have any reason to suspect any inappropriate usage, then store the machine for evidence in any subsequent legal proceedings.

9. Keep all tape backups, sensitive documents, and other media under lock and key, with limited access to them.

10. If portable computers are used, then encrypt the hard drives. Encryption prevents a thief from extracting useable data from a stolen laptop. There are a number of products on the market that accomplish this encryption, including the following:

   • CryptoEx from Navastream (**www.navastream.com**). As Figure 9.5 shows, the CryptoEx family of products has different components to suit different needs. CryptoEx Pocket enables you to protect a personal digital assistant (PDA) and CryptoEx Volume enables you to encrypt hard drives.

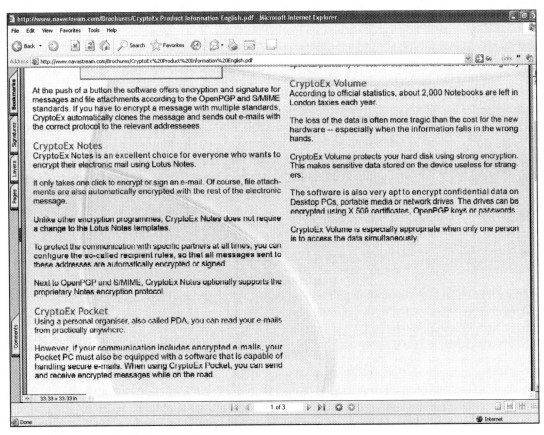

FIGURE 9.5 Navastream's CryptoEx

   • CryptoGram Folder from Imecom Group (**www.secure-messaging.com/products/cgfolder/index.htm**). As Figure 9.6 shows, CryptoGram Folder provides features that enable you to protect your files, hard drive, and e-mail.

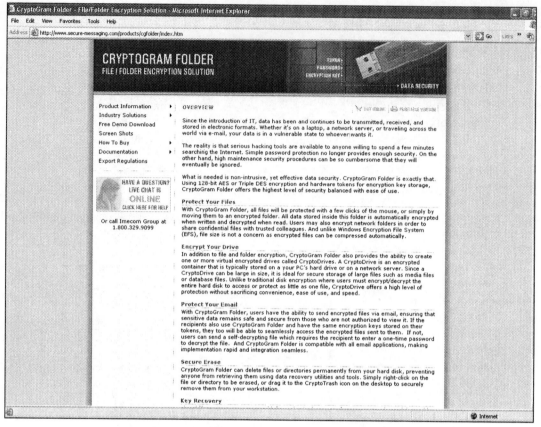

FIGURE 9.6 Overview of CryptoGram Folder.

- Safe House from Envoy Data Corporation (**www.smart-cardsys.com/security/**). As Figure 9.7 shows, SafeHouse also enables you to encrypt data on either a notebook or desktop personal computer.

This list is not exhaustive; therefore, it is highly recommended that you carefully review a variety of encryption products before making a selection.

11. Have all employees with access to any sensitive information sign non-disclosure agreements. Such agreements give you, the employer, a recourse should an ex-employee divulge sensitive data. It is amazing how many employers do not bother with this rather simple protection.

Unfortunately, following these simple rules will not make you totally immune to corporate espionage. However, using these strategies will make any such attempts much more difficult for any perpetrator and, thus, you will improve your organization's data security.

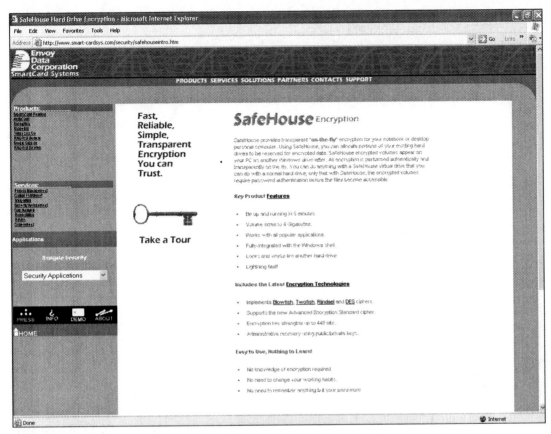

FIGURE 9.7 Overview of Safe House encryption.

Real-World Examples of Industrial Espionage

Now that you have been introduced to the concept of corporate espionage, let's look at five actual cases. These case studies are of real-world espionage found in various news sources. This section should give you an idea for what types of espionage activities actually occur.

Example 1: VIA Technology

VIA Technology actually provides two examples of industrial espionage. In the first instance, the chief executive officer (CEO) of the firm, which was based in Taipei, was indicted for copyright infringement for allegedly stealing technology from one of his own customers, a networking company called D-Link (Lemon, 2003).

According to the allegations, VIA engineer Jeremy Chang left VIA to work for D-Link. For several months while at D-Link, Chang continued to receive a paycheck from VIA. Then he promptly resigned from D-Link and returned to VIA. Once Chang rejoined VIA, a D-Link document that detailed one of their simulation programs for testing integrated circuits was posted to an FTP server owned by VIA.

The prosecutors allege that Chang continued to receive a check from VIA because he had never really resigned. They allege that Chang was in fact a "plant" sent to D-Link to acquire D-Link's technology for VIA. VIA maintains that his continuation to receive a check was simply an oversight, and Chang denies that he posted the document in question. Whatever the truth of the case, it should make any employer think twice about hiring decisions and non-disclosure agreements.

To make matters worse for VIA, another company accused VIA of stealing code for its optical readers. In both cases, the story of the possible theft of technology alone has had a negative impact on the stock value of both companies.

Example 2: General Motors

In 1993, General Motors (GM) and one if its partners began to investigate a former executive, Inaki Lopez. GM alleged that Lopez and seven other former GM employees had transferred GM proprietary information to Volkswagen (VW) in Germany via GM's own network (Szczesny, 2000). The information allegedly stolen included component price data, proprietary construction plans, internal cost calculations, and a purchasing list.

In 1996, GM followed up the ongoing criminal investigation with civil litigation against Lopez, VW, and the other employees. In November of 1996, GM expanded its legal battle by invoking the various Racketeer Influenced and Corrupt Organizations Act (RICO) statutes, originally intended to be used against organized crime conspiracies (Dever, 1996). By May of 2000, a federal grand jury indicted Lopez on six counts related to fraud and racketeering. As of this writing, the case is not resolved (*USA Today*, 2000). At the time Lopez was indicted, he was residing in Spain and the U.S. Justice Department was negotiating for his extradition. Thus, you can see that corporate espionage is neither new nor restricted to technology companies.

Example 3: Interactive Television Technologies, Inc.

On August 13, 1998, someone broke into the computer systems of Interactive Television Technologies, Inc. and stole the data for a project the company was working on (Secur Telecom, 1998). That project involved four years of intense research and a substantial financial investment. The product was to be a way whereby anyone with a television could have Internet access via the Web. This product, code-named "Butler," would have been worth a substantial amount to its inventors. However, with all the research material stolen, it was only a matter of time before several other companies came out with competing products, thus preventing Interactive Television Technologies from pursuing a patent.

To date, no arrests have been made and no leads are available in this case. This situation was a case of very skillful hackers breaking into a computer system and taking exactly what they needed. One can only speculate about their motives. They may well have sold the research data to competitors of Interactive Television Technologies, or they may have simply put the data out in the open via the Internet. Whatever the motives or profits for the perpetrators, the outcome for the victim company was catastrophic.

Example 4: Bloomberg, Inc.

According to the *American Bar Association Journal* (U.S. Department of Justice, 2003), in August 2003, Oleg Zezev, a 29-year-old PC technician from Kazakhstan, broke into the Bloomberg Inc. computer system and used the alias "Alex" to obtain information and then blackmail the firm.

Zezev entered Bloomberg's computer system and accessed various accounts, including Michael Bloomberg's (CEO and founder of Bloomberg L.P.) personal account as well as accounts for other Bloomberg employees and customers. Zezev copied information from these accounts including e-mail inbox screens, Michael Bloomberg's credit card numbers, and screens relating to the internal functions of Bloomberg. He also copied internal information that was only accessible by Bloomberg employees.

Zezev then threatened to expose the data he had stolen to the public and, in essence, tell everyone exactly how he had broken into Bloomberg's network unless he received $200,000.

After deliberating for less than six hours, the jury in the U.S. District Court in Manhattan found the perpetrator guilty of all four charges: conspiracy, attempted extortion, sending threatening electronic messages, and computer intrusion. Although this is not industrial espionage in the classic sense, it does illustrate the compromising situations in which a company and its employees can be placed when security is breached.

Example 5: Avant Software

In 1997, executives at Avant Software in Santa Clara County, California, were charged with attempting to steal secrets from their rival, Cadence Design. The case focused on a former consultant for Avant, Mitsuru "Mitch" Igusa. After Igusa had taken a job at Cadence, he began e-mailing files to his home; it is alleged that he later turned those files over to Avant.

Industrial Espionage and You

These five cases notwithstanding, most companies will deny any involvement in anything that even hints at espionage. However, not all companies are quite so shy about the issue. Larry Ellison, CEO of Oracle Corporation, has openly defended his decision to hire private investigators to sift through Microsoft garbage in an attempt to garner information (Konrad, 2000). Clearly, espionage is no longer a problem just for governments and defense contractors. It is a very real concern in the modern business world. The savvy computer security professional will be aware of this concern and will take the appropriate proactive steps.

Summary

A number of conclusions can be drawn from the examination of industrial espionage. The first conclusion: It does indeed occur. The case studies clearly demonstrate that industrial espionage is not some exotic fantasy dreamed up by paranoid security experts. It is an unfortunate, but quite real, aspect of modern business. If your firm's management chooses to ignore these dangers, then they do so at their own peril.

The second thing that can be concluded from this brief study of industrial espionage is that there are a variety of methods by which espionage can take place. An employee revealing confidential information is perhaps the most common. However, compromising information systems is another increasingly popular means of obtaining confidential and potentially valuable data. You will want to know the best way to protect your company and yourself. In the upcoming exercises at the end of this chapter, you will run screen capture software, key loggers, and anti-spyware.

Test Your Skills

MULTIPLE CHOICE QUESTIONS

1. What is the ultimate goal of espionage?

    A. To subvert a rival government

    B. To obtain information that has value

    C. To subvert a rival business

    D. To obtain information not otherwise available

2. What is the best outcome for a spy attempting an espionage activity?

    A. To obtain information without the target even realizing he did so

    B. To obtain information with or without the target realizing he did so

    C. To obtain information and discredit the target

    D. To obtain information and cause harm to the target

3. What is the usual motivating factor for corporate/industrial espionage?

 A. ideological

 B. political

 C. economic

 D. revenge

4. Which of the following types of information would be a likely target for industrial espionage?

 A. A new algorithm that the company's IT department has generated

 B. A new marketing plan that the company has formulated

 C. A list of all the company's customers

 D. All of the above are correct.

5. Which of the following is a likely reason that an organization might be reluctant to admit it has been a victim of corporate espionage?

 A. It would embarrass the IT department.

 B. It would embarrass the CEO.

 C. It might cause stock value to decline.

 D. It might lead to involvement in a criminal prosecution.

6. What is the difference between *corporate* and *industrial* espionage?

 A. None; they are interchangeable terms.

 B. Industrial espionage only refers to heavy industry, such as factories.

 C. Corporate espionage only refers to executive activities.

 D. Corporate espionage only refers to publicly traded companies.

7. You can calculate the value of information by what formula?

 A. Resources needed to produce the information, plus resources gained from the information

 B. Resources needed to produce the information, multiplied by resources gained from the information

 C. Time taken to derive the information, plus money needed to derive the information

 D. Time taken to derive the information, multiplied by money needed to derive the information

9

8. If a company purchases a high-end Unix server to use for its research and development department, what is probably the most valuable part of the system?

    A. The high-end Unix server

    B. The information on the server

    C. The devices used to protect the server

    D. The room to store the server

9. Information is an asset to your company if it:

    A. Cost any sum of money to produce.

    B. Cost a significant sum of money to produce.

    C. Might have economic value.

    D. Might cost significant money to reproduce.

10. What is the greatest security risk to any company?

    A. disgruntled employees

    B. hackers

    C. industrial spies

    D. faulty network security

11. Which of the following is the best definition for *spyware*?

    A. Software that assists in corporate espionage

    B. Software that monitors activity on a computer

    C. Software that logs computer keystrokes

    D. Software that steals data

12. What is the highest level of security you can expect to obtain?

    A. A level of security that makes the effort required to get information more than the value of the information

    B. A level of security comparable with government security agencies, such as the Central Intelligence Agency

    C. A level of security that has a 92.5% success rate in stopping intrusion

    D. A level of security that has a 98.5% success rate in stopping intrusion

13. In the context of preventing industrial espionage, why might you wish to limit the number of company CD burners and control access to them in your organization?

   A. An employee could use such media to take sensitive data out.

   B. An employee could use such media to copy software from the company.

   C. CDs could be a vehicle for spyware to get on your system.

   D. CDs could be a vehicle for a virus to get on your system.

14. Why would you want to scan an employee's computer when he leaves the organization?

   A. To check the work flow prior to leaving

   B. To check for signs of corporate espionage

   C. To check for illegal software

   D. To check for pornography .

15. What is the reason for encrypting hard drives on laptop computers?

   A. To prevent a hacker from reading that data while you are online

   B. To ensure that data transmissions are secure

   C. To ensure that another user on that machine will not see sensitive data

   D. To prevent a thief from getting data off of a stolen laptop

9

EXERCISES

Exercise 9.1: Learning about Industrial Espionage

1. Using the Web, library, journals, or other resources, look up a case of industrial or corporate espionage not already mentioned in this chapter. The following Web sites might be of some help to you in finding a case:

   - citeseer.ist.psu.edu/320204.html
   - www.newhaven.edu/california/CJ625/p6.html
   - www.fidex.com/hackinglaws.htm

2. Write a brief essay describing the facts in the case. The parties in the case and the criminal proceeding are of interest, but most of your discussion should focus on the technical aspects of the case. Be sure to explain how the espionage was conducted.

Exercise 9.2: Using Anti-Spyware

Note that this exercise may be repeated with different anti-spyware products. It is a good idea for any person interested in computer security to be familiar with multiple anti-spyware products.

1. Go to the Web site of one of the anti-spyware utilities. (See Chapter 5 if you need more direction.)

2. Find instructions on the vendor's Web site.

3. Download the trial version of that software.

4. Install it on your machine.

5. After installation, run the utility. What did it find? Record your results.

6. Let the utility remove or quarantine anything it found.

Exercise 9.3: Learning about Key Loggers

Note that this exercise may only be completed on machines where you have explicit permission to do so (no public computers).

1. Using any Web site, find and download a key logger. The following Web sites might help you locate a key logger:

   • home.rochester.rr.com/artcfox/TinyKL/

   • www.kmint21.com/familykeylogger/

   • www.blazingtools.com/bpk.html

2. Install the key logger on your PC.

3. Examine how it behaves on your machine and if you notice anything that might indicate the presence of illicit software.

4. Run the anti-spyware software you downloaded in Exercise 2. Does the anti-spyware software detect the key logger?

Exercise 9.4: Screen Capture Spyware

1. Using the Web, find and download a screen-capturing spyware application. The following Web sites might be helpful to you in selecting an appropriate product:

   • www.win-spy.com/doorway/index80.htm

   • marketwatch-cnet.com.com/3000-2384-10188787. html?tag=lst-0-2

- www.softforall.com/Multimedia/Screencapture/River_Past_Screen_Recorder07090011.htm

2. Install and configure the application on your computer.

3. Run the application and note what it finds.

4. Run the anti-spyware from Exercise 2 and see whether it detects your spyware program.

Exercise 9.5: Learning about Hardware-Based Key Loggers

In this chapter, as well as Chapter 5, we discussed software-based key loggers. However, there are also hardware-based key loggers.

1. Use the Internet to learn more about hardware-based key loggers. (You may wish to search for "Keykatcher" as a starting point.)

2. Write an essay outlining the way in which these key loggers work and how they could be implemented for either security or industrial espionage.

PROJECTS

Project 9.1: Preventing Corporate Espionage

Using one of the Web sites listed in this book (you can also choose from the preferred resources in Chapter 1) or other resources, find a set of guidelines on general computer security. Write a brief essay comparing and contrasting those guidelines against the ones given in this chapter. Keep in mind that the guidelines in this chapter relate specifically to corporate espionage and not to general computer security.

Project 9.2: Handling Employees

Write a brief essay describing steps regarding the handling of employees. These steps should include all steps that you believe any organization should take to prevent corporate espionage. It is important that you support your opinions with sources and reasons.

If possible, visit a company and talk with someone in either the IT or personnel departments to determine how that company handles issues such as employee termination, rotation of duties, control of access to data, and so forth. Compare and contrast your steps to those used by the company you visited.

Project 9.3: Asset Identification in Your Organization

Using the Asset Identification table found in this chapter or a similar table of your own design, identify the most valuable data in your organization (school or business) and what parties would most likely wish to access that data. Then write a brief guideline on how you might go about securing that data. In this project, you should tailor your security recommendations to the specific type of data you are trying to protect and against the most likely perpetrators of industrial espionage.

▶ Case Study

David Doe is a network administrator for the ABC Company. David is passed over for promotion three times. He is quite vocal in his dissatisfaction with this situation. In fact, he begins to express negative opinions about the organization in general. Eventually, David quits and begins his own consulting business. Six months after David's departure, it is discovered that a good deal of the ABC Company's research has suddenly been duplicated by a competitor. Executives at ABC suspect that David Doe has done some consulting work for this competitor and may have passed on sensitive data. However, in the interim since David left, his computer has been formatted and reassigned to another person. ABC has no evidence that David Doe did anything wrong.

What steps might have been taken to detect David's alleged industrial espionage? What steps might have been taken to prevent his perpetrating such an offense?

Chapter 10

Cyber Terrorism and Information Warfare

Chapter Objectives

After reading this chapter and completing the exercises, you will be able to do the following:

- Explain what cyber terrorism is and how it has been used in some actual cases.
- Understand the basics of information warfare.
- Have a working knowledge of some plausible cyber terrorism scenarios.
- Have an appreciation for the dangers posed by cyber terrorism.

Introduction

Throughout this book, various ways have been examined in which a person might use a computer to commit a crime. This book has also looked into specific methods to make a system more secure. One issue that has not been addressed is that of cyber terrorism. People in countries around the world have grown accustomed to the ever-present threat of a terrorist attack, which could come in the form of a bomb, a hijacking, releasing a biological agent, or other means. Most people have not given much thought to the possibility of cyber terrorism.

The first question might be: What is cyber terrorism? According to the FBI, *cyber terrorism* is the premeditated, politically motivated attack against information, computer systems, computer programs, and data that results in violence against noncombatant targets by sub-national groups or

> ### FYI: The U.S. Government Takes Information Security Seriously
>
> Throughout 2003 and 2004, there have been a number of reports in reliable news sources, such as Cable News Network (CNN), of the U.S. government hiring hackers to test the security of various systems. The job of these hackers is to attempt to breach security of a sensitive system in order to find security flaws so they can be corrected before a more maliciously motivated hacker exploits them. Clearly, the U.S. government considers the concept of cyber terrorism to be a real threat and is taking steps to secure information.

clandestine agents (Dick, 2002). Cyber terrorism is simply the use of computers and the Internet connectivity between them in order to launch a terrorist attack. In short, cyber terrorism is just like other forms of terrorism—it is only the milieu of the attack that has changed. Clearly the loss of life due to a cyber attack would be much less than that of a bombing. In fact, it is highly likely that there would be no loss of life at all. However, significant economic damage, disruptions in communications, disruptions in supply lines, and general degradation of the national infrastructure are all quite possible via the Internet.

It is a strong possibility that, in time, someone or some group will try to use computer methods to launch a military or terrorist attack against our nation. Some experts make the case that the MyDoom virus (discussed in Chapter 4) was an example of domestic economic terrorism. However, an attack such as that may be only the tip of the iceberg. Sometime in the near future, our nation may be the target of a serious cyber terrorism attack. This chapter will examine some possible cyber terrorism scenarios, with the purpose of giving you a realistic assessment of just how serious a threat this is. In the exercises at the end of the chapter, you will have the opportunity to examine current acts of cyber terrorism, as well as potential threats, and the actions you can take to help prevent them.

Economic Attacks

There are a variety of ways that a cyber attack can cause economic damage. Lost files and lost records are one way. Chapter 9 discussed cyber espionage and mentioned the inherent value of data. In addition to stealing that data, it could simply be destroyed, in which case the data is gone and the resources used to accumulate and analyze the data are wasted. To use an analogy, consider that a malicious person could choose to simply destroy your car rather than steal it. In either case, you are without the car and will have to spend additional resources acquiring transportation.

In addition to simply destroying economically valuable data (remember that there is very little data that does not have some intrinsic value), there are other ways to cause economic disruption. Some of those ways include stealing credit cards, transferring money from accounts, and fraud. But it is a fact that anytime IT staff is involved with cleaning up a virus rather than developing applications or administering networks and databases, there is economic loss. The mere fact that companies now need to purchase antivirus software, intrusion-detection software, and hire computer security professionals means that computer crime has already caused economic damage to companies and governments around the world. However, the general damage caused by random virus outbreaks, lone hacking attacks, and online fraud is not the type of economic damage that is the focus of this chapter. This chapter is concerned with a concerted and deliberate attack against a particular target or targets for the exclusive purpose of causing direct damage.

A good way to get a firm grasp on the impact of this type of attack is to walk through a scenario. Group X (which could be an aggressive nation, terrorist group, activist group, or literally any group with the motivation to damage a particular nation) decides to make a concerted attack on our country. They find a small group of individuals (in this case, six) that are well versed in computer security, networking, and programming. These individuals, motivated either by ideology or monetary needs, are organized to create a coordinated attack. There are many possible scenarios under which they could execute such an attack and cause significant economic harm. The example outlined below is just one of those possible attack modalities. In this case, each individual has an assignment, and all assignments are designed to be activated on the same specific date.

- Team member one sets up several fake e-commerce sites. Each of these sites is only up for 72 hours and portends to be a major stock brokerage site. During the brief time they are up, the site's real purpose is only to collect credit card numbers/bank account numbers and so forth. On the predetermined date, all of those credit card and bank numbers will be automatically, anonymously, and simultaneously posted to various bulletin boards/Web sites and newsgroups, making them available for any unscrupulous individual that wishes to use them.

- Team member two creates a virus. This virus is contained in a Trojan horse. Its function is to delete key system files on the predetermined date. In the meantime, it shows a series of business tips or motivational slogans, making it a popular download with people in business.

- Team member three creates another virus. It is designed to create distributed Denial of Service attacks on key economic sites, such as those for stock exchanges or brokerage houses. The virus spreads harmlessly and is set to begin its distributed Denial of Service attack on the predetermined date.

- Team members four and five begin the process of footprinting major banking systems, preparing to crack them on the predetermined date.

- Team member six prepares a series of false stock tips to flood the Internet on the predetermined date.

If each of these individuals is successful in their mission, on the predetermined date, several major brokerages and perhaps government economic sites are taken down, viruses flood networks, and files are deleted from the machines of thousands of businessmen, economists, stock brokers. Thousands of credit cards and bank numbers are released on the Internet, guaranteeing that many will be misused. It is also highly likely that the cracking team members four and five will have some success—meaning that possibly one or more banking systems are compromised. It does not take an economist to realize that this would easily cost hundreds of millions of dollars, perhaps even billions of dollars. A concerted attack of this nature could easily cause more economic damage to our country than most traditional terrorists attacks (i.e., bombings) have ever done.

FIGURE 10.1 A team member of Group X?

You could extrapolate on this scenario and imagine not just one group of six cyber terrorists, but five groups of six—each group with a different mission and each mission designed to be committed approximately two weeks apart. In this scenario, the nation's economy would literally be under siege for two and one-half months.

This scenario is not particularly far-fetched when you consider that, in past decades, nuclear scientists were sought after by various nations and terrorist groups. More recently, experts in biological weapons have been sought by these same groups. It seems extremely likely that these groups will see the possibilities of this form of terrorism and seek out computer security/hacking experts. Given that there are literally thousands of people with the requisite skills, it seems likely that a motivated organization could find a few dozen people willing to commit these acts.

Military Operations Attacks

When computer security and national defense are mentioned together, the obvious thought that comes to mind is the possibility of some hacker breaking into ultra-secure systems at the Department of Defense, Central Intelligence Agency (CIA), or National Security Agency (NSA). However, such an intrusion into one of the most secure systems in the world is very unlikely—not impossible, but very unlikely. The most likely outcome of such an attack would be that the attacker is promptly captured. Such systems are hyper-secure and intruding upon them is not as easy as some movies might suggest. However, there are a number of scenarios in which breaking into less secure systems could jeopardize our national defense or put military plans at risk.

Consider less sensitive military systems for a moment, for example, systems that are responsible for basic logistical operations (e.g., food, mail, fuel). If someone cracks one or more of these systems, he could perhaps obtain information that several C-141s (an aircraft often used for troop transports and parachute operations) are being routed to a base that is within flight distance of some city — a city that has been the focal point of political tensions. This same cracker (or team of crackers) also finds that a large amount of ammunition and food supplies, enough for perhaps 5000 troops for two weeks, is simultaneously being routed to that base. Then, on yet another low-security system, the cracker (or team of crackers) notes that a given unit, such as two brigades of the 82nd airborne division, have had all military leaves cancelled. It does not take a military genius to conclude that these two brigades are preparing to drop in on the target city and secure that target. Therefore, the fact that a deployment is going to occur, the size of the deployment, and the approximate time of that deployment have all been deduced without ever attempting to break into a high-security system.

10

Taking the previous scenario to the next level, assume the hacker gets deep into the low-security logistical systems. Then assume that he does nothing to change the routing of the members of the brigades or the transport planes—actions that might draw attention. However, he does alter the records for the shipment of supplies so that the supplies are delivered two days late and to the wrong base. So there would be two brigades potentially in harms way, without a re-supply of ammunition or food en route. Of course, the situation could be rectified, but the units in question may go for some time without re-supply—enough time, perhaps, to prevent them from successfully completing their mission.

These are just two scenarios in which compromising low-security/low-priority systems can lead to very significant military problems. This further illustrates the serious need for high security on all systems. Given the interconnectivity of so many components of both business and military computer systems, there clearly are no truly "low-priority" security systems.

General Attacks

The previously outlined scenarios involve specific targets with specific strategies. However, once a specific target is attacked, defenses can be readied for it. There are many security professionals that work constantly to thwart these specific attacks. What may be more threatening is a general and unfocused attack with no specific target. Consider the various virus attacks of late 2003 and early 2004. With the exception of My Doom, which was clearly aimed at the Santa Cruz Organization, these attacks were not aimed at a specific target. However, the shear volume of virus attacks and network traffic did cause significant economic damage. IT personnel across the globe dropped their normal projects to clean infected systems and shore up the defenses of systems.

This leads to another possible scenario in which various cyber terrorists continuously release new and varied viruses, perform Denial of Systems attacks, and work to make the Internet in general, and e-commerce in particular, virtually unusable for a period of time. Such a scenario would actually be more difficult to combat, as there would not be a specific target to defend or a clear ideological motive to use as a clue to the identity of the perpetrators.

Information Warfare

Information warfare certainly predates the advent of the modern computer and, in fact, may be as old as conventional warfare. In essence, information warfare is any attempt to manipulate information in pursuit of a military or political goal. When you attempt to use any process to gather information on an opponent or when you use propaganda to influence opinions in a conflict, these are both examples of information warfare. Chapter 9 discussed the role of the computer in corporate espionage. The same techniques can be applied to a military conflict in which the computer can be used as a tool in espionage. Although information gathering will not be re-examined in this chapter, information gathering is only one part of information warfare. Propaganda is another aspect of information warfare. The flow of information impacts troop morale, citizens' outlooks on a conflict, the political support for a conflict, and the involvement of peripheral nations and international organizations.

Propaganda

Computers and the Internet are very effective tools that can be used in the dissemination of propaganda. Many people now use the Internet as a secondary news source, and some even use it as their primary news source. This means that a government, terrorist group, political party, or any activist group could use what appears to be an Internet news Web site as a front to put their own political spin on any conflict. Such a Web site does not need to be directly connected to the political organization whose views are being disseminated; in fact, it is better if it is not directly connected. The Irish Republican Army (IRA), for example, has always operated with two distinct and separate divisions: one that takes paramilitary/terrorist action and another that is purely political. This allows the political/information wing, called Sinn Fein, to operate independently of any military or terrorist activities. In fact, Sinn Fein now has their own Web site shown in Figure 10.2 where they disseminate news with their own perspective (**www.sinnfein.org**). In this situation, however, it is fairly clear to whoever is reading the information that it is biased toward the perspective of the party sponsoring the site. A better scenario (for the party concerned) occurs when there is an Internet news source that is favorably disposed to a political group's position without having any actual connection at all. This makes it easier for the group to spread information without being accused of any obvious bias. The political group (be it a nation, rebel group, or terrorist organization) can then "leak" stories to this news agency.

Information Control

Since World War II, control of information has been an important part of political and military conflicts. Below are just a few examples.

- Throughout the Cold War, Western democracies invested time and money for radio broadcasts into communist nations. This well-known campaign was referred to as Radio Free Europe. The goal was to create dissatisfaction among citizens of those nations, hopefully encouraging defection, dissent, and general discontent. Most historians and political analysts agree that this was a success.

10

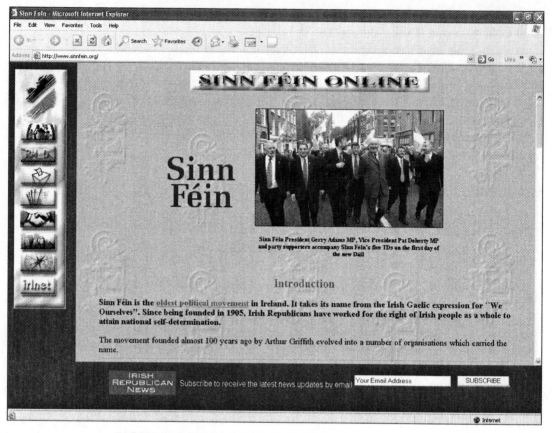

FIGURE 10.2 The Sinn Fein Web site.

- The Vietnam War was the first modern war in which there was strong and widespread domestic opposition. Many analysts believe that opposition was due to the graphic images being brought home via television.

- Today, the government and military of every nation are aware of how the phrases they use to describe activities can affect public perception. They do not say that innocent civilians were killed in a bombing raid. Rather, they state that there was "some collateral damage." Governments do not speak of being the aggressor or starting a conflict. They speak of "preemptive action." Dissenters in any nation are almost always painted as treasonous or cowards.

Public perception is a very important part of any conflict. Each nation wants their own citizens to be totally in support of what they do and to maintain a very high morale. High morale and strong support lead to volunteers for military service, public support for funding the conflict, and political success for the nation's leader. At the same time, you want the enemy to have low morale—to doubt not only their ability to be successful in the conflict, but also their moral position relative to the conflict. You want them to doubt their leadership and to be as opposed to the conflict as possible. The Internet provides a very inexpensive vehicle for swaying public opinion.

Web pages are just one facet of disseminating information. Having people post to various discussion groups can also be effective. One full-time propaganda agent could easily manage 25 or more distinct online personalities, each spending time in different bulletin boards and discussion groups, espousing the views that his political entity wants to espouse. These can reinforce what certain Internet news outlets are posting or they could undermine those postings. They can also start rumors. Rumors can be very effective even when probably false. People often recall hearing something with only a vague recollection of where they heard it and whether it was supported by any data.

Such an agent could have one personality that purports to be a military member (it would take very little research to make this credible) and could post information "not seen in newscasts" that would cast the conflict in either a positive or negative light. She could then have other online personas that entered the discussion who would agree with and support the original position. This would give the initial rumor more credibility. Some people suspect this is already occurring in Usenet newsgroups and Yahoo discussion boards.

FYI: Cyber Information Warfare Now

Anyone familiar with Yahoo news boards has probably noticed an odd phenomenon. At certain times, there will be a flood of posts from anonymous users, all saying essentially the exact same things—even using the exact same grammar, punctuation, and phrasing—and all in support of some ideological perspective. These flurries often happen in times when influence of public opinion is important, such as when an election is nearing. Whether or not these postings are coordinated by any well-known or official organization is debatable. However, they are an example of information warfare. One person or group of people attempt to sway opinion by flooding one particular media (Internet groups) with various items advocating one view. If they are lucky, some individuals will copy the text and e-mail it to friends who do not participate in the newsgroups, thus crossing over to another media and spreading opinions (in some cases entirely unfounded) far and wide.

10

FYI: Disinformation—A Historical Perspective

While disinformation campaigns are certainly easier to conduct since the advent of mass communication, particularly the Internet, such activities did exist prior to the Internet, or even television. For example in the weeks leading up the famous D-Day invasion of World War II, the Allied forces used a number of disinformation techniques:

- They created documents and communiqués listing fictitious military units that would invade from an entirely different location than the real invasion was planned.
- They used Allied double agents to spread similar disinformation to the Germans.
- A few small groups simulated a large scale invasion to distract the German army.

Disinformation

Another category of information warfare that is closely related to propaganda is disinformation. It is a given that a military opponent is attempting to gather information about troop movements, military strength, supplies, and so forth. A prudent move would be to set up systems that had incorrect information and were just secure enough to be credible, but not secure enough to be unbreakable. An example would be to send an encrypted coded message such that, when the message is decrypted, it seems to say one thing, but to those who can complete the code, it has a different message. The actual message is "padded" with "noise." That noise is a weakly encrypted false message, whereas the real message is more strongly encrypted. In this way, if the message is decrypted, there exists a high likelihood that the fake message will be decrypted and not the real one. General Gray USMC put it best when he said, "Communications without intelligence is noise; intelligence without communications is irrelevant." (Institute for the Advanced Study of Information Warfare, 2004)

The goal of any military or intelligence agency is to make certain our communications are clear and that the enemy can only receive noise.

Actual Cases

It should be noted that there are voices in the computer security industry that think cyber terrorism or cyber war are simply not realistic scenarios. Marcus Ranum of Information Security magazine states as much in the

April 2004 issue. He and others claim that there is no danger from cyber terrorism and that, in fact, "The whole notion of cyberwarfare is a scam." (Ranum, 2004) However, computer warfare and cyber terrorism have already been used on a small scale. It seems quite plausible that, in a matter of time, it will be seen on a much larger scale.

Even if you believe that the scenarios outlined in the earlier sections of this chapter are merely the product of an overactive imagination, you should consider that there have already been a few actual incidents of cyber terrorism—although much less severe than the theoretical scenarios. This section examines some of these cases so as to show you how such attacks have been carried out in the past.

The incidents listed below were reported in testimony before the Special Oversight Panel on Terrorism Committee on Armed Services U.S. House of Representatives (Denning, 2000).

- In 1996, a computer hacker allegedly associated with the White Supremacist movement temporarily disabled a Massachusetts ISP and damaged part of the ISP's record-keeping system. The ISP had attempted to stop the hacker from sending out worldwide racist messages under the ISP's name. The hacker signed off with the threat, "You have yet to see true electronic terrorism. This is a promise."

- In 1998, ethnic Tamil guerrillas swamped Sri Lankan embassies with 800 e-mails a day over a two-week period. The messages read, "We are the Internet Black Tigers and we're doing this to disrupt your communications." Intelligence authorities characterized it as the first known attack by terrorists against a country's computer systems.

- During the Kosovo conflict in 1999, NATO computers were blasted with e-mail bombs and hit with Denial of Service attacks by *hacktivists* (the name applied to individuals who work for their causes using cyber terrorism) protesting the NATO bombings. In addition, businesses, public organizations, and academic institutes received highly politicized virus-laden e-mails from a range of Eastern European countries, according to reports. Web defacements were also common. After the Chinese Embassy was accidentally bombed in Belgrade, Chinese hacktivists posted messages such as, "We won't stop attacking until the war stops!" on U.S. government Web sites.

The good news is that these particular attacks caused little damage and were clearly the product of amateurs. However, it may only be a matter of time before more damaging attacks are perpetrated by far more skilled cyber terrorists. Yet it is clear that cyber terrorism, at least on a low-intensity scale, is already beginning. These warnings can be heeded and the issues taken seriously, or they can simply be ignored until disaster strikes.

10

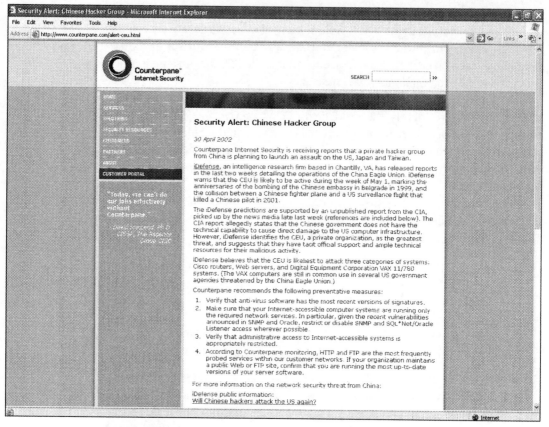

FIGURE 10.3 Counterpane Internet Security report on a planned cyberattack.

In addition to those cases listed above, there have been other credible threats or actual incidents of cyber attacks in the past several years.

■ In 2002, Counterpane Internet Security reported (as shown in Figure 10.3) a credible threat of a Chinese-backed, all-out cyber attack planned on the United States and Taiwan (2002). A private group of Chinese hackers, called the Chinese Eagle Union, planned to attack routers and Web servers across the United States and Taiwan. The attack never materialized, but unconfirmed reports suggested that the CIA took the threat seriously.

■ In June of 2000, Russian authorities arrested a man they accused of being a CIA-backed hacker. As shown in Figure 10.4, this man allegedly hacked into systems of the Russian Domestic Security Service (FSB) and gathered secrets that he then passed on to the CIA (BBC News, 2000). This example illustrates the potential for a

FIGURE 10.4 BBC report on an arrested hacker.

skilled hacker using his knowledge to conduct espionage operations. This espionage is likely occurring much more often than is reported in the media, and many such incidents may never come to light.

Alternative media sources have been reporting that both the CIA and NSA have employed hackers for some time. This might be easily dismissed as false were it not for the fact that such hackers have actually been caught, as in the Russian story. One might even go so far as to say that, in our

FYI: The Threat of Cyber Terrorism

Fortunately, to date, the examples given in this text, are about the most dramatic that have been made public. Cyber terrorism is not a big problem today; it is the problem that is looming on our horizon.

modern age, for intelligence gathering agencies not to employee cyber intelligence-gathering techniques would be a dereliction of their duty.

What is also frightening to consider are reports that our satellites, used for communication, weather, and military operations, could be vulnerable to hacking (Roberts, 2002). Such vulnerabilities seem less likely simply because of the skill level required to execute such an attack. As previously mentioned, hacking/cracking is like any other human endeavor—by the law of averages, most people are mediocre. The level of skill required to compromise security on a satellite system is far greater than that required to compromise the security of a Web site. Of course, that does not mean that such an attack is impossible, but simply that it is less likely.

Future Trends

By carefully analyzing what is occurring presently in cyber crime and terrorism along with the recent history of that field, you can extrapolate and make reasonably accurate estimates for what trends will dominate in the

FIGURE 10.5 The Cyberterrorism Preparedness Act of 2002.

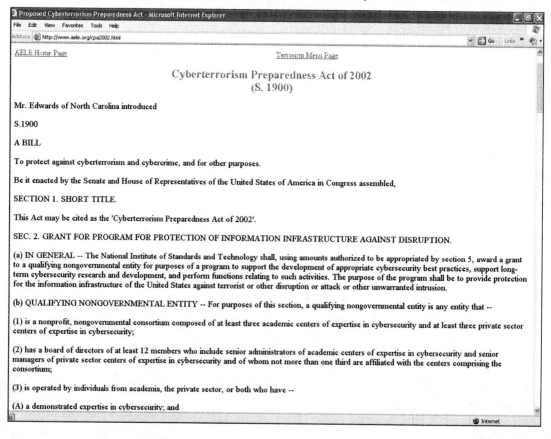

near future. This section will endeavor to do that. There are certainly positive and negative trends that should be considered.

Positive Trends

It does seem that various governments are beginning to take notice of this problem and are taking some steps to ameliorate the dangers. For example, U.S. senator John Edwards (D-NC) proposed two bills in 2002 aimed at allocating $400 million for cybersecurity efforts. The first measure, called the Cyberterrorism Preparedness Act of 2002 (Tech Law Journal, 2002), a portion of which is shown in Figure 10.5, would set aside $350 million over five years for improving network security, first for Federal systems and then for the private sector. It would also create a group assigned to gather and distribute information about the best security practices. The Cybersecurity Research and Education Act of 2002 (The Orator, 2002), a portion of which is shown in Figure 10.6, would provide $50 million over four years for fellowships that would be used to train IT specialists in cyber security. It also

FIGURE 10.6 Cybersecurity Research and Education Act of 2002.

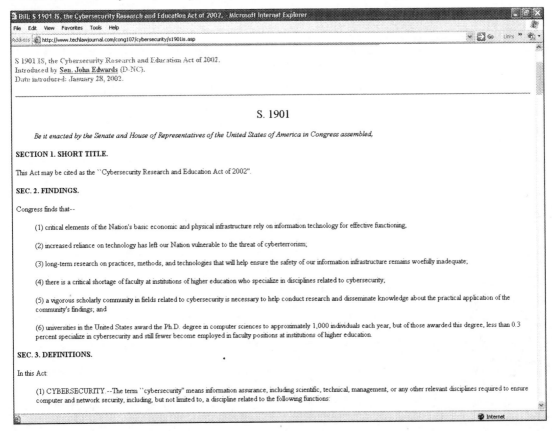

10

calls for the creation of a Web-based university where administrators can get updated training. As of this writing, both bills are in committee and have not come before the entire Senate for a vote. However, the fact that bills such as this, and others, are being considered by various governments, including the U.S. government, is a step in the right direction.

Negative Trends

Unfortunately, as legislative bodies become aware of this problem and focus some resources on the issue, the threats continue to grow. In a paper commissioned by the Rand Corporation (Hoffman, 2003), it is noted that even groups such as Al Queda—who have not used cyber terrorism as one of their attack modalities as of this writing—have used Internet and computer technology resources to plan their various activities and coordinate training.

As early as 2000, the U. S. General Accounting Office warned of several possible cyber terrorism scenarios (Tech Law Journal, 2000). As shown in Figure 10.7, their concerns involved far more lethal attackers than any of

FIGURE 10.7 Rand report on cyber terrorism.

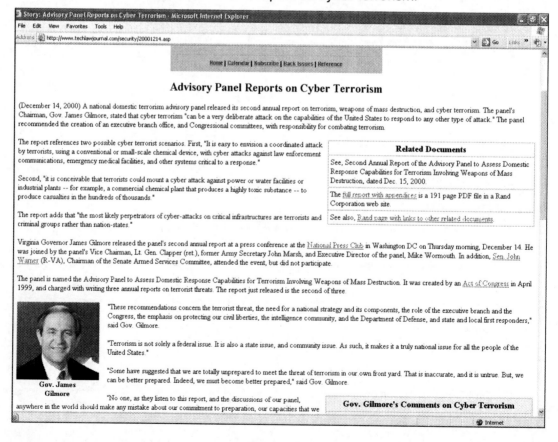

the scenarios that have been outlined in this chapter. They proposed possible attack scenarios in which the computer-controlled machinery in a chemical plant was altered in order to cause a release of toxic chemicals into the environment. This could be done in a variety of ways including simply causing the machinery to drastically over-produce, overheat, or perhaps prematurely shut down equipment. The panel also contemplated scenarios in which water and power supplies were interrupted or compromised via computer systems. In essence, their focus was on the potential for massive casualties as a direct result of a cyber-based attack rather than the economic damage on which this chapter's scenarios focused.

Defense Against Cyber Terrorism

As the world becomes more dependent upon computer systems, the danger of cyber terrorism will grow. Clearly, there must be a much stronger emphasis on computer security. In addition to the basic security measures already recommended in this book, there are also some recommendations for preparing for and protecting systems against cyber terrorism.

- Many recommend a Manhattan Project-level government program designed to prepare for and defend against cyber warfare.

- Major academic institutions must begin dedicated research and academic programs that are devoted solely to computer security.

- Computer crime must be treated far more seriously, with stronger punishments and more active investigation of suspected crimes.

- It is unreasonable to ask every police department to have a computer-crime specialist on staff. However, state-level investigative agencies should be able to hire such personnel. Rather than take law enforcement officers and train them in basic computer crime, the recommendation exists to take highly skilled computer professionals and train them in law enforcement. To adequately combat cyber terrorism, one absolutely must first and foremost be a highly qualified computer expert.

- An emergency reporting system may need to be implemented so that security professionals from various industries have a single source where they can report attacks on their systems and can view the issues with which other security professionals are dealing. This could enable security professionals as a group to more quickly recognize when a coordinated attack is occurring.

In addition, you can make some additions to and variations on your existing security measures. For example, you should have a recovery process in place so that data can be quickly recovered should someone

10

delete important files. You should also, as recommended in Chapter 9, assess what data is of most value and focus your attention on that data. But, as this chapter points out, you must also consider how data that would at first appear to be of less value may actually reveal more information about you personally or your company then is prudent.

Summary

It is clear that there are a variety of ways in which cyber terrorist attacks could be used against any industrialized nation. Many experts, including various government panels, senators, and terrorism experts, believe that this is a very real threat. This means that it is more important than ever to be extremely vigilant in securing your computer systems. You must also look beyond the obvious uses of data and see how someone with an intent to harm or cause economic hardship could use seemingly unimportant information. In the exercises at the end of this chapter, you will have a chance to explore various cyber terrorism and information warfare threats.

Test Your Skills

MULTIPLE CHOICE QUESTIONS

1. What is the most likely damage from an act of cyber terrorism?

   A. loss of life

   B. military strategy compromised

   C. economic loss

   D. disrupted communications

2. Which of the following is not an example of financial loss due to cyber terrorism?

   A. lost data

   B. transferring money from accounts

   C. damage to facilities including computers

   D. computer fraud

3. Which of the following military/government systems would most likely be the target of a successful computer hack?

    A. The most sensitive systems of the CIA

    B. Nuclear systems at NORAD

    C. Low-security logistical system

    D. Military satellite control systems

4. Which of the following might be an example of domestic cyber terrorism?

    A. Sasser virus

    B. Mimail virus

    C. Sobig virus

    D. MyDoom virus

5. What differentiates cyber terrorism from other computer crimes?

    A. It is organized.

    B. It is politically or ideologically motivated.

    C. It is conducted by experts.

    D. It is often more successful.

6. Which of the following is a political group that has already used the Internet for political intimidation?

    A. Internet Black Tigers

    B. Al Queda

    C. Mafia

    D. IRA

7. What is information warfare?

    A. Only spreading disinformation

    B. Spreading disinformation or gathering information

    C. Only gathering information

    D. Spreading disinformation or secure communications

8. Which of the following would most likely be considered examples of information warfare?

    A. Radio Free Europe during the Cold War

    B. radio political talk show

    C. normal news reports

    D. military press releases

10

9. Which of the following is a likely use of Internet newsgroups in information warfare?

A. To spread propaganda

B. To monitor dissident groups

C. To send encoded messages

D. To recruit supporters

10. Sending a false message with weak encryption, intending it to be intercepted and deciphered, is an example of what?

A. poor communications

B. need for better encryption

C. disinformation

D. propaganda

11. Which of the following best describes the communication goal of any intelligence agency?

A. To send clear communications to allies and noise to all other parties

B. To send clear communications to allies and noise only to the enemy

C. To send disinformation to the enemy

D. To send clear communications to allied forces

12. Which of the following conflicts had a cyber warfare component?

A. 1989 invasion of Panama

B. 1990 Kosovo crisis

C. 1990 Somalia crisis

D. Vietnam War

13. Which of the following agencies has allegedly had one of its cyber spies actually caught?

A. NSA

B. KGB

C. FBI

D. CIA

14. According to the October 2002 *InfoWorld* magazine article, which of the following systems may be vulnerable to attack?

    A. NORAD nuclear weapons control

    B. low-level logistical systems

    C. satellites

    D. CIA computers

15. Which of the following is a cyber attack that would likely cause imminent loss of life?

    A. disruption of banking system

    B. disruption of water

    C. disruption of security systems

    D. disruption of chemical plant control systems

EXERCISES

Exercise 10.1: Finding Information Warfare

1. Pick a current political topic.

2. Track that topic on multiple bulletin boards, Yahoo newsgroups, or blogs.

3. Look for signs that might indicate an organized effort to sway opinion or information warfare. This might include posts allegedly made by separate individuals that have highly similar points, grammar, and syntax.

4. Write a brief essay discussing what you found and why you think it constitutes information warfare.

Exercise 10.2: Cyber Terrorism Threat Assessment

1. Pick some activist group (e.g., political, ideological) that you find intriguing.

2. Using only the Web, gather as much information about that organization as you can.

3. Write a brief dossier on that group, including what you think is the likelihood that such a group would engage in information warfare or cyber terrorism and why.

10

Exercise 10.3: Finding Information Policies

1. Using the Web or other resources, locate several examples of organizational policies regarding information dissemination.

2. Find points common to all such policies.

3. Write a brief essay explaining why these policies might be related to either propagating or preventing information warfare.

Exercise 10.4: How Companies Defend Against Cyber Terrorism

1. Interview the IT staff of a company to find out whether they take information warfare or cyber terrorism into direct account when they are securing their systems.

2. Find out what steps they take to protect their company's systems from these threats.

3. Write a brief essay explaining what you have found out.

Exercise 10.5: Pulling it All Together

Pulling together what you have learned from previous chapters, what information can you apply to the protection of a system against cyber terrorism or information warfare? Write a brief outline of the steps you would take to secure a system against these threats.

PROJECTS

Project 10.1: Computer Security and Cyber Terrorism

Consider the various security measures you have examined thus far in this book. Given the threat of cyber terrorism, write an essay discussing how those methods might relate to cyber terrorism. Also discuss whether or not the threat of computer-based terrorism warrants a higher security standard than you might have otherwise used, and explain why or why not.

Project 10.2: The Law and Cyber Terrorism

Note: This is meant as a group project.

Using the Web or other resources, find and examine laws that you feel relate to cyber terrorism. Then write an essay describing legislation you believe needs to be written regarding cyber terrorism. Essentially, your group should act as if it were technical advisors to a congressional committee drafting new legislation.

Project 10.3: Cyber Terrorism Scenario

Considering any of the theoretical cyber terrorism scenarios presented in this chapter, write a security and response plan that you feel addresses that scenario and protects against that specific threat.

▶▶ Case Study

Jane Doe is the network administrator responsible for security for a small defense contractor. Her company does handle some low-level classified material. She has implemented a strong security approach that includes:

- A firewall has all unneeded ports closed.

- Virus scanners are placed on all machines.

- Routers between network segments are secured.

- All machines have the operating systems patched monthly.

- Passwords are long, complex, and change every 90 days.

   What other recommendations would you make to Jane Doe? Explain the reasons for each of your recommendations.

Chapter | 11

Cyber Detective

Chapter Objectives

After reading this chapter and completing the exercises, you will be able to do the following:

- Find contact information on the Web.
- Locate court records on the Web.
- Locate criminal records on the Web.
- Use Usenet newsgroups to gather information.

Introduction

In the preceding chapters we have examined many facets of computer security. Three of those issues lead us to the content of this chapter. The first is identity theft, the second is hacking, and the third is investigating potential employees for sensitive positions.

In order for a criminal to perpetrate identity theft they have to take a small amount of information they find on their target and use that to garner even more information. Perhaps a discarded credit card receipt, or utility bill becomes the starting point from which the perpetrator finds enough information to assume the victim's identity. This chapter will show you some techniques that use the Internet to find additional information about a person. You need to be aware of how this is done, in order to be better prepared to defend against it and so that you are aware of what information about you personally is available.

Hackers, at least skilled hackers, will want information about a target person, organization, and system in order to assist in compromising security. Whether the perpetrator is attempting to use social engineering, or simply trying to guess a password, having information about the target will facilitate the task. Once you realize how easy it is to gain personal information about someone, you will realize why security experts are so adamant that you must not use passwords that are in any way associated with you, your profession, your hobbies, or anything that might be traced back to you.

Finally, when you are hiring employees that might have access to sensitive data, simply calling the references they provide is not an adequate method of checking into their background. And hiring a private investigator may be impractical. The information in this chapter might be of use to you in conducting some level of investigation on your own.

This may surprise some readers, but network administrators are of particular significance to be investigated before hiring. Most companies perform the same cursory check of network administrators as they do of any other person. That usually consists of verifying degrees/certifications and calling references. With some companies it might include a credit check and a local criminal check. However, a network administrator should be more thoroughly investigated. The reason is quite simple, regardless of how tight your security is, it cannot keep out the person who sets it up and maintains it. If you are considering hiring a network administrator for your company, knowing that he or she has been affiliated with hacking groups might be of interest to you. Or simply knowing that they have had lapses in judgment might indicate a stronger possibility that they will have similar lapses in the future. This may seem a bit paranoid, but by this point in this book you should have developed a little healthy paranoia.

The Internet can be a valuable investigation tool. It can be used to find out about potential employees, baby sitters, etc. Much of the information on the Internet is also free. Many states have court records online, and there are many other resources you can use to find information. In this chapter we will examine some of the various resources you can use on the Internet to locate critical information.

Before beginning this discussion, a few points need to be made clear. The first being that this information is a two edged sword. Yes, you can use it to find out if a potential business partner has previously been sued or declared bankruptcy, or if your child's little league coach has a criminal record. However as we briefly mentioned, a less scrupulous person can also use these techniques to gather detailed information about you, either for the purpose of identity theft or perhaps stalking. Some people have suggested to me that perhaps I should not put this information (and some other items that appear in various chapters) in this book. However my opinion is that the hackers, crackers, and perpetrators of identity theft already know about these resources, my hope is to level the playing field. I would also warn all readers that invading other people's privacy is fraught with ethical, moral, and in many cases legal, ramifications. It would be advisable to obtain written permission before running a background check on any person—or, better yet, play it safe and only perform searches on your own name. It must

11

also be stressed that I am neither an attorney nor a law enforcement officer. I am simply providing you with techniques and resources. If you have questions about legality, you should refer those questions to an attorney.

General Searches

Sometimes you simply want to find an address, phone number, or e-mail address for a person. Or perhaps that is the starting point for a more thorough investigation. There are a number of absolutely free services on the Web that will allow you to perform this sort of search. Some are better than others, and obviously the more common the name you are searching for the harder it will be to find the right one. If you do a search for John Smith in California, you might have a tough time dealing with all the results you get.

A fairly easy to use service is the Yahoo People Search. When you go to **www.yahoo.com** you see a number of options on the page. One option is the 'People Search' shown in Figure 11.1.

When you select this option you will see a screen similar to the one shown in Figure 11.2. In this screen you enter a first and last name, as well as a city or state. You can then search for either a phone number/address or an email.

FIGURE 11.1 Yahoo People Search

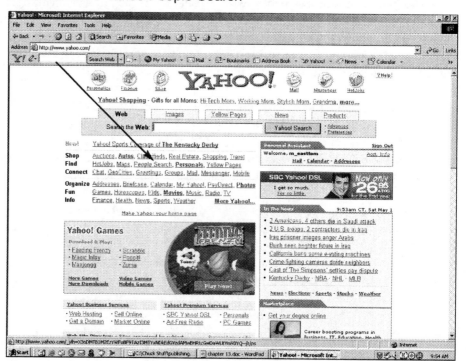

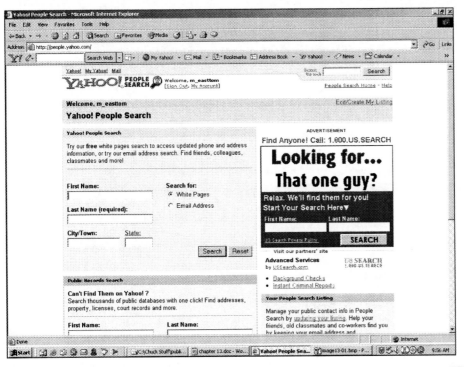

FIGURE 11.2 Search options

To illustrate how this works, I did a search on my own name, in Texas (where I live). As Figure 11.3 shows, that search results in my home address and phone number, as well two listings for my wife, Misty—one that shows our current address and phone number and one that shows our previous address and phone number.

Another useful site for addresses and phone numbers around the world is **www.infobel.com**. This site has the advantage of being international, allowing you to seek out phone numbers and addresses in a variety of countries. As you can see from Figure 11.4, the first step is to select a country to search in.

Once you have selected your country, you can then narrow your search further by providing as much information as you can on the person you are trying to locate. A first and last name, however, is a minimum.

These are just two of the many sites that allow you to investigate and discover a person's home address or telephone number. Several other good sites you should consider are listed below.

- www.smartpages.com

- www.theultimates.com/white/

- www.bigfoot.com/

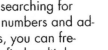

Caution

Multiple Results

When searching for phone numbers and addresses, you can frequently find multiple wrong results, especially when searching for a common name. For example if you search for John Smith in the state of New York, the chances are you will get a huge number of results. The more information you have to narrow your search, the better. Even the search on "Easttom" in "Texas", a fairly uncommon name and, hence, a narrow search, resulted in one right listing and one wrong listing for Misty Easttom.

11

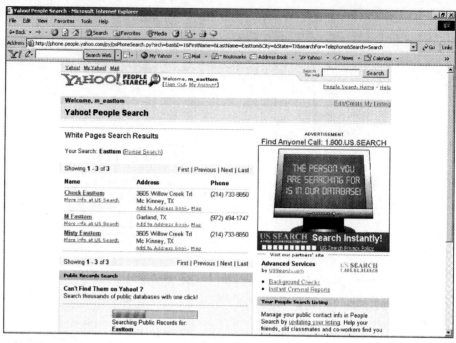

FIGURE 11.3 People Search results

FIGURE 11.4 Infobel home page

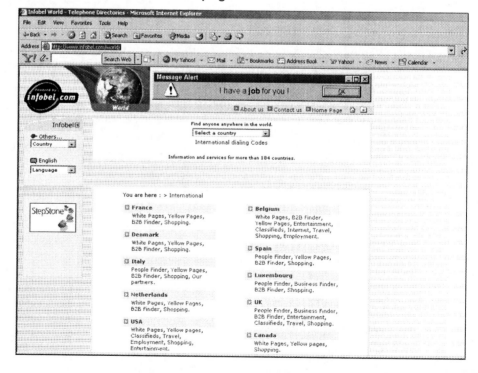

FYI: Respecting Privacy

You might wonder why I would be willing to put my home address and phone number in a published book. To begin with, anyone reading this chapter could easily have done their own search and found my information. And, in order to illustrate the process, I needed a name to use. For the liability reasons mentioned earlier I could not have used someone else's name. However, should readers wish to contact me, they are strongly encouraged to do so via my Web site (**www.chuckeasttom.com**) and email address (**chuckeasttom@yahoo.com**) rather than via phone. I try to answer all my email, but frequently avoid my phone. And I am certainly not encouraging anyone to make a surprise visit to my home!

Caution

Mistaken Identity

There have been cases of mistaken identity with sex offender lists. Any time you find negative information on a person you are investigating—whatever the source—you have an ethical responsibility to verify that information before you take any action on it.

- www.whowhere.com
- www.switchboard.com
- www.people.icq.com/whitepages

It is important to remember that the more information you can provide, and the more you narrow down your search, the greater the likelihood of finding what you are looking for. All of these Web sites can assist you in finding phone numbers and addresses, both current and past. For a background check on an employee this can be useful in verifying previous addresses.

Court Records and Criminal Checks

A number of states are now putting a variety of court records online. Everything from general court documents to specific records of criminal history and even lists of pedophiles. This sort of information can be critical before you hire an employee, use a babysitter, or send your child to little league. In the following sections, we discuss a variety of resources for this sort of information.

Sex Offender Registries

First, you should become familiar with the online sex offender registries. The FBI maintains a rather exhaustive list of individual state registries. You can access this information at **www.fbi.gov/hq/cid/cac/registry.htm**. Every state that has an online registry is listed on this Web site, as shown in Figure 11.5. Obviously some states have done a better job of making accurate information public, than have others. For example, Texas has a rather

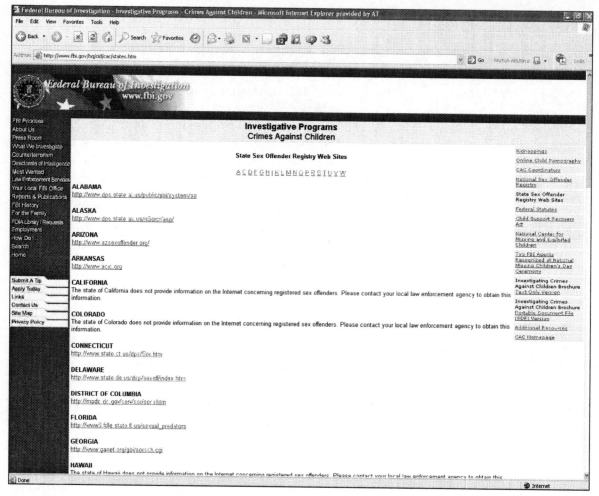

FIGURE 11.5 FBI state registry of sex offenders.

comprehensive site. You can find it at **records.txdps.state.tx.us/**. This site allows you to either look up an individual person, or to put in a zip code (or city name) and find out any registered sex offenders in that area. Figure 11.6 shows the search screen for the Texas site mentioned.

One of the most compelling things about the Texas sex offender registry is that it lists the offense the person was convicted of as well as a photo of the offender. This is important since the term 'sex offender' covers a wide variety of crimes. Some of which may not, for example, impact whether you should hire this person. It is important to know what a person was convicted of before you decide they are unsuitable to be interacting with your children or working in your organization.

Some sex offenders have committed heinous crimes and many parents will want to use this information to find out about potential baby sitters and

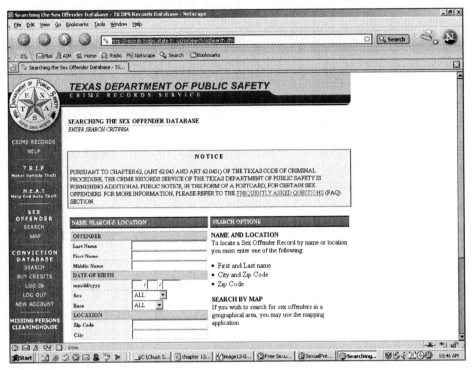

FIGURE 11.6 Texas sex offender search page

coaches. This information may also be applicable to employment screenings. However, anytime any information is used for employment screening it is advisable to check the laws in your area. You may not legally be able to base employment decisions on certain information. As with all legal questions, your best course of action is to consult a reputable attorney.

Civil Court Records

There are a variety of crimes, as well as civil issues, a person might be involved in that would make them unsuitable for a particular job. If you are hiring a person to work in your human resources department and oversee equal opportunity issues, knowing if they had been involved in domestic violence, racially motivated graffiti, or other similar issues, might effect your employment decision. Or, if you are considering a business partnership, it would be prudent to discover if you prospective partner has ever been sued by other business partners, or has ever filed for bankruptcy. Unfortunately, in any of these cases, you cannot simply rely on the other parties honesty. You need to check these things out for yourself.

Unfortunately this area of legal issues has not been transferred to a Web format as well as sex crimes. However many states and federal courts do offer online records. One of the best organized and most complete on this issue, is the state of Oklahoma. You can find their Web site at **www.oscn.net/applications/oscn/casesearch.asp**, and their home search page is shown in Figure 11.7.

This site allows you to search by last name, last and first name, case number, and more. You will get a complete record of any case you find, including current disposition and any filings. This includes both civil and criminal proceedings. Oddly enough, there are at least five different Web sites offering information on Oklahoma court cases for a fee—when all of that information is online and free. This illustrates a key point to keep in mind. There are a number of sites/companies that offer to do searches for you, for fees ranging from $9.95 to $79.95. It is true that they can probably do it faster than you. But it is also true that you can find the exact same information these people do, for free. And hopefully this chapter will equip you with the information you need to do that successfully.

Other Resources

There are many other Web sites that can be quite helpful for your searches. There are a few that deserve particular attention. The National Center for State Courts has a Web site at **www.ncsconline.org/D_KIS/info_ court_Web_sites.html** that lists links to state courts all over the United

FIGURE 11.7 Oklahoma Online Court Records

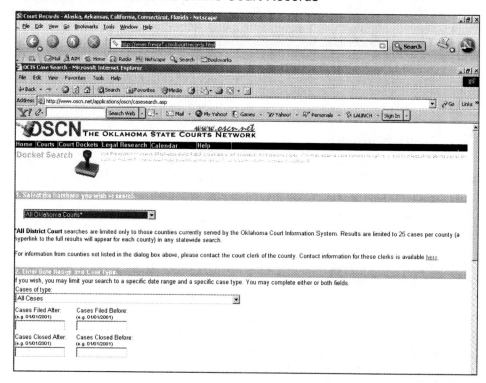

States. It also lists several international courts in countries like Australia, Brazil, Canada, and the United Kingdom. This Web site, as shown in Figure 11.8, is an excellent starting point if you are seeking court records. The Law School at Emory University has an interactive map that will help you find any federal court Web site in the United States. Their Web site is at **http://www.law.emory.edu/FEDCTS/**.

The following list is designed to give you a starting point for online Web searches across the United States. These Web sites should help you start your search for court records:

- Public Record Finder: **www.freeprf.com/courtrecords.html**

- Pacer: **www.pacer.psc.uscourts.gov/**

FIGURE 11.8 National Center for State Courts Web site.

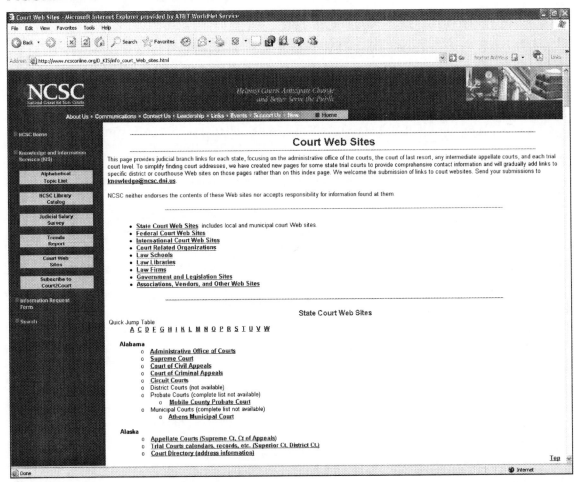

- The Boost: **www.theboost.net/court_records/**

- State Public Access: **www.ncsc.dni.us/NCSC/TIS/TIS99/PUB ACS99/PublicAccesslinks.htm**

- Prison searches: **www.ancestorhunt.com/prison_search.htm**

- Federal Prison Records: **www.bop.gov/**

- Public Records: **www.searchsystems.net/**

- Public Records by State: **www.proagency.tripod.com/statesearch index. html**

- United Kingdom Public Records: **www.pro.gov.uk/**

As you begin searching the Internet, you will find other sites that appeal to you. This may be due to their ease of use, content, or other factors. When you do find such sites, bookmark them. In a short time you will have an arsenal of online search engines. Also, your proficiency with using them will increase and you will learn which to use for which kind of information. This will allow you to become adept at quickly finding information that you need online.

Usenet

Many readers who are new to the Internet (in the past five years) may not be familiar with Usenet. Usenet is a global group of bulletin boards that exist on any subject you can imagine. There are specific software packages used to view these newsgroups, but for sometime now they have been accessible via Web portals. The search engine Google has an option on their main page, called 'Groups'. When you click on that option you are taken to Google's portal to Usenet newsgroups as shown in Figure 11.9.

As you can see, newsgroups are divided into broad categories. For example newsgroups devoted to science topics would be found under the heading *sci*. This includes groups like *sci.anthropology, sci.logic, sci.math.stat,* and more. The heading *alt* is a catch-all for anything and everything. This category includes things ranging from *alt.hacking* to *alt.adoption.*

You may be thinking that, while all this is fascinating, it does not have anything to do with tracking down information. But actually it does. If, for example, you were hiring a network administrator, you could see if she had posted in various network administration groups, and if those postings revealed key information about her network. This tool may be the single most important investigative tool you have, if you are willing to take the time and ferret out the information you need.

Caution

Usenet Information

Anyone can post anything on Usenet. There are no restrictions at all. So simply because you find a negative comment about a person on Usenet it is not wise to automatically assume that comment is true. These postings can only be viewed as part of an investigation and only credible if other facets of the investigation also support the postings you find.

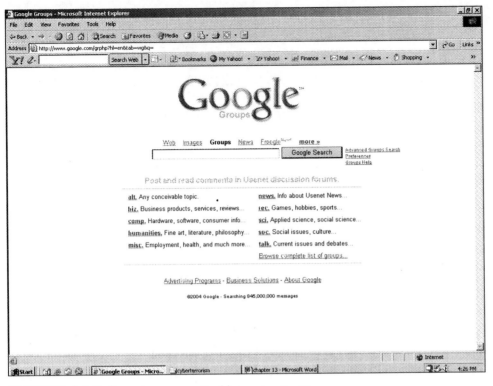

FIGURE 11.9 Google access to Usenet groups

Summary

We have seen in this chapter that the Internet can be a valuable resource for any sort of investigation. It is often one of the tools that hackers and identity thieves use to gain information about their target. However, it can also be a valuable tool for you in researching a prospective employee or business partner. It can also be invaluable for you to routinely find out what information is on the Internet about you. Seeing strange data that is not accurate can be an indication that you have already been the victim of identity theft.

Test Your Skills

MULTIPLE CHOICE QUESTIONS

1. How might an identity thief use the Internet to exploit his or her victim?

   A. He or she might find even more information about the target, and use this information to conduct their crime.

   B. He or she could find out how much the target has in their savings account.

   C. The identity thief usually does not use the Internet to accomplish his or her task.

   D. Identity thieves use the Internet to intercept your email and thus get access to your personal life.

2. Which of the following is not an ideal place to seek out phone numbers and addresses?

   A. Yahoo People Find

   B. People Search

   C. The international phone registry

   D. Infobell

3. Why do you not want too much personal data about you on the Internet?

   A. It might reveal embarrassing facts about you.

   B. It might be used by an identity thief to impersonate you.

   C. It might be used by a potential employer to find out more about you

   D. There is no reason to worry about personal information on the Internet.

4. How could a hacker use information about you found through Internet searches?

   A. To guess passwords if your passwords are linked to personal information such as your birth date, address, or phone number

   B. To guess passwords if your passwords are linked to your interests or hobbies

   C. In social engineering, to ascertain more information about you or your computer system

   D. All of the above

5. If you are hiring a new employee, which of the following should you do?

   A. Verify degrees and certifications

   B. Call references

   C. Perform an Internet search to verify contact information and to check for a criminal record

   D. All of the above

6. Which of the following would be LEAST important to know about a potential business partner?

   A. Past bankruptcies

   B. A 15-year-old marijuana possession arrest

   C. A law suit from a former business partner

   D. A recent DUI

7. What information would provide the most accurate results for locating a person?

   A. First name and state

   B. First name, last name, and state

   C. Last name and state

   D. First name and last name

8. Of the Web sites listed in this chapter, which would be the most useful in obtaining the address and phone number of someone who does not live in the United States?

   A. The FBI Web site

   B. Yahoo

   C. Infobel

   D. Google

11

9. Where would you go to find various state sex offender registries?

    A. The FBI Web site

    B. The national sex offender online database

    C. The interstate online sex offender database

    D. The special victims unit Web site

10. What is most important to learn about a person listed in a sex offender registry?

    A. The extent of his punishment

    B. How old she was when she committed their crime

    C. How long he has been out of prison

    D. The nature of her specific crime

11. Which Web search approach is best when checking criminal backgrounds?

    A. Check primarily the person's state of residence

    B. Check primarily federal records

    C. Check the current and previous state of residence

    D. Check as many places as might have information

12. What advantages are there to commercial Web search services?

    A. They can get information you cannot.

    B. They can get the information faster than you can.

    C. They can do a more thorough job than you can.

    D. They are legally entitled to do searches, you are not.

13. Which would you use to begin a search for information on a United States court case?

    A. The National Center for State Courts Web site

    B. Infobel

    C. Yahoo People Search

    D. Google Groups

14. Which of the following is the most accurate description of Usenet?

    A. A nation wide bulletin board

    B. A repository of computer security information

    C. A large scale chat room

    D. A global collection of bulletin boards

15. Which of the following is the most helpful data you might get from Usenet on a person you are investigating?

    A. Postings by the individual you are investigating

    B. Security tips to help you investigate

    C. Criminal records posted

    D. Negative comments made by others about your target

EXERCISES

For all Exercises and Projects in this chapter, you will concentrate your investigation on some person. It is best if you investigate yourself (which makes it easier to evaluate the accuracy of what you find) or if someone in the class or the instructor volunteers to be the target of the investigation. There are ethical issues with simply investigating random people without their knowledge or permission. It is also important to avoid embarrassing someone in the classroom. So the volunteer targets of the investigation should be certain they will not be embarrassed by whatever is found. Substitute the name of the person you are investigating for John Doe or Jane Doe in the projects and exercises.

Exercise 11.1: Finding Phone Numbers

1. Beginning with Yahoo People search, seek out phone numbers and addresses for John Doe.

2. Use at least two other sources to look up John's phone number.

Did you get too little information or too much information? Were you able to determine the correct, current number?

Exercise 11.2: Criminal Records Checks

1. Using sources listed in this chapter or other Web sites, look for criminal background information about John Doe. Start with the state John currently resides in, then check other states, particularly those that might have shown up with John's name in Exercise 1.

2. Expand your search to check for Federal crimes as well.

Exercise 11.3: Checking Court Cases

1. Search court records for any court cases for Jane Doe's business.

2. Check state licensing agency Web sites, if applicable, for any history or complaints on John's business.

11

Exercise 11.4: Finding Business Information on Usenet

1. Access Usenet.

2. Search bulletin boards and other groups that Jane Doe may have posted to in connection with her business.

Were you able to find out more about Jane's business through her postings to a Usenet group?

Exercise 11.5: Blocking Information

This chapter illustrated the many ways you can access information about someone and pointed out the potential hazards of having too much personal information available on the Internet. So, what can you do to prevent unscrupulous individuals from finding out too much about you? Check the primary Web sites listed in this chapter (i.e., Yahoo and Google) to see if they provide any means to block your information from being distributed. Are there any other means of blocking access to your personal information?

PROJECTS

Project 11.1: Investigating a Person

Using all of the Web resources in this chapter, and any others you come across, do a complete investigation of Jane Doe. Try to determine her address, phone number, occupation, age, and any criminal history. You might even check Usenet postings and find out clues as to Jane's hobbies and personal interests as well. Create a brief report on Jane based on your findings.

Project 11.2: Investigating a Company

Using all of the Web resources in this chapter, and any others you come across, do a complete investigation of John Doe's business. How long has he been in business? Are there any complaints about the business with any regulatory agency? Any complaints on Usenet boards? Any business relationships? Any past court proceedings? Write a report discussing your analysis of this business based on your findings.

Project 11.3: The Ethics of Investigation

Write an essay discussing the ethics of online investigations. Do you feel these investigations are an invasion of privacy? Why or why not? If you do feel they are an invasion of privacy, what do you think can be done about it? Are there problems with getting inaccurate information?

Case Study

Henry Rice, the owner and CEO of a small company, has been conducting a search for a new human resource administrator. After many rounds of interviews, he has narrowed his search down to two individuals that he feels are the best candidates. Each has very similar qualifications so Henry's decision may very well be based on the information he finds when he checks their references and performs a background check.

Henry has received written permission from each to conduct a background check. Where should Henry begin his search? What sites or sorts of information would be most critical for him to check? What type of information could weigh heavily for a person working in human resources? Write a brief essay, outlining what steps Henry should take in conducting his research.

11

Chapter | **12**

Computer Security Hardware and Software

Chapter Objectives

After reading this chapter and completing the exercises, you will be able to do the following:

- Evaluate the effectiveness of a scanner based on how it works.
- Choose the best type of firewall for a given organization.
- Understand anti-spyware methods.
- Employ intrusion-detection systems to detect problems on your system.

Introduction

Throughout this book, various aspects of computer crime and computer security have been discussed. At this point in your studies, you should have a good idea of what the real dangers are and what adequate security policies include, as well as a basic understanding of the various forms of computer crime. However, if you are striving to secure your network, you will need more technical details on the various security devices and software you might choose to employ. This chapter reviews these items with enough detail to allow you to make intelligent decisions on which types of products you will see.

Most of these devices have been mentioned and briefly described in the preceding chapters. The intent of this chapter is to delve more deeply into details of how these devices work. This information is of particular value to those readers who intend to eventually enter the computer security profession. Simply having a theoretical knowledge of computer security is inadequate. You must have some practical skills. This chapter will be a good starting point for gaining those skills, and the exercises at the end of the chapter will give you a chance to practice setting up and evaluating various types of firewalls, IDSs, and antivirus applications.

Virus Scanners

A virus scanner is essentially software that tries to prevent a virus from infecting your system. This fact is probably abundantly obvious to most readers. Knowing how a virus scanner works, however, is another matter. This topic was discussed briefly in Chapter 5, but will be elaborated on in this chapter.

In general, virus scanners work in two ways. The first method is that they contain a list of all known virus files. Generally, one of the services that vendors of virus scanners provide is a periodic update of this file. This list is typically in a small file, often called a *.dat* file (short for data). When you update your virus definitions, what actually occurs is that your current file is replaced by the more recent one on the vendor's Web site.

The antivirus program can then scan your PC, network, and incoming e-mail for known virus files. Any file on your PC or attached to an e-mail is compared to the virus definition file to see whether there are any matches. With e-mails, this can be done by looking for specific subject lines and content. Known virus files often have specific phrases in the subject line and the body of the messages they are attached to. Yet viruses and worms can have a multitude of headers, some of which are very common, such as *re:hello* or *re:thanks.* Scanning against a list of known viruses alone would result in many false positives. Therefore, the virus scanner also looks at attachments to see whether they are of a certain size and creation date that matches a known virus or whether it contains known viral code. The file size, creation date, and location are the telltale signs of a virus.

How Does a Virus Scanner Work?

An article in the July 2004 issue of *Scientific American,* titled "How Does a Virus Scanner Work," stated that a virus scanner is essentially software that searches for the signature or pattern of known virus. Keep in mind that the scanner only works if you keep it updated. And, of course, it only works with known viruses.

The second way a virus scanner works is to watch for certain types of behaviors that are typical of a virus. This might include any program that attempts to write to your hard drive's boot sector, change system files, automate your e-mail software, or self-multiply. Another feature that virus scanners search for is a file that will stay in memory after it executes. This is called a **Terminate and Stay Resident (TSR)** program. Some legitimate programs do this, but it is often a sign of a virus. Additionally, some virus scanners use more sophisticated methods, such as scanning your system files and monitoring any program that attempts to modify those files.

It is also important to differentiate between on-demand virus scanning and ongoing scanners. An ***ongoing virus scanner*** runs in the background and is constantly checking your PC for any sign of a virus. ***On-demand virus scanners*** run only when you launch them. Many modern antivirus scanners offer both options.

Virus-Scanning Techniques

In general, there are five ways a virus scanner might scan for virus infections. Some of these were mentioned in the previous section, but they are outlined and defined below.

E-mail and Attachment Scanning Since the primary propagation method for a virus is e-mail, e-mail and attachment scanning is the most important function of any virus scanner. Some virus scanners actually examine your e-mail on the e-mail server before downloading it to your machine. Other virus scanners work by scanning your e-mails and attachments on your computer before passing it to your e-mail program. In either case, the e-mail and its attachments should be scanned prior to you having any chance to open it and release the virus on your system.

Download Scanning Anytime you download anything from the Internet, either via a Web link or through some FTP program, there is a chance you might download an infected file. Download scanning works much like e-mail and attachment scanning, but does so on files you select for downloading.

File Scanning This is the type of scanning in which files on your system are checked to see whether they match any known virus. This sort of scanning is generally done on an on-demand basis instead of an ongoing basis. It is a good idea to schedule your virus scanner to do a complete scan of the system periodically. I personally recommend a weekly scan, preferably at a time when no one is likely to be using the computer.

Heuristic Scanning This is perhaps the most advanced form of virus scanning. This sort of scanning uses rules to determine whether a file or program is behaving like a virus and is one of the best ways to find a virus that is not a known virus. A new virus will not be on any virus definition list, so you must examine its behavior to determine whether it is a virus. However, this process is not foolproof. Some actual virus infections will be missed, and some non-virus files might be suspected of being a virus.

FYI: How Commercial Scanners Work

Most commercial virus scanners use multiple methods, including most, if not all, of the methods listed here. Any virus scanner that uses only one scanning modality would be virtually worthless from a practical virus defense perspective.

Active Code Scanning Modern Web sites frequently embed active codes, such as Java applets and ActiveX. These technologies can provide some stunning visual effects to any Web site. However, they can also be a vehicle for malicious code. Scanning such objects before they are downloaded to your computer is an essential feature in any quality virus scanner.

Commercial Antivirus Software

There are two brands of antivirus software that virtually dominate the antivirus market today and a number of companies that offer a commercial scanner also offer a free version that does not provide as many features as the commercial product. For example, AVG Anti-Virus, available from **www.grisoft.com**, is a commercial product, but the company also offers the AVG Anti-Virus Free Edition: McAfee and Norton. Both products are very good choices, and both also come with additional options, such as spam filters and personal firewalls. Either product can be purchased for a home machine for about $30 to $60 dollars (depending on options you add). This purchase price includes a one-year subscription to update the virus files so that your antivirus software will recognize all known virus attacks. Organizational licenses are also available to cover an entire network.

Of course, there are other antivirus solutions available. Several free virus scanners can easily be found on the Internet. McAfee and Norton are mentioned here because they are so commonly used, and it is likely that you will encounter them frequently.

Firewalls

A firewall is, in essence, a barrier between your network and the outside world. At a minimum, it will filter incoming packets based on certain parameters such as packet size, source IP address, protocol, and destination port. As was mentioned in the discussion on firewalls in Chapter 2, Linux and Windows XP ship with a simple firewall. Additionally, Norton and McAfee both offer personal firewall solutions for individual PCs.

In an organizational setting, you will want a dedicated firewall between your network and the outside world. This might be a router that also

12

has built-in firewall capabilities. (Cisco Systems is one company that is well-known for high quality routers and firewalls.) Or, it might be a server that is dedicated solely to running firewall software. There are a number of firewall solutions that you can examine, and Appendix B has some links to get you started. Selecting a firewall, however, is an important decision. If you lack the expertise to make that decision, then you should arrange for a consultant to assist you in this respect.

Firewall Types and Components

Up to this point, most discussion of firewalls has focused on packet-filtering firewalls. However, there are several other types of firewalls or components to firewalls that are listed below.

- Screening firewall
- Application gateway
- Circuit-level gateway

The following sections will discuss each of these and assess the advantages and disadvantages of each.

Screening Firewall *Screening firewalls,* the most basic type of firewall, are simply another name for packet-filtering firewalls. This type of firewall works in the "Network" layer of the OSI model (see Chapter 1). It simply examines incoming packets and either allows or denies them entrance based on a set of rules that were put into its configuration. They can filter packets based on packet size, protocol type used, destination IP address, source IP address, destination port, source port, and so forth. For example, a packet filter might deny all traffic on ports 1024 and up, or it might block all incoming traffic using the TFTP protocol. You can use incoming and outgoing filters to dictate what information passes into or out of your local network.

Many routers offer this type of firewall option. These firewalls are usually very easy to configure and quite inexpensive. As mentioned, some operating systems include built-in packet-filtering capabilities.

There are a few disadvantages to the screening/packet-filtering firewall solution. One disadvantage is that they do not actually examine the packet or compare it to previous packets; therefore, they are quite susceptible to either a ping flood or SYN flood. They also do not offer any user authentication. Additionally, in many cases, a packet-filtering firewall will be used as a bastion host. A **bastion host** is a single point of contact between the Internet and a private network. It usually will only run a limited number of services (those that are absolutely essential to the private network) and no others.

Application Gateway An *application gateway* (also known as *application proxy* or *application-level proxy*) is a program that runs on a firewall. When a client program, such as a Web browser, establishes a connection to a destination service, such as a Web server, it connects to an application gateway, or proxy. The client then negotiates with the proxy server in order to gain access to the destination service. In effect, the proxy establishes the connection with the destination behind the firewall and acts on behalf of the client, hiding and protecting individual computers on the network behind the firewall. This process actually creates two connections. There is one connection between the client and the proxy server and another connection between the proxy server and the destination.

Once a connection is established, the application gateway makes all decisions about which packets to forward. Since all communication is conducted through the proxy server, computers behind the firewall are protected.

With an application gateway, each supported client program requires a unique program to accept client application data. This sort of firewall allows for individual user authentication, which makes them quite effective at blocking unwanted traffic. However, a disadvantage is that these firewalls use a lot of system resources and are susceptible to SYN floods and ping floods.

Circuit-Level Gateway A *circuit-level gateway* is similar to an application gateway, but is more secure and generally implemented on high-end equipment. A circuit-level gateway relays a TCP connection, but does no additional processing or filtering of the protocol (Wack, 1995). In this system, your username is checked and granted access before the connection to the router is established. This means that you as an individual, either by username or IP address, must be verified before any further communication can take place. Once this verification takes place and the connection between the source and destination is established, the firewall simply passes bytes between the systems. A virtual "circuit" exists between the internal client and the proxy server. Internet requests go through this circuit to the proxy server, and the proxy server delivers those requests to the Internet after changing the IP address. External users only see the IP address of the proxy server. Responses are then received by the proxy server and sent back through the circuit to the client. While traffic is allowed through, external systems never see the internal systems.

While highly secure, this approach may not be appropriate for some public situations, such as e-commerce sites. This type of firewall does not allow features, such as URL filtering. They also frequently offer only limited auditing capabilities.

12

How Firewalls Examine Packets

In addition to how the firewall operates, you can further differentiate firewalls based on how they examine incoming packets. There are two main approaches to this task, and each is briefly examined below.

Stateful Packet Inspection The ***Stateful Packet Inspection (SPI)*** firewall will examine each packet, denying or permitting access based not only on the examination of the current packet, but also on data derived from previous packets in the conversation. This means that the firewall is aware of the context in which a specific packet was sent. This makes these firewalls far less susceptible to ping floods and SYN floods, as well as being less susceptible to spoofing. For example, if the firewall detects that the current packet is an ICMP packet and a stream of several thousand packets have been continuously coming from the same source IP, it is clearly a Denial of Service attack and the packets will be blocked.

The SPI firewall can also look at the actual contents of the packet. This allows for some very advanced filtering capabilities. Most high-end firewalls use the Stateful Packet Inspection method; when possible, this is the recommended type of firewall.

Stateless Packet Inspection *Stateless packet inspection* does not involve actually examining the contents of each packet, which is a significant weakness in using such an inspection technology. Also, the stateless packet inspection does not examine a packet within the context of an ongoing TCP conversation. It does not know what the preceding or subsequent packets are doing, thus making it vulnerable to ping floods and other Denial of Service attacks.

Firewall Configurations

In addition to the various types of firewalls, there are also various configuration options. The type of firewall tells you how it will evaluate traffic and hence decide what to allow and not to allow. The configuration gives you an idea of how that firewall is set up in relation to the network it is protecting. Some of the major configurations/implementations for firewalls include:

- Network host-based
- Dual-homed host
- Router-based firewall
- Screened host

Each of these is discussed in the following sections.

Network Host-Based A *network host-based firewall* is a software solution installed on an existing machine with an existing operating system. The most significant concern in using this type of firewall is that, no matter how good the firewall solution is, it is contingent upon the underlying operating system. In such a situation, it is absolutely critical that the machine hosting the firewall have a hardened operating system.

Dual-Homed Host A *dual-homed host* is a firewall running on a server with at least two network interfaces. The server acts as a router between the network and the interfaces to which it is attached. To make this work, the automatic routing function is disabled, meaning that an IP packet from the Internet is not routed directly to the network. You can choose what packets to route and how to route them. Systems inside and outside the firewall can communicate with the dual-homed host, but cannot communicate directly with each other.

Router-Based Firewall As was previously mentioned, you can implement firewall protection on a router. In larger networks with multiple layers of protection, this is commonly the first layer of protection. Although one can implement various types of firewalls on a router, the most common type used is packet filtering. If you use a broadband connection in your home or small office, you can get a packet-filtering firewall router to replace the basic router provided to you by the broadband company.

Screened Host A *screened host* is really a combination of firewalls. In this configuration, you use a combination of a bastion host and a screening router. The screening router adds security by allowing you to deny or permit certain traffic from the bastion host. It is the first stop for traffic, which can continue only if the screening router lets it through.

Commercial and Free Firewall Products

There is a variety of commercial firewall products from which you can choose. If all you want is a basic packet-filtering solution, many software vendors offer this. Major antivirus software vendors (including those mentioned previously in this chapter) often offer the firewall software as a bundled option with their antivirus software. Other companies, such as Zone Labs, sell firewall and intrusion-detection software. Zone Labs, for example, offers the ZoneAlarm Security Suite, which provides all the tools for complete Internet security. Major manufacturers of routers and hubs, such as Cisco Systems, also offer firewall products. How much security you need is a difficult question to answer. A bare minimum recommendation is to have a packet-filtering firewall/proxy server between your network and the Internet—but that is a bare minimum. There are also many free firewall

12

applications available. Zone Labs, mentioned above for their commercial product, also offers a free download of the ZoneAlarm firewall protection.

Outpost Firewall, available from **www.agnitum.com/products/outpost/** is a product designed for the home or small office user. Like the Zone Labs product, it has both a free version and an enhanced commercial version. Information on this product is shown in Figure 12.1. Note that the free versions is an older version of the software and does not include many of the enhancements of the commercial version. But it may be sufficient for your needs.

Listed and shown below are a number of other sources for information on free firewall protection. Each of these Web sites offers links to a number of sources for free firewall protection as well as to other useful security tools. You may want to explore these sites as well as add them to your list of resource sites.

- www.free-firewall.org/

- www.homenethelp.com/web/howto/free-firewall.asp

- www.firewallguide.com/freeware.htm

FIGURE 12.1 Firewall protection from Agnitum.

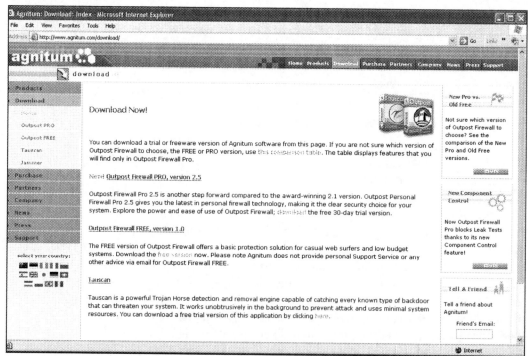

Firewall Logs

Firewalls are also excellent tools when attempting to ascertain what has happened after an incident occurs. Almost all firewalls, regardless of type or implementation, will log activity. These logs can provide valuable information that can assist in determining the source of an attack, methods used to attack, and other data that might help either locate the perpetrator of an attack or at least prevent a future attack using the same techniques. Any security-conscious network administrator should make it a routine habit to check the firewall logs.

Anti-Spyware

Anti-spyware, as discussed earlier in this book, scans your computer to see whether there is spyware running on your machine. This is an important element of computer security software that was at one time largely ignored. Even today, not enough people take spyware seriously or guard against it. Most anti-spyware works by checking your system for known spyware files. Each application must simply be checked against a list of known spyware. This means that you must maintain some sort of subscription service so that you can obtain routine updates to your spyware definition list.

In today's Internet climate, running anti-spyware is as essential as running antivirus software. Failing to do so can lead to serious consequences. Personal data, and perhaps sensitive business data, could easily be leaking out of your organization without your knowledge. And, as was pointed out in Chapter 9, it is entirely possible for spyware to be the vehicle for purposeful industrial espionage.

Barring the use of anti-spyware, or even in conjunction with such software, you can also protect yourself via your browser's security settings as was discussed in a previous chapter. Additionally, several times throughout this book, you have been warned to be cautious about attachments and Internet downloads. You would also be well advised to avoid downloading various Internet "enhancements," such as "skins" and "toolbars." If you are in an organization, prohibiting such downloads should be a matter of company policy.

12

Intrusion-Detection Software

Intrusion-detection software (IDS) has become much more widely used in the last few years. Essentially, an IDS will inspect all inbound and outbound port activity on your machine/firewall/system and look for patterns that might indicate an attempted break-in. For example, if the IDS finds that a series of ICMP packets were sent to each port in sequence, this probably indicates that your system is being scanned by network-scanning software, such as Cerberus. Since this is often a prelude to an attempt to breach your system security, it can be very important to know that someone is performing preparatory steps to infiltrate your system.

Entire volumes have been written on how IDS systems work. This chapter cannot hope to cover that much information. However, it is important that you have a basic idea of how these systems work.

The sections below will first examine the broad categories in which IDS systems tend to be viewed and then will also look at some specific approaches to IDS. While this information is not all-inclusive, it does address the more common terminology used.

IDS Categorization

There are a number of ways in which IDS systems can be categorized. The most common IDS categorizations are:

- misuse detection vs. anomaly detection

- passive systems vs. reactive systems

- network-based systems vs. host-based systems

Misuse Detection vs. Anomaly Detection   An IDS that uses *misuse detection* analyzes the information it gathers and compares it to large databases of attack signatures (*IDS signatures*) (Webopedia, 2004) Much like a virus detection system, this form of IDS looks for specific attacks that have already been documented. However, similar to virus scanners, this form of IDS is only as good as the IDS signatures against which it compares the packets.

On the other hand, *anomaly detection* involves actual software that works to detect intrusion attempts and notify the administrator. This is what many people think of when they talk about intrusion-detection systems. The general process is simple: the system looks for any anomalous behavior. Any activity that does not match the pattern of normal user access is noted and logged. The software compares observed activity against expected normal usage profiles. Profiles are usually developed for specific users, groups of users, or applications. Any activity that does not match the definition of normal behavior is considered an anomaly and is logged.

Passive Systems vs. Reactive Systems   In a *passive system,* the IDS detects a potential security breach, logs the information, and signals an alert. In a *reactive system,* the IDS responds to the suspicious activity by logging off a user or reprogramming the firewall to block network traffic from the suspected malicious source (Webopedia, 2004).

Network-Based System vs. Host-Based System   In a network-based system (NIDS), the individual packets flowing through a network are analyzed. This system can detect malicious packets that are designed to be

FYI: Normal Activity Patterns

With anomaly-based IDS, it can take some time to create what is considered "normal" activity patterns. While these activity patterns are being established, you may experience a high rate of false alarms.

You should also note that, if the network already contains malicious code, then the activity of this code would be considered "normal."

overlooked by a firewall's simplistic filtering rules (Webopedia, 2004). In a host-based system (HIDS), the activity of each individual computer or host is examined.

IDS Approaches

There are many approaches to detection and prevention. Some of these methods are implemented in various software packages, while others are simply strategies that an organization can employ to decrease the likelihood of a successful intrusion.

Preemptive Blocking This approach, sometimes called banishment vigilance, seeks to prevent intrusions before they occur. This is done by noting any danger signs of impending threats and then blocking the user or IP address from which these signs originate. Examples of this technique include attempting to detect the early foot printing stages of an impending intrusion, then blocking the IP or user that is the source of the foot printing activity. If you find that a particular IP address is the source of frequent port scans and other scans of your system, then you would block that IP address at the firewall.

This sort of intrusion detection and avoidance can be complicated. Usually, a software system will simply alert the administrator that suspicious activity has taken place. A human administrator will then make the decision whether or not to block the·person. If the software automatically blocks any addresses it deems suspicious, you run the risk of blocking out legitimate users. It should also be noted that nothing prevents the offending user from moving to a different machine to continue their attack. This sort of approach should only be one part of an overall intrusion-detection strategy and not the entire strategy.

Infiltration This method refers to efforts on the part of the administrator or security specialist to acquire information from various illicit sources. Many administrators rely solely on various security bulletins from vendors.

12

With infiltration, the administrator proactively seeks out intelligence on potential threats and/or groups. In other words, it is not a software or hardware implementation, but rather a process of infiltrating hacker/cracker online groups in order to keep tabs on what sort of vulnerabilities are currently being exploited by these groups and what target systems are considered attractive targets. This form of intrusion detection is not widely used for two reasons. The first reason is that it is quite time-consuming. The second reason is that it requires spying skills, which many administrators may not possess.

Intrusion Deflection This method is becoming increasingly popular among the more security-conscious administrators. The essence of it is quite simple. An attempt is made to attract the intruder to a sub-system set up for the purpose of observing him. This is done by tricking the intruder into believing that he has succeeded in accessing system resources when, in fact, he has been directed to a specially designed environment. Being able to observe the intruder while he practices his art will yield valuable clues and can lead to his arrest.

This is often done by using what is commonly referred to as a *honey pot*. Essentially, you set up a fake system, possibly a server that appears to be an entire subnet. You make that system look very attractive by perhaps making it appear to have sensitive data, such as personnel files, or valuable data, such as account numbers or research. The actual data stored in this system is fake. The real purpose of the system is to carefully monitor the activities of any person who accesses the system. Since no legitimate user ever accesses this system, it is a given that anyone accessing it is an intruder.

Intrusion Deterrence This method involves simply trying to make the system seem like a less palatable target. In short, an attempt is made to make any potential reward from a successful intrusion attempt appear more difficult than it is worth. This approach includes tactics such as

FYI: Using Honey Pots

The use of honey pots and similar technologies is on the rise. In fact, some vendors are now selling pre-packaged, ready-to-use honey pots, including wireless honey pots. These devices are an admission that no system is 100% foolproof and are an attempt to at least capture the hacker after she has intruded the system.

attempting to reduce the apparent value of the current system's worth through camouflage. This essentially means working to hide the most valuable aspects of the system. The other tactic in this methodology involves raising the perceived risk of a potential intruder being caught. This can be done in a variety of ways, including conspicuously displaying warnings and warning of active monitoring. The perception of the security of a system can be drastically improved, even when the actual system security has not been improved.

Commercial IDS Providers

There are a number of vendors who supply IDS systems, each with its own strengths and weaknesses. Which system is best for your environment is contingent on many factors including the network environment, security level required, budget constraints, and the skill level of the person who will be working directly with the IDS. One popular open-source IDS is Snort, which can be downloaded for free from **www.snort.org/**.

Summary

It is absolutely critical that any network have a firewall and proxy server between the network and the outside world. It is critical that all machines in the network (servers and workstations alike) have updated virus protection. It is also a good idea to consider intrusion-detection software and anti-spyware as well. In the upcoming exercises, you will have an opportunity to practice setting up various types of firewalls and IDS systems.

Test Your Skills

MULTIPLE CHOICE QUESTIONS

12

1. Which of the following is the most common way for a virus scanner to recognize a virus?

   A. To compare a file to known virus attributes

   B. To use complex rules to look for virus-like behavior

   C. To only look for TSR programs

   D. To look for TSR programs or programs that alter the registry

2. What is one way of checking e-mails for virus infections?

   A. Block all e-mails with attachments

   B. Block all active attachments (e.g., ActiveX, scripting)

   C. Look for subject lines that are from known virus attacks

   D. Look for e-mails from known virus sources

3. What is a TSR program?

   A. Terminal Signal Registry programs that alter the system registry

   B. Terminate and System Remove that erase themselves when complete

   C. Terminate and Scan Remote that scan remote systems prior to terminating

   D. Terminate and Stay Resident that actually stay in memory after you shut them down

4. What is the name for scanning that depends on complex rules to define what is and is not a virus?

   A. Rules-based scanning (RBS)

   B. Heuristic scanning

   C. TSR scanning

   D. Logic-based scanning (LBS)

5. Which of the following is not one of the basic types of firewalls?

   A. Screening firewall

   B. Application gateway

   C. Heuristic firewall

   D. Circuit-level gateway

6. Which of the following is the most basic type of firewall?

   A. Screening firewall

   B. Application gateway

   C. Heuristic firewall

   D. Circuit-level gateway

7. Which of the following is a disadvantage to using an application gateway firewall?

   A. It is not very secure.

   B. It uses a great deal of resources.

   C. It can be difficult to configure.

   D. It can only work on router-based firewalls.

8. What is SPI?

   A. Stateful Packet Inspection

   B. System Packet Inspection

   C. Stateful Packet Interception

   D. System Packet Interception

9. What is the term for a firewall that is simply software installed on an existing server?

   A. Network host-based

   B. Dual-homed

   C. Router-based

   D. Screened host

10. What is a major weakness with a network host-based firewall?

    A. Its security is dependent on the underlying operating system.

    B. It is difficult to configure.

    C. It can be easily hacked.

    D. It is very expensive.

11. What is the term for blocking an IP address that has been the source of suspicious activity?

    A. Preemptive blocking

    B. Intrusion deflection

    C. Proactive deflection

    D. Intrusion blocking

12. What is the term for a fake system designed to lure intruders?

    A. Honey pot

    B. Faux system

    C. Deflection system

    D. Entrapment

13. Which of the following is the correct term for simply making your system less attractive to intruders?

    A. Intrusion deterrence

    B. Intrusion deflection

    C. Intrusion camouflage

    D. Intrusion avoidance

12

14. What method do most IDS software implementations use?
   A. Anomaly detection
   B. Preemptive blocking
   C. Intrusion deterrence
   D. Infiltration

15. How do most anti-spyware packages work?
   A. By using heuristic methods
   B. By looking for known spyware
   C. The same way antivirus scanners work
   D. By seeking out TSR cookies

EXERCISES

Exercise 12.1: Setting Up a Firewall

Microsoft Windows XP and Linux both offer built-in packet-filtering firewalls of some sort.

1. Using the documentation for whichever operating system you have, decide what packets you wish to block.

2. Set your firewall to filter those packets.

Note: Ideally, if you have access to both operating systems, the best exercise is to experiment setting up firewalls for both.

Exercise 12.2: Router-Based Firewalls

Note: This exercise is for those labs with access to a lab router-based firewall.

1. Consult your router documentation for instructions on how to configure the firewall.

2. Configure your router-based firewall to block the same items you chose to block in Exercise 2.

Exercise 12.3: Evaluating Firewalls

Write a brief essay explaining whether you think the router-based solution or the built-in operating system solution is best. Explain your reasons.

Exercise 12.4: Active Code

Using the Web or other resources, find out why blocking active code (e.g., ActiveX, Scripts) might or might not be a good idea for some situations. Write a brief essay explaining your position.

Exercise 12.5: Hardware Used by a Company

Visit the IT department of a company and ascertain what hardware they use in their computer system's defense. Do they use a hardware firewall in addition to a software firewall? What form of intrusion-detection software do they use? Do they use antivirus and anti-spyware on the workstations within the company? Write a brief report summarizing your findings.

PROJECTS

Project 12.1: How Does the Microsoft Firewall Work?

Using Microsoft documentation, the Web, and other resources, find out what methodologies the Microsoft Windows XP firewall uses. Write a brief essay explaining the strengths and weaknesses of that approach. Also discuss situations in which you feel that approach is adequate and those in which it might be inadequate.

Project 12.2: How Does Anti-Virus Software Work?

Using documentation from the vendor, the Web, or other resources, find out what methodology Norton AntiVirus uses, as well as the methods that McAfee uses. Armed with this information, write a brief essay comparing and contrasting any differences. Also discuss situations in which one might be recommended over the other.

Project 12.3: Using Snort

Note: This is a longer project and appropriate for groups.

Go to the Snort.org Web site (**www.snort.org/**) and download Snort. Using the vendor documentation or other resources, configure Snort. Then use port scanners on the machine that has Snort configured and note whether Snort detects the scan.

12

Case Study

Jane Smith is responsible for security at the ABC Company. She has a moderate budget with which to purchase security solutions. To date, she has installed a router-based firewall between the network and the out-side world. She also has a commercial virus scanner on every machine on the network. What other actions might you recommend to her? Would you recommend a different firewall? Why or why not?

Appendix **A**

Computer Security Professionals: Education and Certifications

This book has been an introduction to the world of computer security. It is not sufficient to make you a security professional. It is rather a gateway into the profession. The question naturally arises: What should you do if you wish to become a computer security professional? What education, training, and certifications will best prepare you to embark on a career in computer security? This appendix answers these questions.

Academic Training and Programs

Clearly a degree is going to be necessary to pursue a career in computer security. There are a variety of computer science, engineering, computer information systems, and even some computer security programs from which you could choose. It is likely that you are currently enrolled in some college program. The question is: What does a program need to provide you the appropriate training?

The first issue to address is the type of degree and length of program. While many institutions offer associates (two-year) degrees, you would be hard put to find many job advertisements that do not require a four-year bachelors degree. In general, with many computer-related jobs, employers view the two-year degree as simply not sufficient. This is often not true for technical support or sales jobs, but generally is true for programming, networking, and computer security positions. Therefore, first and foremost, you will need to obtain a bachelors degree.

The second issue to address is content. While there are some degree programs available in computer security, most institutions do not offer such a specific degree. For security professionals, the difference between computer information systems, computer science, and engineering is not as critical as the content of your degree. In any degree program, you generally have flexibility in choosing both electives and a minor. This flexibility should allow you to formulate an appropriate program. The list below details what training is required.

- **Network:** First, you should take as many network courses as possible. Expertise in computer networks is a cornerstone of computer security.

- **Programming and database:** You will need at least introductory courses in these fields. Security extends well beyond simple firewalls into software development, database management, and all other aspects of IT. It is therefore critical that you have at least a cursory understanding of these topics.

- **Telecommunications:** If at all possible, an introductory course in basic telecommunications should be taken.

- **Security:** Obviously, if your college offers any specific courses in computer security, take them.

- **Math:** If you intend to get a better understanding of encryption, you will need mathematics up to and including number theory. Number theory is generally a post-calculus course.

- **Law/Criminology:** Since computer security often involves data forensics, it can be useful to have a basic understanding of the law and basic criminology.

You can see that network security is a very broad field and touches on a number of other fields. This means a broad educational background is necessary to truly be effective in this endeavor. The real key to any training program, in any field, is an appropriate mix of solid grounding in theory, with hands-on practice. As in this book, you have had numerous hands-on exercises as well as reading/research projects. Any good program will combine theory and research with hands-on practice. Studying how firewalls work is not much use unless you have actual experience installing a firewall.

It is also important to know something about the instructors for security courses. Security is becoming the hottest buzzword in IT; unfortunately, some academic institutions are so eager to provide security courses that they might be tempted to use instructors that may not have adequate backgrounds. Has the instructor/professor had professional, hands-on security experience? What is their background in relation to security? Usually, faculty members are eager to announce their credentials on the college or university's Web site. If you don't see any security-related experience or credentials, this might be a matter of concern to you.

Industry Certifications

Industry certifications are a significant part of the computer industry. Microsoft Certified Software Engineers, Red Hat Certified Engineers, and Certified Java Programmers are all part of the IT profession. However, people's attitudes toward certifications vary a great deal. Some people will tell you that they would never hire a person who was not certified. Some job ads either require or prefer one certification or another. Other professionals will tell you certifications are worthless. Both extremes come from two factors: a misunderstanding of what certification means and the use of "cheat sheets."

■ Misunderstanding what certification means: Some people think certification is meant to show complete mastery of a topic. Thus, if such a person hires a certified CompTIA A+ technician who has not completely mastered PC hardware, then the employer might decide certifications are not worthwhile. The problem is that one or both parties in this case misunderstood what certification means. Certifications indicate that the person holding them has achieved a certain *minimum* level of competency with that product or technology; they do not indicate that the person in question has completely mastered the topic at hand.

■ Use of "cheat sheets": The Internet is replete with "study guides" that are, in fact, cheat sheets for certification exams. These study guides often have the real questions and answers from a particular certification exam. A person could quite easily memorize such a cheat sheet, pass a test, and not truly understand the material. Such study guides are very good resources for identifying areas in which you may need more study. If used in conjunction with hands-on experience and a thorough study of reference material, they are then useful study aids. However, they are often used simply as cheat sheets, thus demeaning the value of certifications.

Once you have a realistic idea of what certifications mean, the next question that arises is: What certifications are truly meaningful in security? Unfortunately, computer certifications are not regulated as are medical licenses, real estate licenses, and so on. Anyone can publish a certification and make bold claims about it. However, over time, certain certifications have gained acceptance in the IT security profession. The following sections will examine a few of these and discuss what they mean.

Security +

This certification is administered by the Computer Technology Industry Association (CompTIA), which is famous for A+, Network+, and Linux+ certifications (as well as others). The test itself covers security concepts. It is not a hands-on test, but rather a test of general security knowledge. This certification is a good gateway to other certifications. In and of itself, it would not be a sufficient indication of whether a person is qualified to be a security professional. However, combined with experience, formal education, and possibly other certifications (e.g., Microsoft Certified Systems Engineer, Certified Novel Engineer), it might be a good indicator. For the novice trying to enter the security profession, this test is an excellent place to start. Details can be found at the CompTIA Web site at **www.comptia.org/certification/security/**.

CIW Security Analyst

This exam is quite similar in content to the Security+ exam. It asks general security knowledge questions, and its content is a bit more broad and inclusive than that of Security+. It does not delve into hands-on security knowledge. However, it has one very significant advantage over Security+: before you can take this exam, you must first pass the CIW Security Professional exam and the CIW Foundations exam, as well as one of the following:

- Microsoft Certified Systems Administrator (MCSA)
- Microsoft Certified Systems Engineer (MCSE)
- Certified Novell Engineer (CNE)
- Cisco Certified Network Professional (CCNP)
- Cisco Certified Network Associate (CCNA)
- Cisco Certified Internetwork Expert (CCIE)
- Linux Professional Institute (LPI) Level 2

This means that, in addition to basic security knowledge, the holder of this certification has had at least two other CIW certifications, as well as at least one major network certification. This combination of certifications is a likely indicator of competence in network security. You can find out more about this exam at **www.ciwcertified.com/**.

MCSE Security Specialization

Microsoft is a widely used operating system, and Microsoft-based networks abound. Many companies prefer to hire Microsoft Certified Systems Engineers (MCSE) for administering such networks. Microsoft has added a specialized track within the MCSE specifically for those people interested in security. In addition to the basic fundamentals of the MCSE, the security specialization requires three security-specific certification tests:

■ Designing Security for a Microsoft Windows 2000 Network

■ Implementing and Administering Security in a Microsoft Windows 2000 Network

■ Installing, Configuring, and Administering Microsoft Internet Security and Acceleration (ISA) Server 2000, Enterprise Edition

If your goal is to secure Microsoft networks, then this particular certification would be very important. You can find out more about it at **www.microsoft.com/learning/mcp/mcse/security/windows2000.asp**.

CISSP

The Certified Information Systems Security Professional (CISSP) designation is the gold standard in security certifications. This designation is simply the most sought-after security certification due to the rigorous standards required to achieve certification. The requirements are as follows:

■ Pass a grueling exam that takes several hours.

■ Have at least four years of security experience, or three years and a bachelors degree. This experience must be certified by either another CISSP or an officer in your corporation.

■ Meet certain continuing education requirements every 36 months to retain your certification.

■ A certain percentage of those who pass the exam are randomly selected for an audit and investigation of their background.

With the CISSP certification, the test itself is not what makes the certification meaningful. It is the requirement for verifiable work experience as well as ongoing continuing education. For someone looking to excel in the computer security profession, this certification is certainly desirable. You can find out more about this test at **www.isc2.org**.

SANS Institute Certifications

The Sans Institute (**www.sans.org**) is a well-respected source for security information. You have probably noticed that both their site and their documents have been referenced more than once in this book; you would probably find the same in other computer security books. However, their computer security certifications have not been widely used within the security industry, probably due to the fact that they are relatively new and not extensively marketed. However, it seems likely that, in the coming years, their certifications will gain wider acceptance. You can find more details at **www.giac.org/subject_certs.php**.

High Tech Crime Network Certifications

This certification is included for a very different reason than the others. The High Tech Crime Network (**www.htcn.org/**) sponsors a number of computer crime certifications; they also have a very professional-looking Web site. They offer seminars, certifications, and more. However, a thorough search did not reveal a single job advertisement on any of the major job boards (e.g., **www.computerjobs.com**, **www.hotjobs.com**, **www.monster .com**) that required or even mentioned their certifications. Also, a review of two dozen top-selling security books and several security journals revealed no reference to these certifications.

This does not mean that the certifications are not valid; they very well may be quite rigorous and demanding certifications. However, they simply have not gained any acceptance in the IT security industry and will not assist you in gaining employment. This certification is mentioned because it is important for you when seeking industry certifications to consider how widely those certifications are accepted in the industry. A plethora of certifications will not help you if no one has heard of the certification vendor.

Appendix | B

Resources

General Computer Crime and Cyber Terrorism

Cyber crime: **www.cybercrime.gov/**

Computer security: **www.cert.org**

Department of Justice Computer Crime **www.usdoj.gov/criminal/cybercrime/compcrime.html**

Symantec's antivirus site: **www.symantec.com/avcenter/**

Computer Associates Virus Information Center **www3.ca.com/virusinfo/**

Department of Defense cyber crime: **www.dcfl.gov/dc3/home.htm**

General Hacking

IRC security: **www.irchelp.org/irchelp/security/**

Hacking link: **www.hideaway.net/home/public_html/index.php**

Hacking link: **www.xs4all.nl/~l0rd/**

Hacking link: **www.hackinthebox.org/**

IP spoofing: **www.iss.net/security_center/advice/Underground/Hacking/Methods/Technical/Spoofing/default.htm**

Hacker history: **www.tranquileye.com/hackerculture/home.html**

Hacker history: **www.sptimes.com/Hackers/history.hacking.html**

Cyber Stalking

www.crimelibrary.com/criminology/cyberstalking/

www.cyber-stalking.net/

Identity Theft

www.consumer.gov/idtheft/

www.idtheftcenter.org/index.shtml

www.usdoj.gov/criminal/fraud/idtheft.html

Port Scanners and Sniffers

Port scanners: www.hackfix.org/software/port.html

Port scanners and other tools: www.all-internet-security.com/security_scanners.html

More port scanners: www.mycert.org.my/resource/scanner.htm

More scanners and sniffers: is-it-true.org/pt/ptips13.shtml

www.prosolve.com/software/winscan.php

Password Crackers

Password crackers: www.password-crackers.com/

More password crackers: www.pcmag.com/article2/0,4149,696,00.asp

Counter Measures

Preventing port scanning: www.nwfusion.com/links/Encyclopedia/P/792.html

Various security and hacking tools: www.insecure.org

Snort, an open source IDS system: www.snort.org/

The Sans Institute IDS FAQ: www.sans.org/resources/idfaq/

The Association of Computing Machinery IDS page: www.acm.org/crossroads/xrds24/intrus.html

Spyware

www.youarethespy.com/spy-software.htm

www.keystrokekeyloggers.com/spy_anywhere.asp

www.keyloggers.com/

www.bestspyware.com/

www.spectorsoft.com/

www.spywareguide.com/

www.spywareinfo.com/

www.softactivity.com/

Counter Spyware

theplanet.tucows.com/preview/305123.html (free, removes spyware.)

www.webroot.com/wb/products/spysweeper/index.php

www.spywarenuker.com/overture.php

www.webroot.com

www.enigmasoftwaregroup.com/jump8.shtml

Cyber Investigation Tools

WhoIs tool: **www.whois.sc/**

Sam Spade for Windows: **www.samspade.org/ssw/**

Various search tools: **www.virtualgumshoe.com/**

General Tools

General tools: **www.maxwells-alley.com/tech/toolkit.html**

General tools: **www.all-internet-security.com/security_scanners.html**

Scanning tool: **www.rawlogic.com/netbrute/**

General tools: **www.totalshareware.com**

Virus Research

CNET Virus Center: **reviews.cnet.com/4520-6600_7-5020382-1.html? legacy=cnet**

Fsecure: **www.fsecure.com**

Symantec virus encyclopedia: **securityresponse.symantec.com/ avcenter/vinfodb.html**

Computer Associates Virus Information Center: **www3.ca.com/ securityadvisor/virusinfo/default.aspx**

Appendix C

Sample Security Policy Documents and Checklists

Throughout this text, you have been given many tips and, at times, lists of things to be done in order to secure a system. This appendix is a compilation of many of those tips and "to-do" lists, brought together in one convenient location. In addition, the material contained within this appendix is available on the companion Web site should you need these documents in electronic format. In particular, you may find the electronic sample Acceptable Use Policy and the sample Password Policy extremely helpful as a starting point for your own policies.

The sections contained within this appendix are:

- Basic Home PC Policies
- Basic PC Security Checklist
- Basic Network Security Checklist
- Online Fraud Checklist
- Sample Acceptable Use Policy
- Sample Password Policy
- Hiring a Security Professional

Basic Home PC Policies

This list of suggested policies is for all home users of PCs. You may wish to add other items to this list of personal recommendation from the author.

General Tips

Following are general tips that, if followed, will help to keep your home PC system secure.

- Virus scanning: You must have virus scanning software on your computer. It must be up to date and properly configured.

- Patches: You must have updated patches for your operating system and all software. I recommend a minimum of a quarterly audit during which you check the patches on all machines, including servers.

- Services: Any service you don't need, shut it off. That goes for all machines.

- Configure: Configure your browser for high security.

- Firewall: If your operating system has a firewall (Windows XP and Linux both do), then make sure it is on and properly configured.

- Anti-spyware: You should definitely consider anti-spyware.

- Information: Don't give out personal information on the Internet unless you must. Do not use your real name or address in any chat room, newsgroup, and so on.

- Attachments: When in doubt, don't open them. Have friends and colleagues use a codeword in the subject of an e-mail when they must send attachments. If you don't see that codeword, don't open the attachment. You can use something simple, yet unique, as a codeword. It can be anything that you agree on with friends and colleagues. For example, the subject line could be:

     Hey, this is the picture you asked for codeword:willow

  or

     Your letter is attached codeword:oaktree

Specific Tips for Windows Users

Much has been made of Microsoft Window's security flaws. It is not my intent to debate the merits of Windows, Linux, or any other operating system. It is simply my intent to help you secure whatever system you are using. If you are using Windows 2000, XP, or 2003, then there are several steps you can take to make your system more secure.

- Make it a scheduled item to routinely visit the Microsoft Windows Update page (**v5.windowsupdate.microsoft.com/v5consumer/**

default.aspx?ln=en-us) to obtain the latest patches/updates. Checking once a month would be sufficient for most people—perhaps even once per quarter.

■ Do the same for Microsoft Office Updates (**office.microsoft.com/en-us/officeupdate/default.aspx**).

■ If you have Windows XP or higher, turn on and configure the firewall as described on the Web site listed above.

■ Run a well-known virus scanner, such as McAffee or Norton.

■ Follow the basic rules (e.g., don't download unknown attachments).

■ Go to Tools and Internet Options on your Internet Explorer and reconfigure it for much higher security. When you go to the security tab, make sure ALL zones are AT LEAST MEDIUM. If you feel more confident in your knowledge of security issues, then you may want to customize it further.

■ If there is a service you don't need, shut it off. This is described in the section on how to find out information on a target system.

■ Microsoft has a security analyzer tool. You should run this on your system a MINIMUM of once per quarter (MS Security Analyzer: **support.microsoft.com/default.aspx?scid+kb%3Ben-us%3Bq320454**).

Microsoft may not have developed the most secure operating system available; however, many "security flaws" are actually people using the operating system that have no idea what they are doing. Start with these basic tips, and your PC will be more secure than a great many people on the Internet.

Basic PC Security Checklist

This checklist is provided to assist you in ensuring that an individual computer—either a home PC or a workstation in a business—has appropriate security. This checklist can form the foundation for a basic audit.

Basic Security

Basic security is the absolute minimum standard that all computers should meet. Many computers will exceed this level.

_____ Patches have been updated within the last 90 days.

_____ Antivirus software is installed, updated, and running.

_____ All unused/unneeded services have been shut down.

_____ If the operating system has built in port filtering or a firewall, it is turned on.

_____ The password is at least eight characters long and has been changed within the last six months.

_____ The browser is configured to default medium-level security.

_____ Only the administrator has full rights to the machine.

Enhanced Security

Enhanced security is for users who are willing to invest more resources in ensuring security. This assumes the basic security level has been met and adds or enhances those with the following steps:

_____ Anti-spyware software is installed, updated, and running.

_____ The browser is configured on a custom basis for levels exceeding medium security.

_____ The password is at least eight characters long, contains a mixture of characters, and has been changed within the last 90 days.

_____ All unneeded operating system components have been uninstalled.

_____ The machine has been scanned for vulnerabilities with a security analyzer or port scanner within the last 120 days.

Basic Network Security Checklist

This checklist is provided to assist you in ensuring that an organizational network has appropriate security. This checklist can form the foundation for a basic audit.

Basic Security

Basic security simply provides minimum standards that any network should employ. If your network does not at least meet these standards, then you are in significant danger. Many networks will actually exceed these standards.

_____ All workstations and servers are in compliance with the Basic PC Security Checklist (Basic Security level).

_____ There is a packet-filtering firewall between the network and the outside world.

_____ There is a proxy server between the network and the outside world.

_____ All routers are configured to not repeat broadcast packets.

_____ All passwords are at least eight characters long and have been changed within the last six months.

_____ Servers are all physically secure, with only necessary personnel having access.

_____ There are policies in place prohibiting downloads of any software from the Internet.

_____ There are policies in place governing how e-mail attachments are handled.

_____ There are policies in place on how to handle terminated employees.

_____ All employees are made aware of security and organizational policies.

_____ Server logs are kept and checked at least once per month.

_____ All servers are backed up at least once per week, with once-per-month backups being moved offsite to a secure location.

_____ Only the administrator has full rights to any machine.

Enhanced Security

Enhanced security is for users who are willing to invest more resources in ensuring security. This assumes that all workstations have enhanced security (see the Basic PC Security Checklist) and that the basic network level is achieved. Enhanced security adds the following:

_____ There is a stateful packet inspection firewall on the perimeter.

_____ All routers to subnets have packet-filtering firewalls built in.

_____ All servers are backed up once per day, with once-per-week backups being moved offsite to a secure location.

_____ A clearly written disaster recovery plan is in place and all IT personnel are familiar with it.

_____ An intrusion detection software system is installed and running.

_____ Server logs are kept and checked weekly.

_____ Patches are checked and updated on all machines every 60 days or less.

_____ All personnel with network administrative privileges have had an extensive background check (e.g., criminal, credit, references).

_____ All browsers are configured on a custom basis for levels exceeding medium security.

_____ All passwords are at least eight characters long, contain a mixture of characters, and have been changed within the last 90 days.

_____ All servers are scanned with a security analyzer and a port scanner at least once every 90 days.

_____ External logins to the network are only done on a very limited basis and are accomplished with a virtual private network.

_____ All sensitive communications and all communications outside the network are encrypted.

_____ All security activities (e.g., backups, scanning, downloading patches, changing passwords, adding/removing users, changing permissions) are logged with the name of the person performing the action, the date/time, and the name of the person authorizing the action.

_____ Once each quarter, a basic audit is performed using a security analyzer on servers, including a check of patches and a spot check of logs and policies.

_____ Once per year, the entire network is carefully audited including a review of administrative personnel backgrounds, a complete simulated breach attempt, packet sniffing to check encryption, review of logs, and so forth.

_____ Users are given routine, brief security updates warning them of current scams, frauds, viruses, Trojan horse, and so forth.

_____ Old media (e.g., hard drives, tapes) are thoroughly destroyed.

Online Fraud Checklist

This checklist is provided to assist you in ensuring that you are taking appropriate precautions to avoid online fraud. It is important to note that there is no way to guarantee you won't be a victim of fraud, but you can take steps to significantly reduce the chance of being a victim.

Investment Offers

_____ Take investment advice only from well-known, reputable brokerage firms/sources.

_____ Independently research and verify all claims.

_____ View all claims/offers with skepticism.

_____ Never invest when someone is using high-pressure tactics.

_____ Only invest money you can afford to lose.

Online Auctions

_____ Only work with well-known auction sites (eBay).

_____ Only bid on items if the seller has a high positive rating (don't bid with unrated sellers).

_____ Ask questions of the seller (usually via e-mail) before bidding.

_____ If the product seems too good to be true, don't bid.

Sample Acceptable Use Policy

Overview

All technology-related systems—including, but not limited to, computer equipment, software, telephone systems, network equipment, operating systems, storage media, network accounts providing electronic mail, and Web browsers—are the property of <organization's name goes here>. These systems are to be used for business purposes in serving the interests of the organization and our clients and customers in the course of normal operations. The purpose of this document is to outline the acceptable use of computer equipment at <Company Name>. These rules are in place to protect the employee and <organizations name goes here>.

Policies

General Use

1. For security and network maintenance purposes, authorized individuals within <organizations name goes here> may monitor equipment, systems, and network traffic at any time, per <organization's name goes here> Audit Policy.

2. <organization's name goes here> reserves the right to audit networks and systems on a periodic basis to ensure compliance with this policy.

Security and Proprietary Information

1. All passwords must be kept secure. Employees are directed to never share accounts. Authorized users are responsible for the security of

their passwords and accounts. System-level passwords should be changed quarterly, and user-level passwords should be changed every six months.

2. All PCs, laptops, and workstations should be secured with a password-protected screensaver, with the automatic activation feature set at ten minutes or less, or by logging off (Ctrl+Alt+Delete for Windows 2000 users) when the host will be unattended.

3. Postings by employees from <organization's name goes here> e-mail address to newsgroups are prohibited unless part of normal business operations.

4. All hosts used by the employee that are connected to <organization's name goes here> Internet/Intranet/Extranet, whether owned by the employee or <organization's name goes here>, shall be continually executing approved virus-scanning software with a current virus database unless overridden by departmental or group policy.

5. Employees must use extreme caution when opening e-mail attachments received from unknown senders, which may contain viruses or Trojan horses.

Unacceptable Use

The following activities are, in general, prohibited. Unless your job duties specifically require you to violate these policies (such as a security administrator performing a vulnerability audit), you are directed to never engage in any of these activities. Under no circumstances is an employee of <organization's name goes here> authorized to engage in any activity that is illegal under local, state, federal, or international law while utilizing <Company Name>-owned resources.

The list below is by no means exhaustive, but attempts to provide a framework for activities which fall into the category of unacceptable use. You should not assume that any activity not listed is acceptable. The activities listed are strictly prohibited, with no exceptions.

1. Violations of the rights of any person or company protected by copyright, trade secret, patent, or other intellectual property, or similar laws or regulations, including, but not limited to, the installation or distribution of any software products that are not appropriately licensed for use by <organization's name goes here>.

2. Unauthorized copying of copyrighted material including, but not limited to, books, copyrighted music, or copyrighted software for which <organization's name goes here> does not have an active license is strictly prohibited.

3. Introduction of any programs into the network or server that are not approved by the appropriate IT personnel.

4. Revealing your account password or allowing use of your account by any other person.

5. Using <organization's name goes here> computing asset to actively engage in procuring or transmitting material that is in violation of sexual harassment laws in the user's local jurisdiction.

6. Making statements about warranty, expressly or implied, unless it is a part of normal job duties.

7. Attempting to perform security breaches or disruptions of network communication. This is a violation even if the attempt is unsuccessful. Security breaches include, but are not limited to, accessing data the employee is not authorized to access, attempting to guess or crack any password, and attempting to access any account or server the employee is not expressly authorized to access unless these duties are within the scope of regular duties.

8. Port scanning or security scanning is expressly prohibited unless it is a direct part of your duties, such as in the case of a network administrator performing an authorized vulnerability scan.

9. Executing any form of network monitoring that will intercept data not intended for the employee's host unless this activity is a part of the employee's normal job/duty.

10. Circumventing user authentication or security of any host, network, or account.

11. Sending unsolicited e-mail messages, including the sending of "junk mail" or other advertising material, to individuals who did not specifically request such material (e-mail spam).

12. Any form of harassment via e-mail, telephone, or paging, whether through language, frequency, or size of messages.

13. Creating or forwarding "chain letters" or "pyramid" schemes of any type.

Enforcement of Policies

Any employee found to have violated this policy may be subject to disciplinary action, up to and including termination of employment. In some cases, the employee who violates these policies may be subject to civil or criminal action.

Password Policy

1.0 Overview

Passwords are an important aspect of computer security. They are the front line of protection for user accounts. A poorly chosen password may result in the compromise of <Company Name>'s entire corporate network. As such, all <Company Name> employees (including contractors and vendors with access to <Company Name> systems) are responsible for taking the appropriate steps, as outlined below, to select and secure their passwords.

2.0 Purpose

The purpose of this policy is to establish a standard for creation of strong passwords, the protection of those passwords, and the frequency of change.

3.0 Scope

The scope of this policy includes all personnel who have or are responsible for an account (or any form of access that supports or requires a password) on any system that resides at any <Company Name> facility, have access to the <Company Name> network, or store any non-public <Company Name> information.

4.0 Policy

4.1 General

- All system-level passwords (e.g., root, enable, NT administration, application administration accounts) must be changed on at least a quarterly basis.

- All production system-level passwords must be part of the InfoSec-administered global password management database.

- All user-level passwords (e.g., e-mail, Web, desktop computer) must be changed at least every six months. The recommended change interval is every four months.

- User accounts that have system-level privileges granted through group memberships or programs such as "sudo" must have a unique password from all other accounts held by that user.

- Passwords must not be inserted into e-mail messages or other forms of electronic communication.

■ Where SNMP is used, the community strings must be defined as something other than the standard defaults of "public," "private," and "system" and must be different from the passwords used to log in interactively. A keyed hash must be used where available (e.g., SNMPv2).

■ All user-level and system-level passwords must conform to the guidelines described below.

4.2 Guidelines

A. General Password Construction Guidelines

Passwords are used for various purposes at <Company Name>. Some of the more common uses include user-level accounts, Web accounts, e-mail accounts, screensaver protection, voicemail password, and local router logins. Since very few systems have support for one-time tokens (i.e., dynamic passwords that are only used once), everyone should be aware of how to select strong passwords.

Poor, weak passwords have the following characteristics:

■ The password contains less than eight characters.

■ The password is a word found in a dictionary (English or foreign).

■ The password is a common-usage word, such as

- Names of family, pets, friends, co-workers, fantasy characters, and so forth

- Computer terms and names, commands, sites, companies, hardware, or software

- The words "<Company Name>," "sanjose," "sanfran," or any derivation

- Birthdays and other personal information, such as addresses and phone numbers

- Word or number patterns such as aaabbb, qwerty, zyxwvuts, 123321, and so forth

- Any of the above spelled backwards

- Any of the above preceded or followed by a digit (e.g., secret1, 1secret)

Strong passwords have the following characteristics:

- Contain both upper- and lowercase characters (e.g., a-z, A-Z)

- Have digits and punctuation characters as well as letters (e.g., 0-9,!@#$%^&*()_+|~-=\`{}[]:";'<>?,./)

- Are at least eight alphanumeric characters long.

- Are not words in any language, slang, dialect, or jargon

- Are not based on personal information, names of family, and so forth

- Passwords should never be written down or stored on line. Try to create passwords that can be easily remembered. One way to do this is create a password based on a song title, affirmation, or other phrase. For example, the phrase might be: ""This May Be One Way to Remember" and the password could be: "TmB1w2R!" or "Tmb1W>r~" or some other variation.

NOTE: Do not use either of these examples as passwords!

B. Password Protection Standards

Do not use the same password for <Company Name> accounts as for other non-<Company Name> access (e.g., personal ISP account, option trading, benefits). Where possible, don't use the same password for various <Company Name> access needs. For example, select one password for Engineering systems and a separate password for IT systems. Also, select a separate password to be used for an NT account and a UNIX account.

Do not share <Company Name> passwords with anyone, including administrative assistants or secretaries. All passwords are to be treated as sensitive, confidential <Company Name> information.

Following is a list of "don't's":

- Don't reveal a password over the phone to ANYONE.

- Don't reveal a password in an e-mail message.

- Don't reveal a password to the boss.

- Don't talk about a password in front of others.

- Don't hint at the format of a password (e.g., "my family name").

- Don't reveal a password on questionnaires or security forms.

- Don't share a password with family members.

- Don't reveal a password to co-workers while on vacation.

If someone demands a password, refer them to this document or have them call someone in the Information Security Department.

Do not use the "Remember Password" feature of applications (e.g., Eudora, OutLook, Netscape Messenger).

Again, do not write passwords down and store them anywhere in your office. Do not store passwords in a file on ANY computer system (including PDAs or similar devices) without encryption.

Change passwords at least once every six months (except system-level passwords, which must be changed quarterly). The recommended change interval is every four months.

If an account or password is suspected to have been compromised, report the incident to Information Security and change all passwords.

Password cracking or guessing may be performed on a periodic or random basis by Information Security or its delegates. If a password is guessed or cracked during one of these scans, the user will be required to change it.

C. Application Development Standards

Application developers must ensure that their programs contain the following security precautions:

- Should support authentication of individual users, not groups

- Should not store passwords in clear text or in any easily reversible form

- Should provide for some sort of role management so that one user can take over the functions of another without having to know the other's password

- Should support TACACS+, RADIUS, and/or X.509 with LDAP security retrieval wherever possible

D. Use of Passwords and Pass Phrases for Remote Access Users

Access to <Company Name> networks via remote access is to be controlled using either a one-time password authentication or a public/private key system with a strong pass phrase.

E. Pass Phrases

Pass phrases are generally used for public/private key authentication. A public/private key system defines a mathematical relationship between the public key that is known by all and the private key that is known only to the user. Without the pass phrase to "unlock" the private key, the user cannot gain access.

Pass phrases are not the same as passwords. A pass phrase is a longer version of a password and is, therefore, more secure. A pass phrase is typically composed of multiple words. Because of this, a pass phrase is more secure against "dictionary attacks."

A good pass phrase is relatively long and contains a combination of upper- and lowercase letters and numeric and punctuation characters. An example of a good pass phrase is "The*?#>*@TrafficOnThe101Was* &#!#ThisMorning."

All of the rules above that apply to passwords apply to pass phrases.

5.0 Enforcement

Any employee found to have violated this policy may be subject to disciplinary action, up to and including termination of employment.

6.0 Definitions

Terms	Definitions
Application Administration Account	Any account that is for the administration of an application (e.g., Oracle database administrator, ISSU administrator)

7.0 Revision History

Hiring a Security Professional

If you should decide to hire a security professional, whether as a permanent position or simply as a short-term consultant to assess your organization's security, the question becomes: How do you find a good one? Security is perceived as one of the more glamorous segments of the IT profession. It also does not take a great deal of knowledge to know more about security than the average person. By reading a few security books, you would probably know more than most people. This leads to a number of unqualified people posing as security experts. Therefore, how do you know if you are getting the real thing? This section contains a few guidelines that will help you.

Experience

The primary item to look for is experience—verifiable experience with references. There is no substitute for real-world experience. A security professional should have a minimum of five years of IT experience (e.g., networking, programming), with three years directly related to security.

Education/Training

It is certainly possible to be a security professional without any college or formal training. However, to be truly proficient at security, one needs to understand operating systems, networks, programming, and so forth. It is likely that a person with these qualifications would have a degree in computer science, engineering, MIS, or some related field. You will find that some colleges now offer security-specific degrees.

Certifications

Certifications are certainly not the end-all and be-all of any branch of IT, including security. You should never hire someone simply based on certifications. However, they can be one part of the entire picture. As with all professional designations, some security certifications mean more than others. Following are a few of the more common certifications. (For more information on certifications and links to more information, see Appendix C.)

- Security+: This is CompTIA's general security certification and is actually a test of general knowledge. Holding this certification alone is probably not sufficient to qualify someone as a security professional. However, it is a good starting place for someone wanting to pursue a computer security career.

- CIW Security Analyst: This test approximates the same level of knowledge as the Security+ test. However, what makes it valuable is that CIW will only award it to those who also have MCSA, MCSE, or CNE. In other words, you must have some solid knowledge of computer networks before you can take the CIW Security Analyst test, giving the holder of this certification a little more credibility.

- MSCE Security Specialist: This is the Microsoft Certified Systems Engineer (MSCE) test, with specific security tests taken as electives. If you are looking for someone to secure a 100% Microsoft network, this is probably a good certification.

- CISSP: This is the gold standard in security. This certification requires three years of real-world experience, a grueling exam, and continuing education credits to maintain. This certification is generally a strong indicator of a qualified security professional.

- Other: As stated earlier, to be good at security, you must understand networks. For this reason, you often see people that started out as Linux, Unix, Microsoft, or Novell administrators eventually specialize in security. This means that people will often have Linux +,

RHCE, MCSA, MCSE, CNE, CCNP, and other certifications related to networking and hardware.

Background

You must do a background check. Any security professional that objects to a criminal, credit, and drug screen should be avoided. You should always check the background of the person you hire, but this caution rings more true in the security field than for any other position.

Documentation

Especially when hiring a consultant, you should agree on documentation of what they do before you sign any contract. For example, if you want a consultant to assess your security system, you should receive both detail and summary documentation. The detail documents should tell you exactly what steps he or she took, what vulnerabilities and strengths were found, and a recommended course of action to follow. It is even better if these recommendations are supported by cited studies and industry standards rather than simply being opinion. The summary document should summarize all of this in easy-to-follow terms.

No set of guidelines is foolproof. However, these simple rules should help you avoid hiring an unqualified security professional who may falsely declare your system to be secure.

Links to Reputable Certifications and Societies

CIW Security Analyst: **www.ciwcertified.com/certifications/professionalcert.asp?comm=home&llm=2#5**

Security + Exam: **www.comptia.org/certification/security/default.aspx**

CISSP Exam: **www.cissp.com/**

Computer Security Institute: **www.gocsi.com/**

SANS Institute: **www.sans.org/**

Part 1
Glossar

Some terms in this section are from the hacker community and others are from the security professional's community. To truly understand computer security, one must be familiar with both worlds. General networking terms are also included in this glossary.

A

admin   Short for system administrator.

adware   Software loaded onto your machine, often without your knowledge, that causes ads to pop up on your screen. This technology often works in a different manner than Web page pop-ups; thus, pop-up blockers will not stop them.

anomaly detection   A process of looking for system behavior that is not normal. This process is used by many intrusion-detection systems.

application gateway   A type of firewall that authenticates entire client applications.

application-level proxy   Another name for an application gateway.

application proxy   Another name for an application gateway.

asset identification   Identifying all of the assets you must protect. This is a critical step in securing any system.

audit   A check of systems security. This usually includes a review of documents, procedures, and system configurations.

authentication   The process of verifying that a user is authorized to access a given resource. This is part of the logon system.

B

back door   A hole in the security system deliberately left by the creator of the system.

backbones   The central Internet connections to which Internet Service Providers must ultimately connect.

bagbiter   Something, such as a program or a computer, that fails to work or works in a remarkably clumsy manner.

bastion host   A gateway between an inside network and an outside network. Used as a security measure, it is designed to defend against attacks aimed at the inside network.

bid shielding   The process of entering fake high bids in an online auction, then withdrawing them just before the auction concludes. This has the effect of protecting one bid (one entered before the fake bidding began) from competition.

bid siphoning   Attempts to lure buyers from a legitimate auction site to an off-site auction that is a fraud.

binary numbers   Numbers using the base 2. Ultimately, all data on a computer is stored in a base 2 format.

black hat hackers   Hackers with malicious intent; synonymous with cracker.

block cipher Ciphers that encrypt blocks of text at a time, for example, 64 bytes at a time.

BlowFish A well known encryption algorithm.

brain dump The act of telling someone everything one knows.

breach To successfully break into a system; to *breach* the security.

brute force To try to crack a password by simply trying every possible combination.

buffer overflow An attack that involves loading a buffer with more data than it is designed to hold.

bug A flaw in a system.

C

Caesar cipher One of the oldest known encryption methods. It simply shifts each character by a given number of characters.

cipher Synonym for cryptographic algorithm.

cipher text Encrypted text.

circuit-level gateway A type of firewall that employs user authentication.

client errors Errors that occur on the client machine rather than the server.

code The source code for a program or the act of programming, as in "to *code* an algorithm."

code grinder An unflattering reference to one who works in an uncreative corporate programming environment.

cookie A small file containing information from a Web site.

cracker One who breaks into a system in order to do something malicious, illegal, or harmful. A hacker with malicious intent; synonymous with black hat hacker.

crash A sudden and unintended failure, as in "my computer *crashed.*"

cryptography The study of encryption and decryption.

cyber fraud Using the Internet to defraud someone.

cyber stalking Using the Internet to harass someone.

cyber terrorism Using the Internet to terrorize someone or some group of individuals.

D

Data Encryption Standard (DES) A widely used block cipher encryption algorithm.

datagram A packet sent using the TCP protocol.

decryption To break encryption and discover the underlying message.

demigod A hacker with years of experience, or one with a national or international reputation.

Distributed Denial of Service (DDoS) A Denial of Service attack launched from multiple machines, often without the knowledge of the owners of those machines.

Domain Name Service (DNS) A protocol that translates names, such as **www.prenticehall. com**, into an IP addresses.

DNS servers/Domain Name Server A server that provides DNS Service.

Denial of Service (DoS) An attack that prevents legitimate users from accessing a resource.

dual-homed host A firewall that actually has two network interface cards, thus participating in two networks (although one might be the Internet itself).

dumpster diving The process of searching through trash looking for information that might be useful in hacking (particularly social engineering) or identity theft.

E

echo/chargen attack A type of Denial of Service attack that attempts to build up to much CPU activity with echos.

encryption   The act of encrypting a message. This usually involves altering a message so that it cannot be read without the key and the decryption algorithm.

espionage   Spying; the act of illicitly gaining confidential information.

ethical hacker   One who hacks into systems in order to accomplish some goal that they feel is ethically valid.

F

firewall   A device or software that provides a barrier between your machine or network and the rest of the world.

flood attack   An attack that involves sending a large number of packets to a server in an attempt to overload the server.

footprinting   A term hackers use for assessing a system looking for vulnerabilities.

G

gray hat hackers   Hackers who normally behave legally but who may, for certain reasons and in limited situations, conduct illegal activities, usually for reasons they feel are ethically compelling.

H

hacker   One who tries to learn about a system by examining it in detail and reverse-engineering it.

hacking   The process of attempting to learn about a system by examining it and often exploiting flaws. This usually involves attempts to compromise the target system in some way.

hactivism   Hacking conducted for ideological purposes.

hardening   The process of securing all aspects of a server. This includes adding patches, shutting off unnecessary services, making sure all settings are secure, and so forth.

hub   A device for connecting computers.

I

ICMP flood attacks   An attack that attempts to overload the target system with too many ICMP packets for it to respond to.

identity theft   The process of getting enough personal information on someone so that you might be able to pose as that person. Often done to secure credit or make purchases in the victim's name.

IDS signatures   Characteristics of specific types of attacks that intrusion-detection systems look for.

industrial espionage   The use of espionage for purely economic purposes.

information warfare   The use of information in any conflict. This often involves propaganda and disinformation campaigns.

Internet Control Message Protocol (ICMP)   A protocol used for a variety of purposes, including "pinging" other computers.

Internet Protocol (IP)   A protocol that is part of the TCP/IP suite of protocols, which is the foundation for most networking and all Internet communications.

Internet Protocol Security (IPSec)   A protocol that is critical for securing virtual private networks.

Internet Service Provider (ISP)   A company that provides Internet access for clients.

intrusion-detection system (IDS)   A system that is designed to detect signs of attacks in progress and to notify the administrator.

IP address   A numerical designation for a computer consisting of four 1-byte binary numbers.

IPConfig   A utility that provides extensive information about a computer's network connection.

K

key logger   Software that logs key strokes on a computer.

L

land attack   Sending a packet to a machine with the source host/port the same as the destination host/port, causing some systems to crash.

Layer 2 Tunneling Protocol (L2TP)   A protocol that is used to create virtual private networks. It is a successor to the older point-to-point tunneling protocol (PPTP).

layered security approach   An approach that attempts to fortify security within the network rather than just the perimeter.

loop back address   An address used to test a machine's own network card, 127.0.0.1.

M

MAC addresses   A unique hexadecimal number that is used to identify a network interface card.

malware   Any software that has a malicious purpose, such as a virus or Trojan horse.

mono-alphabet substitution   A primitive encryption algorithm in which there is one single substitute character for all plain text characters.

multi-alphabet substitution   A primitive encryption algorithm in which there are multiple substitute characters for all plain text characters.

N

Network Access Points (NAP)   Places where one can connect to a network. This often is used to refer to wireless network connectivity points.

network host-based firewall   A firewall that is running software on an existing server.

network scanning   The process of scanning a network looking for vulnerabilities.

NIC   Network interface card, which is the card that allows network connectivity for a computer.

O

on-demand virus scanners   Virus scanning that runs when requested by the user.

ongoing virus scanner   Virus scanning that is continually running in the background.

OSI model   A seven-layer model describing network connectivity, devices, and protocols.

P

packet   A binary piece of data prepared for transmission over a network.

pass phrases   A phrase that is used instead of a simple password.

password age   How long a password is viable before it must be replaced.

password history   How many old passwords a system remembers to prevent a user from re-using them.

penetration testing   Assessing the security of a system by attempting to break into the system. This is the activity most sneakers engage in.

perimeter security approach   An approach that simply tries to secure the barriers between a network and the Internet without concern for security within the network.

phishing   The process of sending e-mails to people in which the e-mail purports to be from some legitimate financial institution, such as a bank or credit card company, and induces the recipient to provide personal information.

phreaking   The process of hacking phone systems.

ping   To send a single ICMP packet to a destination, usually in order to confirm that the destination can be reached.

Ping of Death (PoD) To send an extremely large packet to a target. For some older systems, this would cause the target to crash.

Point-to-Point Tunneling Protocol (PPTP) A protocol used in virtual private networks. It is based on the earlier point-to-point protocol (PPP).

port A numerical designation for a connection point on a computer. There are well defined ports for specific protocols such as FTP port 21, HTTP port 80, and so forth.

port scanning Scanning a target machine to see what ports are open in an attempt to assess vulnerabilities.

Pretty Good Privacy (PGP) A widely used encryption algorithm.

protocols Agreed-upon methods of communication in networking that refer to ways of performing certain types of communication, such as hypertext transfer protocol for Web pages.

proxy server A machine or software that hides all internal network IP addresses from the outside world. It provides a point of contact between a private network and the Internet.

public key encryption Encryption algorithms that use two keys. One is publicly distributed and is used to encrypt messages. The other is kept private and is used to decrypt the messages.

pump and dump Artificially inflating the price of a stock so you may sell your shares at a much higher value than they should have been sold.

R

reactive security Security that simply acts after something has gone wrong.

router A device that separates networks.

RSA A widely used encryption algorithm.

RST cookie A method for preventing Denial of Service attacks that actually uses a type of cookie to authenticate the client's connection.

S

screened host A firewall, usually on the perimeter of a network, that combines a packet-filtering router with an application gateway located on the protected subnet side of the router; also called a *screening firewall*.

script kiddy A hacker term for one who claims much greater hacking skill than they actually have.

server errors Errors that occur on the server rather than the client.

shill bidding A term for a seller putting in fake bids on his own item in order to drive up the price.

single-key encryption An encryption method in which the same key is used to both encrypt and decrypt a message. This is also referred to as *symmetric key encryption*.

smurf A specific type of distributed Denial of Service attack.

sneaker Someone who is attempting to compromise a system in order to assess its vulnerability.

social engineering Using interpersonal skills to extract information about a computer system and its security.

spoofing Pretending to be something else, as when a packet might spoof another return IP address (as in the smurf attack) or when a Web site is spoofing a well known e-commerce site.

spyware Software that monitors computer use.

stateful packet inspection (SPI) A type of firewall process in which each packet and its contents are examined.

stateless packet inspection A type of firewall in which the inspection does not involve actually examining the contents of each packet, nor does it examine a packet within the context of an ongoing TCP conversation.

stream cipher A type of cipher in which the original text is encrypted one byte at a time in a stream of bytes.

subnet   A subsection of a network.

subnet mask   A mask used to determine what subnet an IP address belongs to.

substitution alphabet   The characters used to replace plain text in a substitution or multi-substitution encryption algorithm.

switch   A device that works like a hub, but routes packets only out of the port that they need to go to rather than out of all ports.

SYN cookies   Cookies used to authenticate connection requests and thus avoid certain types of Denial of Service attacks.

SYN flood   A Denial of Service attack in which the target is flooded with connection requests that are never completed.

SYNACK   The response a server sends back to a connection request from a client.

T

teardrop attack   A type of attack against a TCP/IP stack based on using fragmented packets

Terminate and Stay Resident (TSR)   Software that stays loaded in memory even if shuts down.

Tracert   A utility similar to ping that also tells you what hops it made getting to the destination and how long it took to get there.

Transmission Control Protocol (TCP)   A protocol used to send data over the Internet; part of the TCP/IP suite of protocols.

Transmission Control Protocol/Internet Protocol (TCP/IP)   A suite of protocols used for various types of Internet and networking communication.

Trojan horse   Software that appears to have a valid and benign purpose, but really has another nefarious purpose.

U

UDP flood attack   A Denial of Service attack based on sending a huge number of UDP packets.

Uniform Resource Locator (URL)   An Internet address, such as **www.prenticehall.com**.

User Datagram Protocol (UDP)   A protocol very similar to TCP except that transmissions are merely sent without any attempt to confirm their arrival at the destination.

V

virtual private network (VPN)   A network that is constructed by using public wires to connect nodes.

virus   Software that is self-replicating and spreads like a biological virus.

W

war-dialing   Dialing phones waiting for a computer to pick up. This is usually done via some automated system.

war-driving   Driving and scanning for wireless networks that can be compromised.

white hat hackers   Hackers who only hack for legal/ethical purposes.

Z

zone transfers   DNS servers must update their list of what IP addresses go with what URL (Uniform Resource Locator). They periodically perform zone transfers to synchronize those lists.

Part 1
References

Chapter 1

100th Congress. Computer Security Act of 1987. Public Law 100-235. **http://www.net.ohio-state.edu/security/links/csa-1987.html** (accessed 15 December 2004).

CNN/Technology. Hacker Accesses 5.6 Million Credit Cards. February 18, 2003. **http://www.cnn.com/2003/TECH/02/17/creditcard.hack/index.html** (accessed 15 December 2004).

Computer Security Institute. Cyber Crime Bleeds U.S. Corporations, Survey Shows; Financial Losses from Attacks Climb for Third Year in a Row. April 7, 2002. **http://www.gocsi.com/press/20020407.jhtml;jsessionid=J5CTJV4ZKSD3MQSNDBGCKHSCJUMEKJVN?_requestid=219439** (accessed 15 December 2004).

DefCon II. Wardriving Statistics. Las Vegas, NV. August 2003. **http://www.defcon.org/html/defcon-11/defcon-11-postcon.html** (accessed 15 December 15, 2004).

F-Secure. F-Secure Virus Descriptions. 2003. **http://www.f-secure.com/v-descs/_new.shtml** (accessed 15 December 2004).

Glossary of Hacker Terminology. June 2003. **http://www.cs.usask.ca/undergrads/kwm519/490/project/details/glossary.htm** (accessed 15 December 2004).

Lemos, Robert. Mitnick Teaches Social Engineering. *ZDNet News.* July 16, 2000. **http://news.zdnet.com/2100-9595_22-522261.html?legacy=zdnn** (accessed 15 December 2004).

Mitnick, Kevin D., William L. Simon, and Steve Wozniak. 2002. *The Art of Deception: Controlling the Human Element of Security.* Indianapolis, IN: Wiley Publishing Inc.

Online Banking Report. OBR Special Report Series. New Edition—2004 Factbook: Online Banking by the Numbers. November 2003. **http://www.onlinebankingreport.com/resources/sr7.html** (accessed 15 December 2004).

Poulsen, Kevin. War Driving by the Bay. *SecurityFocus.* April 12, 2001. **http://www.securityfocus.com/news/192** (accessed 15 December 2004).

Raymond, Eric S. 1993. *The New Hacker's Dictionary.* 3rd ed. Cambridge, MA: The MIT Press.

Symantec. What Is the Difference Between Viruses, Worms, and Trojans? Security Response FAQ Sheet. 2003. **http://service1.symantec.com/SUPPORT/nav.nsf/aab56492973adccd8825694500552355/024c927836400f528825675100593eb2?OpenDocument&src=sec_web_nam** (accessed 15 December 2004).

Webopedia. Proxy Server. 2004. **http://www.webopedia.com/TERM/p/proxy_server.html** (accessed 15 December 2004).

Chapter 2

Webopedia. IP. 2004. **http://www.webopedia.com/TERM/I/IP.html** (accessed 15 December 2004).

Webopedia. TCP. 2004. **http://www.webopedia. com/TERM/T/TCP.html** (accessed 15 December 2004).

Chapter 4

Gibson, Steve. Description and Analysis of a Potent, Increasingly Prevalent, and Worrisome Internet Attack. *Distributed Reflection Denial of Service*. February 22, 2002. **http://grc.com/ dos/drdos.htm** (accessed 15 December 2004).

Moore, David, Vern Paxson, Stefan Savage, Colleen Shannon, Stuart Staniford, and Nicholas Weaver. Slammer Worm Dissection: Inside the Slammer Worm. *IEEE Security and Privacy*. 2004. **http://www.computer.org/ security/v1n4/j4wea.htm** (accessed 15 December 2004).

Delio, Michelle. My Doom Targets Linux Antagonist. *Wired News*. January 27, 2004. **http:// www.wired.com/news/linux/0,1411,62058,00 .html** (accessed 15 December 2004).

SCO./Linux. 2003. **http://swpat.ffii.org/patente/ wirkungen/sco/index.en.html** (accessed 15 December 2004).

Webopedia. DoS Attack. 2004. **http://www. webopedia.com/TERM/D/DoS_attack.html** (accessed 15 December 2004).

Chapter 5

finjan software. Mobile Code—A Necessary Evil. 2004. **http://www.finjan.com/SecurityLab/ KnowledgeCenter/CurrentTopics/Active- ContentandMaliciousMobileCode.asp** (accessed 15 December 2004).

F-Secure. F-Secure Virus Descriptions: Sobig. April 23, 2003. **http://www.f-secure.com/v- descs/sobig.shtml** (accessed 15 December 2004).

Gudmundsson, Atli, and Scott Gettis. W32.Mi- mail.A@mm. *Symantec*. July 28, 2004. **http:// securityresponse.symantec.com/avcenter/** **venc/data/w32.mimail.a@mm.html** (accessed 15 December 2004).

searchSecurity.com. Buffer Overflow. September 13, 2004. **http://searchsecurity.techtarget. com/sDefinition/0%2C%2Csid14_gci54902 4%2C00.html** (accessed 15 December 2004).

searchSecurity.com. Rootkit. December 7, 2004. **http://searchsecurity.techtarget.com/s Definition/0,,sid14_gci547279,00.html** (accessed 16 December 2004).

SpywareGuide. 2004. **http://www.spywareguide. com/product_list_full.php** (accessed 16 December 2004).

Vmyths.com. jdbgmgr.exe Virus. July 7, 2002. **http://vmyths.com/hoax.cfm?id=275&page= 3** (accessed 16 December 2004).

Yakabovicz, Ed. Expert Knowledgebase. *TechTarget Expert Answer Center*. March 29, 2003. **http://expertanswercenter.techtarget. com/eac/knowledgebaseAnswer/0,,sid63_gci 980661,00.html** (accessed 16 December 2004).

Chapter 7

Burnett, Steve, and Stephen Paine. 2001. *RSA Security's Official Guide to Cryptography*. New York, NY: McGraw-Hill.

Curtin, Matt. Snake Oil Warning Signs: Encryption Software to Avoid. April 10, 1998. **http:// www.interhack.net/people/cmcurtin/snake- oil-faq.html** (accessed 16 December 2004).

Federal Information Processing Standards. Data Encryption Standards (DES). Publication 46-2. December 30, 1993. **http://www.itl.nist.gov/ fipspubs/fip46-2.htm** (accessed 16 December 2004).

International PGP. Home Page. **http://www. pgpi.org/** (accessed March 2004).

McCune, Tom. Tom McCune's Page for Pretty Good Privacy. **http://www.mccune.cc/PGP. htm** (accessed March 2004).

MyCrypto.net. Encryption Algorithms. **http://www.mycrypto.net/encryption/crypto_algorithms.html** (accessed April 2004).

Security in Computing. Letter Frequency Distributions in the English Alphabet. 1988. **http://arapaho.nsuok.edu/~rosener/mis4313/freq-distribution.html** (accessed 16 December 2004).

Singh, Simon. 2001. *The Code Book: How to Make It, Break It, Hack It, Crack It*. New York, NY: Delacorte Press, 10, 241-242.

Zimmermann, Philip. Philip Zimmermann: Creator of PGP. **http://www.philzimmermann.com/EN/background/index.html** (accessed March 2004).

Chapter 8

Garner, Bryan A. 2000. *Black's Law Dictionary*. 7th ed. West Group.

Fraud Bureau. Stock Scams 101. Pump and Dump Classic. 1999. **http://www.fraudbureau.com/investor/101/article15.html** (accessed November 2003).

California Youth Authority. OPVS Bulletin—Stalking Awareness. 2000. **http://www.cya.ca.gov/Staff/stalking.html** (accessed 16 December 2004).

National Conference of State Legislatures. 2004 Pending Identity Theft Legislation. October 14, 2004. **http://www.ncsl.org/programs/lis/privacy/IDTheft2004_Pending.htm** (accessed 16 December 2004).

Romanian Information Technology Initiative. Anti-corruption Law Title III on Preventing and Fighting Cyber-crime. *Romanian Cyber-crime Law*. May 7, 2002. **http://www.riti-internews.ro/cybercrime.htm** (accessed 16 December 2004).

University of Dayton School of Law. Cyber-crimes. 2001. **http://cybercrimes.net/** (accessed 16 December 2004).

U.S. Department of Justice. Cyberstalking: A New Challenge for Law Enforcement and Industry. February 7, 2003. **http://www.usdoj.gov/criminal/cybercrime/cyberstalking.htm** (accessed 16 December 2004).

U.S. Department of Justice. What Are Identity Theft and Identity Fraud? June 5, 2000. **http://www.usdoj.gov/criminal/fraud/idtheft.html** (accessed October 2003).

U.S. Federal Trade Commission. Identity Theft and Assumption Deterrence Act. October 30, 1998. **http://www.ftc.gov/os/statutes/itada/itadact.htm** (accessed December 2004).

U.S. Federal Trade Commission. Internet Auctions: A Guide for Buyers and Sellers. June 2004. **http://www.ftc.gov/bcp/conline/pubs/online/auctions.htm** (accessed 16 December 2004).

U.S. Secret Service. Public Awareness Advisory Regarding "4-1-9" or "Advance Fee Fraud" Schemes. 2002. **http://www.secretservice.gov/alert419.shtml** (accessed November 2003).

U.S. Securities and Exchange Commission. Internet Fraud: How to Avoid Internet Investment Scams. November 15, 2001. **http://www.sec.gov/investor/pubs/cyberfraud.htm** (accessed October 2003).

U.S. Securities and Exchange Commission. Pump&Dump.con: Tips for Avoiding Stock Scams on the Internet. September 28, 2000. **http://www.sec.gov/investor/online/pump.htm** (accessed November 2003).

Working to Halt Online Abuse. Home Page. September 28, 2004. **http://www.haltabuse.org/** (accessed 16 December 2004).

Chapter 9

Briney, Andrew. The Four P's: When It Comes to Security, People Matter Most. *Information Security*. September 2003, 8. **http://infosecuritymag.techtarget.com/ss/0,295796,sid6_iss81_art198,00.html** (accessed 17 December 2004).

Dever, Paul. Federal Judge Says VW Chairman Must Remain Defendant in GM Spy Suit. *The Auto Channel*. October 24, 1996. **http://www. theautochannel.com/news/date/19961024/ news02344.html** (accessed 17 December 2004).

Konrad, R. Leaks and Geeks: International Espionage Goes High-Tech. *CNET News*. September 21, 2000. **http://news.com.com/2100-1001-242620.html?legacy=cnet** (accessed September 2001).

Lemon, Sumner. Top VIA Execs Indicted for Industrial Espionage. *NetworkWorldFusion, IDG News Service*. December 8, 2003. **http:// www.nwfusion.com/news/2003/1208 updattop.html** (accessed 17 December 2004).

Secur Telecom. Introduction to Espionage. Latest Trends in Industrial Espionage. 1998. **http:// www.securtelecom.com/Industrial Espionage/espionage.htm** (accessed 17 December 2004).

Szczesny, Joseph. Lopez Surfaces in Indictment. *CarConnection.com*. May 29, 2000. **http:// www.thecarconnection.com/index.asp?n=15 6,175&sid=175&article=1908** (accessed 17 December 2004).

U.S. Department of Justice. Kazakhstan Hacker Sentenced to Four Years Prison for Breaking into Bloomberg Systems and Attempting Extortion. July 1, 2003. **http://www.usdoj.gov/ criminal/cybercrime/zezevSent.htm** (accessed 17 December 2004).

USA Today. Former GM Exec Indicted in VW Scandal. May 23, 2000. **http://www.usatoday. com/money/consumer/autos/mauto646.htm** (accessed 17 December 2004).

Chapter 10

BBC News. Russians Arrest "CIA Hacker." June 26, 2000. **http://news.bbc.co.uk/1/hi/world/ europe/806984.stm** (accessed 17 December 2004).

Counterpane Internet Security. Security Alert: Chinese Hacker Group. April 30, 2002. **http://www.counterpane.com/alert-ceu.html** (accessed 17 December 2004).

Denning, Dorothy E. Cyberterrorism. May 23, 2000. **http://www.cosc.georgetown.edu/ ~denning/infosec/cyberterror.html** (accessed 17 December 2004).

Dick, Ronald L. Cyber Terrorism and Critical Infrastructure Protection. U.S. Federal Bureau of Investigation. July 24, 2002. **http://www. fbi.gov/congress/congress02/nipc072402.htm** (accessed 17 December 2004).

Hoffman, Bruce. Al Qaeda, Trends in Terrorism and Future Potentialities: An Assessment. Santa Monica, CA: The Rand Corporation, 2003. **http://www.rand.org/publications/P/P8078/P 8078.pdf** (accessed 17 December 2004).

Institute for the Advanced Study of Information Warfare. March 14, 2004. **http://www.psycom. net/iwar.1.html** (accessed April 2004).

Ranum, Marcus. Myths of Cyberwar. *Information Security*. April 2004. **http://infosecuritymag. techtarget.com/ss/0,295804,sid6_iss366,00. html** (accessed 17 December 2004).

Roberts, Paul. Government Report Finds Satellite Security Lax. *InfoWorld*. October 4, 2002. **http://archive.infoworld.com/articles/hn/xml /02/10/04/021004hnsatellites.xml?s=IDGNS** (accessed 17 December 2004).

Tech Law Journal. Advisory Panel Reports on Cyber Terrorism. December 14, 2000. **http:// www.techlawjournal.com/security/ 20001214.asp** (accessed 17 December 2004).

Tech Law Journal. Cyberterrorism Preparedness Act of 2002. January 28, 2002. **http://www. techlawjournal.com/cong107/cybersecurity/s 1900is.asp** (accessed 17 December 2004).

The Orator. Cybersecurity Research and Education Act of 2002. 107th Congress, 2nd Session.

January 28, 2002. **http://www.theorator.com/ bills107/s1901.html** (accessed 17 December 2004).

Chapter 12

How Does a Virus Scanner Work? *Scientific American* (7), 2004.

Wack, John. Circuit-Level Gateways. *Computer Security Resource Center*. February 9, 1995. **http://csrc.nist.gov/publications/nistpubs/800 -10/node53.html** (accessed 8 December 2004).

Webopedia. Intrusion Detection System, 2004. **http://www.webopedia.com/TERM/I/Intrusi on_detection_system.html** (accessed 17 December 2004).

Webopedia. NIDS. 2004. **http://www.webo pedia.com/TERM/N/NIDS.html** (accessed 17 December 2004).

Part 1
Index

Part 2

Part 2 Preface

When teaching a complex and ever-changing discipline like information security, students are best served by beginning with a high-level understanding of the subject before tackling the details. A solid grasp of the objectives, terminology, principles, and framework will help them understand how to place issues in a context to find working solutions. That is the goal of this text: to introduce students to the most important topics of information security and hopefully pique their interest to learn more.

The Body of Knowledge (as it is called in the IT security industry) is vast, deep, and at times baffling. Solutions are not always straightforward, because the problems they address are rarely intuitive. There is no cookbook or universal recipe for IT security success. Ideally, protecting computer systems from attacks and unauthorized access means anticipating problems and devising strategies to address how people, processes, and technologies interact. The goal, while not always realistic, is to prevent these problems from happening and not simply to react to them as so many organizations do today.

This is rarely easy.

This book navigates through the ocean of information technology (IT) security topics and issues while keeping the technical jargon to a minimum. Chapters are ordered to follow the major "domains" of the Common Body of Knowledge to help you organize your course and prepare students for a more detailed examination of the topics if that is their desire. If some students are already familiar with some of the concepts of information security, the book should be sufficiently detailed to hold their interest and discuss topics they may not have previously considered.

IT security specialists are rarely experts in all areas of the discipline. They must focus on carefully selected areas of the field if they want to succeed. This book guides students through the critical topics and helps them to decide which areas are of greatest interest to them.

According to the Bureau of Labor Statistics, the need for IT security specialists will continue to grow into the foreseeable future (**www.bls.gov/oco/ocos042.htm**). With the growth of computers in offices, homes, and public areas, the need for effective security has grown while the availability of trained and experienced personnel is inadequate. Businesses, governments, and civic organizations alike need security experts to help assure that the computing resources they have grown to depend upon are secure and reliable. Should students decide to enter the field of information security, they will find this book helpful in charting their course and joining the ranks of specialists in this discipline. If student interest is more general and part of a broader information science curriculum, they should find the topics covered not only informative but useful in their own lives.

Audience

The book is designed for introductory courses in information security. A background for instructing a course on IT security includes a basic understanding of telecommunications networks and how the Internet operates. The textbook is a useful foundation for advanced studies in CBK Domains and related topics. Content, review material, exercises, and end-of-section questions are designed to test whether section objectives were met.

Overview of the Book

This textbook is designed for anyone who desires a tighter grasp of security principles and practices or is considering entering the field as a practitioner or researcher. Topics were selected and organized using the widely accepted Common Body of Knowledge (CBK) defined by the International Information Systems Security Certifications Consortium, Inc. (**www.isc2.org**). While the CBK is used for organization of the content, the book should not be considered a study guide for the CISSP exam or other ISC^2 exams based on the information security Common Body of Knowledge.

Chapters 13 offers an overview of the fundamental principles and concepts of Information Security (InfoSec) that are needed for setting the context and the objectives for the remainder of the book. Chapter 14 introduces the Information Security Common Body of Knowledge and provides an overview of each of the 10 domains.

Chapters 15-19 follow the content–at the principles and concepts level–of the 10 domains, specifically:

- Security Management (Chapter 15) examines the policies, standards, and other documents that form the basis of an IT Security Management Programme. It includes the principles and industry best practices to codify a successful management system.

- Security Architecture and Models (Chapter 16) provides the framework and fundamental principles of common security architectures and information assurance models that are applied in various security mechanisms described throughout the text.

- Business Continuity Planning/Disaster Recovery Planning (Chapter 17) looks at the principles, methods, and tools needed to assure continued business operations in the event of a loss of access or a disaster that affects a business' information systems.

- Law, Investigations, and Ethics (Chapter 18) covers fundamental principles and practices related to the collection of evidence for forensics purposes when computer security incidents occur. Chapter 18 also looks at the ethical standards that IT Security personnel must uphold. Physical Security (Chapter 19) examines the mechanisms, building, and safety requirements for installations housing computer equipment needed to operate a business.

Each chapter covers the topics at the principles and concepts level and helps students build a foundation and framework to understanding the role of IT Security in the modern, networked world. Appendices included at the end of the book offer a listing of the key areas of knowledge in the Common Body of Knowledge (Appendix D), a taxonomy for security policies and standards (Appendix E), example security policies and standards to use as a model for developing customized documents (Appendix F), an inside look at one popular security management software system (Appendix G), and a review of the HIPPA Security Rules Standards (Appendix H).

Chapter 13

Information Security Principles of Success

Chapter Objectives

After reading this chapter and completing the exercises, you will be able to do the following:

- Build an awareness of 12 generally accepted basic principles of information security to help you determine how these basic principles are applied to real-life situations.
- Distinguish between the three main security goals.
- Learn how to design and apply the principle of "Defense in Depth."
- Comprehend human vulnerabilities in security systems to better design solutions to counter them.
- Explain the difference between functional and assurance requirements.
- Comprehend the fallacy of *security through obscurity* to avoid using it as a measure of security.
- Comprehend the importance of risk analysis and risk management tools and techniques for balancing the needs of business.
- Determine which side of the open disclosure debate you would take.

Introduction

Many of the topics information technology students study in school can be carried directly from the classroom to the workplace. For example, new programming and systems analysis and design skills can often be applied on new systems-development projects as companies espouse object-oriented analysis and programming to internal systems.

Security is a little different. Although their technical skills are certainly important, the best security specialists combine their practical knowledge of computers and networks with general theories about security, technology, and human nature. These concepts, some borrowed from other fields such as military defense, often take years of (sometimes painful) professional experience to learn. With a conceptual and principles view of information security, you'll be able to analyze a security need in the right frame of reference or context so you can balance the needs of permitting access versus the risk allowing such access. No two systems or situations are identical, and there are no cookbooks to consult on how to solve security problems, so it's imperative to rely on principle-based analysis and decision making.

This chapter introduces these key information security principles, concepts, and durable "truths."

Principle 1: There Is No Such Thing as Absolute Security

In 2003, the art collection of the Whitworth Gallery in Manchester, England, included three famous paintings by Van Gogh, Picasso, and Gauguin. Valued at more than $7 million, the paintings were protected by closed-circuit television, a series of alarm systems, and 24-hour rolling patrols. Yet, in late April 2003, thieves broke into the museum, evaded the layered security system, and made off with the three masterpieces. Several days later, investigators discovered the paintings in a nearby public restroom along with a note from the thieves saying, "The intention was not to steal, only to highlight the woeful security."

The burglars' lesson translates to the information security arena and illustrates the first principle of information security (IS): Given enough time, tools, skills, and inclination, a hacker can break through any security measure. This principle applies to the physical world as well and is best illustrated by using the analogy of safes or vaults, which businesses commonly use to protect their assets. Safes are rated according to their resistance to attacks using a scale that describes how long it could take a burglar to open them. They are divided into a number of categories based on the level of protection they can deliver and the testing they undergo. Four common classes of safe ratings are B-Rate, C-Rate, ULTL-15, and ULTL-30:

- **B-Rate:** B-Rate is a catchall rating for any box with a lock on it and describes the thickness of the steel used to make the lockbox. No actual testing is performed to gain this rating.

- **C-Rate:** This is defined as a variably thick steel box with a 1-inch-thick door and a lock. No tests are given to provide this rating either.

- **ULTL-15:** Safes with an Underwriters Laboratory (UL) TL-15 rating have passed standardized tests as defined in UL Standard

13

687 using tools and an expert group of safe-testing engineers. The UL TL-15 label requires that the safe be constructed of 1-inch solid steel or equivalent. The label means that the safe has been tested for a net working time of 15 minutes using ". . . common hand tools, drills, punches hammers, and pressure applying devices." Net working time means that when the tool comes off the safe, the clock is stopped. Engineers exercise more than 50 different types of attacks that have proved effective for safecracking.

■ **ULTL-30:** UL TL-30 testing is essentially the same as the TL-15 testing except for the net working time. Testers get 30 minutes and a few more tools to help them gain access. Testing engineers usually have a safe's manufacturing blueprints and can disassemble the safe before the test begins to see how it works.

As you will see in Chapter 16, security testing of hardware and software systems employs many of the same concepts of safe testing, using computers and custom-developed testing software instead of tools and torches, but the outcomes of testing are just the same—like software, no safe is burglar proof; it will simply buy time. This leads to the second principle.

Principle 2: The Three Security Goals Are Confidentiality, Integrity, and Availability

All information security measures try to address at least one of three goals:

■ Protect the *confidentiality* of data.

■ Preserve the *integrity* of data.

■ Promote the *availability* of data for authorized use.

These goals form the confidentiality, integrity, availability (CIA) triad (see Figure 13.1 for a diagram of the CIA triad). The CIA triad is the basis of all security programs. Information security professionals who create policies and procedures (often referred to as *models*) must consider each goal when creating a plan to protect a computer system.

Caution

Confidentiality Models

Confidentiality models are primarily intended to assure that no unauthorized access to information is permitted and that accidental disclosure of sensitive information is not possible. Common confidentiality controls are user IDs and passwords.

FYI: Confidentiality by Another Name

Confidentiality is sometimes referred to as the "principle of least privilege," meaning that users should only be given enough privilege to perform their duties, and no more. Some other synonyms for confidentiality you may encounter include privacy, secrecy, and discretion.

FIGURE 13.1 The CIA triad.

Integrity Models

Integrity models keep data pure and trustworthy by protecting system data from intentional or accidental changes. Integrity models have three goals:

- Prevent unauthorized users from making modifications to data or programs.

- Prevent authorized users from making improper or unauthorized modifications.

- Maintain internal and external consistency of data and programs.

An example of integrity checks would be balancing a batch of transactions to make sure that all the information is present and accurately accounted for.

Availability Models

Availability models keep data and resources available for authorized use, especially during emergencies or disasters. Information security professionals usually address three common challenges to availability:

- Denial of Service (DoS) due to intentional attacks or because of undiscovered flaws in implementation (e.g., a program written by a programmer who is unaware of a flaw that could crash the program if a certain unexpected input is encountered).

- Loss of information system capabilities because of natural disasters (e.g., fires, floods, storms, or earthquakes) or human actions (e.g., bombs or strikes).

- Equipment failures during normal use

Some of the activities that preserve confidentiality, integrity, and/or availability are the granting of access only to authorized personnel, applying

Caution

CIA Triad

The principle of information security protection of confidentiality, integrity, and availability cannot be overemphasized and is central to all studies and practices in IS. You'll often see the term *CIA triad* to illustrate the overall goals for IS throughout the research, guidance, and practices you encounter.

encryption to information that will be sent out over the Internet, periodic testing of operating system security to uncover new vulnerabilities, and developing a disaster recovery plan to assure that the business can continue to exist in the event of a disaster or loss of access by personnel.

Principle 3: Defense in Depth as Strategy

A bank would never leave its assets inside an unguarded safe alone. Typically, access to the safe requires passing through layers of protection that may include human guards and locked doors with special access controls. Furthermore, the room where the safe resides may be monitored by closed-circuit television, motion sensors, and alarm systems that can quickly detect unusual activity. The sound of an alarm may trigger the doors to automatically lock, the police to be notified, or the room to fill with tear gas.

Layered security, like the example described above, is called *defense in depth*. Defense in depth is security implemented in overlapping layers that provide the three elements needed to secure assets: prevention, detection, and response. Defense in depth also means that the weaknesses of one security layer are offset by the strengths of two or more layers.

In the information security world, defense in depth means you should layer security devices in a series that protects, detects, and responds to attacks on systems. For example, a typical Internet-attached network designed with security in mind includes routers, firewalls, and intrusion detection systems (IDS) to protect the network from would-be intruders; it employs traffic analyzers and real-time human monitors who watch for anomalies as the network is being used to detect any breach in the layers of protection; and it relies on automated mechanisms to turn off access or remove the system from the network in response to detection of an intruder.

Finally, the security of each of these mechanisms must be thoroughly tested before deployment to ensure that the integrated system is suitable for normal operations. After all, a chain is only as good as its weakest link.

Principle 4: When Left on Their Own, People Tend to Make the Worst Security Decisions

The primary reason that identity theft, viruses, worms, and stolen passwords are so common is that people are easily duped into giving up the secrets that technologies use to secure systems. Organizers of Infosecurity Europe 2003, Britain's biggest information technology security exhibition, sent researchers to London's Waterloo Station to ask commuters to hand over their office computer passwords in exchange for a free pen. Three-quarters of respondents revealed the information immediately and an additional 15 percent did so after some gentle probing. Study after study like this one shows how little it takes to convince someone to give up their credentials in exchange for trivial or worthless goods.

Virus writers know all too well how easy it is to fool people into spreading their viruses for them. A good example is the Anna Kournikova VBS.SST computer virus, informally known as "Anna." This viral worm swept through the computing world in 2001. It used Visual Basic to infect Windows systems when a user unwittingly opened an e-mail note with an attachment that appeared to be a graphic image of Russian tennis star Anna Kournikova. When the file was opened, a clandestine code extension enabled the worm to copy itself to the Windows directory and then send the file as an attachment to all the addresses listed in the victim's Microsoft Outlook e-mail address book.

The virus arrived as an e-mail with the following subject, message, and attachment:

```
Subject: Here you have, ;o)
Message body: Hi: Check This!
Attachment: AnnaKournikova.jpg.vbs
```

That's all it took. Despite the primitive nature of this attack, many people were easily convinced to double-click on the attachment hoping for a quick peek at Anna. Because of Anna and other viruses like it, computer users are now much more wary of opening e-mail attachments from unknown sources. However, today's virus writers are far more sophisticated and use dozens of other ways to convince people to open an attachment or visit a rogue Web site.

IN PRACTICE: Phishing for Dollars

Phishing is another good example of how easily intelligent people can be duped into breaching security. Phishing is a dangerous Internet scam, named after the hacking community's use of "ph" instead of "f," which comes from the days of phone *phreaking* in the 1970s. Phone phreakers, with the most famous among them named Captain Crunch (John Draper), discovered that the free whistle that used to come packaged with Captain Crunch cereal produced the identical tone to coins dropped in a pay-phone slot, thus permitting the phreaker to make unlimited and untraceable long-distance telephone calls. A phishing scam typically operates as follows:

■ The victim receives an "official looking" e-mail message purporting to come from a trusted source, such as an online

13

banking site, Paypal, eBay, or other service where money is exchanged, moved, or managed.

- The e-mail tells the user that his or her account needs updating immediately or will be suspended within *X* number of days.

- The e-mail contains a URL (link) and instructs the user to click on the link to access their account and update their information. The link text appears as though it will take the user to the site they expect. The link itself is actually a link to the attacker's site, which is made to look exactly like the site the user expects to see.

- Once at the spoofed site, the user enters his or her credentials (ID and password) and clicks on submit.

- The site returns an innocuous message, such as "We're sorry—we're unable to process your transaction at this time" or a similar message and the user is none the wiser.

- At this point, the victim's credentials are stored on the attacker's site or sent via e-mail to the perpetrator where they can be used to log-in to the *real* banking or exchange site and empty it before the user knows what happened.

Phishing and the resultant ID theft and monetary losses are on the increase and will only begin to slow down once the cycle is broken through awareness and education. Protect yourself by taking the following steps:

- Look for telltale signs of a fraud—rather than addressing you by name, a phishing e-mail will address you as "User" or by your e-mail address—a legitimate message from a legitimate company will use your name as they know it.

- Do not click on links embedded in unsolicited finance-related e-mail messages. It's simple to make a link look legitimate, but when you click on it, you may be redirected to the site of a phisher. If you believe that your account is in jeopardy, type in the known URL of the site in a new browser window and look for messages from the provider after you're logged in.

- Check with your provider for messages related to phishing scams that they are aware of. Your bank or other financial services provider wants to make sure that you don't fall victim and often go out of their way to educate users on preventing problems.

Principle 5: Computer Security Depends on Two Types of Requirements: Functional and Assurance

Functional requirements describe what a system *should* do, and *assurance requirements* describe how functional requirements should be implemented and tested. Both sets of requirements are needed to answer the following questions:

- Does the system do the right things (i.e., behave as promised)?
- Does the system do the right things in the right way?

These are the same questions that others in noncomputer industries face with verification and validation. Verification is the process of confirming that one or more predetermined requirements, or specifications, are met. Validation then is a determination of the correctness or quality of the mechanisms used in meeting the needs. In other words, you can develop software that addresses a need, but it may contain flaws that could compromise data when placed in the hands of a malicious user.

Using car safety testing as an example, verification testing for seat belt functions may include stress tests on the fabric, testing the locking mechanisms, and making certain the belt will fit the intended application, thus completing the functional tests. Validation, or assurance testing, might then include crashing the car with crash-test dummies inside to "prove" that the seat belt is indeed safe when used under normal conditions and can survive under harsh conditions.

With software, you need both verification and validation answers to gain confidence in products prior to launching them into a wild, hostile environment like the Internet. Most of today's *commercial off-the-shelf (COTS)* software and systems stop at the first step, verification, without bothering to test for obvious security vulnerabilities in the final product. Developers of software generally lack the wherewithal and motivation needed to try and break their own software. More often, developers will test that the software meets the specifications in each function that is present but usually do not try to find ways of circumventing the software in an attempt to make it fail. You'll learn more about security testing of software in Chapter 5, Security Architectures and Models.

Principle 6: Security Through Obscurity Is Not an Answer

Many in the information security industry believe that if hackers don't know *how* software is secured, security is better. Although this may seem logical, it's actually untrue. Security through obscurity means that hiding the details of the security mechanisms is sufficient to secure the system alone. An example of security through obscurity might involve closely guarding the written specifications for security functions and preventing all but the most trusted people from seeing it. Obscuring security leads to a *false* sense of security, which is often more dangerous than not addressing security at all.

If the security of a system is maintained by keeping the implementation of the system a secret, once the first person discovers how the security mechanism works, the entire system collapses—and someone is always determined to discover these secrets. The better bet is to make sure that no one mechanism is responsible for the security of the entire system. This again is defense in depth in everything related to protecting data and resources.

It makes no sense to keep an algorithm for cryptography secret when the security of the system should rely on the cryptographic keys used to protect data or authenticate a user. You can also see this in action with the open-source movement where anyone can gain access to program (source) code and analyze it for security problems and then share with the community improvements that eliminate vulnerabilities and/or improve the overall security through simplification (see Principle 9).

Principle 7: Security = Risk Management

It's critical to understand that spending more on securing an asset than the intrinsic value of the asset is a waste of resources. For example, buying a $500 safe to protect $200 worth of jewelry makes no practical sense. The same is true when protecting electronic assets. All security work is a careful balance between the level of risk and the expected reward of expending a given amount of resources. Security is not concerned with eliminating all threats within a system or facility but with eliminating known threats and minimizing losses if an attacker succeeds in exploiting a vulnerability. Risk analysis and risk management are central themes to securing information systems. Once risks are well understood, there are three possible outcomes:

■ The risks are mitigated (countered).

■ Insurance against the losses that would occur should a system be compromised is acquired.

■ The risks are accepted and the consequences are managed.

Risk assessment and risk analysis are concerned with placing an economic value on assets to best determine appropriate countermeasures that protect them from losses.

Likelihood	Consequences				
	1. Insignificant	**2. Minor**	**3. Moderate**	**4. Major**	**6. Catastrophic**
A (almost certain)	High	High	Extreme	Extreme	Extreme
B (likely)	Moderate	High	High	Extreme	Extreme
C (moderate)	Low	Moderate	High	Extreme	Extreme
D (unlikely)	Low	Low	Moderate	High	Extreme
E (rare)	Low	Low	Moderate	High	High

FIGURE 13.2 Consequences/likelihood matrix for risk analysis.

The simplest form of determining the degree of a risk is by looking at two factors:

- What is the consequence of a loss?

- What is the likelihood that this loss will occur?

Figure 13.2 illustrates a matrix you can use to determine the degree of a risk based on these factors.

Once a risk rating has been determined, one of the following actions may be required:

- Extreme risk: immediate action required.

- High risk: senior management attention needed.

- Moderate risk: management responsibility must be specified.

- Low risk: manage by routine procedures.

In the real world, risk management is more complicated than simply making a human judgment call based on intuition or previous experience with a similar situation. Recall that every system has unique security issues and considerations, so it's imperative to understand the specific nature of data the system will maintain, what hardware and software will be used to deploy the system, and the security skills of the development teams. Determining the likelihood of a risk coming to life requires understanding a few more terms and concepts:

- Vulnerability

- Exploit

- Attacker

Vulnerability refers to a known problem within a system or program. A common example in InfoSec is called the *buffer overflow* or *buffer overrun* vulnerability. Programmers tend to be trusting and do not worry about who will attack their programs but rather about who will use their programs legitimately. One feature of most programs is the ability for a user to "input" information or requests. The program instructions (source code) then will contain an "area" in memory (buffer) for these inputs and act upon them when told to do so. Sometimes the programmer won't check to see if the input is proper or innocuous. A malicious user, however, might take advantage of this weakness and overload the input area with more information than it can handle, crashing or disabling the program. This is called **buffer overflow** and might permit the malicious user to gain control over the system. This is a very common vulnerability in nearly all versions of all software and must be addressed when developing systems.

An **exploit** is a program or a "cookbook" on how to take advantage of a specific vulnerability. It might be a program that a hacker can download over the Internet and then use to search for systems that contain the vulnerability it's designed to exploit. It might also be a series of steps that are documented on how to exploit the vulnerability once an attacker finds a system that contains it.

An attacker, then, is the link between a vulnerability and an exploit. The attacker has two characteristics: skill and will. He is either skilled in the art of attacking systems or has access to tools that do the work for him. He has the will to perform attacks on systems he does not own and usually cares little about the consequences of his actions.

In applying these concepts to risk analysis, the IS practitioner must anticipate who might want to attack the system, how capable the attacker may be, how available the exploits to a vulnerability are, and which systems have the vulnerability present.

Risk analysis and risk management are specialized areas of study and practice, and the IS professionals who concentrate in these areas must be skilled and current in their techniques. You'll find more on Risk Management in Chapter 15, Security Management.

Principle 8: The Three Types of Security Controls Are Preventative, Detective, and Responsive

Controls (such as documented processes) and countermeasures (such as firewalls) must be implemented as one or more of these above types, else the controls are not there for the purposes of security. Shown in another triad, the principle of defense in depth dictates that a security mechanism serves a purpose by preventing a compromise, detecting that a compromise or compromise attempt is underway, or responding to a compromise while it's happening or after it has been discovered.

Referring to the example of the bank vault in Principle 3, access to a bank's safe or vault requires passing through layers of protection that may include human guards and locked doors with special access controls (prevention). In the room where the safe resides, closed-circuit televisions, motion sensors, and alarm systems quickly detect any unusual activity (detection). The sound of an alarm may trigger the doors to automatically lock, the police to be notified, or the room to fill with tear gas (response).

These controls are the basic toolkit for the security practitioner who mixes and matches them to carry out the objectives of confidentiality, integrity, and/or availability by using people, processes, or technology (see Principle 11) to bring them to life.

Principle 9: Complexity Is the Enemy of Security

The more complex a system gets, the harder it is to secure. With too many "moving parts" or interfaces between programs and other systems, the system or interfaces become difficult to secure while still permitting them to operate as intended. You'll learn in Chapter 16 how complexity can easily get in the way of comprehensive testing of security mechanisms.

Principle 10: Fear, Uncertainty, and Doubt Do *Not* Work in Selling Security

There was a time where it was effective to "scare" management into spending resources on security to avoid the unthinkable. The tactic of fear, uncertainty, and doubt (FUD) no longer works: Information security management is now too mature. Now, IS managers must justify all investments in security using techniques of the trade. Although this makes the job of information security practitioners more difficult, it also makes them more valuable because of management's need to understand what is being protected and why. When spending resources can be justified with good, solid business rationale, security requests are rarely denied.

Principle 11: People, Process, and Technology Are *All* Needed to Adequately Secure a System or Facility

As described in Principle 3, "Defense in Depth as Strategy," the information security practitioner needs a series of countermeasures and controls to implement an effective security system. One such control might be

13

dual control, a practice borrowed from the military. The U.S. Department of Defense uses a dual control protocol to secure the nation's nuclear arsenal. This means that at least two on-site people must agree in order to launch a nuclear weapon. If one person were in control, she could make an error in judgment or act maliciously for whatever reason. But with dual control, one person acts as a countermeasure to the other: Chances are less likely that both people will make an error in judgment or act maliciously. Likewise, no one person in an organization should have the ability to control or close down a security activity. This is commonly referred to as ***separation of duties***.

Process controls are implemented to assure that different people can perform the same operations exactly in the same way each time. Processes are documented as procedures on how to carry out an activity related to security. The process to configure a server operating system for secure operations is documented as one or more procedures that security administrators use and can be verified as done correctly.

Just as the information security professional might establish process controls to make sure that a single person cannot gain complete control over a system, she should never place all of her faith in technology. Technology can fail, and without people to notice and fix technical problems, computer systems would stall permanently. This type of waste would be illustrated by installing an expensive firewall system (a network perimeter security device that blocks traffic), and then turning around and opening all the ports that are intended to block certain traffic from entering the network.

People, process, and technology controls are essential elements of several areas of practice in information technology (IT) security including operations security, applications development security, physical security, and cryptography. These three pillars of security are often depicted as a three-legged stool (see Figure 13.3).

Process

People   **Technology**

FIGURE 13.3 The people, process, and technology triad.

IN PRACTICE: How People, Process, and Technology Work in Harmony

To illustrate how people, process, and technology work together to secure systems, let's take a look a how the security department grants access to users for performing their duties. The process, called *user access request*, is initiated when a new user is brought into the company or switches her department or role within the company. The user access request form is initially completed by the user and approved by her manager.

Once the user access request is approved, it's routed to information security access coordinators to process using the documented procedures for granting access. Once access is granted and the process for sharing the user's ID and password are followed, the system's technical access control system takes over to protect the system from unauthorized access by requiring a user ID and password and preventing password guessing by an unauthorized person by limiting the number of attempts to three before locking the account from further access attempts.

Principle 12: Open Disclosure of Vulnerabilities Is Good for Security!

A raging and often heated debate within the security community and software developing centers concerns whether to let users know about a problem before a fix or patch can be developed and distributed. Principle 6 tells us that security through obscurity is not an answer: Keeping a given vulnerability secret from users and from the software developer can only lead to a false sense of security. Users have a right to know about defects in the products they purchase, just as they have a right to know about automobile recalls because of defects. The need to know trumps the need to keep secrets in order to give users the right to protect themselves.

IN PRACTICE: To Disclose or Not to Disclose; That Is the Question!

Having specific knowledge of a security vulnerability gives administrators the knowledge to properly defend their systems from related exploits. The ethical question is how should that valuable information be disseminated to the good guys while keeping it away from the bad guys? The simple truth is that you can't! Hackers tend to communicate among themselves *far* better than professional security practitioners ever could. Hackers know about most vulnerabilities long before the general public gets wind of them. By the time the general public is made aware, the hacker community has already developed a workable exploit and disseminated it far and wide to take advantage of the flaw before it can be patched or closed down.

Because of this, open disclosure benefits the general public far more than is acknowledged by the critics who claim that it gives the bad guys the same information.

Bottom Line: If you uncover an obvious problem, raise your hand and let someone who can do something about it know. You'll sleep better at night!

13

Summary

To be most effective, computer security specialists must not only know the technical side of their jobs but also must understand the principles behind information security. No two situations that security professionals review are identical, and there are no recipes or cookbooks on universal security measures. Because each situation calls for a distinct judgment to address the specific risks inherent in information systems, principles-based decision-making is an imperative. There's an old saw that states, "If you only have a hammer, every problem looks like a nail." This approach simply does not serve today's businesses, which are always striving to balance risk and reward of access to electronic records. The goal is to help you create a toolkit and develop the skills to use these tools like a master craftsman. Learn these principles, take them to heart, and you'll start out much farther along than your peers who won't take the time to bother learning them!

As you explore the rest of the Common Body of Knowledge (CBK) domains, try to relate the practices you find to one or more of these. For example, Chapter 19 covers physical security, which addresses how to limit access to physical spaces and hardware to authorized personnel. This helps prevent breaches in confidentiality, integrity, and availability and implements the principle of defense in depth. As you will find, these principles are mixed and matched to describe why certain security functions and operations exist in the real world of IT.

Test Your Skills

MULTIPLE CHOICE QUESTIONS

1. The three goals of information security are:
   A. confidentiality, integrity, and availability.
   B. prevention, detection, and response.
   C. people controls, process controls, and technology controls.
   D. network security, PC security, and mainframe security.

2. Making sure that data has not been changed unintentionally due to an accident or malice is:
   A. availability.
   B. confidentiality.
   C. integrity.
   D. auditability.

3. Related to information security, confidentiality is the opposite of which of the following?
   A. closure
   B. disclosure
   C. disaster
   D. disposal

4. The CIA triad is often represented by a:
   A. triangle.
   B. diagonal.
   C. ellipse.
   D. circle.

5. Defense in depth is needed to assure that which three mandatory activities are present in a security system?
   A. prevention, response, and prosecution
   B. response, collection of evidence, and prosecution
   C. prevention, detection, and response
   D. prevention, response, and management

13

6. The weakest link in any security system is the:

    A. technology element.

    B. process element.

    C. human element.

    D. B and C.

7. The two types of IT security requirements are:

    A. functional and logical.

    B. logical and physical.

    C. functional and assurance.

    D. functional and physical.

8. Security functional requirements describe:

    A. what a security system should do by design.

    B. what controls a security system must implement.

    C. quality assurance description and testing approach.

    D. how to implement the system.

9. Security assurance requirements describe:

    A. how to test the system.

    B. how to program the system.

    C. to what degree the testing of the system is conducted.

    D. implementation considerations.

10. The probability that a threat to an information system will material-
    ize is called _____.

    A. threat

    B. vulnerability

    C. hole

    D. risk

11. The absence or weakness in a system that may possibly be exploited
    is called a(n):

    A. vulnerability.

    B. threat.

    C. risk.

    D. exposure.

12. Controls are implemented to:
    A. eliminate risk and eliminate the potential for loss.
    B. mitigate risk and reduce the potential for loss.
    C. eliminate risk and reduce the potential for loss.
    D. mitigate risk and eliminate the potential for loss.

13. A cookbook on how to take advantage of a vulnerability is called a(n):
    A. risk.
    B. exploit.
    C. threat.
    D. program.

14. The three types of security controls are:
    A. people, functions, and technology.
    B. people, process, and technology.
    C. technology, roles, and separation of duties.
    D. separation of duties, processes, and people.

15. Process controls for IT security include:
    A. assignment of roles for least privilege.
    B. separation of duties.
    C. documented procedures.
    D. All of the above.

EXERCISES

Exercise 13.1: The Importance of Information Confidentiality

Why is confidentiality important to corporate information? What kinds of abuses can you think of in the absence of controls to confidentiality? What criminal activities could be reduced or eliminated if confidentiality controls were effectively implemented?

Exercise 13.2: Real-World Defense in Depth

Find some analogies to the principle of defense in depth in the physical world and make some diagrams of the mechanism that you locate.

Exercise 13.3: Avoiding Security Through Obscurity

Why is security through obscurity a bad idea to the overall security of a system?

Exercise 13.4: Finding Poor Security Within Society

Locate and summarize stories that you find on the Internet about users who make poor security decisions related to viruses, giving up passwords, and so forth.

Exercise 13.5: Risk Management in Action

Every day you make risk management decisions in your daily life. Should you get in the car and drive to the store? Should you jaywalk or cross at the light? Should you get on that airplane or not? Think about the risk management decisions you make when using your PC:

1. What kinds of judgments do you make before downloading a piece of software? Or writing an e-mail to your boss?

2. What are the mental steps you go through before taking some action?

PROJECTS

Project 13.1: E-mail–Borne Viruses

1. Visit one or more of the antivirus software developer sites (Symantec, MacAfee, Computer Associates, Trend Micro, and so forth) and see if you can identify which viruses and worms require a user to click on an e-mail attachment to replicate.

2. Trace the sophistication of the virus writers over time and try to determine how they circumvent any improvements in user awareness of and education toward preventing viruses from spreading.

Project 13.2: Hackers Come in Many Colors

Open disclosure of software vulnerabilities is often associated with *gray-hat hackers*, described as security researchers who aren't particular about who learns of their findings. Research the three types of hackers (white hat, gray hat, and black hat) and try to determine their typical positions on full disclosure of software problems prior to patches or new versions of the software being made available in the marketplace. Use Google.com or your favorite Internet search engine with a query of "Open Disclosure of Software Vulnerabilities" to help you formulate your answers.

Project 13.3: Comparing Physical and Virtual Risk Management Techniques

1. How is risk management for physical systems similar to computer systems? How are they different? What skill sets would be required for each type?

Case Study

The Maginot Line was built between 1929 and 1940 to protect France from her longtime enemy, Germany, and to defend the traditional invasion routes across France's eastern frontier. It was built to provide time for the French army to mobilize and to make up for a potentially disastrous shortfall of manpower that was predicted for the late 1930s. Most of all, it was built to provide a place behind which the French army could hide, a so-called Great Wall of France where the nation could feel secure in a doctrine that would become known as the *Maginot mentality.*

The World War II German invasion plan of 1940 was designed to deal with the line. A decoy force sat opposite the line while a second army group cut through the Low Countries of Belgium and The Netherlands, as well as through the Ardennes Forest, which lay north of the main French defenses, thus bypassing the Maginot Line and going around it. The Germans were able to avoid assaulting the Maginot Line directly. Attacking from May 10, the German forces were well into France within 5 days, and they continued to advance until May 24, when they stopped near Dunkirk. By early June, the German forces had cut the line off from the rest of France, and the French government was preparing for surrender.

This famous story highlights several of the principles found in the chapter, the most notable one being defense in depth.

What other defenses could the French have deployed to protect their entire border? What other principles did the French violate that led to such catastrophic results?

Chapter 14

Certification Programs and the Common Body of Knowledge

Chapter Objectives

After reading this chapter and completing the exercises, you will be able to do the following:

- Analyze the Certified Information Systems Security Professional (CISSP) certificate program as the gold standard in information technology (IT) security certification.

- Define and describe the role of the International Information Systems Security Certifications Consortium.

- Distinguish the contents of the 10 domains of the Common Body of Knowledge.

- Distinguish the CISSP from other security certification programs in the industry.

Introduction

This chapter outlines the more prominent information security certifications available to individuals interested in becoming security professionals or those already in the field who are interested in advancing their careers. To help you in those efforts, we begin with the most prominent and most demanded certification that's available to professionals and practitioners: the Certified Information Systems Security Professional (CISSP) and the System Security Certified Practitioner (SSCP) certificates, administered by The International Information Systems Security Certifications Consortium (*IISSCC*, or *ISC²*).

The CISSP and SSCP are based on formal testing of content knowledge and practical experience found in the security professional's ***Common Body of Knowledge (CBK)***. The CBK is a compilation and distillation of all security information collected internationally that is relevant to information security professionals. This book uses the CBK and its 10 domains as the organizing framework to introduce the field of information security (commonly referred to as *InfoSec*) and to help students decide what area(s) of InfoSec they may wish to pursue.

Once you get an idea of the structure of the CBK, you'll then find other industry certification programs that are complementary to the CISSP and SSCP.

Certification and Information Security

Information security professionals invest corporate resources in information assets, such as technology, architecture, and processes. Industry standards, ethics, and certification of information systems (IS) professionals and practitioners is critical to ensuring that a high standard of security is achieved. Certification benefits both the employer and the employee.

Benefits of ISC^2 certification to employers include the following:

- Establishes best practices.

- Provides a broad, solution-based orientation, particularly of the CBK (covered later in this chapter), which practitioners find useful when faced with solving IT security issues and problems. Many times, great value is derived from knowing what questions to ask and where to locate practical, hands-on solutions to common problems, and the CBK makes that effort simple.

- Allows access to a network of global industry and subject matter/ domain experts.

- Acts as a resource for broad-based security information.

- Adds to credibility of the employee because of the rigor and regimen of the certification examinations.

- Provides a business and technology orientation to risk management.

The benefits of ISC^2 certification to professionals include the following:

- Confirms a working knowledge of information security.

- Confirms the passing of a rigorous examination.

- Differentiates career, with peer networking and added IS credibility.

- Broadens career expectations because of credentials.

Oversight and governance of the professional certification process is needed to help maintain its relevance and currency and to aid professionals in networking with other professionals for collaboration in problem solving and in job seeking. To meet that need, the ISC^2 organization was created.

International Information Systems Security Certifications Consortium

The ISC^2 is a global, not-for-profit organization dedicated to:

- Maintaining a Common Body of Knowledge for information security.

- Certifying industry professionals and practitioners according to the international IS standard.

- Administering training and certification examinations.

- Ensuring credentials are maintained, primarily through continuing education.

Governments, corporations, centers of higher learning, and other organizations worldwide demand a common platform to use in administering and mastering the dynamic nature of information security. ISC^2 helps fulfill these needs. Thousands of IS professionals in more than 60 countries worldwide have attained certification in one of the two primary designations administered by ISC^2:

- Certified Information Systems Security Professional (CISSP)

- System Security Certified Practitioner (SSCP)

Both credentials indicate that those certified have demonstrated experience in the field of information security, passed a rigorous examination (6 hours, 250 questions), subscribed to a Code of Ethics, and will maintain certification with continuing education requirements. The CISSP is intended for those who are in managerial positions or for senior personnel who have oversight for multiple areas of information security, whereas the SSCP is intended for people who specialize in areas of security operations. It's possible to attain both certificates beginning with the SSCP and then, with further exposure to other areas of InfoSec and advanced experience, gain the CISSP.

In 2004, the International Standards Organization (ISO) gave its stamp of approval to the CISSP security certification for IT professionals.

The American National Standards Institute (ANSI), the U.S. representative to the Geneva-based ISO, announced that the standards bodies are granting certificate accreditation to the CISSP credential. Roy Swift, an ANSI program director, said the CISSP is the first IT certification to be accredited under ISO/IEC 17024, the standard that is a global benchmark for workers in various professions.

> ## FYI: ISO/IEC 17024
>
> The ISO/IEC 17024:2003 *"Conformity assessment—General requirements for bodies operating certification of persons"* standard outlines the requirements for bodies operating a certification of persons program and was developed with the objective of achieving and promoting a globally accepted benchmark for organizations offering certifications programs. Certifying people is one means of providing assurance that the certified person meets the requirements of the certification scheme. Confidence in the respective certification schemes is achieved by means of a globally accepted process of assessment, subsequent surveillance, and periodic reassessments of the competence of certified persons.
>
> You can find out more about ISO/IEC 17024 at **www.iso. org/iso/en/CatalogueDetailPage.CatalogueDetail?CS NUMBER=29346&scopelist=**.

ISO's accreditation of CISSP reduces some of the uncertainty that currently exists because of competing certification programs (see **www.computerworld.com/securitytopics/security/story/0,10801,94169, 00.html**).

The Information Security Common Body of Knowledge

The CBK is a compilation and distillation of all security information collected internationally that is relevant to information security professionals. The ISC² was formed, in part, to aggregate, standardize, and maintain this information because no industry standards previously existed.

ISC² works to ensure that accomplished and experienced IS professionals with CISSP certification have a working knowledge of all 10 domains of the CBK as described on the ISC² Web site (**www.isc2.org**). Note that you will not find material in this book that covers all of the information found in the CBK. To do so would require a much more comprehensive text. Rather, you will gain a good understanding of the underlying principles for each of the 10 domains and the topics needed to make an informed decision on whether information security is right for you as a career choice, and if so, which areas of concentration you may find most appealing.

There are many books on specialized areas of InfoSec that you may wish to acquire for a more complete examination of the domains. The goal here is not to prepare you for industry certification exams but rather to provide you sufficient detail to make an informed choice for a possible career in information security.

These ten domains of the CBK are described below.

Security Management Practices

The Security Management Practices domain (covered in Chapter 15) emphasizes the importance of a comprehensive security plan that includes security policies and procedures for protecting data and how it is administered. Topics include:

- Types of security controls

- Components of a security program

- Security policies, standards, procedures, and guidelines

- Risk management and analysis

- Information classification

- Employee management issues

- Threats and corresponding administrative controls

Security Architecture and Models

The Security Architecture domain (covered in Chapter 16), one of the more technical areas of study within the CBK, discusses network layering, configuration, access control lists, and types of attacks. Specific topics cover:

- Critical components of every computer

- Processes and threads

- The OSI model

- Operating system protection mechanisms

- Ring architecture and trusted components

- Virtual machines, layering, and virtual memory

- Access control models

- *Orange Book*, ITSEC, and Common Criteria

- Certification and accreditation

- Covert channels and types of attacks

- Buffer overflows and data validation attacks

Business Continuity Planning

Business Continuity Planning (BCP), along with the Business Impact Assessment (BIA) and the Disaster Recovery Plan (DRP), is the core of this domain. Topics included in this domain are

- Roles and responsibilities

- Business impact analysis

- Development process of BCP

- Backup options and technologies

- Types of off-site facilities

- Implementation and testing of BCP

This domain is covered in Chapter 17.

Law, Investigations, and Ethics

This domain covers the different targets of computer crimes, bodies of law, and the different types of laws as they apply to computer security. Other topics included in this domain are

- Computer criminal profiles

- Types of crimes

- Liability topics

- Privacy laws and concerns

- Complications of computer crime investigation

- Types of evidence and how to collect it

- Forensics

- Legal systems

- The role of ethics in information security professionalism

This domain is covered in Chapter 18.

Physical Security

Topics covered in this domain include securing the physical site using policies and procedures coupled with the appropriate alarm and intrusion detection systems, monitoring systems, and so forth. Topics include:

- Facility location and construction issues

- Physical vulnerabilities and threats

- Doors, windows, and secure room concerns

- Hardware metrics and backup options

- Electrical power issues and solutions

- Fire detection and suppression

- Fencing, lighting, and perimeter protection

- Physical intrusion detection systems

This domain is covered in Chapter 19.

14

Operations Security

This domain covers the kind of operational procedures and tools such as firewalls, antivirus scanners, and network sniffers that may be familiar to IT specialists and users alike. Specific topics include:

- Operations department responsibilities

- Personnel and roles

- Resource protection

- Types of intrusion detection systems

- Vulnerability and penetration testing

Access Control Systems and Methodology

Who may access the system and what can they do once they are signed on? That is the focus of this CBK domain. Specific topics include:

- Identification, authentication, and authorization techniques and technologies

- Biometrics, smart cards, and multifactor authentication

- Password management

- Single sign-on technologies and their risks

- Discretionary versus mandatory access control models

- Rule-based and role-based access control

- Social engineering issues

- Specific attacks and countermeasures

Cryptography

This domain contains the stuff of espionage and spy novels. It involves encrypting data so that authorized individuals may view the sensitive data and unauthorized individuals may not. Cryptography is a highly complex topic. The InfoSec specialist needs to understand the function but not necessarily the mechanics of cryptography. Topics in the Cryptography domain include:

- Historical uses of cryptography
- Block and stream ciphers
- Explanation and uses of symmetric key algorithms
- Explanation and uses of asymmetric key algorithms
- Public key infrastructure components
- Data integrity algorithms and technologies
- IPSec, SSL, and PGP

Telecommunications, Network, and Internet Security

This domain covers another technical segment of the CBK. Topics include not just network topologies but also their weaknesses and defenses. Many of the operational tools such as firewalls are covered in this domain along with the following subject areas:

- Open system interconnect (OSI) seven-layer model
- TCP/IP suite
- LAN, MAN, and WAN topologies and technologies
- Network devices, like routers and firewalls
- Firewall types and architectures
- Dial-up and VPN protocols
- Domain Name Service (DNS)
- Wireless LANs and security issues
- Types of network attacks

Application Development Security

Application development in a networked environment focuses on sound and secure application development techniques. Topics covered in this domain include:

- Software development models

- Software development life cycle

- Object-oriented programming

- ActiveX and Java

- Database security

- Relational database components

- Types of malware

Chapter 15 through Chapter 19 are devoted to the domains listed above in a level of detail that will help you to decide if a career in InfoSec is for you.

Other Certificate Programs in the IT Security Industry

Although the CISSP and SSCP are the gold standards for IT security, many other certification programs also exist. Some of these programs are complementary to the CISSP, and others demonstrate a proficiency in specific areas within information security. A few of these programs are discussed in the following section.

Certified Information Systems Auditor

Once the exclusive domain of IT auditors, the Certified Information Systems Auditor (CISA) has become a sought-after certification for senior-level personnel and management. The subject areas of the CISA have moderate overlap with the CISSP, but it focuses more on business procedures than technology. The CISA certification is administered by the Information Systems Audit and Control Association and Foundation (ISACA) (**www.isaca.org**), founded in 1969. The CISA certification itself has been around since 1978. As of late 2002, about 28,000 individuals worldwide held the CISA certification.

Certified Information Security Manager

In 2003, ISACA deployed the Certified Information Security Manager (CISM) certification. This certification recognizes the knowledge and experience of an IT security manager. The CISM is ISACA's next-generation credential and is specifically geared toward experienced information security managers and those who have information security management responsibilities. The CISM is designed to provide executive management with assurance that those earning the designation have the required knowledge and ability to provide effective security management and consulting. It is business-oriented and focuses on information risk management while addressing management, design, and technical security issues at a conceptual level. Although its central focus is security management, all those in the IS profession with security experience may find value in CISM.

Global Information Assurance Certifications (GIAC)

The SANS Institute (**www.sans.org**) is also on the certification bandwagon with its suite of certifications under the GIAC (Global Information Assurance Certification) program. Although GIAC certifications are intended primarily for practitioners or hands-on personnel such as system administrators and network engineers, there are a few that would be appropriate for early-career managers. The GIAC Information Security Officer (GISO) is an entry-level certification that includes knowledge of threats, risks, and best practices. The GIAC Security Essentials Certification (GSEC) is an intermediate-level certification that requires basic information security knowledge for both practitioners and managers. Information on GIAC certifications can be found at **www.giac.org**.

CompTIA Security+ Certification

The CompTIA Security+ certification exam tests the security knowledge mastery of an individual with two years on-the-job networking security experience. The exam covers industry-wide topics, including communication security, infrastructure security, cryptography, access control, authentication, external attack, and operational and organization security. CompTIA Security+ is taught at colleges, universities, and commercial training centers around the globe. There are approximately 10,000 CompTIA Security+ certified professionals worldwide. The objectives of CompTIA Security+ were derived through input from industry, government, and academia, a job task analysis, a survey of more than 1,100 subject matter experts, and a beta exam with responses from subject matter experts around the world.

Vendor-Specific Certification Programs

Vendor-neutral certification programs like those described above differ in focus and objectives from vendor-specific certification programs. In the IT security industry, dozens of vendor-specific certificates are available for practitioners. A few of these programs are listed below. For a comprehensive list of what's available in the industry, visit **www.certmag.com**.

Check Point Certified Security Principles Associate An entry-level certification, the Check Point Certified Security Principles Associate (CCSPA) focuses on security fundamentals, concepts and best practices, and incorporation of network and systems security with business needs. This credential covers the information security triad, threat and vulnerability assessments, security policies, business-continuity plans, safeguards and countermeasures, security and network architecture, encryption algorithms, and access control technologies (see **www.checkpoint.com**).

Cisco Qualified Specialist Program Cisco Qualified Specialists can pursue midlevel certification across a broad array of subjects and technologies. This program includes several credentials with strong—if not exclusive—security components, including:

- Cisco Firewall Specialist

- Cisco IDS Specialist

- Cisco VPN Specialist

- Cisco Wireless LAN Design Specialist

- Cisco Wireless LAN Support Specialist

For more information, visit **www.cisco.com**.

INFOSEC (Information Systems Security) Professional In early 2003, the National Security Agency and the Committee on National Security Systems granted Cisco the authority to recognize INFOSEC professionals who are responsible for the security of key networks. Candidates must pass four exams based on Cisco products (IOS, PIX Firewall, Cisco VPN, and Cisco IDS). For more information, visit **www.cisco.com**.

Microsoft Certified Systems Engineer Security Specializations (MCSE: Security) These two credentials take the standard MCSE for Windows 2000 and Windows Server 2003 and transform elective exams into security specialization exams (and add one exam to the total count required, so that this credential requires passing eight exams instead of seven for Windows Server 2003, and seven exams instead of six for Windows Server 2000). The idea is to allow MCSEs to demonstrate their interest in and focus on Microsoft-related security topics, tools, and technologies (all Microsoft Certified Systems Administrator [MCSA] requirements also carry over to the MCSE for security specializations). For more information, visit **www.microsoft.com**.

RSA Certified Systems Engineer The RSA Certified Systems Engineer (RSA/CSE) is designed for security professionals who install and configure enterprise security solutions built around RSA SecureID, ClearTrust, and KEON PKI Core products (three separate credentials, one for each product family). Candidates must be able to design client solutions based on analysis of business needs, match implementations to client environments and infrastructures, and carry a solution from design through prototyping, pilot, and full-scale deployment phases. For more information, visit **www.rsa.com**.

Sun Certified Security Administrator for the Solaris Operating System This credential aims to identify experienced Solaris administrators with security interest and experience. It's a midrange credential that focuses on system lockdown, best security practices, a good understanding of file and system resources protection, and encryption and authentication methods. A single exam, 310-301, is required to obtain this credential. For more information, visit **www.sun.com**.

Symantec Technology Architect A single-product-focused and entry-level credential, Symantec Technology Architects must pass any one of the security solutions exams. Security solutions topics include virus protection and content filtering, intrusion detection, vulnerability management, and firewall and VPN technologies. For more information, visit **www.symantec.com**.

Tivoli Certified Consultant Tivoli is part of the IBM family of companies. Tivoli's Certified Consultant credential covers security topics: the IBM Tivoli Access Manager for Business Integration V3.8.1. Certified consultants must have a strong working knowledge of InfoSec concepts, tools, and technologies and understand how to design, deploy, manage, maintain, and troubleshoot Access Manager environments. For more information, visit **www.ibm.com**.

Windows Server 2003 Security Certified Professional This credential recognizes individuals with thorough knowledge of managing and configuring a Windows Server 2003 environment, deploying local and network security, configuring Active Directory to manage organization-wide security, administering patch management and vulnerability scans, and creating and enforcing security policies and procedures. For more information, visit **www.learningtree.com**.

FYI: Is 2005 the Year of the Security Pro?

In late 2004, ISC^2 declared 2005 as the "Year of the Information Security Professional" with the goal of recruiting new candidates to the profession and educating organizations and the public on the growing importance of certification as a measure of competence, commitment, and professionalism.

Summary

The International Information Systems Security Certification Consortium maintains the ever-evolving Common Body of Knowledge through ongoing reviews of references and best practices to ensure its relevance and effectiveness.

The information security CBK consists of 10 domains that cover all the areas of InfoSec that practitioners and managers are encouraged to know in order to excel in their careers and provide their employers with industry best practices that have proved successful.

The benefits of certification and immersion into the CBK are clear to both employers and professionals who commit to life-long learning and to the betterment of themselves and their careers. The role of the security professional is expanding, fueled by growing demands from the IT industry and national governments that are experiencing a growing threat to computing systems and operations.

14

Test Your Skills

MULTIPLE CHOICE QUESTIONS

1. ISC^2 was formed for which of the following purposes?

   A. maintaining a Common Body of Knowledge for information security

   B. certifying industry professionals and practitioners in an international IS standard

   C. ensuring credentials are maintained, primarily through continuing education

   D. all of the above

2. The information security Common Body of Knowledge is

   A. a compilation and distillation of all security information collected internationally of relevance to information security professionals

   B. a volume of books published by ISC^2

   C. a reference list of books and other publications put together by practitioners in information security

   D. an encyclopedia of information security principles, best practices, and regulations

3. The CBK contains:
   A. 5 domains
   B. 10 domains
   C. 7 domains
   D. 3 domains

4. The Security Management Practices domain includes:
   A. identification of security products
   B. documented policies, standards, procedures, and guidelines
   C. managiement of risk to corporate assets
   D. B and C only

5. The Security Architecture and Models domain includes:
   A. concepts and principles for secure operations
   B. concepts and principles for secure programs
   C. concepts and principles for secure designs of computing resources
   D. concepts and principles for secure application development

6. The Access Control Systems and Methodology domain includes:
   A. a collection of mechanisms to create secure architectures for asset protection
   B. instructions on how to install perimeter door security
   C. a methodology for applications development
   D. a methodology for secure data center operations

7. The Application Development Security domain includes:
   A. an outline for the software development environment to address security concerns
   B. a recipe book for developers to follow in building secure application software
   C. a language guide on programming security functions
   D. quality assurance testing of custom-developed software

8. The Operations Security domain includes:
   A. mechanisms for secure access to a data center
   B. identification of controls over hardware, media, and personnel
   C. help-desk support for security incidents
   D. evidence collection and preservation for computer crimes

9. The Physical Security domain includes:

   A. a code of conduct for employees

   B. perimeter security controls and protection mechanisms

   C. data center controls and specifications for physically secure operations

   D. B and C

10. The Cryptography domain includes:

    A. principles, means, and methods to disguise information to assure confidentiality, integrity, and authenticity

    B. tools and techniques to intercept competitive secrets

    C. procedures on how to protect Internet communications

    D. procedures on how to discover cryptographic keys

11. The Telecommunications, Network, and Internet Security domain includes:

    A. technology, principles, and best practices to secure telephone networks

    B. technology, principles, and best practices to secure corporate networks

    C. technology, principles, and best practices to secure Internet-attached networks

    D. all of the above

12. The Business Continuity domain includes:

    A. plans for recovering business operations in the event of loss of access by personnel

    B. management practices to determine business risks

    C. documented plans for interacting with law enforcement

    D. maintenance of current versions of all software in use by the organization

13. The Law, Investigations, and Ethics domain includes:

    A. teams of lawyers to determine the legality of security decisions

    B. private law-enforcement personnel

    C. methods to investigate computer crime incidents

    D. a council to determine the ethical behavior of security personnel

14

14. People more interested in certifying themselves as security experts in a business context should consider preparing for which certification?

    A. GIAC

    B. CISA

    C. CompTIA Security+

    D. SSCP

15. People more interested in certifying themselves as security technical practitioners should consider preparing for which certification(s)?

    A. CISM and GIAC

    B. GIAC and CompTIA Security+

    C. CISSP and CISM

    D. SSCP and CISA

16. The growth in the security profession is driven by:

    A. new technology

    B. growth of the Internet

    C. demands by industry and government for scarce resources

    D. overseas hackers

EXERCISES

Exercise 14.1: Benefits Gained Through Industry Certification

1. Think about how certification benefits employees and employers in job-seeking efforts. (Refer to advantages listed in this chapter if necessary.)

2. Name three advantages certified professionals have over noncertified professionals when applying for a job.

3. Explain how an employer could use information about certifications to evaluate potential employees.

Exercise 14.2: Preparing for Certification Tests

1. Search your favorite online bookstore for books in print that help prepare professionals to sit for the CISSP and CISM certificates.

2. Aside from the organization of the books, what can you find in common among them?

3. Do you believe that drills from exam test banks is a good method for the beginner to prepare for certifications? Why or why not?

Exercise 14.3: Hot Topics in Information Security

1. Off the top of your head, list some of the current topics and issues in information security that you think concern IT and business managers.

2 Visit the Search Security Web site (**www.searchsecurity.com**) to see how your list maps to hot topics found on the Web site.

3. As a practitioner, how would you respond to these concerns when company management looks to you for information and recommendations?

Exercise 14.4: Growth in Internal Security Departments

1. Describe the composition and size of the security department at your place of employment or at your school. You may need to talk to the IT professionals within your organization to develop this description as well as to address the following steps.

2. Explain whether the department has grown in size during the past few years. If it has grown, by how much and for what reasons? (Has the organization grown? Or is there more work for the security professionals to do?)

3. Explain whether the managers feel that it has been difficult to recruit qualified employees. What sort of experience or certifications do the managers look for in potential employees?

Exercise 14.5: BS7799 and CBK Domains

1. Research the British Standard 7799 Part One (**www.bsi-global.com/ Education/Information_Security/explained.xalter**).

2. Determine how its organization is similar to the CBK. List the similarities.

3. List the area(s) that are different and how they are different.

14

PROJECTS

Project 14.1: Comparing Certificate Programs

1. Consider security industry certification like the SSCP and CISSP versus security vendor certifications like those from Cisco Systems (**www.cisco.com**) and Symantec Corporation (**www.symantec.com**). Why do you think someone might pursue vendor certification rather than industry certification?

2. Are there any situations in which it would be beneficial to have both? If so, describe the situations in which having both would be beneficial.

3. What certifications would make good combinations for certain domain areas?

4. Which certificates do you think would be more valuable to hiring managers?

5. Which certificates do you think employers are demanding for security personnel?

Project 14.2: Supplemental ISC^2 Certifications

In addition to the CISSP and SSCP, ISC^2 offers specialty concentration certifications for management (ISSMP), security architecture (ISSAP), and one specific for the United States National Security Agency (NSA): the ISSEP.

1. Research these concentrations at the ISC^2 Web site (**www.isc2.org**).

2. Try to determine why professionals might want to attain one or more of them beyond the CISSP credential.

3. Do you see additional personal value beyond the CISSP for these certificates? If so, list the values you see.

4. Explain why employers might seek personnel who hold these certificates.

5. Why would the NSA require a concentration specific only to their organization?

Project 14.3: Information Privacy and Information Security

Information privacy and information security are two sides of the same coin. You can't have privacy without security.

1. Using an Internet search engine, distinguish between those issues related to privacy versus those related to security.

2. What overlapping issues do you find?

3. Why are U.S. lawmakers seemingly more concerned with privacy controls and protections than requiring U.S. companies to maintain effective IT security programs?

4. What are some of the controls being mandated through legislation?

5. Do you believe these controls are (will be) effective?

14

▶▶ Case **Study**

Sue and Barbara both have an equivalent of eight years of IT security consulting experience in the banking industry. Barbara has earned her CISSP and has held it for five years. Sue decided not to pursue the certificate because she could not find the time, and she has focused her efforts solely on internal company issues. A headhunter in IT security has recently contacted both of them for an opportunity that has recently come along, and both have decided to interview for the position.

Which candidate do you think will be more appealing to the hiring manager? What is it about professional certification that makes the difference among employers?

Some of the resources you may find helpful to research in finding the answers include:

- *Infoworld* Magazine Online (**http://iwsun4.infoworld.com/**).

- *Internet Week* Magazine Online (**www.internetweek.com**).

- *Windows IT Pro* Magazine Online (**www.win2000mag.com/**).

- *Tech Republic* Magazine Online (**http://techrepublic.com/**).

Chapter | 15

Security Management

Chapter Objectives

After reading this chapter and completing the exercises, you will be able to do the following:

- Choose the appropriate type of policies to document a security programme.
- Distinguish between the roles of standards, regulations, baselines, procedures, and guidelines.
- Organize a typical standards and policies library.
- Classify assets according to standard principles.
- Incorporate the separation of duties principle when creating a security policy.
- Outline the minimum preemployment hiring practices for organizations.
- Analyze and manage risk.
- Outline the elements of employee security education, awareness, and training.
- List the eight types of people responsible for security in an information technology (IT) setting.

Introduction

This chapter describes the first domain of the Certified Information Systems Security Professional (CISSP) Common Body of Knowledge (CBK): Security Management Practices. This domain appears first because it establishes the framework and foundation for all the other domains to build upon.

Security management is a broad set of executive support and management activities that define an IT security programme. (*Note:* This spelling is used to distinguish a management programme from a computer program.)

A ***programme***, unlike a project, is an ongoing management activity that is constantly funded and intended for the preservation and advancement of the organization.

Like any programme, an IT security programme begins with statements of management's intent. These goals are translated into security ***policies*** (statements of management intent) and then used to drive the details of how the programme will run, who will be responsible for day-to-day work, how training and awareness will be conducted, and how compliance to policies will be handled.

Other areas addressed within the Security Management Practices domain are activities related to information classification, risk management concepts and techniques, and security roles and responsibilities to assure ongoing organizational security consciousness.

Security Policies Set the Stage for Success

Policies are the most crucial element in a corporate information security infrastructure and must be considered long before security technology is acquired and deployed. Security industry expert Marcus Ranum explains, ". . . If you haven't got a security policy, you haven't got a firewall. Instead, you've got a thing that's sort of doing something, but you don't know what it's trying to do because no one has told you what it should do" (Ranum 2003). Implementing security technology with no predetermined rules about what it *should* do results in accidental protection at best—even a broken clock is right twice a day!

Effective policies can rectify many of the weaknesses from failures to understand the business direction and security mission and can help to prevent or eliminate many of the faults and errors caused by a lack of security guidance.

An organization faces many technology and strategic choices when deciding how to protect its computer assets. Some choices are made based on trade-offs, but others involve conflicting trade-offs, questions about an organization's strategic direction, and other factors that don't easily lend themselves to quantitative analysis. Technology providers are at times overly anxious to push product out the door that unwitting managers may choose to buy without determining what problem(s) it might solve. Once established, policies become the basis for protecting both information and technology resources and for guiding employee behavior but are not sufficient on their own. Familiarity with these types of policies is required to aid people within a company in addressing computer security issues that are important to the organization as a whole. Effective policies ultimately result in the development and implementation of better computer security and better protection of systems and information.

Policies may be published on paper or electronically via a corporate intranet. Tools used to automate the mechanics of policy creation, management, maintenance, and dissemination are commercially available. (For more information about these tools, visit Archer Technologies at **www.archer-tech.com** and NetIQ for the Vigilent Policy Center at **www.netiq.com**).

Figure 15.1 illustrates a typical structure of a corporate policy and standards library.

An effective policy contains the following information:

- Title

- Purpose

- Authorizing individual

- Author/sponsor

- Reference to other policies

- Scope

- Measurement expectations

- Exception process

- Accountability

- Compliance management and measurements description

- Effective/expiration dates

- Definitions

This structure is a best practice within the industry for comprehensive coverage of the topics found in security policies. As people gain experience and exposure to policies, a common structure helps them to quickly locate the information they seek.

Four Types of Policies

According to the National Institute of Standards and Technology (NIST) Computer Systems Laboratory (CSL)—a division of the U.S. Department of Commerce—there are four types of computer security policies. Policies and the follow-up documents in the library start out at a very high level of understanding and become more specific (granular) at the lower levels.

- *Programme-level policy* is used for creating a management-sponsored computer security program. A programme-level policy, at the highest level, might prescribe the need for information security and may delegate the creation and management of the program to a role within the IT department. Think of this as the mission statement for the IT security program.

15

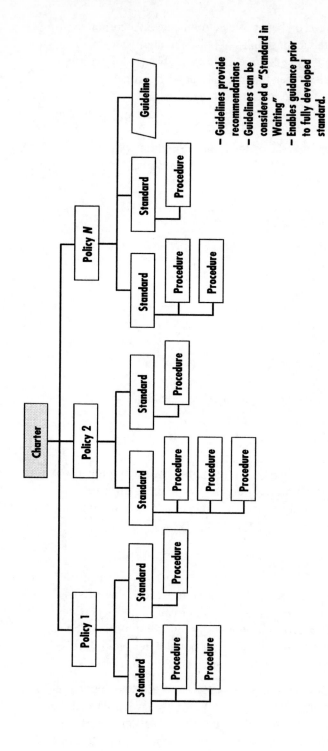

FIGURE 15.1 A typical policies and standards library structure.

- *Programme-framework policy* establishes the overall approach to computer security (i.e., a computer security framework). A framework policy adds detail to the program by describing the elements and organization of the program and department that will carry out the security mission.

- *Issue-specific policy* addresses specific issues of concern to the organization.

- *System-specific policy* focuses on policy issues that management has decided for a specific system.

A complete IT security policy and standards library taxonomy may be found in Appendix E. Specific types of policy and standards examples may also be found in Appendix F at the back of this book.

Each policy type is described in greater detail in the following sections.

Programme-Level Policies

Management needs programme-level policy to help establish a security programme, assign programme management responsibilities, state an organization-wide computer security purpose and objectives, and establish a basis for policy compliance.

The head of the organization or other senior officials, such as the organization's top management officers, typically will issue programme-level policy. Programme-level policy, sometimes called an information security charter, establishes the computer security program and its basic framework. This high-level policy defines the purpose of the programme and its scope within the organization, assigns responsibilities for direct programme implementation (to the computer security organization) as well as responsibilities to related offices, and addresses compliance issues.

The components of programme-level policy are

- **Purpose** clearly states the purpose of the programme. This includes defining the goals of the computer security programme as well as its management structure. Security-related needs, such as integrity, availability, and confidentiality, can form the basis of organizational goals established in policy. For instance, in an organization responsible for maintaining large mission-critical databases, reduction in errors, data loss, or data corruption might be specifically stressed. In an organization responsible for maintaining confidential personal data (as in most e-commerce systems), the goals might emphasize stronger protection against unauthorized disclosure. A programme management structure should be organized to best address the goals of the programme and respond to the particular operating and risk environment of the organization. Important issues for the structure of the central computer security programme include management and coordination of security-related resources, interaction with diverse communities, and the ability to relay issues of concern to upper management. The policy could also establish operational security offices for major systems, particularly those at high risk or most critical to organizational operations.

■ **Scope** specifies which resources (including facilities, hardware, and software), information, and personnel the programme covers. Often, the programme will cover all systems and agency personnel, but this is not always the case. In some instances, a policy may name specific assets, such as major sites and large systems. Sometimes, tough management decisions arise when defining the scope of a program, such as determining the extent to which the programme applies to contractors and outside organizations using or connected to the organization's systems. Scope should also consider home-based employers (telecommuters) and mobile employees who access company resources from remote locations.

■ **Responsibilities** addresses the responsibilities of officials and offices throughout the organization, including the role of line managers, applications owners, users, and the information processing or IT organization. The policy statement distinguishes between the responsibilities of computer services providers and the managers of applications using the computer services. It can also establish the basis for employee accountability. Overall, the programme-level assignment of responsibilities covers those activities and personnel who will be vital to the implementation and continuity of the computer security policy.

■ **Compliance** authorizes and delineates the use of specified penalties and disciplinary actions for individuals who fail to comply with the organization's computer security policies. Because the security policy is a high-level document, penalties for various infractions are normally not detailed therein. However, the policy may authorize the creation of compliance structures that include violations and specific penalties. Infractions and associated penalties are usually defined in issue-specific and system-specific policies.

When establishing compliance structures, an organization must consider that employee violations of policy can be unintentional. For example, nonconformance can be due to a lack of knowledge or training. Each policy and standard should contain a section on compliance management and metrics to help management educate employees on their responsibilities and provide a measurement tool to help determine the document's effectiveness. The Web-based policy and standards management systems (mentioned above), offer facilities to "push" a new or revised standard or policy to the audience that needs to be aware of changes, and then provide awareness training (if needed), quizzes to gauge user understanding of the changes, and a mechanism to record a user's decision to comply with the new standard or request intervention from the security department.

Programme-Framework Policies

Programme-framework policies provide an organization-wide direction for broad areas of programme implementation. These policies may be issued to assure that everyone complies with acceptable use rules (e-mail, Internet, and so on) or that they address disaster planning and risk analysis issues correctly. Managers or departments with sufficient authority to direct all organization components on computer security issues create programme-framework policies. This may be the organization's management official or the head of the computer security programme (e.g., chief information officer or more commonly chief information security office).

Programme-framework policies define the organization's security programme elements that form the foundation for the computer security programme. The programme-framework policy reflects information technology management's decisions about priorities for protection, resource allocation, and assignment of responsibilities.

The areas addressed by programme-framework policy vary within each organization, as does the way in which the policy is expressed. Some organizations issue policy directives, whereas others issue handbooks that combine policy, regulations, standards, and guidance.

Many organizations issue policy on "key" areas of computer security, such as life-cycle management, contingency planning, and network security. If the policy and associated standards and guidance are too rigid, cost-effective implementations and innovation could be negatively affected. For an example of programme-framework policy, consider a typical organization policy on contingency planning. An organization may require that all contingency plans categorize the criticality of computer programs and IT processes according to a standard scale. This will assist the organization in preparing a master plan (in the event the physical plant is destroyed) by supporting prioritization across departmental boundaries. Programme-framework policies may be composed of components similar to those contained in programme-level policy but may be in different formats (organizational handbooks, and so forth) Examples of possible programme-framework policies include

- Business continuity planning (BCP) framework (see Chapter 17).

- Physical security requirements framework for data centers (see Chapter 18).

- Application development security framework.

Issue-Specific Policies

Issue-specific and system-specific policies identify and define specific areas of concern and state an organization's position or posture on the issue. Depending on the issue and its controversy—as well as potential impact—issue-specific policy may come from the head of the organization, the top management official, the chief information officer (CIO), or the computer security programme manager (e.g., CISO).

System-specific policy is normally issued by the manager or owner of the system (which could be a network or application) but may originate from a high-level executive or official. This is especially true if all affected departments don't agree with the policy and may be tempted to create conflicting policies addressing their own needs to the detriment of the overall organization.

IN PRACTICE: An Issue-Specific Policy Scenario

Trying to stay on top of ever-evolving technology and the security risks posed by these technologies is one of the most challenging aspects of being an IT security professional. For example, hand-held PDAs and laptop computers have become ubiquitous in private medical offices, clinics, hospitals, and even blood banks because of the convenience and ease of wireless local area networks (WLANs). They allow physicians and nurses to access patient records remotely, add observations and diagnoses, and check on medications—among other things. This increased access poses new and difficult security questions:

- How can office managers be sure that no unauthorized computers can eavesdrop on the wireless communications?

- How can patients be sure that the doctor's convenience is not at the price of patient record privacy?

Covered health care entities need to consider whether they should postpone deploying an initial WLAN until planned improvements in wireless network security standards are adopted and have been implemented in commercial products. Those who are charged with maintaining the security of health care information systems carry a heavy burden. As technology changes constantly, covered entity managers and their lawyers are required to regularly evaluate the impact of those changes on the security of their networks. (*Source:* **www.dwt.com/practc/hc_ecom/bulletins/05-03_BNAarticle.htm.**)

System-specific policies

- State security objectives of a specific system.

- Define how the system should be operated to achieve the security objectives.

- Specify how the protections and features of the technology will be used to support or enforce the security objectives.

Issue-specific policies focus on areas of current relevance and concern to an organization. Although programme-level policy is usually broad enough that it requires little modification over time, issue-specific policies require more frequent revision due to changes in technology and related factors. As new technologies are developed, some issues diminish in importance, and new ones continually appear. It may be appropriate, for example, to issue a policy on the proper use of a cutting-edge technology (like Wi-Fi networks)—the security vulnerabilities of which are still largely unknown.

A useful structure for issue-specific policy is to break the policy into its basic components:

- **Issue statement** defines a security issue, along with any relevant terms, distinctions, and conditions. For example, an organization might want to develop an issue-specific policy on the use of "Internet access," which may define what Internet activities it will permit and those it won't permit. Additionally, other distinctions and conditions may need inclusion, for instance, Internet access that's gained using a personal dial-up or broadband ISP connection from an employee's desktop PC that makes the internal network vulnerable to interlopers when the connection is alive.

- **Statement of the organization's position** clearly states an organization's position on the issue. Continuing with the example of Internet access, the policy should state what types of sites are prohibited in all or some cases (e.g., porn sites or brokerage sites), whether or not there are further guidelines for approval and use, or whether case-by-case exceptions will be granted, by whom, and on what basis.

- **Applicability** clearly states where, how, when, to whom, and to what a particular policy applies. For example, the hypothetical policy on Internet access may apply only to the organization's own on-site resources and employees and not to contractor organizations with offices at other locations. Additionally, the policy's applicability to employees traveling among different sites or working at home who will require Internet access from multiple sites might require further clarification.

- **Roles and responsibilities** assigns roles and responsibilities to the issue. Continuing with the Internet example above, if the policy permits private ISP access given the appropriate approvals, then the approving authority should be identified. The office or department(s) responsible for compliance should also be named.

■ **Compliance** gives descriptions of the infractions and states the corresponding penalties. Penalties must be consistent with organizational personnel policies and practices and need to be coordinated with appropriate officials, offices, and, perhaps, employee bargaining units.

■ **Points of contact and supplementary information** lists the names of the appropriate individuals to contact for further information and lists any applicable standards or guidelines. For some issues, the point of contact might be a line manager; for other issues it might be a facility manager, technical support person, or system administrator. For yet other issues, the point-of-contact might be a security programme representative. Using the Internet access example, employees need to know whether the point of contact for questions and procedural information would be the immediate superior, a system administrator, or a computer security official. Examples of an issue-specific policy include:

  ■ E-mail acceptable use

  ■ Internet acceptable use

  ■ Laptop security policy

System-Specific Policies

Programme-level policies and issue-specific policies both address policies from a broad level, usually involving the entire organization. System-specific policies, on the other hand, are much more focused, as they address only one system. Many security policy decisions apply only at the system level. Examples include

■ Who is allowed to read or modify data in the system?

■ Under what conditions can data be read or modified?

■ Are users allowed to dial into the computer system from home or while on travel?

Development and Management of Security Policies

To develop a comprehensive set of system security policies, a management process is required that derives security rules from security goals such as a three-level model for system security policy:

■ Security objectives

- Operational security
- Policy implementation

Security Objectives

The first step is to define the security objectives. This step must extend beyond analyzing the need for integrity, availability, and confidentiality. Security objectives must be more specific and concrete. They should be clearly stated in order to achieve the objective. The security objectives should consist of a series of statements to describe meaningful actions about specific resources. These objectives should be based on system functionality or mission requirements but should also state the security actions to support the requirements.

Operational Security

The next section is concerned with the operational policies that list the rules for operating a system. Using data integrity as an example, the operational policy would define authorized and unauthorized modification: who, (by job category, by organization placement, or by name) can do what (modify, delete, and so forth) to which data (specific fields or records) and under what conditions. Managers need to make decisions in developing this policy, as it is unlikely that all security objectives will be fully met. Cost, operational, technical, and other constraints will intervene.

Also worth consideration is the degree of formality needed in documenting the policy. Once again, the more formal the documentation, the easier it will be to enforce and follow policy. Formal policy is published as a distinct policy document; less formal policy may be written in memos. Informal policy may not be written at all. As would be expected, unwritten policy is extremely difficult to follow or enforce. On the other hand, very granular and formal policy at the system level can also be an administrative burden. In general, good practice suggests a granular formal statement of the access privileges for a system due to its complexity and importance. Documenting access control policy makes it substantially easier to follow and to enforce.

Another area that normally requires a granular and formal statement is the assignment of security responsibilities. Some less formal policy decisions may be recorded in other types of computer security documents such as risk analyses, accreditation statements, or procedural manuals. However, any controversial or uncommon policies may need formal policy statements. Uncommon policies include any areas where the system policy is different from organization policy or from normal practice within the organization—being either more or less stringent. Uncommon policies should also contain a statement explaining the reason for deviating from the organization's standard policy.

An example of the need for an uncommon policy or standard is where a specialty-computer system may be unable to meet the organization's overall policy on password lengths. Suppose this oddball system allows only five-character passwords using only letters of the alphabet, but the organizational policy on passwords dictates that passwords be eight or more characters in length and must contain at least one number. In this case, a standard that requires additional controls over this system to mitigate the risk of the inability to comply with the organizational policy may be developed.

Policy Implementation

Finally, the organization must determine the role technology plays in enforcing or supporting the policy. Security is normally enforced through a combination of technical and traditional management methods. This is especially true in the areas of Internet security where security devices protect the perimeter of the company's information management systems. Although technical means are likely to include the use of access control technology, there are other automated means of enforcing or supporting security policy.

For example, technology can be used to block telephone systems users from calling certain numbers. Intrusion detection software can alert system administrators to suspicious activity or take action to stop the activity. Personal computers can be configured to prevent booting from a floppy disk. Automated security enforcement has both advantages and disadvantages. A computer system, properly designed, programmed, and installed, consistently enforces policy, although users can't be forced to follow all procedures. In addition, deviations from the policy may sometimes be necessary and appropriate. This situation occurs frequently if the security policy is too rigid.

Policy Support Documents

Although policies are defined as statements of management's intent, the embodiment of policies and details on how to comply with them show up in other documents that are derived from policy statements. These documents provide levels of detail supporting the policy and explaining the system development, management, and operational requirements. Procedures then provide a recipe for the execution of steps that are intended to comply with a policy directive. These supporting documents include

- **Regulations:** laws passed by regulators and lawmakers.

- **Standards and baselines:** topic-specific (standards) and system-specific (baselines) documents that describe overall requirements for security.

- **Guidelines:** documentation that aids in compliance with standard considerations, hints, tips, and best practices in implementation.

- **Procedures:** step-by-step instructions on how to perform a specific security activity (configure a firewall, install an operating system, and others).

Regulations

Often, the standards related to information security (InfoSec) are dictated by the nature of an organization's business. The Federal Trade Commission (FTC) and Department of Commerce govern U.S. retail operators, among others. Federal banking standards regulate U.S. banks (FFIEC), U.S. medical device manufacturers or suppliers fall under Federal Drug Administration (FDA) regulations, and so forth. By selecting the most robust or strictest sets of published standards governing a particular business, an organization is most likely to meet the requirements outlined by any applicable less-stringent standards.

In 2004, the Sarbanes–Oxley Corporate Responsibility and Accountability Act—passed by the U.S. Senate in the wake of the collapse of Enron, Arthur Anderson, Worldcom, and several other large firms—gained the attention of all U.S. corporate CEOs. The act requires internal controls in order to foster regulator confidence in the integrity of financial statements to the Securities and Exchange Commission (SEC) and shareholders. It also requires that CEOs attest to the integrity of financial statements to the SEC.

Because of this mandate, controls related to information processing and management have been placed under a magnifying glass. As the effective date of the regulation draws closer, the need for a comprehensive library of current operating documents is underscored.

Many of the regulations on the books are drawn from existing and evolving sources of information security industry standards and best practices. Policies and standards are always changing as best practices are learned, documented, and shared with others in the same industry.

15

IN PRACTICE: HIPAA Privacy

The Health Insurance Portability and Accountability Act of 1996 (HIPAA) includes a section titled "Medical Privacy Rule," which specifies new privacy protections for patients and lays out the privacy obligations for employers and health care providers. Because of the privacy rule, health care providers and health plan providers can no longer release protected health information to patients' employers unless certain conditions are met. Human resources

CONTINUED ON NEXT PAGE

departments in all companies that offer employee health-care coverage must now look at HIPAA as it relates to workers compensation, drug testing, physical exams, Family Medical Leave Act (FMLA), maternity leaves, sick days, and health care plan communications.

Suddenly, developers of HR systems are no longer immune from privacy and security controls, and retrofitting existing (legacy) systems is not only costly but also detracts from new development work and adds new risks of security controls that may not be well implemented. Demands on security specialists are increased, too, as companies are forced to bring these old systems into compliance.

IT security policies and standards have been around for many years, and many are already available as **de facto** (accepted practices in the industry) and **dejure** (official standards passed by international and industry standards committees). One such standard that is regularly used in IT security is ISO/IEC 17799—Code of Practice for Information Security Management. ISO/IEC 17799 is based on British Standard (BS) 7777 Part I. It defines a series of domains or subject areas—similar to the CISSP CBK—that management is expected to address and is more suggestive in nature (e.g., management *should* address the area of preemployment background checks). On the other hand, British Standard 7799 Part II is the actual standard that prescribes activities that management must address in order to be compliant to the standard. It refers to dictates, such as management SHALL put into place preemployment background checks, and may be used as an assessment tool to verify compliance.

Although ISO/IEC 17799 and BS 7799 are widely used throughout the industry, other documents prepared by international and industry bodies are available for the asking. The National Institute of Standards and Technology, formerly the National Bureau of Standards, has a complete library of documents that serve as the basis for IT security within U.S. federal agencies and the Federal Information Processing Standards (FIPS).

The Control Objectives for Information and Related Technology (COBIT) is another widely accepted set of documents that is commonly found as the basis for an information security programme throughout the world. COBIT is an initiative from the Information Systems Audit and Control Association (ISACA) and is preferred among IT auditors.

The U.S. National Security Telecommunications and Information Systems Security Committee (NSTISSC) Standard 4011, otherwise known as National Training Standard for Information Systems Security Professionals, establishes the minimum training standard for the training of information systems security professionals in the disciplines of telecommunications and automated information systems security. The body of knowledge listed in the standard may be obtained from a variety of sources (e.g., the National Cryptologic School, contractors, adaptations of existing department/agency training programs) or a combination of experience and formal training. The instruction is applicable to all departments and agencies of the U.S. government, their employees, and contractors who are responsible for the security oversight or management of national security systems during each phase of the life cycle. For more on NSTISSC Number 4011, see **www.cnss.gov/As sets/pdf/nstissi_4011.pdf**.

Standards and Baselines

There's an old saw within the IT industry about standards being great because there are so many to choose from. But the point is that there's little need to reinvent your own standards when you can simply reuse what people have found to be best practices.

15

FYI: Security Experts Are Never Alone

You cannot invent best practices—you simply adopt them from others and thank those who have documented them for making mistakes that you can avoid. This is a primary reason for being fully involved in the IT security industry when you're a practitioner. It's folly to operate in a corporate vacuum, especially when others who share your concerns and problems have already traversed the trails that led them to improved processes and technologies. Security is not an area where competition is admired. Companies are better served by not competing on security when interdependence is present. For example, a bank offering better security on credit card payments is not helping the industry as a whole if it uses security as a market differentiator. If any bank suffers a breach in security, the entire banking industry is adversely affected.

Below the layer of policies, you'll find a more populated layer of standards and baselines (refer to Figure 15.1). Often, you'll see the terms *standards* and *baselines* interchanged. A *standard* refers to specific security requirements, or what is needed for a system or process to be considered secure. An example is a password standard that covers the requirements for password creation, distribution, use, changing, and revocation in support of the policy that mandates appropriate access controls and accountability measures. A *baseline* is a specific set of requirements for a technology implementation, such as Windows 2003 Server security settings or Oracle DBMS protection mechanisms.

Baselines and standards are the enforceable element in the security programme. Compliance with standards and baselines is what the auditors check, and exceptions are filed against a baseline or a standard. If a standard cannot be met because of time or budget constraints to implementing a control, an exceptions or variance process is usually present to accommodate the messy reality of software development and implementation. Exceptions should be temporary and include a plan for meeting compliance to the standard. In any event, the risks of failing to comply with a standard must be understood, and compensating controls to contain these risks should be implemented.

Guidelines

Guidelines, guidance documents, or advisories provide the people who need to implement a standard or baseline more detailed information and guidance (hints, tips, processes, advice, and so forth) to aid in compliance. These documents are optional in a library but are often helpful.

Procedures

Procedures are the detailed, step-by-step activities that are followed to implement a process or configure a system for compliance to a guideline. They may also be step-by-step security processes that assure repeatability and accountability of personnel performing the procedure.

Suggested Standards Taxonomy

Standards are formal written documents that describe several security concepts that are fundamental to all successful programmes. The highest level includes

- Asset and data classification
- Separation of duties
- Pre-employment hiring practices
- Risk analysis and management
- Education, awareness, and training

For a complete taxonomy of standards that would be expected in a comprehensive library, see Appendix E.

Asset Classification

Asset and data classification is needed by businesses and agencies to help determine how much security is needed for appropriate protection. A rule of thumb states that one should never spend more on security than the value of the asset being protected. Sometimes determining value is straightforward, but other times—for example, when trying to place a value on a brand icon—it is not so clear. That's where classification helps.

Some of the obvious benefits to a classification system are

- Data confidentiality, integrity, and availability are improved because appropriate controls are used throughout the enterprise.

- Protection mechanisms are maximized.

- A process exists to review the values of company business data.

- Decision quality is increased because the quality of the data upon which the decision is being made has been improved.

In the military, a strict classification system exists to protect national secrets and information. This classification system is covered in-depth in Chapter 16, but a common taxonomy for commercial businesses may provide for the following classes:

- **Public information:** information intended for public dissemination. This may include marketing content on a Web site, direct mail inserts, directories of contact information, published annual reports, and so forth.

- **Business sensitive or business confidential:** information needed by employees and other insiders to perform their duties. This may include company directories (address books, e-mail addresses, and so forth), invoice information, department budget information, internal policies, and so forth.

- **Customer confidential:** information that identifies individual customers of the business or institution and may include their purchase activity, account-specific information, credit card numbers, social security numbers (when needed), grades or course information in the case of a university, or any other information considered personally identifiable information (PII) that dictates *need to know* or least privilege controls to assure confidentiality and integrity.

- **Trade secret:** information in this classification is severely restricted and protected through more strict need to know controls than customer confidential information. Some examples of trade secret information may include the recipe for Coca-Cola, employee disciplinary actions, prereleased financial statement information, or proprietary secrets that offer a competitive advantage to the business.

Separation of Duties

Separating duties within a business or organization helps limit any individual's ability to cause harm or perpetrate theft. For an illegal act to succeed, two or more employees would be forced to conspire. This concept is similar to accounting controls, where it's imprudent, for example, for a person approving an invoice to also be responsible for preparing a vendor payment.

FYI: U.S. Regulations Covering PII

Many of the newly enacted regulations by the U.S. Congress are aimed at protecting PII. Two notable regulations are the Gramm–Leach–Bliley Act (GLBA) for banking, insurance, and finance, and the Health Insurance Portability and Accountability Act (HIPAA) for health care providers, pharmacies, and health care insurance providers. HIPAA caused a flurry of activity throughout 2002 to 2004. In order to comply with the act, health care providers required all patients to sign a release form that authorized them to share personal health-related information for purposes of treatment. You may remember signing these forms each time you used a health care service (dentists, doctors, pharmacy visits, and so forth).

You may also remember a mass mailing in 2003 by your credit card issuers of privacy statements that detailed your rights as a user of a credit product. This activity was in response to the enforcement date of GLBA, which took effect in late 2003.

No single person should be responsible for completing a task involving sensitive, valuable, or critical information from beginning to end. Likewise, a person must not be responsible for approving his own work. Following are some suggestions for separating critical activities:

- Separate development, testing, and production environments and different personnel to manage and operate these environments.

- Separate security management and audit mechanisms and personnel.

- Separate accounts payable and accounts receivable processing and personnel.

- Separate controls over encryption key generation or changing of keys.

- Separate encryption keys into two (or more) components, each of which does not reveal the contents to the two (or more) key signing officers.

Preemployment Hiring Practices

Policies, standards, and procedures issued by human resources should address internal information security processes and functions. These documents should address preemployment screening and background checks, how to handle employee termination, creating and revoking employee accounts, forwarding e-mail and voice mail after departure, lock keys and safe combination changes, system password changes, and collecting company property upon departure (badges, credit cards, and so forth).

Employee Screening Companies hiring people into areas of responsibility (especially security personnel!) should have policies and practices in place to perform background checks or to get a new employee cleared by the government with security clearances when acting as a contractor for the government. Preemployment background checks should refer to public records because they often provide critical information needed to make the best hiring decision. Conducting these and other simple checks verifies the information provided on the application is current and true and gives the employer an immediate measurement of an applicant's integrity.

Other items that can easily be checked include

- Credit report
- SSN searches
- Worker's compensation reports
- Criminal records
- Motor vehicle report
- Education verification and credential confirmation
- Reference checks
- Previous employer verification

Military Security Clearance One of the most meticulous background checks is the U.S. Department of Defense (DOD) security clearance. The steps are contained in the 30-page Defense Industrial Personnel Security Clearance Review. A defense security clearance is generally only requested for individuals in the following categories whose employment involves access to sensitive government assets:

- Members of the military.
- Civilian employees working for the Department of Defense or other government agencies.
- Employees of government contractors.

A DOD review, known as the ***personnel security investigation***, can take a year or longer and includes these activities:

- Search of investigative files and other records held by federal agencies, including the FBI and, if appropriate, international checks.
- Financial check.

- Field interviews of references (in writing, by telephone, or in person), to include coworkers, employers, personal friends, educators, neighbors, and other individuals.

- A personal interview with the applicant conducted by an investigator.

Risk Analysis and Management

Security in any system should be in proportion to the risk under which it operates. The process to determine which security controls are appropriate and cost effective is quite often a complex and sometimes a subjective matter. One of the prime functions of security risk analysis is to put this process onto a more objective basis.

There are two basic types of risk analysis: quantitative and qualitative.

Quantitative Risk Analysis Quantitative, or a quasisubjective, risk analysis attempts to establish and maintain an independent set of risk metrics and statistics. Some of the calculations used for quantitative risk analysis include

- **Annualized loss expectancy (ALE):** single loss expectancy multiplied by annualized rate of occurrence.

- **Probability:** chance or likelihood, in a finite sample, that an event will occur or that a specific loss value may be attained should the event occur.

- **Threat:** an event, the occurrence of which could have an undesired impact.

- **Control:** risk-reducing measure that acts to detect, prevent, or minimize loss associated with the occurrence of a specified threat or category of threats.

- **Vulnerability:** the absence or weakness of a risk-reducing safeguard.

To compute risk value, multiply the probability of an event occurring by the likely loss it would incur. The result is a single value called the annual loss expectancy. Risk managers use the ALE to rank events by magnitude of risk and to make investment decisions based on this ranking. The problems with quantitative risk analysis are usually associated with the unreliability and inaccuracy of the data. Probability can rarely be precise and can, in some cases, promote complacency. In addition, controls and countermeasures often tackle a number of potential events, and the events themselves are frequently interrelated.

Qualitative Risk Analysis Qualitative risk analysis is the most widely used approach to risk analysis. Probability data is not required, and only estimated potential loss is used. Most qualitative risk analysis methodologies make use of a number of interrelated elements:

- Threats
- Vulnerabilities
- Controls

Threats are things that can go wrong or that can "attack" the system. Examples might include fire or fraud. Threats are present for every system no matter what you try to do to eliminate them completely.

Vulnerabilities make a system more prone to attack or make an attack more likely to have some success or impact. For example, fire vulnerability would be the presence of flammable materials (e.g., paper).

Controls are the countermeasures for vulnerabilities and come in five types:

- Deterrent controls reduce the likelihood of a deliberate attack.
- Preventative controls protect vulnerabilities and make an attack unsuccessful or reduce its impact.
- Corrective controls reduce the effect of an attack.
- Detective controls discover attacks and trigger preventative or corrective controls.
- Recovery controls restore lost computer resources or capabilities to recover from security violations.

A risk is real when there is a presence of threat (e.g., a willing and capable attacker), a vulnerability that the attacker can exploit, and a high likelihood that the attacker will carry out the threat.

Figure 15.2 illustrates the qualitative risk analysis process.

Risk analysis is required because it's impossible to protect assets if you do not know what you are protecting against. A risk analysis answers three fundamental questions:

- What am I trying to protect?
- What is threatening my system?
- How much time, effort, and money am I willing to spend?

After risks are classified either as metrics or relative to one another, you can then develop policies and procedures needed to reduce them.

Education, Training, and Awareness

Because people are the weakest link in any security-related process, it's crucial that a security programme address user education, awareness, and

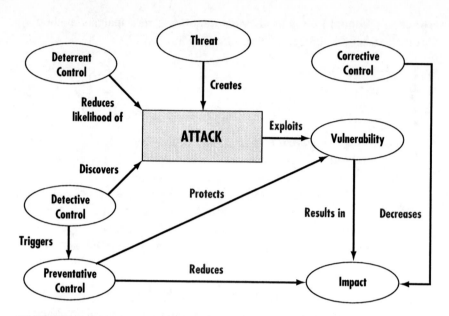

FIGURE 15.2 A model of the risk analysis process.

training on policies and procedures that affect them. Education must be driven top-down and must be comprehensive, all the way from high-end servers down to the desktop systems, peripherals, and hard copies of business documents.

Training may be offered in any number of forms and formats, including paper-based, intranet-based, classroom-based, self-study, and so forth. It should also include mechanisms to make sure that management keeps track of which employees have completed security training and which have agreed to live up to the programme expectations. Furthermore, training must be ongoing (at least annually) and also take place whenever policies change. All employees (including contractors and third-party service providers) need to be made aware of changes.

Training materials and content will vary by the roles or job duties of personnel. A computer user, for example, may only need basic security training (do not write down or share passwords, and so forth), whereas a developer would require application development security training, and IT support personnel or administrators would require more technical security training on the specific assets for which they're responsible.

Who Is Responsible for Security?

Everyone who uses information technology is responsible for maintaining the security and confidentiality of information resources and must comply with security policies and procedures. Certain individuals, however, have specific information security responsibilities that are established by the security programme:

■ **Chief information security officer (CISO):** establishes and maintains security and risk management programmes for information resources.

■ **Information resources manager:** maintains policies and procedures that provide for security and risk management of information resources.

■ **Information resources security officer:** directs policies and procedures designed to protect information resources (e.g., identifies vulnerabilities, develops security awareness programme, and so forth).

■ **Owners of information resources:** responsible for carrying out the programme that uses the resources. This does not imply personal ownership. These individuals may be regarded as programme managers or delegates for the owner.

■ **Custodians of information resources:** provide technical facilities, data processing, and other support services to owners and users of information resources.

■ **Technical managers (network and system administrators):** provide technical support for security of information resources.

■ **Internal auditors:** conduct periodic risk-based reviews of information resources security policies and procedures.

■ **Users:** people who have access to information resources in accordance with the owner-defined controls and access rules.

For a comprehensive example of a policy and standards library that is open to the public, visit the University of Houston Security Manual Web site at: **www.uh.edu/infotech/php/template.php?nonsvc_id=268**.

Summary

The Security Management Practices domain is most concerned with the establishment and ongoing operation of the organization's security programme. This programme begins with documentation in the form of policies, standards, baselines, procedures, and guidance for compliance.

An effective security programme includes top-down sponsorship to establish and enforce these policies and standards and to develop and maintain procedures within a comprehensive library of documents that clearly spell out the responsibilities and consequence of noncompliance for all users of IT resources.

The library of documents is arranged as a hierarchy with the highest level consisting of a few policies, followed by an increasing number of standard and baseline documents and further supplemented with guidance documents to aid in implementation, and finally lots of procedure documents that explicitly describe how to implement a security control or process.

The library should be developed and managed by dedicated personnel who are experts in the subject matter related to the organization's industry or mission. Because information security does not stand still for long, policies and standards libraries must be living and breathing in order to be effective for use in preventing, detecting, and responding to security risks.

Test Your Skills

MULTIPLE CHOICE QUESTIONS

1. Which of the following choices is *not* part of a security policy?

    A. definition of overall steps of information security and the importance of security

    B. statement of management intent, supporting the goals and principles of information security

    C. definition of general and specific responsibilities for information security management

    D. description of specific technologies used in the field of information security regulations

2. Which of the following would be the first step in establishing an information security programme?

    A. adoption of a corporate information security policy statement

    B. development and implementation of an information security standards manual

    C. development of a security awareness–training program for employees

    D. purchase of security access control software

3. An effective information security policy should not have which of the following characteristics?

    A. include separation of duties

    B. be designed with a short- to mid-term focus

    C. be understandable and supported by all stakeholders

    D. specify areas of responsibility and authority

4. What is the difference between advisory and regulatory security policies?

   A. There is no difference between them.

   B. Regulatory policies are high-level policy, whereas advisory policies are very detailed.

   C. Advisory policies provide recommendations.

   D. Advisory policies are mandated, whereas regulatory policies are not.

5. What can best be defined as high-level statements, beliefs, goals, and objectives?

   A. standards

   B. policies

   C. guidelines

   D. procedures

6. A deviation or exception from a security standard requires which of the following?

   A. risk acceptance

   B. risk assignment

   C. risk reduction

   D. risk containment

7. Why would an information security policy require that communications test equipment be controlled?

   A. The equipment is susceptible to damage.

   B. The equipment can be used to browse information passing on a network.

   C. The equipment must always be available for replacement if necessary.

   D. The equipment can be used to reconfigure network devices.

8. Step-by-step instructions used to satisfy control requirements are called a

   A. policy.

   B. standard.

   C. guideline.

   D. procedure.

15

9. Which of the following embodies all the detailed actions that personnel are required to follow?

   A. standards

   B. guidelines

   C. procedures

   D. baselines

10. Which of the following would be defined as an absence or weakness of a safeguard that could be exploited?

    A. a threat

    B. a vulnerability

    C. a risk

    D. an exposure

11. Within IT security, which of the following combinations best defines risk?

    A. threat coupled with a breach

    B. threat coupled with a vulnerability

    C. vulnerability coupled with an attack

    D. threat coupled with a breach of security

12. IT security measures should

    A. be complex.

    B. be tailored to meet organizational security goals.

    C. make sure that every asset of the organization is well protected.

    D. not be developed in a layered fashion.

13. Which of the following should *not* be addressed by employee termination practices?

    A. removal of the employee from active payroll files

    B. return of access badges

    C. employee bonding to protect against losses due to theft

    D. deletion of assigned logon ID and passwords to prohibit system access

14. What would best define risk management?

    A. the process of eliminating the risk

    B. the process of assessing the risks

    C. the process of reducing risk to an acceptable level

    D. the process of transferring risk

15. Controls are implemented to

    A. eliminate risk and reduce the potential for loss.

    B. mitigate risk and eliminate the potential for loss.

    C. mitigate risk and reduce the potential for loss.

    D. eliminate risk and eliminate the potential for loss.

16. Which of the following is an advantage of a qualitative over a quantitative risk analysis?

    A. It prioritizes the risks and identifies areas for immediate improvement in addressing the vulnerabilities.

    B. It provides specific quantifiable measurements of the magnitude of the impacts.

    C. It makes a cost–benefit analysis of recommended controls easier.

    D. It can easily be automated.

17. What can be defined as an event that could cause harm to the information systems?

    A. a risk

    B. a threat

    C. a vulnerability

    D. a weakness

18. One purpose of a security awareness program is to modify

    A employees' attitudes and behaviors.

    B. management's approach.

    C. attitudes of employees with sensitive data.

    D. corporate attitudes about safeguarding data.

19. Which of the following should be given technical security training?

    A. operators

    B. security practitioners and information systems auditors

    C. IT support personnel and system administrators

    D. senior managers, functional managers, and business unit managers

15

EXERCISES

Exercise 15.1: Security Organizational Structures

1. Using your school or employer, document the organization structure of the department responsible for IT security management.

2. Which security concepts (separation of duties, risk management, and so forth) do you find that influenced the current structure?

3. Which security concepts (if any) appear to be missing from the structure?

Exercise 15.2: Policy Manual Analysis

1. Locate the security policy manual for your organization or school.

2. How does its content compare to the content described in this chapter?

3. How does its structure compare to the structure described in this chapter?

Exercise 15.3: Security Awareness and Training

1 Describe the education, awareness, and training activities that you have encountered as an employee or student.

2. Describe the opportunities for education and awareness that are offered to you as an employee or student.

Exercise 15.4: Finding Analogies to Separation of Duties

1. Explain the principle of separation of duties.

2. How does this principle compare to checks and balances found within the U.S. government?

3. How does this principle compare to checks and balances found within your state government?

Exercise 15.5: Risk Analysis Application

1. Apply the information related to qualitative risk analysis to your personal or family's vehicle as an asset.

2. Which risks can you determine, and how would you manage each one?

3. What might you do differently once you complete the exercise?

PROJECTS

Project 15.1: Comparing Standards Libraries Across Organizations

1. Visit the University of Houston Information Security Manual Web site at **www.uh.edu/infotech/php/template.php?nonsvc_id=268**.

2. Compare what you find there to the taxonomy of documents presented in this chapter.

3. Do you find many differences? How might you attribute differences between security manuals for corporations over those for educational organizations?

4. What are some of the similarities?

Project 15.2: Best Practices Standards

1. Visit the InfoSec Reading Room at SANS.org (**www.sans.org/rr**).

2. Search for documented best practices in information security.

3. What types of best practices are commonly documented?

4. How could you incorporate these best practices into the development of a security manual?

5. How would you distribute these to personnel requiring the information?

Project 15.3: Employee Prescreening and Termination Processes

1. Develop a list of recommended steps to include in a preemployment hiring process.

2. Develop a list of recommended steps to include in an employee termination process.

3. Which areas within the organization need to be included?

4. Suggest some ways for the security department to communicate with these other departments to assure that nothing falls through the cracks.

5. How would you help to assure that outside departments follow these recommendations?

15

Case Study

A small medical office of four physicians and support staff decides they want to set up a wireless LAN to permit them to take their laptops with them from room to room for real-time data entry on patient records. The doctors know they need to comply with HIPAA controls over patient records and are concerned that a Wi-Fi LAN could compromise security.

What advice would you offer to the medical office manager about implementing a Wi-Fi access point on the network? What elements would a policy contain? Develop a high-level standard to address the considerations for implementing Wi-Fi under HIPAA security rule constraints.

There are several ways that wireless access points are being deployed to make them more secure.

You may find these sites helpful when developing your policy:

Wi-Fi Planet: **www.wi-fiplanet.com/columns/article.php/ 1550241**

HIPAA Advisory: **www.hipaadvisory.com/tech/wireless.htm**

Chapter | 16

Security Architecture and Models

Chapter Objectives

After reading this chapter and completing the exercises, you will be able to do the following:

- Summarize the concept of a trusted computing base (TCB).
- Illustrate the concept of rings of trust.
- Distinguish among the protection mechanisms used in a TCB.
- Defend the purposes of security assurance testing.
- Apply the Trusted Computer Security Evaluation Criteria (TCSEC) for software evaluations.
- Apply the Trusted Network Interpretation of the TCSEC.
- Categorize the role of the Federal Criteria for Information Technology Security.
- Apply the Common Criteria for Information Security Evaluation.
- Summarize the principles behind confidentiality and integrity models and their role in security architectures.

Introduction

The Security Architecture and Models domain of the Common Body of Knowledge contains the concepts, principles, structures, and standards used to design, monitor, and secure operating systems, equipment, networks, and applications. It also contains the controls used to enforce various levels of availability, integrity, and confidentiality. These ideas and controls stem from research in computer science and the development of systems requiring strict attention to computer security.

Several new terms and concepts are introduced in this domain, including the concepts of trusted computing base (TCB), formal security evaluations and testing, and, finally, models of access control behavior.

Defining the Trusted Computing Base

The *trusted computing base* (TCB) is the totality of protection mechanisms within a computer system including hardware, firmware, and software. A TCB consists of one or more components that together enforce a unified security policy over a product or system. It describes the isolation of objects on which the protection is based, following the concept of the *reference monitor*. The reference monitor is a software model or *abstract machine* that mediates all access from any subject (user or other device) to any object (resource, data, and so forth) and cannot be bypassed. An abstract machine mediates accesses to objects by subjects. In principle, a reference monitor should be

- complete in that it mediates every access.

- isolated from modification by other system entities (objects and processes).

- verifiable in that it only does what it's programmed to do and cannot be circumvented by malicious acts or programmer error.

A security kernel is an implementation of a reference monitor for a specific hardware base such as Sun Solaris, Red Hat Linux, or Mac OS X. The TCB, reference monitor, and security kernel are essential for military- and government-grade information technology (IT) security to prevent unauthorized access or threats to the integrity of programs, operating systems, or data.

A trusted system, according to the TCB, is a system that can be expected to meet users' requirements for reliability, security, and effectiveness due to having undergone formal testing and validation. Trusted computing is an essential element for governments and agencies managing national secrets. Because no single person is responsible for data ownership when it comes to national secrets (as they are in a commercial setting), the operating systems that are relied on use a concept called *mandatory access control* (MAC) for deciding who may gain access to what. MAC requires that access control policy decisions are beyond the control of the individual owner of an object, thus requiring the system to make the decisions. The reference monitor makes these decisions and permits or denies access based on labels and clearance levels.

An *object* is something within a trusted system that people wish to access or use (such as a program). Objects are labeled with a sensitivity level

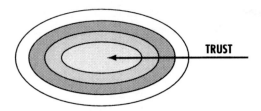

FIGURE 16.1 The unidirectional layered model of trust.

(see Chapter 16). *Subjects* (people or other processes) that wish to access these objects must be cleared to the same level of classification or higher. Several security models covered later in this chapter have been developed to address confidentiality and integrity.

Rings of Trust

The TCB concept is illustrated using what is called a *ring of trust*. Trust in a system moves from the outside to the inside in a unidirectional mode. The ring model of security was originally derived from the concept of execution domains developed by the Multics project. Figure 16.1 illustrates the concept of rings of trust.

FYI: What Is Multics?

Multics (Multiplexed Information and Computing Service) was a timesharing operating system project begun in 1965. The system was started as a joint project by MIT Project MAC, Bell Telephone Laboratories, and General Electric. Multics never caught much in the way of commercial attention, but it had a powerful impact in the computer field, due to its many novel and valuable ideas. In particular, the Unix system (produced by Bell Labs personnel who had worked on Multics), the GNU project, and much later the Linux kernel, are in part descended from Multics.

Among its new ideas, Multics was the first operating system to provide a hierarchical file system, a feature that now can be found in virtually every operating system. It had numerous features intended to result in high availability, so that it would produce a computing utility, similar to the telephone and electricity services.

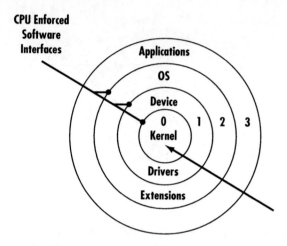

FIGURE 16.2 Rings of trust in stand-alone systems.

Figure 16.2 shows the rings of trust concept in the context of a single computer system. In this model, outer rings contain a lower level of security, and systems requiring higher levels of security are located inside the inner rings. Extra security mechanisms must be navigated to move from an outer ring into an inner ring. The operating system (OS) enforces how communications flow between layers using the reference monitor (within the kernel) to mediate all access and protect resources.

It's also possible to use the concepts of rings of trust to design security domains or operating environments for networks of systems. This concept is illustrated in Figure 16.3.

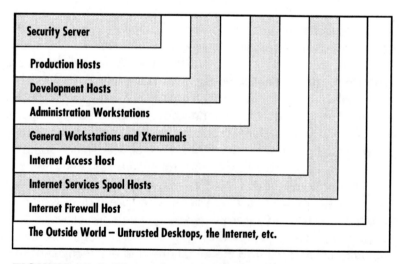

FIGURE 16.3 Rings of trust in networked environments.

This model divides the hosts into rings, based on the security rating of the services they provide to the network, and then uses these rings as the basis for trust between hosts.

To help determine the hierarchy of the rings, some questions must be answered:

- Is the host in a physically secured computer room?

- Does the host have normal (as opposed to privileged) user accounts?

- Is this host at a remote site and hence less trustworthy than the ones in the central computer room?

- Does this host operate software that relies on data obtained from the Internet?

- Does this host provide mission-critical services? How many people in the company would be affected by downtime on this host?

The following general rules apply to constructing rings of trust in networked systems:

- Each host trusts those hosts in a more inner ring than itself.

- No host trusts any host in a more outer ring than itself.

- Each host may trust those hosts in the same ring as itself.

- Where a ring has been segmented into separate subnetworks, a host in one segment does not trust hosts in other segments.

As you can see, rings of trust apply equally well for stand-alone systems, small business or home networks, and large-scale corporate and government networks where security requirements are absolute.

To implement the rings of trust model, a number of software constructs and design objectives are used for security and protection of resources.

Protection Mechanisms in a Trusted Computing Base

There are a number of standard design concepts and software processes that are often found in a TCB and are described below.

Process isolation is a design objective in which each process has its own distinct address space for its application code and data. In this way, it is possible to prevent each process from accessing another process's data. This prevents data or information leakage and prevents modification of the data while it is memory.

Principle of least privilege dictates that a process (program) has no more privilege than what it really needs in order to perform its functions.

Any modules that require "supervisor" or "root" access (that is, complete system privileges) are embedded in the operating system kernel. The kernel handles all requests for system resources and mediates the access from external modules to privileged modules when required.

Hardware segmentation specifically relates to the segmentation of memory into protected segments. The kernel allocates the required amount of memory for the process to load its application code, its process data, and its application data. The system prevents user processes from being able to access another process's allocated memory. It also prevents user processes from being able to access system memory.

Layering is a process operation that is divided into layers by function. Each layer deals with a specific activity. The lower (outer) layers perform basic tasks, whereas the higher (inner) layers perform more complex or protected tasks.

Abstraction is a process that defines a specific set of permissible values for an object and the operations that are permissible on that object. This involves ignoring or separating implementation details in order to concentrate on what is important to maintain security.

Data hiding—also known as information hiding—is a mechanism to assure that information available at one processing level is not available in another, regardless of whether it is higher or lower. It is also a concept in the object-oriented programming (OOP) technique when information is encapsulated within an object and can be directly manipulated only by the services provided within the object.

Information storage refers to the parts of a computer system that retain a physical state (information) for some interval of time, possibly even after electrical power to the computer is removed. There are a number of different types used for data or information storage. These include the following types:

- *Primary storage* is the computer's main memory that is directly addressable by the central processing unit (CPU). Primary storage is a volatile storage medium, meaning that the contents of the physical memory are lost when the power is removed.

- *Secondary storage* is a nonvolatile storage format, where application and system code plus data can be stored when the system is not in use. Examples of secondary storage are disk drives or other persistent data storage mechanisms (e.g., Flash [USB] drives, memory sticks, and tapes).

- *Real memory* is where a program has been given a definite storage location in memory and direct access to a peripheral device. This is common with database management systems that control how storage is used outside of the control of the operating system.

- ■ *Virtual memory* extends the volume of primary storage by using secondary storage to hold the memory contents. In this way, the operating system can run programs larger than the available physical memory. Virtual memory (memory contents stored on disk) is swapped in and out of primary memory when needed for processing.

- ■ *Random memory* is the computer's primary working and storage area. It is addressable directly by the CPU and stores application or system code in addition to data.

- ■ *Sequential storage* is computer memory that is accessed sequentially. An example of this is magnetic tape.

- ■ *Volatile memory* means that there is a complete loss of any stored information when the power is removed.

Closed systems are of a proprietary nature. They use specific operating systems and hardware to perform the task and generally lack standard interfaces to allow connection to other systems. The user is generally limited in the applications and programming languages available.

An *open system*, on the other hand, is based on accepted standards and employs standard interfaces to allow connections between different systems. It promotes interoperability and allows the user to have full access to the total system capability.

Multitasking is a technique used by a system that is capable of running two or more tasks in a concurrent performance or interleaved execution.

A *multiprogramming system* allows for the interleaved execution of two or more programs on a processor.

Multiprocessing provides for simultaneous execution of two or more programs by a processor (CPU). This can alternatively be done through parallel processing of a single program by two or more processors in a multiprocessor system that all have common access to main storage.

A *finite-state machine* is any device that stores the status or state of something at a given time that can operate based on inputs to change the stored status and/or cause an action or output to take place. The importance of finite-state machines is that the machine has distinct states that it remembers. In Multics, for example, there was a state associated with each ring of trust. Each computer's data register also stores a state. The read-only memory from which a boot (computer start-up) program is loaded stores a state. In fact, the boot program is an initial state. The operating system is itself a state, and each application that it runs begins with some initial state that may change as it handles input. Thus, at any moment in time, a computer system can be seen as a very complex set of states and each program in it as a state machine. In practice, however, state machines are used to develop and describe specific device or program interactions for purposes of discovery or evaluation.

System Security Assurance Concepts

When considering IT security systems (firewall software, intrusion detection devices, access control mechanisms, and so forth), the requirements or needs, decided by those who sponsor the development, appear in two forms: functional requirements and assurance requirements.

Functional requirements describe what a system should do by design, and *assurance requirements* describe how the functional requirements should be implemented and tested. Both sets of requirements are needed to answer the following questions:

- Does the system do the right things?

- Does the system do the right things in the right way?

These are the same questions that others in noncomputer industries face with verification and validation. You need both answers to gain confidence in products prior to launching them into a wild, hostile environment, like the Internet, or to use them to protect national secrets and data (like income tax returns). Both types of requirements must be tested (and retested) and are included in the scope of security assurance testing.

Software testing focused only on functionality testing for user acceptance will uncover errors (bugs) in how the software operates. If the system responds to input in the ways the users expect it to respond, it's stamped as ready to ship. If the system responds differently, the bugs are worked out in successive remediation and retesting until it behaves as desired.

Goals of Security Testing

Security testing flips this technique on its head and takes it a step further. It not only verifies that the functions designed to meet a security requirement operate as expected but also validates that the implementation of the function is not flawed or haphazard.

This kind of security testing can only be performed effectively by experts—never by casual users or developers. Programmers can't uncover flaws in their own programs that affect security—they can only find the flaws in its operation.

Security assurance and testing is laced with lots of odd concepts and principles that truly do fly in the face of conventional thinking and are foreign to most people involved in IT development. Gaining confidence that a system does not do what it's not supposed to do is akin to proving a negative, and most everyone knows that you can't prove a negative! What you can do, however, is subject a system to brutal security testing, and with each resistance to an attack, gain additional confidence that it was developed with security in mind.

Formal Security Testing Models

Beginning with the widespread adoption of affordable computers by both the military and government bodies, the *Trusted Computer System Evaluation Criteria* (TCSEC) was born in the United States in the early 1980s. Over the succeeding decade, other countries around the world began the work of developing their own evaluation criteria, building upon the concepts of the TCSEC but adding more flexibility to adapt to evolving computing technology.

In Europe, the *Information Technology Security Evaluation Criteria* (ITSEC) version 1.2 was published in 1991 by the European Commission after joint development by France, Germany, the Netherlands, and the United Kingdom. In Canada, the *Canadian Trusted Computer Product Evaluation Criteria* (CTCPEC) version 3.0 was published in early 1993 as a combination of the ITSEC and TCSEC approaches.

Back in the United States, the draft *Federal Criteria for Information Technology Security* (FC) version 1.0 was published in early 1993 as an attempt to develop criteria to replace the TCSEC and harmonize North American and European concepts for security evaluation criteria. A draft version of the Federal Criteria was released for public comment in December 1992 but was supplanted by the *Common Criteria* standardization efforts.

Beginning with TCSEC, in the next few sections we'll examine the evolution of security testing models that led to today's Common Criteria standard.

16

Trusted Computer Security Evaluation Criteria

The U.S. Department of Defense (DOD) Trusted Computer System Evaluation Criteria (TCSEC) was a collection of criteria used to grade or rate the security claimed for a computer system product. The now-obsolete TCSEC was often called the *Orange Book* because of its orange cover. The last version is dated 1985 (DOD 5200.28-STD, Library No. S225,711). TCSEC is one part of a series of DOD documents called the "Rainbow Series" because of the multiple colored covers on each document.

TCSEC is most interested in confidentiality and sets forth criteria used to rate the effectiveness of trusted systems in terms of how well they can protect the secrecy of objects contained within them.

The TCB described by the *Orange Book* is a complete description of all the protection mechanisms used within computer systems. The combination of all protection mechanisms are used to enforce security policy. The TCB consists of the hardware, software, and firmware that make up the system. Security policy is a formal description of the rules for subjects and objects that a trusted system needs to determine if a given subject is authorized to access a specific object. Trusted systems are evaluated products (hardware, software, or combinations of the two) that are expected to meet the requirements for reliability, security, and operational effectiveness. They're both verified and validated as being implemented correctly through formal evaluation methods that use established criteria for testing.

The earlier efforts to formalize security assurance included groupings of requirements that described the desired levels of security for a product or a system. TCSEC and other assurance criteria documents outlined both security functional requirements (what functions must be present) along with security assurance requirements (i.e., how thoroughly the functions should be tested) to arrive at an overall rating.

TCSEC provided classes (or divisions) of trust that are roughly equivalent to object classifications of Unclassified, Secret, Top Secret, and beyond Top Secret, using the letters D, C, B, and A, respectively.

Division D: Minimal Protection

Division D is reserved by the TCSEC for those systems that have either been formally evaluated but fail to meet the requirements for a higher evaluation class or it is used on unrated or untested systems. TCSEC does not contain specific requirements for Division D evaluations, but some of the TCSEC interpretations documents (other Rainbow Series documents) do permit specifying Division D levels of evaluation.

Division C: Discretionary Protection

Classes in Division C provide for discretionary protection, based on the need-to-know, or least privilege, principle and for audit control mechanisms that enforce the personal accountability of subjects for the actions they take while using the system. Discretionary protection is what is seen in the commercial world protecting objects from unauthorized subjects through the assignment of privilege to the subject by the object's owner. In other words, a data owner (human being) gets to decide who is authorized to access his or her objects (data, programs, and so forth).

Class C1: Discretionary Security Protection The TCB of a Class C1 system satisfies the discretionary access control requirements by separating users and data. It incorporates mechanisms that are capable of enforcing access limitations on an individual basis. C1 requirements are suitable for allowing users the ability to protect project or private information and to keep other users from accidentally reading or destroying their data. Class C1 systems are typically used among a group of users who share the same level of clearance (e.g., workgroups).

Class C2: Controlled Access Protection Systems in this class enforce a more finely grained discretionary access control than C1 systems, making users individually accountable for their actions through login procedures, auditing of security-relevant events, and resource isolation. This means that no program can gain access to the memory areas used by other programs.

Security assurance divisions above Division C are usually reserved for governmental systems and are rarely found in the commercial world unless the company acts as a subcontractor to government agencies requiring such protections. Similarly, assurance levels in the Common Criteria above Evaluation Assurance Level (EAL) 4 are typically reserved for national government systems.

Division B: Mandatory Protection

A major requirement in this division is that a TCB preserves the integrity of sensitivity labels and uses them to enforce a set of mandatory access control rules. Systems in this division must carry the sensitivity labels (secret or top secret, for example) with major data structures in the system. The system developer provides the security policy model on which the TCB is based and furnishes a specification of the TCB. Evidence is needed to demonstrate that the reference monitor concept has been implemented. The reference monitor refers to the concept of an abstract machine (a machine within a machine) that mediates the access of subjects to objects. The reference monitor must be protected from unauthorized changes, must always be used to mediate all access (cannot be circumvented), and must be verified as implemented correctly.

Mandatory protections are what the military is most interested in to protect national secrets. With mandatory access controls, the system or TCB decides who can access what according to the security policy that's implemented by the reference monitor.

Class B1: Labeled Security Protection Class B1 systems require all the features required for Class C2. In addition, an informal statement of the security policy model, data labeling, and mandatory access control over named subjects and objects must be present. The capability must exist for accurately labeling exported information from the system, and any flaws identified during testing must be removed.

Class B2: Structured Protection In Class B2 systems, the TCB is based on a clearly defined and documented formal security policy model that requires the discretionary and mandatory access control enforcement found in Class B1 systems be extended to all subjects and objects in the system. In addition, covert channels are addressed. Covert channels are possible wherever there's an opportunity for a system to provide unintended communications. One example of a covert channel is a back door in a system that circumvents the security mechanisms and enables the movement of data from a higher classification level to an area where lower classifications of data are accessible.

The TCB must be carefully structured into protection-critical and non-protection-critical elements. The TCB interface is well defined and well understood, and the TCB design and implementation should enable the system to be subjected to more thorough testing and more complete review. During this testing and review, authentication mechanisms are strengthened, trusted facility management is offered via an interface for system administrator and operator functions, and strict configuration management controls are imposed. The system is then deemed relatively resistant to penetration.

Class B3: Security Domains For Class B3, the TCB must satisfy the reference monitor requirements to

- mediate all accesses of subjects to objects.
- be tamperproof.
- be small enough to be subjected to analysis and tests.

To this end, the TCB is structured to exclude program code that's not essential to security policy enforcement. This requires significant system engineering during TCB design and implementation with the goal of minimizing its complexity. A security administrator role is supported, audit mechanisms are expanded to signal (trace) security-relevant events, and system recovery procedures are required. This system is deemed highly resistant to penetration.

Division A: Verified Protection

Division A is characterized by the use of formal security verification methods to assure that the mandatory and discretionary security controls employed within the system effectively protect classified or other sensitive information stored or processed by the system. Extensive documentation is required to demonstrate that the TCB meets the security requirements in all aspects of design, development, and implementation.

Class A1: Verified Design Systems in Class A1 are functionally equivalent to those in Class B3, with no additional architectural features or policy requirements added. The distinguishing feature of systems in this class is the analysis derived from formal design specification and verification techniques and the resulting high degree of assurance that the TCB is correctly implemented. This assurance is developmental in nature, starting with a formal model of the security policy and a formal top-level specification of the design. There are five important criteria for Class A1 design verification independent of the particular specification language or verification system used:

- A formal model of the security policy must be clearly identified and documented, including a mathematical proof that the model is consistent with its axioms and is sufficient to support the security policy.

■ A formal top-level specification must be produced that includes abstract definitions of the functions the TCB performs and of the hardware and/or firmware mechanisms that are used to support separated execution domains.

■ The formal top-level specification of the TCB must be shown to be consistent with the model using formal techniques where possible (i.e., where verification tools exist) or informal ones where formal techniques are unavailable.

■ The TCB implementation (i.e., in hardware, firmware, and software) must be informally shown to be consistent with the formal top-level specification. The elements of the formal top-level specification must be shown, using informal techniques, to correspond to the elements of the TCB. The formal top-level specification must express the unified protection mechanism required to satisfy the security policy. It is the elements of this protection mechanism that are mapped to the elements of the TCB.

■ Formal analysis techniques must be used to identify and analyze covert channels. Informal techniques may be used to identify covert timing channels (unwanted communications based on temporal activities). Any continued existence of identified covert channels in the system must be justified by the developer.

To preserve the extensive design and development analysis of the TCB required of systems in Class A1, additional stringent configuration management is required along with procedures for securely distributing the system to sites. System security administrator functions are also required.

The Trusted Network Interpretation of the TCSEC

The Trusted Network Interpretation (TNI) of the TCSEC is also referred to as the *Red Book* of the Rainbow Series. The TNI restates the requirements of the TCSEC in a network context as contrasted with TCSEC on standalone and non-networked environments.

Information Technology Security Evaluation Criteria

The Information Technology Security Evaluation Criteria (ITSEC) is a European-developed criterion that fills a role roughly equivalent to the TCSEC for use throughout the European Community. Although the ITSEC and TCSEC have many similar requirements, there are some important distinctions. The ITSEC places increased emphasis on integrity and availability and attempts to provide a uniform approach to the evaluation of both products and systems.

ITSEC introduces the concept of the ***target of evaluation*** (TOE), which refers to the product or system under evaluation. It adds to the TCB security-relevant functions in addition to security-enforcing functions (like TCSEC). ITSEC provides for functionality classes, assurance classes, and profiles for systems. It also introduces the security target (ST), a written document that contains

- a system security policy.

- required security enforcing functions.

- required security mechanisms.

- claimed ratings of minimum strength.

- target evaluation levels, expressed as both functional and evaluation (F-xx and E-yy).

Comparing ITSEC and TCSEC

ITSEC functionality and assurance classes map closely to the TCSEC divisions and classes and are shown below in Table 16.1. You can use these to roughly compare implementations and testing requirements between products manufactured in the U.S. and Europe.

ITSEC classes are hierarchical; each class adds to the class above it and contains specific functions and mechanisms that correspond to TCSEC. ITSEC also supports other specialized classes that stand alone (nonhierarchical):

- F-IN for high-integrity

- F-AV for high-availability

- F-DI for high data integrity

- F-DC for high data confidentiality

- F-DX for networks that require high demands for confidentiality and integrity during data exchanges

These five classes only describe additional functional requirements above the preset requirements found in Table 16.1.

ITSEC Assurance Classes

The assurance classes, listed as the second value in Table 16.1 for ITSEC, describe the testing requirements and are listed in Table 16.2.

TABLE 16.1 TCSEC and ITSEC classes compared.

TCSEC Classes	ITSEC Functional and Assurance Classes
C1	F-C1, E1
C2	F-C2, E2
B1	F-B1, E3
B2	F-B2, E4
B3	F-B3, E5
A1	F-B3, E6

TABLE 16.2 ITSEC assurance classes.

ITSEC Assurance Class	Description
E0	Inadequate assurance: fails to meet E1 requirements
E1	Security target document that provides an informal description of the TOE's architectural design and functional testing that the TOE satisfies target requirements
E2	E1 requirements plus an informal description of detailed designs, testing evidence, configuration control requirements, and approved distribution procedures
E3	E2 requirements plus source code and drawings that are evaluated and testing evidence of security mechanisms that are evaluated
E4	E3 requirements plus a formal model of security policy, semiformal specification of security enforcing functions, architectural design documents, and detailed design documents
E5	E4 requirements plus evidence of close correspondence between detailed design and source code (traceability of design into implementation)
E6	E5 requirements plus a formal specification of security enforcing functions and architectural design, along with consistency with the formal security policy model

16

Canadian Trusted Computer Product Evaluation Criteria

In August 1988, the Canadian System Security Centre (CSSC) at the Communications Security Establishment of the Government of Canada was formed to develop a set of criteria and to set up a Canadian evaluation capability among other tasks. In April 1992, a draft of version 3.0 of the Canadian Trusted Computer Product Evaluation Criteria (CTCPEC) was published.

The Canadian Trusted Computer Product Evaluation Criteria is the Canadian equivalent of the TCSEC. It is somewhat more flexible than the TCSEC (along the lines of the ITSEC) while maintaining fairly close compatibility with individual TCSEC requirements. The CTCPEC and its approach to structure security functionality separate from assurance functionality influenced international standardization through the Common Criteria. In January 1993, the final and last version (version 3) of CTCPEC was published.

Federal Criteria for Information Technology Security

To further meet organizational needs for handling both classified and unclassified information, the Federal Criteria for Information Technology Security (Federal Criteria, or FC) was developed as a joint project by the National Institute of Standards and Technology (NIST) and the National Security Agency (NSA). The Federal Criteria was an attempt to develop a set of newer criteria to replace the aging TCSEC. It introduces the concept of a protection profile (PP) that empowers users or buyers of technology to specify their security requirements for hardware and software.

A draft version of the FC was released for public comment in December 1992. The effort was supplanted by the international Common Criteria development efforts, and the Federal Criteria never moved beyond the draft stage (although many of its ideas are retained in the Common Criteria). No final version of the FC was ever published.

The Common Criteria

Joint efforts between the United States (TCSEC), Canada (CTCPEC), and Europe (ITSEC) began in 1993 to harmonize security evaluation criteria to enable true comparability between the results of independent security evaluations. These joint activities were designed to align international separate criteria into a single set of IT security criteria that could be broadly used. The activity was named the Common Criteria (CC) Project, and its purpose was to resolve the conceptual and technical differences found in the various source criteria and to deliver the results to the International Organization for Standardization (ISO) as a proposed international standard under development.

> ## FYI: Formal Security Testing in the Real World
>
> While these concepts and processes may seem a bit of overkill, assurance of commercial products is nothing that serious buyers of security products should ever ignore. To better understand how security evaluations work in practice and what their value is to government and commercial buyers of security products, visit the Common Criteria Portal at **www.commoncriteriaportal.org**.

16

Representatives of the sponsoring organizations formed the CC Editorial Board (CCEB) to develop the CC, and a liaison relationship was established between the CCEB and ISO Working Group 3 (WG3). The CCEB contributed several early versions of the CC to WG3 via the liaison. As a result of the interaction between WG3 and the CCEB, successive versions of the CC were adopted as working drafts of the various parts of the CC beginning in 1994. Work continued for the next 5 years on harmonizing requirements. In June 1999, the Common Criteria for IT Security Evaluation became ISO International Standard 15408. It focuses on security objectives, the related threats (malicious or otherwise), and the functional requirements relevant to security.

The market force driving the need for harmonized criteria is best understood by an example. Say a vendor of firewalls in Germany wanted to sell its ITSEC evaluated product to an American government agency. If the U.S. agency required the product for a classified government system, the German firewall vendor would have no choice but to sponsor a separate evaluation of its product in the United States using TCSEC criteria—adding tremendous cost and time to the process of successfully selling its products outside the German border.

The Common Criteria addresses this problem through a mutual recognition of the final certificates granted to successfully evaluated products and eliminates the need for multiple evaluations and their associated costs and time requirements.

The Common Criteria, also known as ISO 15408, combines the best features of the TCSEC with the ITSEC and the CTCPEC and synergizes them into a single international standard.

Many countries and organizations participated in the development of the Common Criteria:

- **Canada:** Communications Security Establishment
- **France:** Service Central de la Securite des Systèmes d'Information
- **Germany:** Bundesamt fur Sicherheit in der Informationstechnik

- **The Netherlands:** Netherlands National Communications Security Agency

- **United Kingdom:** Communications-Electronics Security Group

- **United States:** National Institute of Standards and Technology and the National Security Agency

The CC provides a common language and structure to express IT security requirements and enables the creation of catalogs of standards broken down into components and packages. The CC breaks apart the functional and assurance requirements into distinct elements that users can select for customized security device implementation.

Packages permit the expression of requirements that meet an identifiable subset of security objectives. Packages are reusable and can be used to construct larger packages as well. Using the CC framework, users and developers of IT security products create ***protection profiles*** (PPs) as an implementation-independent collection of objectives and requirements for any given category of products or systems that must meet similar needs (e.g., firewalls). Protection profiles are needed to support defining functional standards and serve as an aid in specifying needs for procurement purposes.

Whereas protection profiles serve as a generic description of product and environmental requirements, targets of evaluation (TOE) are the specific products or systems that will fall into an evaluation against an existing PP. The sets of evidence about a TOE and the TOE itself form the inputs to a security target (ST) that's used by certified independent evaluators as the basis for evaluation.

Once again, there are two types of security requirements: functional and assurance. Functional requirements describe what a product needs to do, and assurance requirements describe how well it meets the functional requirements. Consumers need both of these pieces of data to effectively judge the merits of one product over another.

In defining security requirements for a trusted product or system, users and developers need to consider the threats to the environment. The Common Criteria provides a catalog of components (Part 2 of the CC) that developers of PPs use to form the requirements definition. Assurance requirements (defined in Part 3 of the CC) contain two classes from which evaluation assurance requirements may be selected, along with a class for assurance maintenance.

Protection Profile Organization

A protection profile is organized as follows:

- Introduction section, which provides descriptive information that's needed to identify, catalog, register, and cross-reference a PP. The overview provides a summary of the PP as a narrative.

- Target of evaluation (TOE) description, which describes the TOE to aid in understanding its security requirements and addresses the product type and the general features of the TOE, providing a context for the evaluation.

- Security environment, which consists of three subsections:
  - Assumptions
  - Threats
  - Organizational security policies

These sections describe the security aspects of the environment in which the TOE will be used and the manner in which it will be used. Assumptions describe the security aspects of the environment in which the TOE will be used, including information about the intended usage, aspects about the intended applications, potential asset value, and possible limitations of use. The threats section covers all the threats where specific protection within the TOE or its environment is needed. Only those threats that are relevant to secure TOE operation are included. Organizational security policies identify and explain any security policies or rules that govern the TOE or its operating environment.

- Security objectives address all of the security environment aspects identified in earlier sections of the PP. These objectives define the intent of the TOE to counter identified threats and include the organizational security policies and assumptions. This section defines in detail the security requirements that must be satisfied by the TOE or its environment. TOE security requirements describe what supporting evidence is needed to satisfy security objectives. Functional requirements are selected from the CC functional components (Part 2).

- Assurance requirements are stated as one of the evaluation assurance levels (EALs) from the CC Part 3 assurance components.

- Rationale presents the evidence used by a PP evaluation. This evidence supports the claims that the PP is a complete and cohesive set of requirements and that a compliant TOE provides an effective set of IT security countermeasures within the security environment.

Security Functional Requirements

The classes of security functional requirements (component catalog) include

- **Audit:** Security auditing functions involve recognizing, recording, storing, and analyzing information related to security-relevant activities. The resulting audit records can be examined to determine which security-relevant activities took place and which user is responsible for them.

- **Cryptographic support:** These functions are used when the TOE implements cryptographic functions in hardware, firmware, or software.

- **Communications:** These functional requirements are related to assuring the identity of a transmitted information originator and assuring the identity of the recipient. These functions ensure that an originator cannot deny having sent the message, nor can the recipient deny having received it.

- **User data protection:** This class of functions is related to protecting user data within a TOE during import, export, and storage.

- **Identification and authentication:** These functions ensure that users are associated with the proper security attributes (e.g., identity, groups, roles).

- **Security management:** These functions are intended to specify the management of several aspects of the TOE security functions security attributes and security data.

- **Privacy:** These requirements provide a user protection against discovery and misuse of identity by other users.

- **Protection of the TOE security functions (TSF):** These requirements relate to the integrity and management of the mechanisms that provide the TSF and to the integrity of TSF data.

- **Resource utilization:** Support the availability of required resources such as CPU and/or storage capacity. Fault tolerance provides protection against unavailability of capabilities caused by failure of the TOE. Priority of service ensures that the resources will be allocated to the more important or time-critical tasks and cannot be monopolized by lower priority tasks.

- **TOE access:** Control the establishment of a user's session.

Evaluation assurance classes include

- Configuration management to help ensure that the integrity of the TOE is preserved through required discipline and control in the processes of refinement and modification of the TOE and other related information. Configuration management prevents unauthorized modifications, additions, or deletions to the TOE and provides assurance that the TOE and documentation used for evaluation are the ones prepared for distribution.

- Delivery and operation classes define the requirements for the measures, procedures, and standards concerned with secure delivery, installation, and operational use of the TOE, assuring that the security protection offered by the TOE is not compromised during transfer, installation, start-up, and operation.

- Development classes define the requirements for the stepwise (proceeding in steps) refinement of the TOE security functions (TSF) from the summary specification in the security target down to the actual implementation. Each of the resulting TSF representations provides information to help the evaluator determine whether the functional requirements of the TOE have been met.

- Guidance documents define the requirements for understandability, coverage, and completeness of the operational documentation provided by the developer. This documentation, which provides two categories of information—for users and for administrators—is an important factor in the secure operation of the TOE.

- Life-cycle support defines the requirements for the adoption of a well-defined life-cycle model for all the steps of the TOE development, including flaw remediation procedures and policies, correct use of tools and techniques, and the security measures used to protect the development environment.

- Tests cover the testing requirements needed to demonstrate that the TSF satisfies the TOE security functional requirements. This class addresses coverage, depth of developer testing, and functional tests for independent lab testing.

- Vulnerability assessment defines the requirements directed at identifying exploitable vulnerabilities. Specifically, it addresses those vulnerabilities introduced in the construction, operation, misuse, or incorrect configuration of the TOE.

- Protection profile evaluation is used to demonstrate that the PP is complete, consistent, technically sound, and that an evaluated PP is suitable as the basis for developing an ST.

- Security target evaluation: The goal of an ST evaluation is to demonstrate that the ST is complete, consistent, technically sound, and is suitable as the basis for the corresponding TOE evaluation.

- Maintenance of assurance provides the requirements intended for application after a TOE has been certified against the Common Criteria. Maintenance of assurance requirements help to assure that the TOE will continue to meet its security target as changes are made to the TOE or its environment. Such changes include the discovery of new threats or vulnerabilities, changes in user requirements, and the correction of bugs found in the certified TOE.

16

TABLE 5.3 Security criteria compared.

Common Criteria Assurance Level	Orange Book Criteria Level	ITSEC Criteria Level
—	D: Minimal protection	E0
EAL1	—	—
EAL2	C1: Discretionary security protection	E1
EAL3	C2: Controlled access protection	E2
EAL4	B1: Labeled security protection	E3
EAL5	B2: Structured protection	E4
EAL6	B3: Security domains	E5
EAL7	A1: Verified design	E6

Evaluation Assurance Levels

Assurance levels define a scale for measuring the criteria for evaluating PPs and STs. Evaluation Assurance Levels (EALs) provide an increasing scale that balances the levels of assurance claimed with the cost and feasibility of acquiring such assurance. Table 16.3 indicates the CC EAL levels, along with backward compatibility to the Orange Book and ITSEC criteria levels.

Evaluation Assurance Level 1 EAL1 applies where some confidence in correct operation is required but the threats to security are not viewed as serious. It is of value where independent assurance is required to support the contention that due care has been exercised in protecting personal or similar types of information. It's intended that an EAL1 evaluation could be successfully conducted without assistance from the developer of the TOE at a low cost. An evaluation at this level provides evidence that the TOE functions in a manner consistent with its documentation and that it provides useful protection against identified threats. Think of EAL1 as kicking the tires on a vehicle that you're considering for purchase.

Evaluation Assurance Level 2 EAL2 requires the cooperation of a developer in terms of the delivery of design information and test results but does not demand more effort on the part of the developer than is consistent with good commercial practice and should not require a substantially increased investment of money or time. EAL2 is applicable where developers or users require a low to moderate level of independently assured security in the absence of ready availability of the complete development record. Such a situation may arise when securing legacy systems or where access to the developer may be limited.

Evaluation Assurance Level 3 EAL3 permits a conscientious developer to gain maximum assurance from positive security engineering at the design stage without substantial alteration of existing sound development practices. EAL3 applies in those circumstances where developers or users require a moderate level of independently assured security and requires a thorough investigation of the TOE and its development without substantial reengineering.

Evaluation Assurance Level 4 EAL4 permits a developer to gain maximum assurance from positive security engineering based on good commercial development practices that, though rigorous, do not require substantial specialist knowledge, skills, and other resources. EAL4 is applicable in those circumstances where developers or users require a moderate to high level of independently assured security in conventional off-the-shelf TOEs and are prepared to incur additional security-specific engineering costs.

Evaluation Assurance Level 5 EAL5 permits a developer to gain maximum assurance from security engineering based on rigorous commercial development practices supported by moderate application of specialist security engineering techniques. Such a TOE will likely be designed and developed with the intent of achieving EAL5 assurance. EAL5 is applicable in those circumstances where developers or users require a high level of independently assured security in a planned development and require a rigorous development approach without incurring unreasonable costs for special security engineering techniques.

Evaluation Assurance Level 6 EAL6 permits developers to gain high assurance from the application of security engineering techniques to a rigorous development environment in order to produce a premium TOE for protecting high-value assets against significant risks. EAL6 is applicable to the development of security TOEs for application in high-risk situations, where the value of the protected assets justifies additional costs.

Evaluation Assurance Level 7 EAL7 applies to the development of security TOEs for application in extremely high-risk situations where the value of such assets justifies the costs for higher assurance levels.

Once an ST is independently evaluated and is found to meet the desired assurance level, the CC provides for a certification process that's recognized across all CC-using countries. The implication is that products developed and tested abroad can compete on equal footing with similar products developed within the United States.

The Common Evaluation Methodology

The Common Evaluation Methodology Editorial Board (CEMEB), with members from all of the organizations that produced the Common Criteria for Information Technology Security Evaluation, is responsible for producing an agreed upon methodology for conducting evaluations to apply the CC to security targets.

The Common Evaluation Methodology (CEM) is a companion document to the CC. It is focused on the actions that evaluators must take to determine that CC requirements for a TOE are present. CEM is a tool that's used by evaluation schemes to ensure consistent application of the requirements across multiple evaluations and multiple schemes. As such, it is an important component of the Mutual Recognition Arrangement (MRA) that enables any country to accept a certified evaluation from any other member country. So far, agreement has been reached for evaluation levels EAL1 to EAL4, which are deemed adequate for most commercial security products. The CCMEB is continuing the work on common evaluations for levels EAL5, EAL6, and EAL7.

The CEM contains three parts:

- **Part 1:** Introduction and General Model: Describes agreed upon principles of evaluation and introduces agreed upon evaluation terminology dealing with the process of evaluation.

- **Part 2:** CC Evaluation Methodology: This is based on CC Part 3 evaluator actions. It uses well-defined assertions to refine CC Part 3 evaluator actions and tangible evaluator activities to determine requirement compliance. In addition, it will offer guidance to further clarify the intent evaluator actions. Part 2 provides for

    Methodology to evaluate PPs

    Methodology to evaluate STs

    Methodology to evaluate to EAL1

    Methodology to evaluate to EAL2

    Methodology to evaluate to EAL3

    Methodology to evaluate to EAL4

    Methodology to evaluate to EAL5

    Methodology to evaluate to EAL6

    Methodology to evaluate to EAL7

    Methodology to evaluate components not included in an EAL

- **Part 3:** Extensions to the Methodology: These extensions are needed to take full advantage of the evaluation results. It will include topics such as guidance on the composition and content of evaluation document deliverables.

The Common Criteria is currently in use worldwide and is rapidly gaining acceptance and use in common commercial off-the-shelf (COTS) systems. Several large software and hardware developers have embraced the CC, and their products (including Oracle databases, Apple Computer's MAC OS X, Windows Server 2003, and others) are poised for widespread government procurement activities.

Confidentiality and Integrity Models

Security models are mathematical representations of abstract machines that describe how a reference monitor is designed to operate and to help evaluators determine if the implementation meets the design requirements. The following are some of the more commonly used models:

- Bell-LaPadula model
- Biba integrity model
- Clark and Wilson
- Noninterference
- State machine model
- Access matrix model
- Information flow model

The Bell-LaPadula model and the Biba integrity model are explained in-depth below, as they were major influencing models for TCSEC and ITSEC. Other models that follow are minor improvements to Bell-LaPadula and Biba or provide more analysis tools.

Bell-LaPadula Model

An early and popular security model, called Bell-LaPadula, was developed by Leonard J. LaPadula and David E. Bell in the 1970s and forms the basis of the TCSEC. It is a formal model of security policy that describes a set of access control rules. By conforming to a set of rules, the model inductively proves that the system is secure. A subject's (usually a user's) access to an object (usually a file) is allowed or disallowed by comparing the object's security classification with the subject's security clearance.

Bell-LaPadula is a *confidentiality model* intended to preserve the principle of least privilege. It is a formal description of allowable paths of information flow in a secure system and is used to define security requirements for systems handling data at different sensitivity levels. The model defines a secure state and access between subjects and objects in accordance with specific security policy.

Biba Integrity Model

The Biba model covers integrity levels, which are analogs to the sensitivity levels from the Bell-LaPadula model. Integrity levels cover inappropriate modification of data and prevent unauthorized users from making modifications to resources and data.

The Biba model uses a *read up, write down* approach. Subjects cannot read objects of lesser integrity and subjects cannot write to objects of higher integrity. Think of CIA analysts and the information that they need to perform their duties. Under Biba, an analyst with top secret clearance can only see information that's labeled at top secret with respect to integrity (confirmed by multiple sources, and so forth) and can only contribute information at their clearance level. Those with higher clearances will not be "poisoned" with data from a lower level of integrity and cannot poison those with clearances higher than theirs.

Advanced Models

Some of the other models improve upon earlier models or provide more in-depth analysis tools.

- **Clark and Wilson model:** Proposes "Well Formed Transactions." It requires mathematical proof that steps are performed in order exactly as they are listed, authenticates the individuals who perform the steps, and defines separation of duties.

- **Noninterference model:** Covers ways to prevent subjects operating in one domain from affecting each other in violation of security policy.

- **State machine model:** An abstract mathematical model consisting of state variables and transition functions.

- **Access matrix model:** A state machine model for a discretionary access control environment.

- **Information flow model:** Simplifies analysis of covert channels. A covert channel is a communication channel that allows two cooperating processes of different security levels (one higher than the other) to transfer information in a way that violates a system's security policy.

As you see, security models are required to help developers and evaluators with widely accepted criteria and functions that are proven reliable and acceptable for even a nation's most closely guarded secrets.

FYI: How Does a Covert Channel Work?

Following is an example of a human covert channel: A group of managers decide they don't want to waste too much time with an interview of a prospective employee and have come up with a communications protocol to let other interviewers know of their impression of the interviewee to either continue the interview or cut it short. The managers decide to cough if they decide to end the interview and sneeze if they are interested in pursuing the candidate. Without the candidate having any idea what they're up to, the managers can quickly agree to make the best use of their time.

Now here's an example of a computer-based covert channel: A program written by one programmer wants to communicate with another program written by a different programmer in collusion to violate the system's security policy. One possible motivation for doing so would be to span across a "Chinese Wall" that separates a banking company from a brokerage company to share information about a high-value customer with the intent of defrauding them outside the scope of the business. These programs may be written to agree beforehand on a protocol based on the programmers' desires. When program PostCreditToBill wants to send covert data to program SellStock, program PostCreditToBill may be programmed to cause lots of sudden CPU activity that program SellStock can detect and begin reading memory channels or communication channels to gain information about checking account data that would not be found in the brokerage system.

Summary

The Security Architecture and Models domain of the Common Body of Knowledge embodies the study of formal models for design and evaluation of systems needed for the highest levels of information security, including those that protect national secrets and other government property.

The trusted computing base, or TCB, is the portion of a computer system that contains all elements of the system responsible for supporting the security policy and supporting the isolation of objects on which the protection is based. Included are several mechanisms, properties, and concepts that are required for a formal evaluation prior to being used to protect resources and information.

Several evolving models of evaluation and assurance cover various aspects of confidentiality, integrity, and availability. TCSEC, otherwise known as the *Orange Book*, is primarily concerned with confidentiality and is based on the Bell-LaPadula model. ITSEC adds concerns about integrity and availability. The Canadian Criteria (CTCPEC) advances the work of TCSEC and ITSEC.

Finally, the Common Criteria harmonizes the work of the various international efforts into a unified evaluation methodology that replaces the former methods.

Test Your Skills

MULTIPLE CHOICE QUESTIONS

1. What can best be defined as the sum of protection mechanisms inside the computer, including hardware, firmware, and software?

   A. trusted system

   B. security kernel

   C. trusted computing base

   D. security perimeter

2. Which of the following statements pertaining to protection rings is false?

   A. They provide strict boundaries and definitions on what the processes that work within each ring can access.

   B. Programs operating in inner rings are usually referred to as existing in a privileged mode.

   C. They support the CIA triad requirements of multitasking operating systems.

   D. They provide users with a direct access to peripherals.

3. Which of the following places the *Orange Book* classifications in order from most secure to least secure?

   A. Division A, Division B, Division C, Division D

   B. Division D, Division C, Division B, Division A

   C. Division D, Division B, Division A, Division C

   D. Division C, Division D, Division B, Division A

4. The *Orange Book* describes four hierarchical levels to categorize security systems. Which of the following levels require mandatory protection?

   A. Divisons A and B

   B. Divisions B and C

   C. Divisions A, B, and C

   D. Divisions B and D

5. Which of the following *Orange Book* ratings represents the highest security level?

   A. B1

   B. B2

   C. F6

   D. C2

6. Which *Orange Book* security rating introduces security labels?

   A. C2

   B. B1

   C. B2

   D. B3

7. The *Orange Book* is founded upon which security policy model?

   A. the Biba model

   B. the Bell-LaPadula model

   C. Clark-Wilson model

   D. TEMPEST

8. The Information Technology Security Evaluation Criteria (ITSEC) was written to address which of the following that the *Orange Book* did not address?

   A. integrity and confidentiality

   B. confidentiality and availability

   C. integrity and availability

   D. none of the above

9. What does CC stand for?

   A. enCrypted Communication

   B. Common Criteria for Information Security Evaluation

   C. Certificate Creation

   D. Circular Certificate rollover

16

10. What is it called when a computer uses more than one CPU in parallel to execute instructions?

    A. multiprocessing

    B. multitasking

    C. multithreading

    D. parallel running

11. Which of the following choices describe a condition when RAM and secondary storage are used together?

    A. primary storage

    B. secondary storage

    C. virtual storage

    D. real storage

12. What is the Biba security model concerned with?

    A. confidentiality

    B. reliability

    C. availability

    D. integrity

13. Which of the following is not a method to protect subjects, objects, and the data within the objects?

    A. layering

    B. data mining

    C. abstraction

    D. data hiding

14. What is the main concern of the Bell-LaPadula security model?

    A. accountability

    B. integrity

    C. confidentiality

    D. availability

15. What would best define a covert channel?

    A. an undocumented back door that has been left by a programmer in an operating system

    B. an open system port that should be closed

    C. a communication channel that allows transfer of information in a manner that violates the system's security policy

    D. a Trojan horse

EXERCISES

Exercise 16.1: Trusted Computing Base

1. Describe the concept and main features of the trusted computing base (TCB).

2. What elements are found in the TCB?

3. What types of software should implement the concept of the TCB?

Exercise 16.2: Security Evaluations

1. Describe the concept of security evaluation (security assurance).

2. What are some of the general criteria used for evaluation?

Exercise 16.3: TCSEC (*Orange Book*)

1. Describe TCSEC in terms of its overall purposes.

2. What are the different TCSEC divisions and classes?

3. Why are different classes needed for different types of security classifications?

Exercise 16.4: ITSEC

1. Describe ITSEC in terms of purposes and differences in classes.

2. How does ITSEC differ from TCSEC?

Exercise 16.5: Common Criteria (CC)

1. Describe the Common Criteria in terms of its purpose.

2. How does the CC differ from TCSEC and ITSEC?

16

PROJECTS

Project 16.1: Security Testing for Obvious Vulnerabilities

1. Research the Internet for several common software vulnerabilities (examples: buffer-overflow conditions, cross-site scripting).

2. Describe several ways that security testing can uncover the conditions.

3. Describe the limitations of security testing.

4. To what degree should testing be performed if the software is intended for commercial uses?

5. To what degree should testing be performed if the software is intended for commercial, governmental, and military uses?

Project 16.2: MS Windows and Common Criteria Testing

1. Visit the Microsoft Web Site at **www.microsoft.com**.

2. Search for what MS is doing with the Common Criteria for Windows Operating Systems.

3. How does their involvement in CC testing fit into their Trustworthy Computing Initiatives?

4. What advantages does a CC-certified version of Windows bring about?

5. What criticisms of the CC-certified versions of Windows can you find?

Project 16.3: Trusted Computing in the Marketplace

1. Research a few of the user authentication products in the marketplace:
   - Netegrity Siteminder: **www.netegrity.com**
   - Computer Associates eTrust: **www.ca.com**
   - BMC Software's Control SA: **www.bmc.com**

2. What elements of trusted computing can you find in these products?

3. What kinds of commercial security testing have these products undergone?

4. Which product(s) are certified?

Case **Study**

A manufacturer of intrusion detection systems that is based in Canada wishes to offer its product for sale to the U.S. government. The marketing group has asked your advice on the requirements for selling information assurance products to the United States. As a lead security analyst for the firm, prepare a list of the steps that the manufacturer should go through to prepare the product for a Common Criteria evaluation. What documents do you need to prepare in advance of an evaluation? How long would an evaluation be expected to take?

Use the following Web sites to assist your research:

- Common Criteria Portal: **www.commoncriteriaportal.org**

- Science Applications International Corporation (a U.S.-based CC Lab): **www.saic.com**

- CGI Information Systems and Management Consultants: **http://infosec.cgi.com**

16

Chapter | 17

Business Continuity Planning and Disaster Recovery Planning

Chapter Objectives

After reading this chapter and completing the exercises, you will be able to do the following:

- Distinguish between the business continuity plan (BCP) and the disaster recovery plan (DRP).

- Follow the steps in the BCP.

- Inform business executives why planning is important.

- Define the scope of the business continuity plan.

- Identify types of disruptive events.

- Outline the contents of a business impact analysis (BIA).

- Discuss recovery strategies and the importance of crisis management.

- Explain backup and recovery techniques including shared-site and alternate site agreements.

Introduction

Upon reading this chapter, you may feel like you are preparing for a project management role rather than an information security role, but you'll soon see that the interests of those who manage the business and those who safeguard it are intertwined. This chapter, more so than any of the other domains of the Common Body of Knowledge, deals with business management concerns: how to prepare for an emergency or calamity and how to respond and continue operations under suboptimal business conditions.

In this chapter, you will learn about the goals of sound business continuity planning and disaster recovery planning, how these two types of planning differ, the types of threats that could invoke emergency planning and procedures, and several of the more prominent techniques organizations are using to plan for and hopefully prevent a disruption in business activities.

Overview of the Business Continuity Plan and Disaster Recovery Plan

In the early 1990s, the focus of most businesses concerned about the health and safety of their organization and its continued operation centered on disaster recovery planning. This type of planning primarily included information technology (IT) systems and applications, application data, and the networks supporting the IT infrastructure. In the case of highly regulated industries such as government, health care, and financial services, organizations had to meet recovery-time objectives and recovery-point objectives to minimize the loss of operations and the transaction data upon which they depend.

As the millennium change (or, Y2K) approached, such organizations began to broaden their approach to disaster recovery planning, implementing more encompassing business continuity planning to address fail points not in just IT operations but throughout the organization. Such a shift in view from a strictly IT-centric to a company-wide plan accelerated after the September 11 terrorist attack, when the loss of life dramatically emphasized the need to protect an organization's most important resource, its employees.

The business continuity plan (BCP) describes the critical processes, procedures, and personnel that must be protected in the event of an emergency and uses the business impact analysis (BIA) to evaluate risks to the organization and to prioritize the systems in use for purposes of recovery. Mission-critical systems—those systems that are essential for the ongoing operation of the business—are at the top of the list, followed by less critical systems and those down the line that are "nice to have" systems but nonessential for the business to remain in business.

The disaster recovery plan (DRP) describes the exact steps and procedures personnel in key departments, specifically the IT department, must follow in order to recover critical business systems in the event of a disaster that causes the loss of access to systems required for business operations. For example, one credit card company's mission-critical system is the authorization system for charge requests at the point of sale: Without this capability, no revenue could be generated and the company would be out of business in a matter of days or weeks.

Business continuity planning and disaster recovery planning share the common goal of keeping a business running in the event of an emergency or interruptions. They are alike in that both the BCP and DRP strive to prevent costly disruptions in critical business processes after disaster strikes.

Anticipating, planning for, and preventing problems is generally less costly than simply reacting to them after they occur. At a minimum, outages to IT systems can cost millions of dollars in lost revenue, lost productivity, and lost resources because of legal issues. At the extreme, a sustained outage can threaten the viability of an organization. According to the Gartner Group, "two out of every five enterprises that experience a disaster go out of business within five years." Failing to plan is indeed planning to fail when it comes to business and IT operations.

The following steps must be included when business and security experts create a business continuity plan. They are designed to ensure continued operations and to protect people and property within the business in the event of an emergency. They must:

1. Identify the scope and boundaries of the business continuity plan while communicating the importance of such a plan throughout the organization. What are the critical aspects of the business that must be considered as part of the plan? This step typically involves an audit analysis of the organization's assets including people, facilities, applications, and IT systems, and a risk analysis that identifies the types of threats to the organization, both man-made and natural.

2. The result of the thorough analysis in step 1 is the creation of the business impact assessment. The BIA measures the operating and financial loss to the organization resulting from a disruption to critical business functions (the BIA will be explained more thoroughly later in this chapter).

3. Once the BIA is complete, those responsible for creating the plan must sell the concept of the BCP to key senior management and obtain organizational and financial commitment. Without the support of top management, the BCP will remain an abstraction, mere words on a page, and nothing more. The presenters must be prepared to answer such questions as, is the BCP cost-effective and practical? If the cost of implementing the plan outweighs the benefit derived from it, the BCP will need to be reviewed and modified where appropriate. And if the plan is too cumbersome and impractical to implement, chances of its succeeding are slim.

4. Once the BCP has gained the approval of upper management who have signed off on the plan and released the necessary resources to implement it, each department will need to understand its role in the plan and support and help maintain it. This happens through a thorough examination of "best practices" within the organization and the tasks, processes, roles, and resources needed to meet the stated objectives of the continuity plan.

17

5. Finally, the BCP project team must implement the plan. This includes the necessary training, testing, and ongoing review and support of the BCP, both in financial and practical terms. Business processes are rarely static, and the project team must ensure that the BCP adapts to changes within the organization.

Why the BCP Is So Important

Although never an absolute guarantee, the BCP reduces the risk to the business in the event of a disruption in the continuity of business (more below on exactly what these disruptions can be). Many of the same reasons we plan for emergencies in our personal lives apply to the BCP: to save time and money, reduce stress, maintain a steady flow of income, protect lives, and to minimize disruptions.

Businesses, however, have responsibilities beyond personnel and property. They are chartered with protecting shareholder investments while meeting federal and state legal requirements. They also have to worry about public image. Any significant disruption in business will quickly drive away partners, investors, and consumers. You may have heard the phrase "due diligence" in the work place or in other course work. Although the phrase has no precise definition, the intent is that a business will act responsibly and protect its assets according to generally accepted business practices and management. In fulfilling this responsibility, being "proactive" is preferable to being "reactive."

According to AbleOne Systems, a provider of high-tech consulting services, some telling statistics related to business continuity planning and disaster recovery planning include

- Eighty percent of businesses without a recovery plan went bankrupt within 1 year of a major data loss.

- Fifty-nine percent of companies cannot conduct business during unscheduled IT downtime.

- Forty percent of companies that cannot conduct business during a major IT outage go out of business within 5 years.

- Fifty percent of companies in the World Trade Center went out of business after September 11, 2001.

(Source: **www.ableone.com/Web%20PDF%20files/Business%20Continuity%20Plan-no%20pic.pdf.**)

Types of Disruptive Events

You will learn about some of the specific types of threats to a business in Chapter 19 in a discussion of the Physical Security Domain. Part of the definition of business continuity planning involves identifying realistic threats to the business. Keep in mind that the BCP defines plans and processes to be invoked after an event occurs.

Natural events capable of disrupting a business could include

- earthquakes, fires, floods, mudslides, snow, ice, lightning, hurricanes, tornadoes, and so forth

- explosions, chemical fires, hazardous waste spills, smoke and water damage

- power outages caused by utility failures, high heat and humidity, solar flares, and so forth

Examples of natural events causing dramatic challenges to continuity planning include the 1989 San Francisco earthquake, Hurricane Hugo, the 1997 floods in the Midwestern United States, the 1998 Florida tornadoes, and the series of summer 2004 hurricanes in Florida and on the Gulf Coast of the United States.

Events where man and not nature is directly responsible for disruptive events could include

- strikes, work stoppages, walkouts

- sabotage, burglary, and other forms of hostile activity

- massive failure of technology including utility and communication failure caused by human intervention or error

Memories of the Tylenol scare in 1982, the bombings in 1992 in the London Financial District, the 1993 bombing of the World Trade Center, the Oklahoma City bombing in 1995, the Tokyo sarin gas attack in 1995, and the September 11, 2001, attacks on the World Trade Center in New York and the Pentagon in Washington, D.C., loom large in the minds of millions. Although these are some of the most dramatic examples of recent man-made actions resulting in significant loss of lives and money, a relatively minor event such as theft or sabotage performed by a disgruntled employee can seriously jeopardize a business and go unnoticed for a long period of time.

Defining the Scope of the Business Continuity Plan

The formal implementation of the BCP requires a close examination of business practices and services that constitute the boundaries and define the scope of the plan. Obviously, for a large business or organization, this process can be time consuming and labor intensive. For that reason, one of the most overlooked but important steps is obtaining executive management buy-in and sign-off for the plan. The project team must make a business case for continuity planning, especially in those instances where the BCP is not mandatory. They will have to compare the cost of implementing the BCP with the benefits derived from meeting its objectives.

Other steps involved in defining the scope of the BCP include

- Identifying critical business processes and requirements for continuing to operate in the event of an emergency.

- Assessing risks to the business if critical services are discontinued. This process is sometimes referred to as *business impact analysis*.

- Prioritizing those processes and assigning a value to each process. Which processes are absolutely critical and must be kept "online" without interruption? For example, keeping a continuous supply of power in a hospital emergency room is obviously more important than in the employee cafeteria.

- Determining the cost of continuous operation and the value ascribed to each service.

- Establishing the priority of restoring critical services. Which must be restored within the hour? the day? within a week? Which services cannot withstand any interruption?

- Once executive management has approved the concept of the BCP and the scope and definition of the project is identified, the BCP team must establish the rules of engagement. This involves identifying roles and responsibilities of the project team members and establishing the means of communication and the mechanisms for tracking progress.

Creating the Business Impact Analysis

The BIA identifies the risks that specific threats pose to the business, quantifies the risks, establishes priorities, and performs a cost versus benefit analysis for countering risks. In pursuit of these goals, the three most important steps include

1. Prioritize the business processes, most likely at the department level, possibly using a scoring system to assign a weight or value to each process. For example, in a manufacturing environment, processes such as materials receipt, inventory, production, shipping, and accounting among others would deserve consideration. This makes the task of prioritizing easier and hopefully less subjective, assuming that all business units accept the scoring method. This approach gives prioritization more objective scientific validity.

2. Once critical processes have been identified and prioritized, determine how long each process can be down before business continuity is seriously compromised. Keep in mind that processes usually are interrelated and may need to be grouped together in order to assess downtime tolerance.

3. Identify the resources required to support the most critical processes. What equipment, which people, and how much money beyond normal operating costs do you need to maintain critical ("life support" in industry jargon) systems?

The committee responsible for drafting the BIA must present it to the executive team for evaluation and recommendation when it is complete. Senior management will review the contents of the document including the identification and prioritization of critical processes, cost-benefit analyses and the method of supporting the plan once implemented. Then, most importantly, the plan is communicated to all employees and support personnel including outside vendors and contractors. All personnel, not just those individuals supporting the critical processes, must have a basic awareness of what the business continuity plan contains. This is one case where "on the job" training does not work.

Disaster Recovery Planning

In order to keep the business running, what actions must be taken until normal operations can be restored? In most organizations today, IT plays a critical role in supporting key business processes, thus the importance of the disaster recovery plan. The DRP most typically involves running operations at a remote off-site location until the business deems it safe to restart at its primary location.

The goals of the DRP include

- Keeping the computers running. Computer services are an integral part of most businesses, especially those such as Internet service providers where it is the business.

- Meeting formal and informal service-level agreements with customers and suppliers.

- Being proactive rather than reactive. A carefully rehearsed DRP must be second nature to critical personnel. The DRP should include a comprehensive checklist of activities to perform through practice runs to help make sure those people who are responsible for recovery are not caught by surprise.

Identifying Recovery Strategies

The BCP will identify the critical business processes that must be protected through the BIA documents. The function of the DRP is to identify the exact strategy for recovering those processes, specifically IT systems and services that are struck by a disaster. Because information technology is critical to almost every business these days and is the focus of this text, you will need to understand several disaster recovery strategies that are available to an organization.

Shared-Site Agreements

Shared-site agreements are arrangements between companies with similar if not identical data processing centers. This compatibility in hardware, software, and services allows companies who enter into an agreement to back up each other when one of the partners has an emergency. Rather than build an entire infrastructure to back up its applications and data, Company A enters an agreement with Company B to share resources in the event of a disaster. Such an arrangement can save substantial time and money because the computers and software already exist and do not have to be procured. In theory, when Company A loses its data processing center resources, a figurative switch flips and it begins to run its applications on Company B's computers as if nothing ever happened.

Despite the advantages of reduced costs, there are problems with this scenario. First, the data centers must be highly compatible in terms of the hardware and software they run. In fact, if Company A is not a subsidiary of Company B or if they aren't regional offices of the same corporation, a shared-site agreement is difficult to implement. If the companies are not part of the same corporate charter, other difficulties arise such as assured data security, privacy protection, and data synchronization. Shared-site agreements are feasible when companies are closely related and share common processing platforms, but the challenges are greater when this is not the case.

Alternate Sites

A company seeking DRP assistance can also use a third-party vendor to provide emergency backup services. Instead of entering a reciprocal agreement with another business, the company uses the services of a vendor whose business is to provide DRP services. You might be wondering who provides backup services for the third-party vendor. The vendor is responsible for providing backup services in case they experience a critical failure in their systems.

These alternate-site services providers are the most commonly used form of DRP assistance and generally take on one of three forms: a hot site, a warm site, or a cold site.

Hot Site A hot-site facility assumes the entire burden of providing backup computing services for the customer. This includes hosting the application software and data in a so-called mirror site. The vendor should be prepared to assume all responsibility for processing transactions for the customer, with little to no interruption of service. The vendor is responsible for maintaining the facility including all environmental controls such as heating, air conditioning, and power; hardware, including servers and printers; data backups; and all other services you would associate with a data processing center.

Although a hot-site facility offers several advantages, most importantly providing uninterrupted service in a relatively quick time, it can also be the most expensive solution as a DRP. Also, the hot site poses some security risk as the data is now stored, backed up, and theoretically accessible to a third party. Still, for those companies that can afford a hot-site facility, it is the most attractive solution.

Cold Site Unlike the hot site, the cold site provides the facilities including power, air conditioning, heat, and other environmental systems necessary to run a data processing center without any of the computer hardware or software. The customer must literally deliver the hardware and software necessary to bring their site up. The cold site is a cheaper solution than hot-site services, but you get what you pay for. When you consider the logistical problems of moving hardware that is highly sensitive to both temperature fluctuations and movement and quickly installing software on it, you will appreciate the challenges that a cold-site facility poses. In the event of a true disaster, where a company cannot afford to suffer a protracted outage, the cold-site alternative, although economically feasible, may give the customer the illusion of security that may not be grounded in reality. Unfortunately, this lesson may be learned the hard way.

Warm Site As you might suspect, the warm-site facility is a compromise between the services offered by hot- and cold-site vendors. A warm-site facility provides the building and environmental services previously mentioned, with the addition of the hardware and communication links already established. However, the customer's applications are not installed nor are workstations provided. In this case, the customer restores application software from backups using workstations it provides. Warm sites are cheaper than hot sites but require more effort. On the other hand, they are more expensive than cold-site facilities but less labor intensive and more likely to be effective in a disaster.

An important part of the BCP is determining the constraints, both financial and operational, under which the company is working and choosing the most realistic solution that meets the minimal needs of the BCP.

Additional Arrangements

Several other arrangements exist, affording a company more options with their business continuity planning. They are:

- Multiple centers: in this case, processing is distributed across multiple sites that may be in-house or part of a shared-site agreement. As with distributed networks, a multiple center arrangement spreads the processing across sites and offers redundancy in processing as an added safeguard. Although less costly than a hot site, administering multiple centers could be a burdensome chore and cost-prohibitive.

17

- **Service bureaus:** Known for their quick response but high cost, service bureaus provide backup processing services at a remote location. Service bureaus also perform primary application processing such as payroll systems and have extra capacity available for DRP services.

- **Mobile units:** In this scenario, a third-party vendor provides a data processing center on wheels, complete with air conditioning and power systems.

How to Test a Disaster Recovery Plan

Testing the DRP thoroughly is an absolutely necessary and non-negotiable step in planning for a disaster. A plan may look great on paper, but until it is tested in a situation that resembles a true disaster, its value cannot be determined. Testing the plan not only shows that the plan is viable, but it also prepares personnel for a disaster by teaching them their responsibilities and removing all uncertainty and thus mitigating risk.

The Certified Information Systems Security Professional, or CISSP, recognizes five methods of testing the DRP. They are

- **Walk-throughs:** Members of the key business units meet to trace their steps through the plan, looking for omissions and inaccuracies.

- **Simulations:** During a practice session, critical personnel meet to perform a "dry run" of the emergency, mimicking the response to a true emergency as closely as possible.

- **Checklists:** A more passive type of testing, members of the key departments "check off" the tasks for which they are responsible and report on the accuracy of the checklist. This is typically a first step toward a more comprehensive test.

- **Parallel testing:** The backup processing occurs in parallel with production services that never stop. This is a familiar process for those who have installed complex computer systems that run in parallel with the existing production system until the new system proves to be stable. An example of this might be when a company installs a new payroll system: Until the new system is deemed ready for full cut-over, the two systems are operated in parallel.

- **Full interruption:** Also known as the true/false test, production systems are stopped as if a disaster had occurred to see how the backup services perform. They either work (true) or they fail (false) in which case the lesson learned can be as painful as a true disaster.

Without the Walls and Within

A well-tested DRP should anticipate the unanticipated. It should predict how employees will behave in the event of an emergency within its walls and consider how they will interact with external agents such as firemen, ambulance drivers, and policemen. The goal of the DRP is to reassure and not alarm personnel about the outcome of a disaster and to remind them, above all, that the company will make every effort to protect them. The company must also protect its image to outsiders by proving that the DRP procedures are well thought-out and tested. Should the company survive a disaster in spite of its DRP rather than because of it, the message sent to customers, suppliers, and investors is not a comforting one.

Summary

Buisness continuity planning (BCP) and disaster recovery planning (DRP) are formal processes in any business that is concerned about maintaining its operation in the face of a disaster or interruption that prevents people from gaining access to their place of employment.

The DRP has its roots in the early 1990s when securing IT operations was the focus of most organizations. This concern spread to other areas of the organization with dramatic punctuation after the September 11 attack.

To implement its DRP, a company typically uses outside services such as a shared-site arrangement or third-party vendor to replicate critical data processing services. Several of the alternatives are hot-site, cold-site, and warm-site arrangements.

Regardless of which arrangement a company chooses, the plan must be thoroughly tested using one or more of the five testing techniques such as simulation or parallel testing. Although a true disaster cannot absolutely be recreated, a close approximation should reassure employees that their safety is the company's highest priority and also serve to clarify their responsibilities in the event of a true disaster.

Test Your Skills

MULTIPLE CHOICE QUESTIONS

1. Which of the following is NOT true about the BCP and DRP?

    A. Both plans deal with security infractions after they occur.

    B. Both plans describe preventative, not reactive, security procedures.

    C. The BCP and DRP share the goal of maintaining "business-as-usual" activities.

    D. They belong to the same domain of the Common Body of Knowledge.

2. According to the Gartner Group:

   A. Organizations with sound business continuity plans will never experience an interruption of business.

   B. Approximately 40 percent of businesses experiencing a disaster of some sort go out of business.

   C. The BCP and DRP are interchangeable in most organizations.

   D. Organizations with fewer than 100 employees generally do not need a DRP.

3. Place the following steps of the BCP in the correct sequence: (a) create the BIA; (b) obtain signoff of the tested BCP; (c) identify the scope of the BCP; (d) write the BCP:

   A. a, c, d, b

   B. c, b, a, d

   C. c, a, d, b

   D. d, b, c, a

4. Why is the BCP important?

   A. It minimizes disruption in business continuity.

   B. It eliminates risk in an organization.

   C. It has spawned a new cottage industry for business planning experts.

   D. The public will be unaware of problems within the organization.

5. What is the purpose of the BIA?

   A. To create a document that's used to help management understand what impact a disruptive event would have on the business.

   B. To define a strategy that minimizes the effect of disturbances and to allow for the resumption of business processes.

   C. To emphasize the organization's commitment to employees and vendors.

   D. To work with executive management to develop a DRP.

6. The scope definition of the BCP should include all of the following *except*:

   A. prioritizing critical business processes.

   B. calculating the value and cost of continuing important business processes.

   C. performing a dry run of emergency fire and medical evacuation procedures.

   D. assessing the cost to the business if critical services are disrupted.

7. Which of the following would be considered a man-made disaster?

   A. earthquake

   B. tornado

   C. flooding caused by a broken water main

   D. wildcat strike

8. What is the number one priority of disaster response?

   A. protecting hardware

   B. protecting software

   C. transaction processing

   D. personnel safety

9. What is *not* a benefit of cold sites?

   A. no resource contention with other organizations

   B. quick recovery

   C. geographical location that is not affected by the same disaster

   D. low cost

10. Which of the following computer recovery sites is only partially equipped?

    A. nonmobile hot site

    B. mobile hot site

    C. warm site

    D. cold site

11. An organization short on funding but long on its ability to assume risk would most likely use what kind of recovery site?

    A. alternate site

    B. cold site

    C. global site

    D. tepid site

12. Which of the following is an advantage of using hot sites as a backup alternative?

    A. The costs associated with hot sites are low.

    B. Hot sites can be made ready for operation within a short period of time.

    C. Hot sites can be used for an extended amount of time.

    D. Hot sites do not require that equipment and systems software be compatible with the primary installation being backed up.

13. Using multiple centers as a recovery site has what main disadvantage?

    A. Multiple centers are more difficult to administer than other types of recovery sites.

    B. Processing is shared by multiple sites.

    C. Multiple centers offer redundant processing.

    D. Services may be shared between in-house and outside services.

14. What is a mobile unit site?

    A. a convenient means for employees to give blood

    B. a fully equipped recovery site on wheels

    C. a SWAT team that provides first-response services

    D. a backup power supply, typically a diesel or gasoline generator

15. The primary goal of the DRP is to:

    A. alarm employees as a call to arms.

    B. protect the image of the organization above all.

    C. educate employees about emergency evacuation procedures.

    D. reassure employees that the organization puts their safety above all else.

16. The most extensive type of disaster recovery testing is

    A. checklists

    B. full interruption

    C. simulation

    D. parallel testing

EXERCISES

Exercise 17.1: Define the Attributes of an Effective DRP

1. Develop a DRP for an elementary school to respond to the building catching fire. Remember that the DRP must address the following concerns:

   - **It's practical.** Include useful information. Leave out unnecessary information.

   - **It's understandable.** Test instructions before implementing them.

   - **It's accessible.** Give copies to all concerned individuals, offices, and service points.

   - **It's kept current.** Revise pages as needed.

2. Share your DRP with other students in the class. What are the similarities? What are the differences?

Exercise 17.2: Investigate September 11 Emergency Procedures

1. Investigate BCP/DRP disaster recovery stories from the September 11, 2001, catastrophe in New York and Washington, D.C. (for example, visit the following Web site: **www.recoverychronicles.com/eNewsletter/ August2004/378/Article.asp**).

2. What did companies that successfully recovered do right?

3. What did companies that failed do wrong?

4. What lessons have we learned from such a calamity?

Exercise 17.3: Determine Local DRP Considerations

1. Identify the types of natural disasters prevalent in the area in which you live.

2. Research the types of disaster recovery services ready to respond to such disasters (you might research your local government Web site devoted to emergency management and homeland security).

3. Do you feel your community is prepared for such events?

17

Exercise 17.4: Revisit a Family Emergency

Think about a particular time in your own life, for example a family emergency, when you feel you were not adequately prepared to respond to the event. For example, imagine you went on an overnight backpacking trip with a small child and didn't take adequate supplies to get you through the hike.

1. What could you have done beforehand to avert some of the consequences of a lack of preparedness?

2. What could you have done to foresee events requiring contingency responses?

PROJECTS

Project 17.1: Create an Imaginary Company

1. Create a fictitious company or organization and describe the nature of its business, its location, the number of employees, and so forth.

2. Identify the challenges you would face in keeping your company running in the event of a disaster or interruption.

3. Prioritize the assets and determine what mission-critical functions and systems would need to be recovered first, second, and so forth.

4. Decide on some strategies on how to recover these systems and processes.

Project 17.2: Your BCP and DRP

1. Search the Internet to locate a business continuity plan or disaster recovery plan checklist for a small business. Several online sites you may want to visit include

   - The Business Continuity Planning & Disaster Recovery Planning Directory: **www.disasterrecoveryworld.com/**
   - Disaster Recovery Made Easy: **www.disaster-recovery-plan.com/**
   - Disaster Recovery Journal: **www.drj.com**

2. Draft your own business continuity plan or disaster recovery plan including a checklist of critical recovery tasks.

3. Share your plans with your classmates.

4. What are the similarities between the plans? What are the differences?

5. How would you revise your plan(s) now that you've seen some others?

Project 17.3: Compare Off-Site Services

1. Using the Internet, identify two or more off-site companies providing third-party backup services and compare their services and costs.

2. What kind of common services do they offer?

3. How do their costs compare?

4. Does one company offer services that another doesn't?

5. How do you account for this difference?

> # Case Study

You have just been hired as the chief information officer (CIO) for a high-tech firm in Silicon Valley. You know that the Bay Area in California is susceptible to earthquakes as it sits on top of a major fault line. However, what you didn't know was that your first project in your new position is to relocate the company's data center to a more geographically stable area that is not as susceptible to seismic disturbances. Your quandary, as you see it, is how to do so without losing your highly talented staff.

Most of your employees live in your current location for the lifestyle it offers and would be unlikely to move with the company to what they would consider a less desirable location. Your company provides highly specialized data processing services, and finding replacements for your current staff in a less urban setting would be difficult.

Weighing the financial health of the organization and the safety of your employees, how would you proceed?

17

Chapter 18

Law, Investigations, and Ethics

Chapter Objectives

After reading this chapter and completing the exercises, you will be able to do the following:

- Identify the types and targets of computer crime.
- Summarize the major types of attacks performed by cyber criminals.
- Understand the context of the computer in the legal system.
- Appreciate the complexities of intellectual property law.
- Discuss the issues surrounding computer security and privacy rights.
- Articulate the challenges of computer forensics.
- Recognize ethical issues related to information security.

Introduction

This chapter focuses on the obligations and responsibilities of the information security (IS) specialist. It will cover appropriate ethical behavior for working with sensitive data and systems and the laws governing the profession. It is a constant challenge for IS specialists to keep up with the latest laws, codes of ethics, and other rules governing the use of information technology. They rely on legal experts from both the private and public sectors who scramble to understand and respond to issues created by emerging technologies—issues that may have never existed before. The speed of technological change in most cases simply outstrips the speed in which our governing bodies can create applicable laws.

This gap between technology and the laws governing its use makes the IS specialist's role even more critical. She is duty-bound to her employers, the public, and to governing bodies such as the Information Systems Security Certification Consortium (ISC²) to uphold the law and act ethically in all cases. In this chapter, you will be exposed to some of the legal and ethical implications of being an information security specialist through an overview of the nature and types of computer crime, the laws created to deal with it, and the IS specialist Code of Ethics that governs professional behavior.

Types of Computer Crime

The pervasiveness of sensitive customer, government, and corporate information on the Web has created a million-dollar cottage industry of computer crime. The losses are difficult to gauge accurately, partly because many businesses, and individuals, are reluctant to advertise vulnerabilities. Letting the world know that the company site has been hacked simply is not good advertising. Corporations shun bad news such as this because it undermines public confidence, rattles stockholders, and can result in a sell-off on Wall Street.

Still, the 2004 Computer Security Institute (CSI)/FBI Computer Crime and Security Survey estimated that, based on 489 responses from information security practitioners across a broad range of industries, more than $141 million was lost through computer crimes (*source*: **http://i.cmp net.com/gocsi/db_area/pdfs/fbi/FBI2004.pdf**). The graph in Figure 18.1 reveals the dollar amount lost as a result of each type of computer crime.

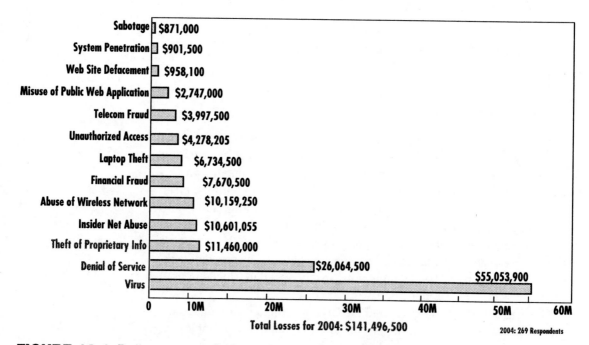

Total Losses for 2004: $141,496,500

2004: 269 Respondents

FIGURE 18.1 Dollar amount of losses by type of computer crime.

The CSI/FBI report also revealed that:

- The greatest financial loss ($55 million) came from virus attacks.

- The second most prevalent crime ($26 million) was the Denial of Service (DoS) attacks (more on this later in this chapter).

- Only 20 percent of companies experiencing an attack reported it to the authorities—down 10 percent from 2003.

The last point is telling. No one knows exactly how much is lost through computer crime, but it would be safe to say that the dollar amount is significantly higher than the amount reported by surveys.

Who are the victims of these acts? Practically everyone, as it turns out. According to the Certified Information Systems Security Professional (CISSP) Common Body of Knowledge, computer crimes are so widespread that identifying specific targets is too cumbersome. Instead, the CISSP has identified these major categories of computer crimes:

- **Military and intelligence attacks:** Criminals and intelligence agents illegally obtain classified and sensitive military information and police files.

- **Business attacks:** Increasing competition between companies frequently leads to illegal access of proprietary information. Even higher education is not immune from these activities. Yale accused Princeton of hacking its admissions site to obtain candidate information in July 2002 (see **www.usatoday.com/tech/news/comput ersecurity/2002-07-25-ivy-hack_x.htm**).

- **Financial attacks:** Banks and other financial institutions provide attractive targets for computer criminals for obvious reasons.

- **Terrorist attacks:** The U.S. Department of Homeland Security monitors the level of "chatter" on the Internet, looking for evidence of planned terrorist attacks against computer systems and geographic locations.

- **"Grudge" attacks:** Companies are increasingly wary of disgruntled employees who feel mistreated and exact their revenge using computer systems.

- **"Thrill" attacks:** Unlike grudge attackers who want some kind of revenge, thrill attackers hack computer systems for the "fun of it," bragging rights, or simply for a challenge.

Now that we've categorized the types of crimes that take place, we can take a look at the means of how these crimes are pulled off and what the consequences may be.

18

How Cyber Criminals Commit Crimes

The methods available to the computer criminal are extensive and too numerous for a complete treatment in this text, but several of the most prevalent types of computer crimes are listed below.

- **Denial of Service (DoS) attacks:** This is an overloading of a computer's resources (in particular, the temporary storage area in computers called "buffers") from any number of sources until the system is so bogged down that it cannot honor requests. The distributed Denial of Service attack in February 2000 on Yahoo! took the site down for three hours. A day later, eBay, Amazon.com, Buy.com, and CNN.com were hit with the same type of attack. The following day, ETrade and ZDNet were struck.

- **Rogue code:** The user inadvertently launches software that can log a user's keystrokes and send them to a remote server or perform other undesirable activities such as deleting files or destroying the operating system, rendering the computer useless.

- **Software piracy:** Copying or downloading software and using it without permission.

- **Social engineering:** Using deception to solicit information such as a password or personal identification number (PIN) from an unwitting victim; for example, a thief calls up a help desk pretending to be a user whose password needs resetting.

- **Dumpster diving:** A no-tech criminal technique that is pointed to as the primary cause of ID theft, where a criminal digs through your trash and recycling bins looking for receipts, checks, and other personal and sensitive information. Tip: If you don't shred all your receipts or lock up your recycling bin where you dispose of protected information, someone may be rummaging through your personal or proprietary information at this very moment.

- **Spoofing of Internet Protocol (IP) addresses:** Sending a message with a false originating IP address to convince the recipient the sender is someone other than who he really is. Every computer on the Internet is assigned a unique IP address. In this case, the attacker masquerades as a legitimate Internet site by using that site's IP address.

- **Emanation eavesdropping:** Intercepting radio frequency (RF) signals emanated by wireless computers to extract sensitive or classified information. This problem is addressed by the U.S. Government's TEMPEST program (requiring shields on computers transmitting such data). Operated by the U.S. Department of Defense (DOD), the

TEMPEST program has created a cottage industry of companies who create protective equipment to prevent foreign spies from collecting stray computer signals issued from DOD labs or U.S. embassies.

- **Embezzlement:** In the movie *Office Space*, three disgruntled employees modify computer software to collect round-off amounts (i.e., fractions of a penny) from a company's accounting program. This is an old crime in a new garb. Now criminals steal money by manipulating software or databases.

- **Information warfare:** A concern of the newly created U.S. Department of Homeland Security, information warfare includes attacks upon a country's computer network to gain economic or military advantage. You can learn more about information warfare at the Institute for the Advanced Study of Information Warfare (**www.psycom.net/iwar.1.html**).

The more highly publicized instances of these attacks are generally dramatic because they are so far-reaching. Some of these with which you might be familiar are the DoS attack against 3Com Corp and Nike.com in 2000, Kevin Mitnick's well-documented hacker exploits against phone companies, the Nigerian e-mail fraud, the Melissa Microsoft Word virus, the Bubbleboy worm, and the theft of 300,000 credit card numbers by the Russian hacker Maxus in 1999.

Then there are the more pedestrian methods: chain letters, pyramid schemes, outright fraud, cyberstalking, and phishing, where a scammer poses as a legitimate enterprise or organization in order to extract personally identifying information from a naïve or gullible user.

A common theme among most of these methods is the presence of vulnerabilities because of flaws in popular computer operating systems and application software or flaws in system implementation (i.e., failing to activate security controls or not configuring a system properly). The Application Development Domain covers specific vulnerabilities, but it is important to recognize now that most computer crime is preventable with sufficient, and competent, attention to security detail when deploying software.

The Computer and the Law

There are many laws that address computer crime. Legal issues have become more complex in the past decade with the extension of the U.S. economy to nations with emerging economies and the proliferation of companies with international or offshore sites. Computer crime issues were once strictly a matter of national law, but the movement of data across time zones and international boundaries has complicated the issue of legal jurisdiction.

As a consequence, an entirely new set of international computer security and privacy laws has been forged, often with conflicting goals. When the European Union passed the 1998 EU Data Protection Directive, it caused a great deal of controversy in the United States. This directive contains protections and safeguards of individual privacy that are generally much stricter than they are in the United States. Rather than examine the conflicts between countries over competing computer security regulations, this text will focus primarily on the legal system within the United States, discussing international law only in the context of how it may differ from U.S. laws.

Legislative Branch of the Legal System

As you are undoubtedly aware, the three branches of government that create and administer the laws defining the legal system in the United States are the legislative, executive, and judicial branches. The legislative branches (Congress and Senate) are responsible for passing statutory laws. A statutory law is a law written through the act of a legislature declaring, commanding, or prohibiting something. They are arranged by subject matter in the order in which they are enacted, thus they are referred to as *session laws*. Federal and state law codes incorporate statutes into the body of laws, and the judiciary system interprets and enforces them. State statutes govern matters such as wills, probate administration, and corporate law; federal statutes cover matters such as patent, copyright, and trademark laws.

Later in this chapter, you will read about copyright law and see how a basic understanding of statutory law is important to the information security specialist.

Administrative Branch of the Legal System

Administrative law is also referred to as *natural justice*. We owe this legal concept to the Romans, who believed certain legal principles were "natural" or self-evident and did not need to be codified by statute. In this case, disputes are resolved before an administrative tribunal and not in a court. For example, the Workmen's Compensation Board reviews and resolves disputes between the employee and his employer, aiming to provide workers and their dependents financial relief in the case of injuries arising out of job-related accidents without requiring a formal court proceeding. Administrative law is expanding rapidly because it normally offers a more expeditious and inexpensive resolution to disputes.

Judicial Branch of the Legal System

Common law arose from unwritten law that developed from judicial cases based on precedent and custom. The United States inherited the common law system from England as the basis for most of its legal systems. Common law is either unwritten or written as statutes or codes. The three primary categories of laws within the common law system are

- **Civil law:** Civil laws are written to compensate individuals who were harmed through wrongful acts known as *torts*. A tort can be either intentional or unintentional in the case of negligence. Common law is generally associated with civil disputes whereby compensation is financial but does not involve imprisonment.

- **Criminal law:** Criminal law punishes those who violate government laws and harm an individual or group. Unlike civil law, criminal law includes imprisonment in addition to financial penalties.

- **Regulatory law:** Administrative laws that regulate the behavior of administrative agencies of government. Considered part of public law, regulatory law addresses issues that arise between the individual and a public entity. Regulatory laws may also exact financial penalties and imprisonment.

The common laws governing matters of information systems include laws regulating intellectual property and privacy, which are discussed next in this chapter.

Intellectual Property Law

If you have ever downloaded music from a Web site without paying for it, you have likely broken one of the laws that protect intellectual property; that is, committed *copyright infringement*. Such an act may seem, at first, innocuous. But multiply this event by millions of users, then by the cost of the CDs they would have purchased, and the sum of the lost revenue is staggering. The magnitude of the problem is immense, costing the recording industry millions of dollars in revenue yearly. According to the Irish Recorded Music Association, a nonprofit organization facilitating discussion between the Irish recording industry and the government, annual losses from downloaded music exceed 3.8 million euros—at the current exchange rate about US$5 million—within the European Union. The association estimates the worldwide music piracy problem to be $5 billion annually (**www.irma.ie/piracy.htm**). This is why the artists and their recording labels go to court.

It is also why you need to know something about the legal framework protecting intellectual property, as the computer and its Internet connection makes the theft of music, video, and software files possible. The Internet also makes plagiarism a breeze. With the sheer volume of content on the Internet, it's difficult at times to determine what's covered by copyright and what is not, but more than one term paper turned in by students is certain to have violated someone's copyrights!

Besides copyright protection, designed to protect the distribution and reproduction rights of the owner, intellectual property law includes several other categories: patent law, trademarks, and trade secrets. These are discussed in detail in the following sections.

Patent Law

Inventors rush to patent their ideas to prevent others from using them. *Patents* "grant an inventor the right to exclude others from producing or using the inventor's discovery or invention for a limited period of time" (**www.uspto.gov**). In the United States, a patent is good for 17 years. The Patent and Trademark Office (PTO) oversees patent law for the federal government. However, the PTO has historically resisted patenting software. In the 1970s, the PTO would not grant a patent if the invention required a computer to perform a computation. The PTO was geared to the world of processes, manufactured articles, and machinery and did not recognize original claims to scientific truth or mathematical expressions. (Mathematical formulas or algorithms still cannot be patented.) This reluctance on the part of the PTO did not prevent a number of companies from filing patent applications for software. In 1963, for example, Bell Telephone Laboratories filed an application on behalf of its employees entitled "Conversion of Numerical Information" for its method of processing data, specifically the programmatic conversion of numeric data to other data types. The patent examiner from the PTO rejected the claim because of a "lack of novelty or non-obviousness." He felt that "mental processes" or "mathematical steps" were not the stuff of statutory law (**http://digital-law-online.info/lpdi1.0/treatise61.html**).

With the rapid advance of computer technology and its rapid spread from government offices to business and public use, the PTO had to devise new guidelines to address the issue of software patents. After numerous U.S. Supreme Court challenges in the early 1980s, the PTO had, by the mid-1990s, developed new guidelines to determine when a software invention was protected by patent law. For example, the PTO now grants patents for software such as instructions on a disk that guide machines or computers.

More famously, Amazon.com won an injunction against Barnes & Noble, who used the "one click" software similar to the software Amazon.com introduced for storing buyer preferences and other identifying information. The courts overturned the injunction in 2001, but Amazon still holds six patents related to ordering books (*source*: **www4.ncsu.edu/~baumerdl/Burgunder.04/Ch.%205.ppt#11**).

Trademarks

The Trademark Act defines *trademark* as "any word, name, symbol, or device, or any combination thereof" that the individual intends to use commercially and wants to distinguish as coming from a unique source. Again, the PTO was originally reluctant to sail the uncharted waters of granting trademarks to intellectual property such as software. But over time they have. Software giant Microsoft currently holds more than 200 trademarks, from "Actimates" to "Zoo Tycoon."

Trade Secrets

If you just gulped down your favorite sports drink, answered a telemarketing survey, or performed a routine task on your computer that used an obscure algorithm, chances are you have unwittingly taken advantage of a company trade secret. Unlike trademarks or patents, *trade secrets* do not benefit from legal protection. As long as no one but you knows about your idea, it belongs to you. Usually, a trade secret is a patent in process, an embryonic but unofficial and legally unprotected idea.

The story of the protection of software as intellectual property is a book unto itself. Enter the keyword search "software intellectual property" on Amazon.com and you should receive more than 20,000 hits, beginning with the contentious issue of "open sourcing." The courts are still debating the question of when an idea manifested as software moves from protection under intellectual property law to the public domain.

18

Privacy and the Law

Perhaps you have received privacy statements from your bank or other financial lenders explaining exactly what they plan on doing with your personally identifying information (e.g., a PIN). Maybe you have signed a statement at your doctor's office agreeing that you have read and fully comprehend the fine print contained in the Health Insurance Portability and Accountability Act (HIPAA) of 1996. These privacy documents often give rise to confusion. Do you "opt in" or "opt out" when being asked to share personally identifying information? What about privacy issues you might not be aware of like cookies (text files that remember information about you) stored on your hard drive without your knowledge? There are many privacy issues confronting companies that keep personal information about customers and employees.

The Federal Trade Commission's May 2000 report, "Fair Information Practices in the Electronic Marketplace," is pertinent to this discussion. Although the FTC does not mandate privacy practices, the report lists four privacy practices that all companies engaged in electronic commerce should observe, namely:

- **Notice/awareness:** In general, the Web site should tell the user how it collects and handles user information. The notice should be conspicuous, and the privacy policy should clearly state how the site collects and uses information.

- **Choice/consent:** Web sites must give consumers control over how their personally identifying information is used. Abuse of this practice is the gathering of information for a stated purpose but using it in another way, one to which the consumer might object.

- **Access/participation:** Perhaps the most controversial of the fair practices, users would be able to review, correct, and in some cases delete personally identifying information on a particular Web site. Most companies that currently collect personal information have no means of allowing people to review what the company collected, nor do they provide any way for a person to correct incorrect information. Implementing this control would be a burden to companies to retrofit onto an existing system. As you have likely seen with commercial credit reports, inaccurate information or information used out of context can make people's lives problematic.

- **Security/integrity:** Web sites must do more than reassure users that their information is secure with a "feel-good" policy statement. The site must implement policies, procedures, and tools that will prevent unauthorized access and hostile attacks against the site.

International Privacy Issues

The issue of protecting privacy in the United States has grown more complicated with the expansion of e-commerce across international borders and into the domain of different and sometimes much more rigorous and exacting privacy protection laws. The European Union's Data Protection Directive of 1998 was the result of several years of tough negotiation among EU members. The directive addressed the disparity between European privacy protection laws and what the EU viewed as the more porous and inconsistent state and federal privacy laws in the United States.

The U.S. Department of Commerce, wishing to head off a privacy law impasse with the European Union, negotiated the Safe Harbor Privacy Principles, a framework that allowed U.S. entities wishing to do business in the European Union to meet the minimum privacy controls of the EU directive. The International Safe Harbor Principles include the following privacy guidelines:

- **Notice:** Companies must notify individuals what personally identifying information they are collecting, why they are collecting it, and how to contact the collectors.

- **Choice:** Individuals must be able to choose whether and how their personal information is used by, or disclosed to, third parties.

- **Onward transfer:** Third parties receiving personal information must provide the same level of privacy protection as the company from whom the information is obtained.

- **Security:** Companies housing personal information and sensitive data must secure the data and prevent its loss, misuse, disclosure, alteration, and unauthorized access.

- **Data integrity:** Companies must be able to reassure individuals that their data is complete, accurate, current, and used for the stated purposes only.

- **Access:** Individuals must have the right and ability to access their information and correct, modify, or delete any portion of it.

- **Enforcement:** Each company must adopt policies and practices that enforce the aforementioned privacy principles.

Privacy Laws in the United States

Unless you are an employee of a U.S. corporation working in the European Union, you are probably more aware of privacy matters in your day-to-day life. For example, the Kennedy-Kassenbaum Health Insurance Portability and Accountability Act (HIPAA), passed in August 1996, codifies the right of individuals to control and protect their own health information. Although the European continent has adopted a more comprehensive and consistent set of privacy principles, the United States has been more willing to allow different industries, such as banking and health care, and different levels of government, to draft their own privacy guidelines. The effect has been a more piecemeal and disjointed approach to privacy protection. The following partial list of computer security and privacy laws shows a less than holistic approach to privacy protection in the United States:

- 1970 U.S. Fair Credit Reporting Act: a federal law that regulates the activities of credit bureaus.

- 1986 U.S. Electronic Communications Act: protects the confidentiality of private message systems through unauthorized eavesdropping.

- 1987 U.S. Computer Security Act.

- 1996 U.S. Kennedy-Kassenbaum Health Insurance and Portability Accountability Act (HIPAA): protects the confidentiality and portability of personal health care information.

- 2000 National Security Directive 42 (NSD-42): signed by President Bush, this directive established the Committee on National Security Systems (CNSS). The CNSS gives guidance on the security of national defense systems, among other roles.

- 2001 U.S. Patriot Act HR 3162, a.k.a. "Uniting and Strengthening America by Providing Appropriate Tools Required to Intercept and Obstruct Terrorism (USA PATRIOT ACT) Act of 2001."

- 2002 Federal Information Security Management Act: defines the basic statutory requirements for protecting federal computer systems.

The sheer numbers of laws related to computers has made it difficult for owners, operators, legislators, and law enforcement to stay on top of all regulations because of a number of factors:

- Enactment of new laws in a rapidly changing technology environment at times causes more problems than are solved.

- Globalization of the economy results in unclear international legal boundaries and jurisdiction questions.

- Standards are not always adopted by all countries, and conflicting security standards and practices result in varying levels of compliance and enforcement.

Without a more comprehensive and consolidated approach to privacy law, legislation in the United States most likely will continue to be a series of industry-specific rules and regulations.

Computer Forensics

Investigating crimes committed with computers is known as *computer forensics*. According to the National Data Conversion Institute, an organization specializing in facilitating the conversion and exchange of data between disparate computer systems as well as providing litigation data management services to law firms, corporations, and governments, an increasing number of civil and criminal lawsuits involve computerized data stored on some form of computer medium. Sherlock Holmes never could have envisioned that the physical evidence he once detected such as a lock of hair, a smudge on a topcoat, or mud caked on boots would evolve into the nearly invisible world of computer evidence.

The intangibility of computer evidence makes the job of prosecuting cyber crime even more difficult than traditional crime. Specialized expert knowledge is usually required, and jurisdictions become murky because of the difficulty of determining the locus of the crime. Furthermore, gathering evidence is complicated by the high-tech sleight-of-hand that computer criminals have mastered. Many know how to cover their tracks and distract investigators from their true locations.

The National Data Conversion Institute (NDCI) makes a case for using expert investigative services to solve computer crimes. Among the many arguments for such services are

- Successful litigation frequently depends on obtaining irrefutable computer evidence. Without solid computer evidence, you may not have a case.

■ Your evidence may not be as good as the opposition's if you are using less sophisticated data-detection techniques.

■ Your adversaries do not want you to obtain the data you need.

■ The technology used to create the data you need may have already disappeared. Time is of the essence.

Additionally, all of the other requirements of successful litigation are still in play: the admissibility of evidence, the types of legal evidence, and the legal search and seizure of evidence. Those prosecuting a crime must still play by the rules when conducting an investigation. But instead of looking for a smoking gun, they may be trying to restore a hard drive that was "permanently" erased.

The Information Security Professional's Code of Ethics

Security specialists are held to a high standard because they have access to a vast amount of information that, if used improperly, could ruin lives and even nations. Ethical behavior is easier to define than display. Although most people intuitively know what proper conduct is, it is difficult for anyone to admit that they are wrong or have done something wrong. It is very tempting to find ways to reinterpret behavior when caught committing a crime. For example, is an IT security specialist with access to sensitive payroll information acting unethically when confirming that a coworker is making substantially less money than another employee with the same job grade and performance rating?

In an effort to make the ethical behavior of information security specialists more explicit, the International Information Systems Security Certification Consortium (ISC^2) developed the code of conduct for Certified Information Systems Security Professionals (CISSPs).

According to the ISC^2 Web site, "All information systems security professionals who are certified by ISC^2 recognize that such certification is a privilege that must be both earned and maintained. In support of this principle, all Certified Information Systems Security Professionals (CISSPs) commit to fully support this Code of Ethics. CISSPs who intentionally or knowingly violate any provision of the Code will be subject to action by a peer review panel, which may result in the revocation of certification" (**www.isc2.org**). The ISC^2 Code of Ethics is mandatory for certified professionals. There are four mandatory canons in the code listed below. General guidance is not intended to substitute for the sound ethical judgment of the professional.

■ Protect society, the commonwealth, and the infrastructure.

■ Act honorably, honestly, justly, responsibly, and legally.

- Provide diligent and competent service to principals.

- Advance and protect the profession.

FYI: A Security Professional's Ethical Dilemma

Suppose you're an IT employee at a pharmaceutical manufacturer, and a high-level manager's PC has been hit hard with a virus attack that requires a desk-side visit to determine the prognosis. You find that the system will no longer boot up but, with your hard-drive recovery and antivirus tools, you're able to recover her files. In the process, you discover an internal memo that the company is trying to suppress from the FDA that discusses the surprising number of deaths during the field trials of a new anticancer drug.

What should you do? Should you ignore what you've found? Should you notify someone? Should you blow the whistle through the media? How can you apply the Code of Ethics to this dilemma? Which canon(s) apply?

This type of dilemma is one you might face as an IT security professional at some point in your career. Your decision at that point will be easier if this is a scenario that you have already thought about.

Although the tools used to commit crimes may change over the years with the advances in technology, the principles of investigation and prosecution, as well as the standards of ethical behavior, remain the same.

Other Ethics Standards

The ISC^2 Code of Ethics is one of the more prominent attempts at specifying ethical conduct for computer specialists. Other codes include

- Computer Ethics Institute's Ten Commandments of Computer Ethics

- Internet Activities Board's Ethics and the Internet

- U.S. Department of Health, Education, and Welfare Code of Fair Information Practices

Each of these efforts to codify ethical behavior share a common goal: establishing a code of conduct for anyone using computer resources. We will now cover each in more detail.

Computer Ethics Institute

The Ten Commandments of Computer Ethics was originally presented by Dr. Ramon C. Barquin in a paper titled "In Pursuit of a 'Ten Commandments' for Computer Ethics" (Computer Ethics Institute, May 7, 1992; **www.brook.edu/its/cei/cei_hp.htm**). They are

1. Thou Shalt Not Use a Computer to Harm Other People.
2. Thou Shalt Not Interfere with Other People's Computer Work.
3. Thou Shalt Not Snoop Around in Other People's Computer Files.
4. Thou Shalt Not Use a Computer to Steal.
5. Thou Shalt Not Use a Computer to Bear False Witness.
6. Thou Shalt Not Copy or Use Proprietary Software for Which You Have Not Paid.
7. Thou Shalt Not Use Other People's Computer Resources Without Authorization or Proper Compensation.
8. Thou Shalt Not Appropriate Other People's Intellectual Output.
9. Thou Shalt Think About the Social Consequences of the Program You Are Writing or the System You Are Designing.
10. Thou Shalt Always Use a Computer in Ways That Ensure Consideration and Respect for Your Fellow Humans.

Although many of these commandments are just good common sense, it's useful to remind people that there are consequences for unacceptable behavior. You may consider including these Ten Commandments in a security training and awareness program (see Chapter 15).

Internet Activities Board: Ethics and the Internet

Computer uses are pervasive; no industry or profession can survive this day and age without the aid of computer technology. Because of the potential for abuse of information or damage to resources from malicious uses of computer technology, the Internet Activities Board published a standard—Ethics and the Internet—intended for wide distribution and acceptance from the Internet-using communities. The introduction to RFC 1087 - Ethics and the Internet reads:

> At great human and economic cost, resources drawn from the U.S. Government, industry and the academic community have been assembled into a collection of interconnected networks called the Internet...
>
> ...As is true of other common infrastructures (e.g., roads, water reservoirs and delivery systems, and the power generation and distribution network), there is widespread dependence on the Internet by its users for the support of day-to-day research activities.

The reliable operation of the Internet and the responsible use of its resources is of common interest and concern for its users, operators and sponsors…

…Many of the Internet resources are provided by the U.S. Government. Abuse of the system thus becomes a Federal matter above and beyond simple professional ethics.

The complete RFC 1087 is available at **www.faqs.org/rfcs/rfc1087 .html**. It outlines a statement of policy and lists a number of unacceptable behaviors that would violate ethical behavior.

Code of Fair Information Practices

The Code of Fair Information Practices was adopted in 1973 by the U.S. Department of Health, Education and Welfare—now called the U.S. Department of Health and Human Services. It states that:

1. There must be no personal data record-keeping systems whose very existence is secret.

2. There must be a way for an individual to find out what information is in his or her file and how the information is being used.

3. There must be a way for an individual to correct information in his or her records.

4. Any organization creating, maintaining, using, or disseminating records of personally identifiable information must assure the reliability of the data for its intended use and must take precautions to prevent misuse.

5. There must be a way for an individual to prevent personal information obtained for one purpose from being used for another purpose without his or her consent.

(*Source*: **www.epic.org/privacy/consumer/code_fair_info.html.**)

The Code of Fair Information Practices, related more to the privacy of individuals on computerized record-keeping systems, complements the ethics standards for people to consider when using information systems. Because no one stands alone when connected to public networks, it's vital to lay the ground rules for what's acceptable and what's not acceptable.

Source: **U.S. Department of Health, Education, and Welfare (1973).**

Summary

Laws, investigative principles, and professional ethics, often thought of as abstract topics, are as important to information security professionals as knowing how to design firewall architecture. Understanding how different laws affect security practices across the globe gives the practitioner the correct perspective with which to operate internationally with the same confidence as working close to home. Understanding the relationships of computer crime investigations and the laws that govern property is critical to becoming a productive member of a team that can effectively protect, detect, and respond to security incidents.

Ethics are the ties that bind one's behavior to the world of computer security—balancing the authority one is given while working in the field with the checks and balances that prevent the abuse of power.

Test Your Skills

MULTIPLE CHOICE QUESTIONS

1. Business losses that are a result of computer crime are difficult to estimate for which of the following reasons?

   A. Companies are not always aware that their computer systems have been compromised.

   B. Companies are sometimes reluctant to report computer crime because it is bad advertising.

   C. Losses are often difficult to quantify.

   D. All of the above.

2. According to a 2004 Computer Security Institute CSI/FBI Computer Crime and Security Survey, what percentage of organizations experiencing computer attacks reported them to law enforcement agencies?

   A. 75 percent

   B. 20 percent

   C. 10 percent

   D. 90 percent

3. The CISSP categorizes computer attacks by type. Which of the following is not one of the categories identified by the CISSP?

   A. terrorist attack

   B. thrill attack

   C. subterfuge attack

   D. business attack

18

4. What type of individual is most likely to perform a "grudge attack?"

   A. an employee who feels he has been mistreated by his employer

   B. a political exile

   C. a libertarian

   D. all of the above

5. Computer crime is generally made possible by which of the following?

   A. the perpetrator's obtaining advanced training and special knowledge

   B. victim carelessness

   C. collusion with others in information processing

   D. system design flaws

6. The computer criminal who calls a help desk trying to obtain another user's password is most likely a:

   A. dumpster diver

   B. black-hat hacker

   C. social engineer

   D. spammer

7. Which of the following computer crimes involves overtaxing a computer's resources until it is no longer functional?

   A. spoofing IP addresses

   B. Denial of Service (DoS)

   C. rogue code

   D. information warfare

8. We inherited which of our legal systems from England?

   A. administrative law

   B. patent law

   C. Ccommon law

   D. byways

9. Computer laws have become increasingly difficult to enforce for which of the following reasons?

    A. the inability of legislation in the United States to keep pace with technological advances

    B. the globalization of the economy resulting in unclear international legal boundaries

    C. conflicting security standards within the United States and between the United States and other nations

    D. all of the above

10. "Natural justice" is

    A. primitive and thus "natural."

    B. enforced by judge and jury.

    C. considered self-evident and thus requires no statutes.

    D. unsuited for arbitration.

11. The Patent and Trademark Office (PTO) resisted patenting software for years for what primary reason?

    A. Software was too intangible.

    B. Software was the product of scientific truth or mathematical expressions.

    C. The average shelf life of software was estimated to be less than the life span of a patent (17 years).

    D. It was too interconnected with the computer's operating system.

12. Which of the following statements is true about a "trade secret"?

    A. It offers legal protection just as a trademark does.

    B. It is a patent "in the works."

    C. It is widely known but rarely discussed.

    D. All of the above.

13. Which of the following *is not* one of the FTC's four Fair Information Practices?

    A. Individuals should be given the choice of "opting out" when sharing their personal information.

    B. Personal information should be accurate and stored securely.

    C. Web sites must have 100 percent availability in case the user wishes to change his personal information.

    D. Web sites must tell the user how his personal information will be used and notify him of any changes to that policy.

18

14. What can be said about the European Union Data Protection Directive of 1998?

    A. The United States was exempted from privacy standards in the EU.

    B. The directive's goal was to standardize privacy protection among the EU members.

    C. It resulted in the "Safe Harbor Privacy Principles" that allowed the United States to meet minimum privacy controls in the European Union.

    D. Both B and C are correct.

15. Which of the following definitions best describes "computer forensics"?

    A. using computers to investigate crime

    B. investigating crimes committed using computers

    C. probing the operating system for signs of malfeasance

    D. predicting behaviors of cyber criminals

16. The ISC^2 Code of Ethics is intended to

    A. help certificate holders in resolving dilemmas related to their practice.

    B. provide guidance on encouraging good behavior.

    C. provide guidance on discouraging poor behavior.

    D. All of the above.

17. What bearing does ethics have on the information security specialist?

    A. Ethical conduct is expected of all IS specialists.

    B. It helps define a high moral code of professional behavior.

    C. It speaks to the credibility of the individual.

    D. All of the above.

18. Which of the following is not one of the provisions of the ISC^2 Code of Ethics?

    A. Act honorably, responsibly, and legally.

    B. Provide thorough and competent service to your customers and peers.

    C. Judge not lest you be judged.

    D. Strive to protect society and its components.

EXERCISES

Exercise 18.1: Research Current Computer Crimes

1. Perform a Google search on computer crime and compile a list of recent attacks and data compromises.

2. Where possible, identify the nature and source of the attacks.

Exercise 18.2: Research the Details of a Computer Crime

1. Select one of the types of computer attacks (e.g., DoS) and research the details of the attack.

2. What has the industry done in response to these attacks?

3. What became of the perpetrators of the crime(s)?

Exercise 18.3: Investigate the Current State of the EU Directive

1. Investigate further the current status of the European Union's Data Protection Directive on information privacy.

2. How many countries currently belong to the Safe Harbor group?

3. If you can determine, how well is Safe Harbor working out for information providers based in the United States?

Exercise 18.4: Investigate the Different Types of Computer-Based Legal Evidence

1. Research the different kinds of legal evidence used in computer crime investigations.

2. What are the differences between admissible and inadmissible evidence?

3. Who should be responsible for maintaining the chain-of-custody for computer crimes evidence?

18

Exercise 18.5: Brainstorm Unethical Uses of the Computer

1. Try to think of 10 examples of what you would consider to be unethical uses of the computer.

2. How might you mitigate these threats?

3. How would a set of codified ethics that users of the computer must subscribe to for using the system help in mitigating these threats?

PROJECTS

Project 18.1: Interview an IS Specialist

1. Identify and interview an IS specialist whose job it is to gather evidence for computer crimes.

2. Ask him/her to discuss as fully as possible the nature of the crimes. (*Note*: Investigators *love* talking about their jobs!)

3. What tools and techniques did he or she use to determine the culprit(s)?

4. How successful were any prosecutions of lawsuits brought against the perpetrators?

Project 18.2: Investigate the Complexities of Intellectual Property Law

1. Research the topic of intellectual property as related to copyright law.

2. What are some of the difficulties in proving a copyright infringement case, such as that brought by the RIAA against those who download free MP3 files?

3. What are some of the other recent and famous cases related to copyright, trademark, or trade secret infringements?

4. Who should govern the Internet to prevent intellectual property law infringements?

5. Can anyone or any one country govern how the Internet is used (and abused)?

Project 18.3: Examine a Recent Governmental Privacy Act

1. Select a recent governmental regulation such as HIPAA or the Gramm-Leach-Bliley Act (GLBA) to research the privacy aspects of the act.

2. What are some of the conflicting interests to business and the individual related to privacy matters?

3. What privacy concerns do you have as an Internet user and shopper?

4. How will your behavior change as a result of reading this chapter?

▶▷ Case Study

In fall 2003, The University of Calgary began offering a new course called "Computer Viruses and Malware," intended for fourth-year students. In the course, students learn to write and test their own viruses. The move touched off a wave of criticism within the antivirus community.

As a school administrator, you wound up getting the phone calls from both the supporters·and the protesters who accuse you of being irresponsible and demand that you cancel the class immediately.

Will you cancel the class? Can you defend the course and the reasoning behind offering it to students? Is there an ethical dilemma here? Write a press release that you would want to share with the local papers and TV stations that reflects your decision to continue or cancel the course.

18

Chapter | 19

Physical Security Control

Chapter Objectives

After reading this chapter and completing the exercises, you will be able to do the following:

- Distinguish between logical and physical security, and explain the reasons for placing equal emphasis on both.

- Recognize the importance of the Physical Security domain.

- Outline the major categories of physical security threats.

- Classify the techniques to mitigate risks to an organization's physical security.

- Classify the five main categories of physical security controls, including their strengths and limitations.

- Propose how smart cards can be used for physical access control.

- Categorize the different types of biometric access controls and determine their respective strengths and weaknesses.

Introduction

An often overlooked connection between ***physical systems*** (computer hardware) and ***logical systems*** (the software that runs on it) is that in order to protect logical systems, the hardware running them must be physically secure. If you can't physically protect your hardware, you can't protect the programs and data running on your hardware!

Physical security deals with who has access to buildings, computer rooms, and the devices within them. Controlling physical security involves protecting sites from natural and man-made physical threats through proper location and by developing and implementing plans that secure devices from unauthorized physical contact.

Information security experts, however, usually focus more on the problems related to logical security because of the greater likelihood that remotely located computer hackers will analyze, dissect, or break into computer networks. A hacker's physical proximity to a network has less to do with its vulnerability than porous interfaces or operating systems with more holes in them than Swiss cheese.

The idea of physical security may seem almost arcane and anachronistic in an age of remote high-tech stealth and subterfuge, but no aspect of computer security can be taken for granted. We are reminded by surveys, including the National Retail Security Survey (NRSS), that employee (insider) theft is on the rise and shows no sign of abating in light of downsizing, rightsizing, and layoffs. According to the 2001 NRSS, retailers attributed more than 45 percent of their company's losses to employee theft, including the trafficking of proprietary information. As you shall see, physical security applies not only to external attacks but also to "inside jobs" perpetrated by disgruntled employees who frequently feel that the company "owes them something" or by employees who are simply thieves.

The NRSS describes the more traditional view of loss of tangible goods (e.g., clothing, DVDs, manufacturing parts, etc.) through theft; however, loss of intellectual property and company information complicates the more traditional definition of property and has forced organizations to take internal theft as seriously as external theft.

Some of the information in this chapter may seem intuitive or obvious. Unfortunately, too many organizations, big and small, neglect some of the most basic aspects of physical security. That is why physical security is one of the 10 domains of the Certified Information Systems Security Professional (CISSP) Common Body of Knowledge (CBK).

Understanding the Physical Security Domain

The Physical Security domain includes the more traditional safeguards against threats, both intentional and unintentional, to the physical environment and the surrounding infrastructure. If you have ever worked for a large company or entered a municipal building, you most likely have experienced some of these security checks first-hand: badge readers, television monitors, bag and "airport" X-ray devices, and the ever-present armed security guards. The level of physical security is typically proportional to the value of the property that is being protected. Organizations such as the government or corporations conducting high-level research generally use more sophisticated physical security checks, including biometrics (explained later), as the property inside might be highly classified. Organizations that keep less sensitive information, however, still must worry about compromising fatal lawsuits. Regardless of the size or the nature of the organization, the goal of the Physical Security domain is to set safeguards in place to protect an organization's assets and assure the continuity of business in the event of man-made or natural disasters.

Challenges related to physical security lay in the need to make it simple for people who belong in a building to get in and get around but make it difficult for those who do not belong to enter and navigate. Thus, physical security, like many other areas of security, is a careful balancing act that requires trusted people, effective processes that reduce the likelihood of harm from inadvertent and deliberate acts, and appropriate technology to maintain vigilance.

If you have an interest in the security field, you'll need to understand the following areas of physical security:

- How to choose a secure site (location) and guarantee the correct design.

- How to secure a site against unauthorized access.

- How to protect equipment, for example personal computers and the information contained on them, against theft.

- How to protect the people and property within an installation.

These four areas of physical security are the focus of this chapter.

Physical Security Threats

You need to understand the threats physical security control systems address before learning about design and implementation. As you will learn later in this chapter, site selection depends heavily on a list of potential physical security threats for a given location. The goal of identifying these threats beforehand is to help assure uninterrupted business and/or computer service, lessen the risk of physical damage to a site from natural or man-made causes, and reduce the risk of internal and external theft. Most importantly, the safety of personnel takes precedence over the safety of structures, computers, data, and other systems.

The major categories of physical security threats, as defined in the CBK, are

- **Weather:** tornadoes, hurricanes, floods, fire, snow, ice, heat, cold, humidity, and so forth.

- **Fire/chemical:** explosions, toxic waste/gases, smoke, fire.

- **Earth movement:** earthquakes, mudslides.

- **Structural failure:** building collapse because of snow/ice or moving objects (cars, trucks, airplanes, and so forth).

- **Energy:** loss of power, radiation, magnetic wave interference, and so forth.

- **Biological:** virus, bacteria, infestations of animals or insects.

- **Human:** strikes, sabotage, terrorism, and war.

A number of factors such as geographic locale determine the likelihood of specific physical security threats. A data center located in the San Francisco Bay area should be more concerned about earthquakes than a comparable data center in Kansas. And because tornados are more prevalent in Kansas than on the West Coast, data centers in the Great Plains should be more concerned about wind shears and snow and ice storms.

Providing Physical Security

The remainder of this chapter discusses in some detail the five areas of physical security that address the aforementioned types of physical security threats. These areas are

- educating personnel

- administrative controls, such as site selection

- physical controls, such as keys and locks, fencing, lighting, and guards

- technical controls, such as smart cards, audit trails, intrusion detection systems, and biometrics

- environmental/life-safety controls

Educating Personnel

An educated staff, made aware of the potential for theft and misuse of facilities and equipment, is the best weapon a company can have against illegitimate and accidental acts by others. Just as the staff should be prepared for the potential of unforeseen acts of nature, employees should be reminded periodically of the importance of helping to secure their surroundings, including

- Being mindful of physical and environmental considerations required to protect the computer systems.

- Adhering to emergency and disaster plans.

- Monitoring the unauthorized use of equipment and services and reporting suspicious or unusual activity to security personnel.

- Recognizing the security objectives of the organization.

- Accepting individual responsibilities associated with their own security and that of their coworkers as well as the equipment they use and how they use it.

An organization can educate its staff on the importance of their physical security through the use of self-paced or formal instruction, security education bulletins, posters, training films and tapes, or awareness days that drive home the importance of constant vigilance.

Administrative Access Controls

The second category of physical access controls, administrative access controls, addresses the procedural and codified application of physical controls. For example, you will learn about several different physical control devices that make a site more secure. And one of the administrative access controls that will be reviewed in this section, site selection, involves the planning for and the design of the site before it is constructed.

Restricting Work Areas A *physical security plan*, developed by executive management, department managers, and physical security site personnel as one of the many policy and standards documents that all effective security programmes require (see Chapter 15), should first identify the access rights to the site (e.g., campus) in general and then the various access rights required by each location (building) within the site. Within a manufacturing plant, an individual may need different access privileges depending on the department or area they are attempting to enter even though they have gained general admittance to the plant. A single mechanism usually controls various levels of security access. This could be a badge reader encoded to allow the individual into specific areas of the facility based on function or business need. The important point to remember is that, just as security experts assign data to specific security classes, there can also be varying degrees of physical access based on security requirements within the facility.

Escort Requirements and Visitor Control Controlling visitor access to a building is not a new concern. Most companies have long had some kind of procedure for requiring visitors to "sign in" and specify a purpose for their visit and wait for an escort that authorizes their presence before granting access to the visitor. However, with heightened post–September 11 security and the formation of the U.S. Department of Homeland Security, visitor control has taken on increased importance because of concern over foreign nationals in the workplace. The U.S. Department of Commerce (DOC) defines a foreign national as "a person who was born outside the jurisdiction of the United States, who is subject to some foreign government, and who has not been naturalized under U.S. law." In many government facilities or facilities with strong government ties, foreign nationals are not allowed unescorted access to any site within the facility. To gain access to any DOC site, for example, a foreign national must provide more than 17 identifying pieces of information including passport number, country of issuance, and sponsor information.

19

For less secure and nongovernment sites, visitors typically must have a clear purpose for their visit and a confirmed contact within the site such as an employee or another individual with the appropriate clearance. Visitors are usually required to sign in at the security desk and are given a temporary badge or other identifying moniker that clearly defines them as a visitor.

In addition, visitors may be required to pass through a metal detector and should be prepared to have handbags, satchels, and laptop briefcases checked and to surrender, at least temporarily, recording devices such as cameras, tape recorders, and other questionable items (e.g., pocketknives).

Site Selection Site designers and planners must make at least the following considerations when deciding on the location for a facility. As an example, the location of a data operations center for a major corporation will be used.

■ **Visibility:** How conspicuous will the facility be at a particular site? Most data centers look nondescript for a reason. They don't want to advertise what they are and attract undue attention. You will never find signs along the highway stating, "Highly Secure but Anonymous-Looking Data Operations Facility, Exit Here!" Low-key is the byword.

■ **Locale considerations:** The wise prospective homeowner should always inspect the neighborhood before purchasing a new house. The same rules apply in many ways to site-selection committees. What are the local ordinances and variances? What is the crime rate of the surrounding neighborhood? Are potentially hazardous sites nearby, such as landfills, hazardous waste dumps, or nuclear reactors?

■ **Natural disasters:** Several major corporations (e.g., Charles Schwab) have moved their computer operations centers from the West Coast, particularly the San Francisco Bay area, to more geologically stable locations because of the risk of earthquakes. Other obvious natural threats to consider are tornadoes, hurricanes, floods, wildfires, chemical fires, vermin, pest damage, and snow and ice. Mother Nature's hand is far-reaching, but site planners can minimize risk by examining local weather patterns, the history of weather-related disasters, and determining their risk tolerance.

■ **Transportation:** Are transportation routes such as airports, highways, and railroads nearby, and if so, are they navigable? A good transportation system is important not only for the delivery of goods and services but also for emergency evacuation procedures as part of a disaster recovery plan (DRP).

Physical Security Controls

A spectrum of physical controls are needed to support the principle of defense in depth. These include controls for the perimeter of the data center, employee and visitor badging, guard dogs when deemed appropriate, and building lighting.

Perimeter Security Controls Controls on the perimeter of the data center are designed to prevent unauthorized access to the facility. These types of controls may have different "states" or behaviors based on the time of day or the day of the month. A gate may allow controlled access during the day but be locked or closed at night, for example.

Fences in some respects model the various levels of security in the virtual world. A fence 3 to 4 feet high will discourage the casual passerby. A fence 6 to 7 feet high will deter general intruders. A fence 8 feet high topped with razor-edge wire signals an even greater need to keep intruders out (and sometimes, unfortunately, to keep people in). A perimeter intrusion and detection assessment system (PIDAS) is fencing that uses passive vibration sensors to detect intruders or any attempts to compromise the system.

Turnstiles are less effective than either gates or fences. They dissuade rather than prevent intruders from entering a site without authorization. Anyone who has ever taken the New York City subway system undoubtedly has witnessed individuals leaping over the turnstile without depositing a token or, in today's age, swiping a Metrocard. Turnstiles usually do not authenticate a user but simply control access based on the use of a token.

Mantraps, as the name implies, are enclosed areas with a secure door on either end that literally "trap" an individual between doors. They address the problem of "piggybacking" whereby an individual without proper authorization will enter a secure area behind a person who enters legitimately. In order to pass through the second door of the Mantrap, the individual must pass a second level of validation—perhaps the authorization of a security guard, the entering of a password, or some other mechanism (see Figure 19.1 for an example of a mantrap).

Badging Issued by a site security office, the photo identification badge is a perimeter security control mechanism that not only authenticates an individual but also continues to identify the individual while inside the facility. Most sites issuing photo identification require that the individual displays the badge where it is most visible, usually on the upper torso. The badge alone is no guarantee that unauthorized individuals are denied access—badges can be stolen and photos replaced—but combined with other perimeter controls, the badge offers a familiar and comfortable sense of security in most organizations.

19

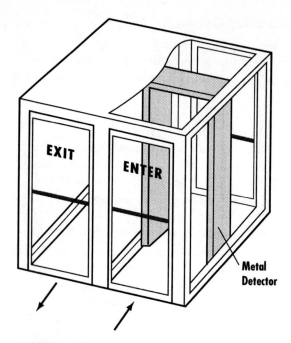

FIGURE 19.1 Example of a mantrap.

Keys and Combination Locks Keys and combination locks are how most people know physical security, mainly because they are the least complicated and expensive devices. Beyond the mechanical door lock opened with a key, locks are now programmable and opened with a combination of keys (e.g., the five-key pushbutton lock once popular in IT operations), a security badge with a magnetic strip, or some other mechanism. Locks are typically unguarded and are meant to delay an intruder, not absolutely deny him access. For that reason, you rarely find these devices any more in areas where a high level of access authorization is required.

Security Dogs What some home security experts don't tell you is that dogs are not just a man's best friend, but they can also make great security guards! Dogs can be unflinchingly loyal and rely on all of their senses to detect intruders. They can also be trained to perform specialized services such as sniffing out drugs or explosives at airports or alerting the blind to fire before it engulfs them. The image of the German shepherd tethered to the door behind an auto junkyard may be the first thing that comes to mind when thinking about security dogs, but dogs are a highly effective and threatening perimeter security control when handled properly and humanely.

Lighting Lighting is another form of perimeter protection that discourages intruders or other unauthorized individuals from entering restricted areas. You are likely familiar with how shopping malls use streetlights to discourage parking lot break-ins, and many homeowners have motion-detector lights installed on garages and back porches. Critical buildings and installations should use some form of lighting as a deterrent, whether it be floodlights, streetlights, or searchlights. According to the National Institute of Standards and Technology, critical areas (e.g., fire escapes, emergency exits, and so forth) require safety lighting to be mounted 8 feet high and burn with a candlepower of 2 candelas (the equivalent of a strong spotlight).

Technical Controls

The next group of physical security controls involves the use of computer hardware and software to protect facilities as opposed to some of the other more traditional physical security techniques described earlier in the chapter. The more prominent technical controls include:

- smart/dumb cards
- audit trails/access logs
- intrusion detection
- biometric access controls

Smart Cards A *smart card* resembles a regular payment (credit) card with the major difference that it carries a semiconductor chip with logic and nonvolatile memory (see Figure 19.2). Unlike a security access card (badge with magnetic strip), the smart card has many purposes, including storing value for consumer purchases, medical identification, travel ticketing and identification, and building access control. The card may also store software that detects unauthorized tampering and intrusions to the chip itself and, if

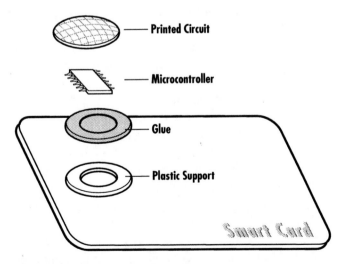

FIGURE 19.2 A smart card.

19

detected, can lock or destroy the contents of the chip to prevent disclosure or unauthorized uses.

FYI: A Taxonomy of Smart Cards

Smart cards are essentially working computers with an infinite possibility of uses. On the physical level, smart cards are classified as contact, contact-less, or as combinations of the two. Contact smart cards require a reader (and/or writer) in which the card is inserted when it's needed. Contact-less cards contain an antenna that may be read by remote receivers. Combination cards may be used both ways, depending on the applications intended. Logically, you'll find smart cards classified three different ways. Memory cards (the simplest form) are used to store values for future uses.

The most common example of a memory card is a prepaid phone card redeemable through the bright-yellow reader slot found on modern pay phones. Protected memory cards require the entry of a secret code or PIN before a stream of data can be sent to or received from the chip. Microprocessor cards contain a semiconductor chip to hold microcode that defines command structures, data file structures, and security structures. They're present when more "intelligence" or storage of information is needed and are often found used in multiapplication products and services, such as combined access and stored-value cards.

Smart cards—used much more extensively in Asia and Europe than in the United States—can also store banks of passwords. A user, for example, can store network, application, and Internet URLs and login passwords on a smart card. When smart cards are integrated with a biometrics (see Chapter 16) login (such as a fingerprint; discussed in more detail later in this chapter), security can further be enhanced.

Smart cards can also facilitate file encryption by storing the user's private key for use with a public key infrastructure (or PKI, a mechanism allowing the use of multiple "keys," one private, one public, to lock and unlock files). They work well for mobile users because such users are inclined to carry their smart card with them as they would one of their credit cards. This means that the user's encryption keys are not stored on a workstation, thus providing a more secure environment than when the cryptographic functions are performed on the workstation itself, which is subject to Trojan Horse attacks, or attacks where a seemingly innocuous object contains something harmful to the interests of the recipient.

Still, smart cards alone are not completely secure. If an attacker were to steal a user's PIN number or password along with the card, he could gain complete access to the network. However, using a fingerprint along with the card to authenticate the user greatly reduces the chance for intrusion.

The use of smart cards in conjunction with biometrics authentication, for example fingerprint readers or retinal scan techniques, can be extremely effective, especially in situations where controlling physical access is of the utmost importance. This kind of layered security goes beyond the use of passwords or passwords and smart cards alone. A company that has already committed to using smart cards for many of its applications could benefit from adding an additional level of security using a biometrics logon.

So why aren't these techniques more widely used? Several factors, namely cost, reliability, and practicality, have hampered the deployment of smart cards and biometrics. However, as more companies build smart card readers into their workstations and as the use of biometrics increases in manageability and flexibility and decreases in price, their use will become increasingly important and prevalent.

Audit Trails/Access Logs In financial settings such as banks, audit trails allow examiners to trace or follow the history of a transaction through the institution. Bank auditors or examiners, for example, are able to determine when information was added, changed, or deleted within a system with the purpose of understanding how an irregularity occurred and hopefully how to correct it. The immediate goal is to detect the problem in order to prevent similar problems in the future. The audit trail should contain the following information:

- The user ID or name of the individual who performed the transaction.

- Where the transaction was performed (hopefully using a fixed terminal ID).

- The time and date of the transaction.

- A description of the transaction, that is, what function did the user perform, and on what.

Creating an audit log is not enough, however, to protect a site. The retention period of the audit logs, recovery time (i.e., how long does it take to recall an archived log file), and, perhaps most importantly, the integrity of the data must also be considered and the logging system designed appropriately.

Intrusion Detection *Intrusion detection* is another type of technical control. In this case, intrusion detectors and alarms alert security personnel when an unauthorized person attempts to access a system or building. Unlike security guards, guard dogs, and security fencing discussed in the section on facility access control, this type of physical security control distinguishes itself by using technology. The burglar alarm is the most commonly known intrusion detection device, but, as you can imagine, the technology has become much more sophisticated since the first devices were used. The two categories of devices are

- **Perimeter intrusion detectors:** These devices are based on dry contact switches or photoelectric sensors. The former consists of metallic foil tape placed on windows or doorframes using contact switches. An alarm is set off when the switches are disturbed. Dry contact switches are used in residential homes and shop fronts where cost is important. Photoelectric sensors receive light beams, typically infrared, from a light-emitting device. When an intruder breaks the beams of light, he trips an alarm. This type of intrusion detection device is more expensive and usually found in larger facilities.

- **Motion detectors:** These devices detect unusual movements within a well-defined interior space. Included in this category of intrusion detection devices are wave pattern detectors that detect changes to light-wave patterns and audio detectors that passively receive unusual sound waves and set off an alarm.

Alarm Systems The implementation of a series of the aforementioned intrusion detectors is referred to as an alarm system. A local alarm system sets off an alarm on the premises, alerting guards on the premises to respond. Private security firms manage central-station systems, such as home alarms from ADT and other well-known home security companies. They monitor a system 24 hours a day and respond to alerts from a central location.

Company established, owned, and operated alarm systems (also called dedicated alarm systems) resemble a commercial central station system in that it serves many customers but differs because the focus is on the company exclusively. Dedicated systems may be more sophisticated than a local alarm system and share many of the same features as the centralized version. Additional alarms may be triggered at police or fire stations, with the permission and knowledge of the company being protected.

Biometrics The use of biometrics (Greek for "life measurements") in conjunction with more standard forms of authentication such as fixed passwords and PINs is beginning to attract attention as the cost of the technology decreases and its sophistication increases. In fact, the traditional scheme of password-based computer security could lose stature as the use of smart card–based cryptographic credentials and biometrics authentication become commercially viable. Some companies such as the American Biometrics Corporation claim that using an individual's unique physical characteristics along with other identification and authentication (I&A) techniques can almost unequivocally authenticate a user. Biometrics authentication uses characteristics of the human face, eyes, voice, fingerprints, hands, signature, and even body temperature, each technique having its own strengths and weaknesses.

Once the domain of TV spy shows and science fiction stories, the use of human characteristics to allow access to secure systems is quickly becoming a reality. (If you have ever seen Tom Cruise in any of his *Mission Impossible* movies, you will recognize many of these devices; oftentimes, science fiction is several decades ahead of reality.)

Any security system, especially biometrics systems, must balance convenience with security. A system that is too intrusive or cumbersome will discourage or prevent an authorized user from accessing a system. A security system should also be scaleable. In other words, not all systems and users need the same level of security, and security procedures and techniques should be flexible enough to reflect this. Still, any computer system requires a minimal level of security, and that is where authenticating the user at system logon becomes an issue.

A user's first access to a PC is during system logon, thus much attention focuses on the use of passwords, PINs, and more recently biometrics. With older versions of PC desktop operating systems, such as Windows 98 and Windows ME, no system logon was required, so whoever had physical access had complete control over the operating system and all the programs and data on the PC. Windows NT, however, was one of the first popular PC operating systems that required a network-level logon, which can be secured by authenticating a user's credentials on an authentication server before he can access the operating system and its file system.

How Best Can Authentication Be Achieved? Today, the use of fingerprints appears to be the cheapest and most reliable form of biometrics authentication, although other techniques such as retina scanning and thermal patterns are currently being developed. The tip of the finger has characteristics called "friction ridges," enclosures, and bifurcation points that uniquely differentiate one print from the print of any other individual. Because the fingerprint can vary in appearance throughout the day due to changes in temperature, skin moisture, dryness, oiliness, or cuts and abrasions, any direct comparison of digital images of the fingerprint cannot guarantee true authentication. Doing so would also require storing a complete image of the fingerprint in a database, something that attracts the attention of civil liberties groups and government agencies.

Instead, fingerprints are compared based on their characteristics described above and are thus characterized. How does this process work? The following steps generally describe the use of authenticating an individual using a fingerprint:

1. Multiple images of the individual's fingerprint are taken, using the center of the image as the reference point for the orientation and placement of other features.

2. The minutia features (ridges and other points) of importance surrounding the center of the image are computed as coordinate (XY) points and are catalogued in a database.

3. Each sample is scored based on the number and quality of coordinate values. The image with the highest (best sample) score becomes the "template" for the individual. This template is stored on a database and becomes the user's baseline or foundational template. Because it only contains a subset of the fingerprint detail, the template cannot be used to reconstruct the fingerprint or be used to impersonate a sample fingerprint.

4. When a user wants to authenticate, an algorithm is used to process the template stored in the database against the minutiae of his sample fingerprint. The level of security required determines the number of coordinate values that must match.

Environmental/Life-Safety Controls

Think of the infrastructure required to maintain the optimal operating environment for man and machine and you have environmental and life-safety controls. The three most critical areas are

- power (electrical, diesel)

- fire detection and suppression

- heating, ventilation, and air conditioning (HVAC)

Each of these areas will be discussed briefly below. For a more complete discussion, see the CISSP Common Body of Knowledge description (**www.isc2.org/**).

Power Whereas human beings can light candles when the power goes out, computers depend on an uninterrupted and regulated supply of power to assure constant voltage and current—computer equipment is highly sensitive to fluctuations in either voltage or current. We hardly need mention the importance of electricity in our working and private lives, but whereas the consumer patiently waits for the lights to come back on, businesses count the minutes in terms of lost revenue and productivity. As part of their DRP (see Chapter 17), most sites have backup power sources such as diesel generators, a kind of private energy source that kicks in when the primary power source is interrupted or inadequate. Threats to power systems include "noise," more specifically electrical radiation in the system, brownouts when a prolonged drop in voltage occurs, and humidity. When the humidity is too high, normally above 60 percent, condensation on computer parts can occur, resulting in lost efficiency.

Fire Detection and Suppression It is outside the scope of this book to discuss at length the details surrounding this extremely important technical control. Those planning on studying more about physical security will need to understand these particulars. Below we briefly touch on the main areas of this control, but you should consult one of the Web sites or CISSP exam prep books recommended at the end of this text for further information.

- **Fire types:** Fires are classified according to the types of combustibles and recommended methods of suppression. The four types of fires include common combustibles (e.g., wood, paper, and so forth), liquids (e.g., petroleum products, coolants, and so forth), electrical, and combustible metal (e.g., magnesium).

- **Fire detectors:** Fire detectors can be one of several types. Heat-sensing systems respond either to a predetermined threshold or a rapid rise in temperature. Flame detectors sense infrared energy or the pulsation of the flame. Smoke detectors use photoelectric sensors to respond to variations in the light hitting the photoelectric cells.

- **Fire-extinguishing systems:** When a fire occurs, the heating, ventilation, and air conditioning system (HVAC) must be stopped immediately to prevent the flow of oxygen. To extinguish the fire, either a water-sprinkler system or a gas-discharge system is used.

Water-sprinkler systems have four classifications: wet pipe, dry pipe, deluge, and preaction. Wet-pipe systems hold water in the pipes that is released when heat opens a valve. Dry-pipe systems do not have standing water in the pipes. Dry-pipe systems are used to eliminate the potential damage of a flood from a burst pipe in a wet-pipe system. When water is needed, a central valve outside the data center is opened (automatically when a fire is sensed), and water flows into the plumbing only when it's required to extinguish a fire. The deluge system is a dry-pipe system where the volume of water is substantially higher. The preaction system combines elements of both wet- and dry-pipe systems and is the recommended fire-extinguishing system for computer rooms.

Heating, Ventilation, and Air Conditioning The classifieds always seem to have ads for HVAC repairmen. That's because reliable and uninterrupted heating, ventilation, and air-conditioning systems are critical environmental controls. Computers are particularly sensitive to the smallest fluctuations in temperature and humidity. We frequently take the HVAC environmental controls for granted, but the IT manager or the person or persons responsible for these systems should know exactly what to do and whom to contact in the event of failure. Routine maintenance of critical infrastructure systems should prevent any significant failure of HVAC systems.

19

Summary

Physical security is often underemphasized by security experts when discussing strategies for protecting critical resources such as computers and the data stored on them. The ability of intruders and unauthorized personnel to access computer systems remotely does not take anything away from the need to secure physical sites. The Physical Security domain includes traditional safeguards against intentional and unintentional threats. Physical security threats can be man-made (e.g., labor strikes) or natural (e.g., earthquakes). Educating personnel about the importance of emergency response and accepting responsibility for their actions is critical. One type of physical security control is administrative access controls that use procedural and codified applications of physical security controls.

Another type of physical security control involves the use of mechanisms such as fences and gates to control access to a facility. Yet another type of physical security control, technical controls, uses computer hardware and software such as smart cards to protect facilities. One rapidly growing area of technical security controls is biometrics—the use of human traits such as fingerprints to identify and authenticate an individual.

Test Your Skills

MULTIPLE CHOICE QUESTIONS

1. Physical security pertains to
   A. guaranteeing the safety of equipment before people.
   B. annual health checkups for all employees.
   C. protecting an organization's assets and assuring the continuity of business in the event of a disaster.
   D. installing smoke alarms in every doorway of every building.

2. The level of physical security
   A. has no limits.
   B. is proportional to the value of the property being protected.
   C. depends on management involvement.
   D. is indexed to employee insecurities.

3. Which of the following does not pertain to physical security?

    A. site selection

    B. securing a site against unauthorized access

    C. protecting people and property

    D. installing firewalls on all computers

4. Natural disasters include

    A. earthquakes.

    B. chemical fires.

    C. rat infestations.

    D. All of the above.

5. Why is it important to educate personnel on the physical security of their facility?

    A. Doing so makes them more employable should they seek a career in facility management.

    B. They are protecting shareholder investments.

    C. They become more aware of the safety of coworkers and equipment.

    D. They become more "in tune" with their environment.

6. Which of the following is *not* a major concern when reviewing site selection?

    A. local crime rate

    B. proximity of restaurants, banks, and other conveniences for employees

    C. transportation systems

    D. weather

7. Why might San Francisco not be an optimal site for a data center?

    A. The cost of doing business is higher than in other parts of the country.

    B. San Francisco is near a major fault zone.

    C. Employees are easily distracted by local attractions.

    D. A and B.

19

8. Which of the following is not considered a physical security protection device?

   A. mantrap

   B. razor-edge wire

   C. German shepherd

   D. police helicopter

9. Security dogs

   A. are always German shepherds.

   B. once trained provide effective perimeter control.

   C. bark but don't bite.

   D. pose a biohazard.

10. Which of the following is true about smart cards?

    A. They are used more extensively in Europe and Asia than in the United States.

    B. They can store passwords such as personal identification numbers (PINs).

    C. Although promising great strides in authenticating users, smart cards are not infallible.

    D. All of the above.

11. What is an audit trail?

    A. a fitness path for quality inspectors

    B. a sound recording of conversations taped through perimeter devices

    C. a history of transactions indicating data that has been changed or modified

    D. all of the above

12. Which of the following is *not* true about the use of fingerprints for identification and authentication (I&A)?

    A. They are an infallible physical security control.

    B. They contain friction ridges and minutia points.

    C. They change based on fluctuations in temperature, skin moisture, and dryness.

    D. The practice has alarmed civil libertarians.

13. Environmental controls include

    A. heating and air conditioning.

    B. barometers.

    C. diesel backup generators.

    D. Both A and C.

14. Power supplies

    A. need to be clean and uninterrupted.

    B. come in unlimited quantities.

    C. are not a major physical security concern because municipalities are responsible for supplying power.

    D. are becoming increasingly inexpensive.

15. What is an HVAC system?

    A. a growing career choice for unemployed IT workers

    B. a medical response team

    C. backup computer power supply

    D. a type of environmental control system

EXERCISES

Exercise 19.1: Examine Your Personal Security Systems

1. Develop a checklist for your home or place of employment to help you decide if the level of physical security is adequate to protect your personal assets or your business's assets and data.

2. Complete the checklist by taking a walk around your site.

3. Recommend what you think needs to be done to improve the physical site's security.

Exercise 19.2: Explain the Codependency of Physical and Logical Security Controls

1. Describe how physical security controls are needed to augment logical security controls in a typical data center.

2. What physical security controls would you recommend for server rooms or network switching equipment closets if a full-blown data center is not practical?

Exercise 19.3: Observe the Security Controls Around You

1. Pick a typical day, and from dawn to dusk make note of the ways in which you interacted with security controls (e.g., you used a badge reader to enter an office building) and record your reaction. Remember that security controls include the unseen as well as the visible.

2. After you complete your list of security controls, describe how you feel about your observations.

3. Do you feel like your personal privacy is being invaded or are the security controls necessary in the highly technological age in which we live?

Exercise 19.4: Evaluate a Locale for a Data Center Operation

1. Select a specific geographic location, perhaps your hometown or the place where a friend or relative lives, and describe the suitability of the location for a major data center operation.

2. What criteria does the location meet for a viable operations center?

3. What are the drawbacks/limitations?

4. How do you go about weighing the advantages against the disadvantages?

Exercise 19.5: Evaluate the Practicality of Biometrics

1. Research in greater detail an aspect of biometrics (e.g., palm print recognition) and discuss the practicality of the security control.

2. Are specific biometric devices more realistic than others?

3. If so, what factors determine the reliability of a biometric control?

PROJECTS

Project 19.1: Tour Your School's Enrollment Systems

1. Arrange for a tour of your local school's information-keeping systems for student and faculty records.

2. Determine if their systems of controls seem appropriate for the nature and sensitivity of their record keeping.

3. Write down your impressions of their physical security controls to share with the class.

4. How do your findings differ from the findings by other students in the class?

Project 19.2: Compare Built-in and Add-on Physical Security

Masonryarts (**http://physicalsecurity.masonryarts.com/default.aspx**) is just one example of a company specializing in the design and implementation of blast-resistant building materials for government buildings (the U.S. embassy in Moscow is their "signature" project).

1. Examine how a company such as Masonryarts or a similar company "builds in" physical security.

2. How does their approach differ from "add-on" physical security devices and protections?

3. For what types of installations is their approach required?

4. Who is their largest customer?

19

Project 19.3: Research the Effectiveness of Home Alarm Systems

Americans spend millions of dollars each year on antitheft systems for their homes and offices from companies like ADT (**www.adt.com**) and Brinks Security (**www.brinkshomesecurity.com**).

1. How effective are these systems?

2. Are Americans shelling out hard-earned dollars for no reason or do such systems truly work?

3. What impacts do home alarm systems have on homeowner insurance premiums?

4. How much security is enough security? How can you determine how much of a system you should buy?

▶ Case Study

A software development firm currently located in Wichita, Kansas, is becoming increasingly concerned about the safety and reliability of their data center, which has been struck by tornadoes over the past three summer seasons. They are considering relocating their data center and operations to another state with fewer risks of natural disasters. Management has asked you to prepare a proposal for three alternative sites within the continental United States.

How do you begin to determine what's best for the company? What do the company's competitors do for their data center operations? Which three locations would you choose?

Appendix D

Common Body of Knowledge

The ISC^2 Common Body of Knowledge (CBK) is an organization and collection of topics that are relevant to information security professionals. The CBK establishes a common framework of information security terms and principles collected to assist worldwide information security professionals with discussions, debates, and to resolve matters within a common understanding. The 10 Domains of the CBK, along with the major topics and major subject areas follows.

Security Management Practices

Key Areas of Knowledge

Security Management Concepts and Principles

- Privacy
- Confidentiality
- Integrity
- Availability
- Authorization
- Identification and Authentication
- Accountability
- Non-Repudiation
- Documentation
- Audit
- CIA Triad

Protection Mechanisms

- Layering
- Abstraction
- Data Hiding
- Encryption
- Change Control/Management
- Hardware Configuration
- System and Application Software
- Change Control Process

Data Classification

- Objectives of a Classification Scheme
- Criteria by Which Data Is Classified
- Commercial Data Classification
- Government Data Classification
- Information/Data
- Worth/Valuation
- Collection and Analysis Techniques

Employment Policies and Practices

- Background Checks/Security Clearances
- Employment Agreements
- Hiring and Termination Practices
- Job Descriptions
- Roles and Responsibilities
- Separation of Duties and Responsibilities
- Job Rotations
- Policies, Standards, Guidelines, and Procedures

Risk Management

- Principles of Risk Management
- Threats and Vulnerabilities

- Probability Determination
- Asset Valuation
- Risk Assessment Tools and Techniques
- Qualitative vs. Quantitative Risk Assessment Methodologies
- Single Occurrence Loss
- Annual Loss Expectancy (ALE) Calculations
- Countermeasure Selection
- Countermeasure Evaluation
- Risk Reduction/Assignment/Acceptance

Roles and Responsibilities

- Management
- Owner
- Custodian
- Users
- IS/IT Function
- Other Individuals
- Security Awareness Training
- Security Management Planning

Security Architecture and Models

Key Areas of Knowledge

Principles of Common Computer and Network Organizations, Architectures, and Designs

- Addressing (Physical and Symbolic)
- Address Space versus Memory Space
- Hardware, Firmware, and Software
- Machine Types (Real, Virtual, Multi-State, Multi-Tasking, Multi-Programming, Multi-Processing, Multi-Processor, Multi-User)
- Network Protocol Functions (OSI 7 Layer Model)
- Operating States (Single State, Multi-State)

- Operating Modes (User, Supervisor, or Privileged)

- Resource Manager Functions

- Storage Types (Primary, Secondary, Real, Virtual, Volatile, Non-Volatile, Random, Sequential)

- Protection Mechanisms (Layering, Abstraction, Data Hiding, Process Isolation, Hardware Segmentation, Principle of Least Privilege, Separation of Privilege, Accountability)

- System Security Techniques (Preventive, Detective, and Corrective Controls)

Principles of Common Security Models, Architectures, and Evaluation Criteria

- Certification and Accreditation

- Closed and Open Systems

- Confinement, Bounds, and Isolation

- Controls (Mandatory and Discretionary)

- IETF Security Architecture (IPSEC)

- ITSEC Classes and Required Assurance and Functionality

- Objects and Subjects (Purpose and Relationship)

- Security Perimeter and DMZ

- Reference Monitors and Kernels (Purpose and Function)

- Trusted Computing Base (TCB)

- Security Models (Bell-LaPadula, Clark-Wilson, Biba) (Confidentiality, Integrity, and Information Flow; Commercial versus Government Requirements)

- TCSEC Classes and Required Functionality

- Tokens, Capabilities, and Labels (Purpose and Functions)

Common Flaws and Security Issues Associated with System Architectures and Designs

- Covert Channels (Memory, Storage, and Communications)

- Initialization and Failure States

- Input and Parameter Checking

- Maintenance Hooks and Privileged Programs (Superzap/Su)

- Programming (Techniques, Compilers, APIs, and Library Issues)
- Timing (TOC/TOU), State Changes, and Communication Disconnects
- Electro-Magnetic Radiation

Business Continuity Planning (BCP) and Disaster Recovery Planning (DRP)

Key Areas of Knowledge

Business Continuity Planning

- Project Scope and Planning
- Business Organization Analysis
- Resource Requirements
- Legal and Regulatory Requirements
- Business Impact Assessment
- Emergency Assessment
- Business Success Factors
- Critical Business Functions
- Establishment of Priorities
- Development of Alternative Means of Accomplishing Objectives

Containment Strategy

- Developing a Strategy, Provisions, and Processes

Recovery Strategy

- Business Unit Priorities
- Crisis Management
- Work Group Recovery
- Alternatives
- Cold/Warm/Hot/Mobile Sites
- Electronic Vaulting
- Selection Criteria

- Processing Agreements
- Reciprocal/Mutual

Recovery Plan Development

- Emergency Response
- Developing Emergency Response Teams and Procedures

Personnel Notification

- Handling Personnel Notification and Communications to Management

Backups and Off-Site Storage

- Determining What to Back Up (Data, Software, Parameters, Tables, Formulas, Documentation) and How Often (Backup Cost versus Cost to Recreate or Update)
- Selecting a Proper Storage Facility for Backups

Software Escrow Arrangements

External Communications

Utilities

- Determining Proper Applications of UPSs
- Logistics and Supplies
- Fire and Water Protection
- Documentation
- Implementation
- Work Group Recovery

Recovery Techniques

- Developing a Containment Strategy
- Determining Provisions to Stock and Where to Store Them
- Developing Recovery Processes (Facilities, Telecommunications, Software, Data)
- Developing a Recovery Strategy (Networks, Systems, Applications, Training/Testing/Maintenance)
- Developing a Training Strategy

- Testing the Plans and Frequency
- Keeping the Plans Up to Date

Disaster Recovery Planning

- Recovery Plan Development
- Emergency Response
- Developing Emergency Response Teams and Procedures
- Personnel Notification
- Handling Personnel Notifications and Communications to Management
- System Software, Application Software, and Data
- Reconstruction from Backups
- Movement of Files from Off-Site Storage
- Loading All Software and Installation of Applicable Updates
- Loading of Data, Parameter, and Supporting Files
- External Communications
- Crisis Management
- Utilities
- Logistics and Supplies
- Documentation
- Implementation
- Work Group Formation
- Recovery Techniques
- How to Develop Recovery Processes
- Facilities
- Telecommunications
- Software
- Data
- How to Develop a Recovery Strategy
- Networks
- Systems

- Applications
- Restoration
- Cleaning
- Procurement
- Data Recovery
- Software Recovery
- Training/Testing/Maintenance
- How to Develop a Training Strategy
- How to Test the Plans and How Often
- How to Keep the Plans Up to Date
- Relocation to Primary Site
- Elements of Business Continuity Planning
- Awareness and Discovery
- Contingency Planning Goals
- Statement of Importance
- Statement of Priorities
- Statement of Organizational Responsibility
- Statement of Urgency and Timing
- Risk Assessment
- Vital Records Program
- Emergency Response Guidelines
- Emergency Response Procedures
- Mitigation
- Preparation
- Testing

BCP/DRP Events

- Bombings
- Explosions
- Earthquakes
- Fires

- Floods
- Power Outages
- Other Utility Failures
- Storms
- Hardware/Software Failures
- Strikes
- Testing Outages
- Hazardous Material Spills
- Employee Evacuation/Unavailability

Law, Investigations, and Ethics

Key Areas of Knowledge

Laws
- Licensing
- Intellectual Properties
- Import/Export
- Liability
- Transborder Data Flow

Major Categories and Types of Laws
- Criminal Law
- Civil Law
- Administrative Law

Investigations
Evidence
- Types of Admissible Evidence
- Collection and Preservation of Evidence
- Chain of Evidence

Investigation Processes and Techniques
- Target

- Object/Subject
- Team Composition
- Forensics
- Privacy
- Interrogation
- Internal/External Confidentiality

Major Categories of Computer Crime

- Military and Intelligence Attacks
- Business Attacks
- Financial Attacks
- Terrorist Attacks
- Grudge Attacks
- "Fun" Attacks

Incident Handling

- Common Types of Incidents
- Abnormal and Suspicious Activity
- Generally Accepted Guidelines for Confiscating Equipment, Software, and Data
- Generally Accepted Guidelines for Incident Data Integrity and Retention
- Generally Accepted Guidelines for Reporting Incidents

Ethics

- (ISC^2) Code of Ethics
- Request for Comment 1087 — Internet Activity Board "Ethics and the Internet"

Physical Security

Key Areas of Knowledge

Facility Requirements

- Restricted Areas/Work Areas

- Escort Requirements/Visitor Control
- Fences, Gates, Turnstiles, Mantraps
- Security Guards/Dogs
- Badging
- Keys and Combination Locks
- Lighting

Site Selection, Facility Design, and Configuration

- Motion Detectors, Sensors, and Alarms
- CCTV
- Technical Controls
- Smart/Dumb Cards
- Audit Trails/Access Logs
- Intrusion Detection
- Biometric Access Controls
- Environment/Life Safety
- Power and HVAC Considerations
- Water Leakage and Flooding
- Fire Detection and Suppression
- Natural Disasters
- Physical Security Threats
- Fire and Smoke
- Water (Rising/Falling)
- Earth Movement (Earthquakes, Slides, Volcanoes)
- Storms (Wind, Lightning, Rain, Snow, Sleet, Ice)
- Sabotage/Vandalism
- Explosion
- Building Collapse
- Toxic Materials
- Utility Loss (Power, Heating, Cooling, Air, Water)
- Communications Loss (Voice, Data)

- Equipment Failure
- Personnel Loss (Strikes, Illness, Access, Transport)
- Elements of Physical Security

Threat Prevention, Detection, and Suppression

- Fire (Sensors, Sprinklers, Flooding Systems, Extinguishers)
- Water (Leakage and Flooding)
- Toxic Materials (Detection and Control)
- Electrical (UPS and Generators)
- Environmental (Location, Air Temperature, Humidity, Contamination, HVAC, Water)
- Public, Private and Restricted Areas (Perimeter Security, Prevention, Detection)
- Guns, Guards, Fences and Gates
- Swat Teams, Armored Personnel Carriers
- Guard Towers, PIDAS Fences
- Man Traps and Turnstiles
- Locks
- Enclosures, Safes, Cabling Systems
- Dogs and X-Ray Equipment
- CCTV
- Detectors (Motion, Heat, Laser Beam, Glass-Breakage)
- Alarms (Silent and Audio)

Operations Security

Key Areas of Knowledge

Administrative Management

- Job Requirements/Specifications
- Background Checking
- Separation of Duties and Responsibilities
- Least Privilege

- Job Rotation
- Mandatory Vacation in One-Week Increments
- Terminations

Concepts

- Antivirus Management
- Backup of Critical Information
- Changes in Workstation/Location
- Need-to-Know/Least Privilege
- Privileged Operations Functions
- Standards of Due Care/Due Diligence
- Privacy and Protection
- Legal Requirements
- Illegal Activities (Fraud Detection, Collusion)
- Record Retention

Sensitive Information and Media

- Marking
- Handling
- Storage
- Destruction

Control Types

- Directive Controls
- Preventive Controls
- Detective Controls
- Corrective Controls
- Recovery Controls
- Operations Controls
- Resource Protection
- Privileged Entity Controls
- Change Control Management

- Hardware Controls

- Input/Output Controls

- Media Controls

- Administrative Controls (Separation of Duties and Responsibilities, Rotation of Duties, Least Privilege)

Trusted Recovery Process

- Communications Hardware/Software

- Processing Equipment

- Password Files

- Application Program Libraries

- Application Source Code

- Vendor Software

- Operating System

- System Utilities

- Directories and Address Tables

- Proprietary Packages

- Main Storage

- Sensitive/Critical Data

- System Logs/Audit Trails

- Violation Report

- Backup Files

- Sensitive Forms and Printouts

Auditing

- Compliance Checks

- Internal and External

- Frequency of Review

- Standard of Due Care

- Audit Trails

- Individual Accountability

- Reconstruction of Events

- Problem Identification (Intrusion Detection)
- Problem Resolution
- Reporting Concepts (Content, Format, Structure, Hierarchy, Escalation, Frequency)
- Reporting Mechanisms
- Audit Logging
- Security Events
- System Audit Trails
- Sampling and Data Extraction
- Retention Periods
- Media
- Protection Against Alteration
- Protection Against Unavailability
- Audit Log Backup (Importance of System Backups, Frequency, Availability, Media, Off-Site Storage Location and Protection Mechanisms, Quality, Readability)

Monitoring

- Event Monitoring
- Hardware Monitoring (Fault Detection, Port)
- Illegal Software Monitoring

Monitoring Tools and Techniques

- Warning Banners
- Keystroke Monitoring
- Traffic Analysis
- Trend Analysis
- Available Tools
- Real Time
- Ad Hoc
- Passive
- Closed Circuit Television (CCTV)

Failure Recognition, Response, and Alternatives

- Problem Identification

- Problem Resolution

- Reporting Concepts (Content, Format, Structure, Hierarchy, Escalation, Frequency)

- Reporting Mechanisms

Intrusion Detection

- Intrusion Prevention (Identification, Authentication)

- Intrusion Detection (Data Extraction, Sampling, Recognition, Traffic)

- Intrusion Response

Types of Intrusion Detection

- Pattern Recognition and Baselines

- Anomaly Identification

- Attack Signature Identification

- Penetration Testing Techniques

- War Dialing

- Sniffing

- Eavesdropping

- Radiation Monitoring

- Dumpster Diving

- Social Engineering

Inappropriate Activities

- Fraud

- Collusion

- Sexual Harassment

- Pornography

- Waste

- Abuse

- Theft

Threats and Countermeasures

- Errors and Omissions
- Fraud and Theft (Internal or External)
- Employee Sabotage
- Loss of Physical and Infrastructure Support
- Malicious Hackers/Crackers
- Espionage
- Malicious Code
- Violations, Breaches, and Reporting

Access Control Systems and Methodology

Key Areas of Knowledge

Accountability

- Access Control Techniques
- Discretionary Access Control
- Mandatory Access Control
- Lattice-Based Access Control
- Rule-Based Access Control
- Role-Based Access Control

Access Control Lists

- Access Control Administration
- Account Administration
- Account, Log, and Journal Monitoring
- Access Rights and Permissions
- Establishment (Authorization)
- File and Data Owners, Custodians, and Users
- Principle of Least Privilege

Segregation of Duties and Responsibilities

- Maintenance
- Revocation

Access Control Models

- Bell-LaPadula
- Biba
- Clark and Wilson
- Non-Interference Model
- State Machine Model
- Access Matrix Model
- Information Flow Model

Identification and Authentication Techniques

- Knowledge-Based Passwords, Personal Identification Numbers (PINs), Phrases
- Passwords
- Selection
- Management
- Control
- Characteristic-Based (Biometrics, Behavior)
- Tokens
- Tickets
- One-Time Passwords
- Token-Based (Smart Card, Key Card)
- Administrative
- Single Sign-On (SSO)

Access Control Methodologies and Implementation

Centralized/Remote Authentication Access Controls

- RADIUS
- TACACS

Decentralized Access Control

- Domains
- Trust
- File and Data Ownership and Custodianship

Methods of Attack

- Brute Force
- Denial of Service
- Dictionary
- Spoofing
- Man-in-the-Middle Attacks
- Spamming
- Sniffers
- Crackers
- Monitoring

Intrusion Detection

- Types of Intrusions
- Intrusion Prevention (Identification, Authentication)
- Intrusion Detection (Data Extraction, Sampling, Recognition, Traffic)
- Attack Signature Identification
- Intrusion Reactive Response
- Anomaly Identification

Intrusion Response

- Alarms
- Signals
- Audit Trails
- Violation Reports
- Corrections
- Penetration Testing

Cryptography

Key Areas of Knowledge

Use of Cryptography

- Confidentiality
- Integrity
- Authentication
- Non-Repudiation

Cryptographic Concepts, Methodologies, and Practices

- Symmetric Algorithms
- Asymmetric Algorithms

Message Authentication

- Digital Signatures
- Non-Repudiation

Encryption/Decryption

- Basic Functionality of Cryptographic Algorithms (DES, RSA, SHA, MD5, HMAC, and DSA)
- Strengths and Weaknesses of Cryptographic Algorithms and Effects of Key Length

Basic Functions Involved in Key Management

- Key Distribution Methods and Algorithms (Manual, Kerberos, and ISAKMP)
- Error Detecting/Correcting Features
- Hash Functions
- Message Digests (MD5, SHA, and HMAC)
- One-Time Cipher Keys (Pads)
- Stream Ciphers and Block Ciphers
- Key Escrow and Key Recovery

Private Key Algorithms

- Applications and Uses
- Algorithm Methodology
- Key Distribution and Management
- Key Generation/Distribution
- Key Recovery
- Key Storage and Destruction
- Key Strength
- Complexity
- Secrecy
- Weak Keys

Public Key Algorithms

- Applications and Uses
- Algorithm Methodology
- Key Distribution and Management
- Key Generation
- Key Recovery
- Key Storage and Destruction
- Key Strength
- Complexity
- Secrecy
- Weak Keys
- Public Key Infrastructure (PKI)
- Certificate Authorities
- Components
- Hierarchical Structure

Certificates

- Types and Classes
- How Certificates Are Issued, Verified, Distributed, and Revoked
- Hierarchy Chain

System Architecture for Implementing Cryptographic Functions

- Use of Application and Network-Based Protocols (PEM, S/MIME, SSL, HTTPS or SHTTP, SET, IPSEC)
- Application of Hardware Components (Smart Cards and Tokens)
- Application of Cryptographic Components (IPSEC)
- Nodes/ISAKMP

Methods of Attack

- COA
- KPA
- CTA (CPA, ACPA, and CCA)
- Brute Force
- CRACK
- Replay
- MIM
- Birthday

Telecommunications and Network Security

Key Areas of Knowledge

International Standards Organization/Open Systems Interconnection (ISO/OSI) Layers and Characteristics

- Physical Layer
- Data Link Layer
- Network Layer
- Transport Layer
- Session Layer
- Presentation Layer
- Application Layer

Communications and Network Security

- Physical Media Characteristics (Fiber Optics/Coaxial/Twisted Pair)
- Network Topologies (Star/Bus/Ring)

- IPSEC Authentication and Confidentiality
- TCP/IP Characteristics and Vulnerabilities
- Local Area Networks (LANs)
- Wide Area Networks (WANs)
- Remote Access/Telecommuting Techniques
- Secure Remote Procedure Call (S-RPC)
- Remote Access Dial-In User System/Terminal Access Control
- Access System (RADIUS/TACACS)
- Network Monitors and Packet Sniffers
- Internet/Intranet/Extranet
- Firewalls
- Routers
- Switches
- Gateways
- Proxies

Protocols

- Transmission Control Protocol/Internet Protocol (TCP/IP)
- Network Layer Security Protocols (IPSEC, SKIP, SWIPE)
- Transport Layer Security Protocols (SSL)
- Application Layer Security Protocols (S/MIME, SSL, SET, PEM)
- Challenge Handshake Authentication Protocol (CHAP) and Password Authentication Protocol (PAP)
- Point-to-Point Protocol (PPP)/Serial Line Internet Protocol (SLIP) Services
- HDLC
- Frame Relay
- SDLC
- ISDN
- X.25

Communications Security Techniques

- Tunneling

- Virtual Private Network (VPN)
- Network Monitors and Packet Sniffers
- Network Address Translation
- Transparency
- Hash Totals
- Record Sequence Checking
- Transmission Logging
- Transmission Error Correction
- Retransmission Controls
- E-mail Security
- Facsimile Security
- Secure Voice Communications
- Security Boundaries and How to Translate Security Policy to Controls

Network Attacks and Countermeasures

- ARP
- Brute Force
- Worms
- Flooding
- Eavesdropping
- Sniffers
- Spamming
- PBX Fraud and Abuse

Applications and Systems Development Security

Key Areas of Knowledge

Application Issues

- Distributed Environment
- Agents

- Applets
- ActiveX
- Java
- Objects
- Local/Non-Distributed Environment
- Viruses
- Trojan Horses
- Logic Bombs
- Worms

Databases and Data Warehousing

- Aggregation
- Data Mining
- Inference
- Polyinstantiation
- Multi-Level Security
- Database Management System (DBMS) Architecture

Data/Information Storage

- Primary
- Secondary
- Real
- Virtual
- Random
- Volatile
- Sequential
- Knowledge-Based Systems
- Expert Systems
- Neural Networks
- Systems Development Controls
- System Development Life Cycle

- Conceptual Definition
- Functional Requirements Determination
- Protection Specifications Development
- Design Review
- Code Review or Walk-Through
- System Test Review
- Certification
- Accreditation
- Maintenance

Security Control Architecture

- Process Isolation
- Hardware Segmentation
- Separation of Privilege
- Accountability
- Layering
- Abstraction
- Data Hiding
- System High
- Security Kernel
- Reference Monitor
- Modes of Operation
- Supervisor
- User
- Integrity Levels
- Network/System
- Operating System
- Database
- File
- Service Level Agreement

Malicious Code
- Definitions
- Jargon
- Myths/Hoaxes

Hackers, Crackers, Phreaks, and Virus Writers
- Antivirus Protection
- Antivirus Software

Computer Viruses
- Multi-Partite
- Macro
- Boot Sector Infectors
- Macintosh
- File Infectors
- Logic Bombs
- Trojan Horses
- ActiveX
- Java
- Trap Doors

Methods of Attack
- Brute Force or Exhaustive Attack
- Denial of Service
- Dictionary Attacks
- Spoofing
- Pseudo Flaw
- Alteration of Authorized Code
- Hidden Code
- Logic Bomb
- Trap Door
- Interrupts

Remote Maintenance

- Browsing
- Inference
- Traffic Analysis
- Flooding
- Cramming
- Time of Check/Time of Use (TOC/TOU)

Appendix E

Security Policy and Standards Taxonomy

As described in Chapter 15 (Security Management Domain), a complete Policy and Standards Library is essential to a comprehensive security programme. An outline of the policies and standards that one would expect to see, derived from ISO/IEC 17799–Code of Practice for Information Security Management, follows. The first level indicates where a policy would be expected, the second level where a standard would be expected, and the third level indicates which topics within the standard should be covered.

Security Management Policy

Information Security Organization

- Mission, Purpose, and Charter
- Authority and Responsibility
- Information Security Oversight
- Information Security Council
- Security-Related Organizational Responsibilities
- Cooperation Between Organizations
- Policy Framework
- Information Security Strategy

Training and Awareness

- Information Security Training and Awareness
- Communication of Policies

Risk Management Policy

Information Ownership

- Information Owners
- Resource Administrators
- Information Users

Information Classification

- Classification Levels
- Data Classification Prefixes
- Classification Reviews

Risk Assessments

- Risk Assessment Process
- Inventory of Information Resources
- Initial Risk Assessment
- Re-evaluation Process
- Risk Classification Process

Security Baselines
Security of Hard Copy Media

- Handling and Labeling
- Copying
- Distribution
- Storage
- Transport
- Disposal
- Printing

Security of Electronic Media

- Handling and Labeling
- Duplication
- Distribution
- Storage
- Transport
- Disposal

Personnel Security Policy

Pre-Employment Controls

- Personnel Screening
- User Acknowledgement of Security Awareness

Separation of Duties

- Separation of Duties Requirements
- Critical Functions to be Separated

During Employment Controls

- Security in Job Definitions
- Confidentiality Agreements
- Information Security Training
- Periodic Re-Screening
- Acknowledgement of Information Security Responsibilities

Personnel Administration

- Performance Monitoring
- Disciplinary Actions
- Third Party Compliance with Security Policies
- Depth of Expertise
- Mandatory Vacation Time
- Rotation of Critical Personnel

Transfer/Resignation/Termination Controls

- Transfers
- Terminations
- Resignations

Physical Security Policy

Security of Facility

- Securing Computing Facilities
- Construction and Design
- Physical Entry Controls
- Securing Offices, Rooms and Facilities
- Working in Secure Areas
- Isolated Delivery and Loading Areas

Security of Information Systems

- Workplace Protection
- Power/Telecommunications Cabling
- Power Supplies
- Network/Server Equipment
- Equipment Maintenance
- Security of Equipment Off-Premises
- Secure Disposal or Re-Use of Equipment
- Removal of Equipment
- Unused Ports and Cables

Fire Protection

- Non-Smoking Restriction
- Fire Detection
- Fire Suppression
- Monitoring Systems

- Systems Testing
- Fire Prevention Training
- Storage of Flammables
- Computing Facility Separation Requirements

Water Protection

- Water Detection
- Waterproof Covering
- Equipment Location
- Water Monitoring Systems
- Systems Testing
- Water Protection Training
- Computing Facility Water Protection

Environmental Controls

- Electrical Protection
- Emergency Lighting
- Climate Controls
- Backup Ventilation
- Monitoring Environmental Controls
- Environmental Controls Training
- Emergency Shutdown Controls

Operations Management Policy

Operational Management and Controls

- Organization and Management
- Operations Manual
- Information Resource Configuration
- Network Documentation
- Emergency Access

- Patches, Fixes and Updates
- Vendor Supplied Operational Software
- Operational Change Control
- System Logs
- System Documentation
- System Acceptance
- Capacity Planning
- Single Points of Failure
- Separation of Development, Test and Protection Environments
- Segregation of Duties
- Never Alone Principle
- Security Diagnostic Tools
- Developer Access to Production Systems

Malicious Code and Viruses

- Responsibilities, Training and Actions
- Antivirus Software

Backup and Recovery

- Periodic Backup
- Off-site Storage
- Record Retention Schedules
- Destruction of Records
- Annual Review/Testing

Software Support

- Use of Approved Software products
- Control of Proprietary Software
- Use of Public Domain Software
- Software Escrow
- Ownership of Software

Security Monitoring and Response Policy

Monitoring Activities

- Network/System Monitoring
- Access Monitoring
- Intrusion Detection Systems (IDSs)
- Internal Communications Monitoring
- Control of Monitoring Devices
- Review of Monitoring Activities

Incident Response

- Reporting Security Incidents/Violations
- Documenting Security Incidents
- Investigation of Incidents/Violations
- Learning from Incidents
- Public Relations

Communications Management Policy

Encryption

- Use of Encryption
- Digital Signatures
- Key Management

Exchange of Information

- Information Exchange Agreements
- Electronic Data Interchange (EDI
- Publically Available Information

E-mail, Internet and Other Electronic Communications

- Business Use
- Use of Encryption

- Acceptable Use
- Retention/Deletion of Electronic Mail
- Personal Web Sites

Voice/Fax/Video Communications

- Business Use
- Acceptable Use
- Phone Calls
- Voice Mail
- Facsimile
- Conference Calls/Video Teleconferences
- Limitations on Confidential and Restricted Information

Meetings and Conversations

- Meetings and Conferences
- Public Conversations

Access Control Policy

User Enrollment and Authorization

- User Enrollment Process
- User Registration
- Review of User Access Privileges
- Password Management Systems

Identification

- User IDs
- Shared/Group IDs
- Default User IDs
- Temporary User IDs
- Group Membership

Authentication

- Access Control Features
- Password Length/Composition
- Password Expiration
- User Password Change
- Password Storage
- One-Time Use of Initial Passwords
- Password Resets
- Default Passwords
- Inactive Accounts
- Failed Login Attempts
- Password History
- Display and Printing of Passwords and User IDs
- Simultaneous Logins
- Automatic Logoff/Timeout
- Duress Alarms

Privileged and Special Account Access

- Special Privileges
- Need to Know
- Least Privilege
- Identification of Privileges
- Use of System Routines
- Logging Privileged Account Activity
- System Utilities/Commands
- Third Party Access

Remote Access

- Requesting/Granting Access
- Remote Computing Devices

- Remote Control Software
- Modem Connections

Network Security Policy

Network Access

- Use of Network Services
- Enforced Path
- Inventory of Network Access Points
- Authentication
- Remote Diagnostic Ports
- Network Segregation
- Network Connections
- Network Routing
- Limitation of Connection Time
- System Login Banner
- Avoidance of Trust Relationships

Network Security Control Devices

- Use of Firewalls
- Use of Demilitarized Zones (DMZs)
- Packet Filter Configuration
- Router Configuration
- Host Configuration
- E-mail
- Remote login
- File Transfer Protocol (FTP)
- Hyper Text Transfer Protocol (HTTP)
- Network News Transfer Protocol (NNTP)
- Trivial File Transfer Protocol (TFTP)
- Non-Essential Services
- UNIX-to-UNIX Copy Protocol (UUCP) Restrictions

- Domain Name Server (DNS)
- Logging and Auditing
- Automatic Terminal Identification
- Requirements for Network Traffic Filtering
- Honey Pots
- Network Address Translation

Third Party Services Policy

Third Party Services

- Selection Process
- Third Party Service Agreements
- Outsourcing Contract Requirements
- Monitoring Outsourcing Contracts

Application Development Policy

Application Development Process

- Methodology
- Development Environment
- Access to Program Source Library
- Business Requirements
- Risk Assessment
- Installation Process
- Electronic Commerce Development
- Software Acquisition
- Restrictions on Changes to Software Packages
- User Procedures and Training

System Business Requirements

- Design
- Design Exceptions

- Input Data Validation
- Control of Internal Processing
- Message Authentication
- Output Data Validation
- Application Auditing/Logging

Application Testing

- Application Review
- Acceptance Testing Criteria
- User Acceptance Testing
- Post Implementation Review
- Protection of System Test Data

Recovery and Business Continuity Area

Business Continuity Management Process

- Roles and Responsibilities
- Business Continuity Planning Framework
- Business Continuity Impact Analysis
- Business Continuity Plan Development
- Annual Inventory

Recovery/Business Continuity Plan Testing Requirements

- Recovery/Business Continuity Plan Testing
- Documentation of Plan Testing
- Testing Requirements for Highly Critical Systems
- Testing Requirements for Moderately Critical Systems
- Third Party Testing

Recovery Sites

- Hot Recovery Sites
- Cold Recovery Sites

Legal, Compliance, and Regulatory Requirements

- Intellectual Property Rights
- Safeguarding of Organizational Records
- Privacy of Personal Information
- Customer Privacy

Security Compliance Testing

- Testing Concepts and Processes
- Testing Results
- Compliance Tools

Appendix F

Sample Policies

Appendix F provides real-world examples of security policies you're likely to find in use in a typical security program as described in Chapter 15. These standards are illustrative of the types of security documentation that you can find at the SANS Security Policy Project, where boiler-plate documentation is available for the taking to reduce the need to reinvent the wheel each time a new policy is required. You can find the Security Policy Project at: **www.sans.org/resources/policies/**

Sample Computer Acceptable Use Policy

1.0.0 Acceptable Use Policy

1.1.0 Overview

<Company Name Here> intentions for publishing an Acceptable Use Policy are not to impose restrictions that are contrary to <Company Name Here> established culture of openness, trust and integrity. <Company Name Here> is committed to protecting <Company Name Here> employees, partners and the company from illegal or damaging actions by individuals, either knowingly or unknowingly. Internet/Intranet/Extranet-related systems, including but not limited to computer equipment, software, operating systems, storage media, network accounts providing electronic mail, WWW browsing, and FTP, are the property of <Company Name Here>. These systems are to be used for business purposes in serving the interests of the company, and of our clients and customers in the course of normal operations. Please review Human Resources policies for further details. Effective security is a team effort involving the participation and support of every <Company Name Here> employee and affiliate who deals with information and/or information systems. It is the responsibility of every computer user to know these guidelines, and to conduct their activities accordingly.

1.2.0 Purpose

The purpose of this policy is to outline the acceptable use of computer equipment at <Company Name Here>. These rules are in place to protect the employee and <Company Name Here>. Inappropriate use exposes <Company Name Here> to risks including virus attacks, compromise of network systems and services, and legal issues.

1.3.0 Scope

This policy applies to employees, contractors, consultants, temporaries, and other workers at <Company Name Here>, including all personnel affiliated with third parties. This policy applies to all equipment that is owned or leased by <Company Name Here>.

1.4.0 Policy

1.4.1 General Use and Ownership

- While <Company Name Here> network administration desires to provide a reasonable level of privacy, users should be aware that the data they create on the corporate systems remains the property of <Company Name Here>. Because of the need to protect <Company Name Here> network, management cannot guarantee the confidentiality of information stored on any network device belonging to <Company Name Here>.

- Employees are responsible for exercising good judgment regarding the reasonableness of personal use. Individual departments are responsible for creating guidelines concerning personal use of Internet/Intranet/Extranet systems. In the absence of such policies, employees should be guided by departmental policies on personal use, and if there is any uncertainty, employees should consult their supervisor or manager.

- <Company Name Here> recommends that any information that users consider sensitive or vulnerable be encrypted.

- For security and network maintenance purposes, authorized individuals within <Company Name Here> may monitor equipment, systems and network traffic at any time, per <Company Name Here> Audit Policy.

- <Company Name Here> reserves the right to audit networks and systems on a periodic basis to ensure compliance with this policy.

1.4.2 Security and Proprietary Information

- The user interface for information contained on Internet/Intranet/Extranet-related systems should be classified as either confidential or not confidential, as defined by corporate confidentiality guidelines, details of which can be found in Human Resources policies. Examples of confidential information include but are not limited to: company private, corporate strategies, competitor sensitive, trade secrets, specifications, customer lists, and research data. Employees should take all necessary steps to prevent unauthorized access to this information.

- Keep passwords secure and do not share accounts. Authorized users are responsible for the security of their passwords and accounts. System level passwords should be changed quarterly; user level passwords should also be changed quarterly.

- All PCs, laptops and workstations should be secured with a password-protected screensaver with the automatic activation feature set at 10 minutes or less, or by logging-off (*control+ alt + delete* for Win2K users) when the host will be unattended.

- Use encryption of information in compliance with <Company Name Here> Acceptable Encryption Use policy.

- Because information contained on portable computers is especially vulnerable, special care should be exercised.

- Postings by employees from a <Company Name Here> e-mail address to newsgroups should contain a disclaimer stating that the opinions expressed are strictly their own and not necessarily those of <Company Name Here>, unless posting is in the course of business duties.

- All hosts used by the employee that are connected to the <Company Name Here> Internet/Intranet/Extranet, whether owned by the employee or <Company Name Here>, shall be continually executing approved virus-scanning software with a current virus database. Unless overridden by departmental or group policy.

- Employees must use extreme caution when opening e-mail attachments received from unknown senders, which may contain viruses, e-mail bombs, or Trojan horse code.

1.4.3 Unacceptable Use

The following activities are, in general, prohibited. Employees may be exempted from these restrictions during the course of their legitimate job responsibilities (e.g., systems administration staff may have a need to disable the network access of a host if that host is disrupting production services). Under no circumstances is an employee of <Company Name Here> authorized to engage in any activity that is illegal under local, state, federal or international law while utilizing <Company Name Here> -owned resources.

The lists below are by no means exhaustive, but attempt to provide a framework for activities, which fall into the category of unacceptable use.

1.4.3.1 System and Network Activities The following activities are strictly prohibited, with no exceptions:

- Violations of the rights of any person or company protected by copyright, trade secret, patent or other intellectual property, or similar laws or regulations, including, but not limited to, the installation or distribution of "pirated" or other software products that are not appropriately licensed for use by <Company Name Here>.

- Unauthorized copying of copyrighted material including, but not limited to, digitization and distribution of photographs from magazines, books or other copyrighted sources, copyrighted music, and the installation of any copyrighted software for which <Company Name Here> or the end user does not have an active license is strictly prohibited.

- Exporting software, technical information, encryption software or technology, in violation of international or regional export control laws, is illegal. The appropriate management should be consulted prior to export of any material that is in question.

- Introduction of malicious programs into the network or server (e.g., viruses, worms, Trojan horses, e-mail bombs, etc.).

- Revealing your account password to others or allowing use of your account by others. This includes family and other household members when work is being done at home.

- Using a <Company Name Here> computing asset to actively engage in procuring or transmitting material that is in violation of sexual harassment or hostile workplace laws in the user's local jurisdiction.

- Making fraudulent offers of products, items, or services originating from any <Company Name Here> account.

- Making statements about warranty, expressly or implied, unless it is a part of normal job duties.

- Effecting security breaches or disruptions of network communication. Security breaches include, but are not limited to, accessing data of which the employee is not an intended recipient or logging into a server or account that the employee is not expressly authorized to access, unless these activities are within the scope of regular duties. For purposes of this section, "disruption" includes, but is not limited to, network sniffing, pinged floods, packet spoofing, Denial of Service, and forged routing information for malicious purposes.

- Port scanning or security scanning is expressly prohibited unless prior notification to <Company Name Here> is made.

- Executing any form of network monitoring which will intercept data not intended for the employee's host, unless this activity is a part of the employee's normal job/duty.

- Circumventing user authentication or security of any host, network or account.

- Interfering with or denying service to any user other than the employee's host (for example, Denial of Service attack).

- Using any program/script/command, or sending messages of any kind, with the intent to interfere with, or disable, a user's terminal session, via any means, locally or via the Internet/Intranet/Extranet.

- Providing information about, or lists of, <Company Name Here> employees to parties outside <Company Name Here>.

1.4.3.2 E-mail and Communications Activities The following activities are strictly prohibited, with no exceptions:

- Sending unsolicited e-mail messages, including the sending of "junk mail" or other advertising material to individuals who did not specifically request such material (e-mail spam).

- Any form of harassment via e-mail, telephone or paging, whether through language, frequency, or size of messages.

- Unauthorized use, or forging, of e-mail header information.
- Solicitation of e-mail for any other e-mail address, other than that of the poster's account, with the intent to harass or to collect replies.
- Creating or forwarding "chain letters," "Ponzi" or other "pyramid" schemes of any type.
- Use of unsolicited e-mail originating from within <Company Name Here> networks of other Internet/Intranet/Extranet service providers on behalf of, or to advertise, any service hosted by <Company Name Here> or connected via <Company Name Here> network.
- Posting the same or similar non-business-related messages to large numbers of Usenet newsgroups (newsgroup spam).

1.5.0 Enforcement

Any employee found to have violated this policy may be subject to disciplinary action, up to and including termination of employment.

1.6.0 Definitions

Term   Definition

Spam Unauthorized and/or unsolicited electronic mass mailings.

1.7.0 Revision History

7/24/2004: Initial Section Creation.

Sample E-mail Use Policy

1.0.0 E-mail Use Policy

1.1.0 Purpose

The purpose of this policy is to prevent tarnishing the public image of <Company Name Here>. When e-mail goes out from <Company Name Here> the general public will tend to view that message as an official policy statement from <Company Name Here>.

1.2.0 Scope

This policy covers appropriate use of any e-mail sent from a <Company Name Here> e-mail address and applies to all employees, vendors, and agents operating on behalf of <Company Name Here>

1.3.0 Policy

1.3.1 Prohibited Use

The <Company Name Here> e-mail system shall not to be used for the creation or distribution of any disruptive or offensive messages, including offensive comments or attachments about race, gender, hair color, disabilities, age, sexual orientation, pornography, religious beliefs and practice, political beliefs, or national origin. Employees who receive any e-mails with this content from any <Company Name Here> employee should report the matter to their supervisor immediately.

1.3.2 Personal Use

Using a reasonable amount of <Company Name Here> resources for personal e-mails is acceptable, but non-work related e-mail should be saved in a separate folder from work related e-mail. Sending chain letters or joke e-mails from a <Company Name Here> e-mail account is prohibited. Virus or other malware warnings and mass mailings from <Company Name Here> shall be approved by <Company Name Here> VP Operations before sending. These restrictions also apply to the forwarding of mail received by a <Company Name Here> employee.

1.3.3 Monitoring

<Company Name Here> employees shall have no expectation of privacy in anything they store, send or receive on the company's e-mail system. <Company Name Here> may monitor messages without prior notice. <Company Name Here> is not obliged to monitor e-mail messages.

1.4.0 Enforcement

Any employee found to have violated this policy might be subject to disciplinary action, up to and including termination of employment.

1.5.0 Definitions

E-mail The electronic transmission of information through a mail protocol such as SMTP or IMAP. Typical e-mail clients include Eudora and Microsoft Outlook.

Forwarded e-mail E-mail resent from an internal network to an outside point.

Chain e-mail or letter E-mail sent to successive people. Typically the body of the note has direction to send out multiple copies of the note and promises good luck or money if the direction is followed.

Sensitive information Information is considered sensitive if it can be damaging to <Company Name Here> or its customers' reputation or market standing.

Virus warning A warning consists of an e-mail containing warnings about virus or malware. The overwhelming majority of these e-mails turn out to be a hoax and contain bogus information usually intent only on frightening or misleading users.

Unauthorized disclosure The intentional or unintentional revealing of restricted information to people, both inside and outside <Company Name Here>, who do not have a need to know that information.

1.6.0 Revision History

Sample Password Policy

1.0.0 Password Policy

1.1.0 Overview

Passwords are an important aspect of computer security. They are the front line of protection for user accounts. A poorly chosen password may result in the compromise of <Company Name Here>'s entire corporate network. As such, all <Company Name Here> employees (including contractors and vendors with access to <Company Name Here> systems) are responsible for taking the appropriate steps, as outlined below, to select and secure their passwords.

1.2.0 Purpose

The purpose of this policy is to establish a standard for creation of strong passwords, the protection of those passwords, and the frequency of change.

1.3.0 Scope

The scope of this policy includes all personnel who have or are responsible for an account (or any form of access that supports or requires a password) on any system that resides at any <Company Name Here> facility, has access to the <Company Name Here> network, or stores any non-public <Company Name Here> information.

1.4.0 Policy

1.4.1 General

- All system-level passwords (e.g., root, enable, NT admin, application administration accounts, etc.) must be changed on at least a quarterly basis.
- All production system-level passwords must be part of the VSI administered global password management database.
- All user-level passwords (e.g., e-mail, Web, desktop computer, etc.) must be changed at least every three months. The recommended change interval is every month.
- User accounts that have system-level privileges granted through group memberships must have a unique password from all other accounts held by that user.
- Passwords must not be inserted into e-mail messages or other forms of electronic communication.
- Where SNMP is used, the community strings must be defined as something other than the standard defaults of "public," "private" and "system" and must be different from the passwords used to log in interactively. A keyed hash must be used where available (e.g., SNMPv2).

■ All user-level and system-level passwords must conform to the guidelines described below.

1.4.2 Guidelines

A. General Password Construction Guidelines

Passwords are used for various purposes at <Company Name Here>. Some of the more common uses include: user level accounts, Web accounts, e-mail accounts, screen saver protection, voicemail password, and local router logins. Since very few systems have support for one-time tokens (i.e., dynamic passwords which are only used once), everyone should be aware of how to select strong passwords.

Poor, weak passwords have the following characteristics:

■ The password contains less than eight characters.

■ The password is a word found in a dictionary (English or foreign).

■ The password is a common usage word such as:

  ■ Names of family, pets, friends, co-workers, fantasy characters, etc.

  ■ Computer terms and names, commands, sites, companies, hardware, software.

  ■ The words "<Company Name Here>" or any derivation.

  ■ Birthdays and other personal information such as addresses and phone numbers.

  ■ Word or number patterns like aaabbb, qwerty, zyxwvuts, 123321, etc.

  ■ Any of the above spelled backwards.

  ■ Any of the above preceded or followed by a digit (e.g., secret1, 1secret)

Strong passwords have the following characteristics:

■ Contain both upper- and lowercase characters (e.g., a-z, A-Z).

■ Have digits and punctuation characters as well as letters (e.g., 0-9, !@#$%^&*()_+|~-=\`{}[]:";'<>?,./)

■ Are at least eight alphanumeric characters in length.

■ Are not comprised of any words in any language, slang, dialect, jargon, etc.

■ Are not based on personal information, names of family, etc.

■ Passwords should never be written down or stored online. Try to create passwords that can be easily remembered. One way to do this is create a password based on a song title, affirmation, or other phrase. For example, the phrase might be: "This May Be One Way To Remember" and the password could be: "TmB1w2R!" or "Tmb1W>r~" or some other variation.

NOTE: Do not use either of these examples as passwords!

B. Password Protection Standards

Do not use the same password for <Company Name Here> accounts as for other non-<Company Name Here> access (e.g., personal ISP account, option trading, benefits, etc.). Where possible, don't use the same password for various <Company Name Here> access needs. For example, select one password for the Engineering systems and a separate password for IT systems. Also, select a separate password to be used for an NT account and a UNIX account.

Do not share <Company Name Here> passwords with anyone, including administrative assistants or secretaries. All passwords are to be treated as sensitive, confidential <Company Name Here> information.

Here is a list of "don'ts":

- Don't reveal a password over the phone to ANYONE.
- Don't reveal a password in an e-mail message.
- Don't reveal a password to the boss.
- Don't talk about a password in front of others.
- Don't hint at the format of a password (e.g., "my family name").
- Don't reveal a password on questionnaires or security forms.
- Don't share a password with family members.
- Don't reveal a password to co-workers while on vacation.
- If someone demands a password, refer them to this document or have them call someone in the Information Security Department.
- Do not use the "Remember Password" feature of applications (e.g., Eudora, Outlook, Netscape Messenger).
- Again, do not write passwords down and store them anywhere in your office. Do not store passwords in a file on ANY computer system (including Palm Pilots or similar devices) without encryption.
- Change passwords at least once every three months (just as system-level passwords which must be changed quarterly). The recommended change interval is every month.
- If you suspect that an account or password has been compromised, report the incident to someone in the Information Security Department immediately and change all the passwords.
- Password cracking or guessing may be performed on a periodic or random basis. If a password is guessed or cracked during one of these scans, the user will be required to change it.

C. Application Development Standards

Application developers must ensure their programs contain the following security precautions. Applications:

- Support authentication of individual users, not groups.

- Do not store passwords in clear text or in any easily reversible form.

- Provide for some sort of role management, such that one user can take over the functions of another without having to know the other's password.

- Support TACACS+ , RADIUS and/or X.509 with LDAP security retrieval, wherever possible.

D. Use of Passwords and Pass Phrases for Remote Access Users

Access to the <Company Name Here> networks via remote access is to be controlled using either a one-time password authentication or a public/private key system with a strong pass phrase.

E. Pass phrases

Pass phrases are generally used for public/private key authentication. A public/private key system defines a mathematical relationship between the public key that is known by all, and the private key, that is known only to the user. Without the pass phrase to "unlock" the private key, the user cannot gain access.

Pass phrases are not the same as passwords. A pass phrase is a longer version of a password and is, therefore, more secure. A pass phrase is typically composed of multiple words. Because of this, a pass phrase is more secure against "dictionary attacks."

A good pass phrase is relatively long and contains a combination of upper- and lowercase letters and numeric and punctuation characters. An example of a good pass phrase:

"The*?#>*@TrafficOnThe101Was*&#!#ThisMorning"

All of the rules above that apply to passwords apply to pass phrases.

1.5.0 Enforcement

Any employee found to have violated this policy might be subject to disciplinary action, up to and including termination of employment.

1.6.0 Definitions

Application Administration Account Any account that is for the administration of an application (e.g., Oracle database administrator, NT administrator, etc.).

1.7.0 Revision History

Sample Wireless (Wi-Fi) Use Policy

1.0.0 Wireless Communication Policy

1.1.0 Purpose
This policy prohibits access to <Company Name Here> networks via unsecured wireless communication mechanisms. Only wireless systems that meet the criteria of this policy or have been granted an exclusive waiver are approved for connectivity to <Company Name Here> networks.

1.2.0 Scope
This policy covers all wireless data communication devices (e.g., personal computers, cellular phones, PDAs, etc.) connected to any of <Company Name Here> internal networks. This includes any form of wireless communication device capable of transmitting packet data. Wireless devices and/or networks without any connectivity to <Company Name Here> networks do not fall under the purview of this policy.

1.3.0 Policy

1.3.1 Register Access Points and Cards
All wireless Access Points / Base Stations connected to the corporate network must be registered and approved. These Access Points / Base Stations are subject to periodic penetration tests and audits. All wireless Network Interface Cards (i.e., PC cards) used in corporate laptop or desktop computers must be registered.

1.3.2 Approved Technology
All wireless LAN access must use corporate-approved vendor products and security configurations.

1.3.3 VPN Encryption and Authentication
All computers with wireless LAN devices must utilize a corporate-approved Virtual Private Network (VPN) configured to drop all unauthenticated and unencrypted traffic. To comply with this policy, wireless implementations must maintain point-to-point hardware encryption of at least 56 bits. All implementations must support a hardware address that can be registered and tracked, i.e., a MAC address. All implementations must support and employ strong user authentication which checks against an external database such as TACACS+, RADIUS or something similar.

1.3.4 Setting the SSID

The SSID shall be configured so that it does not contain any identifying information about the organization, such as the company name, division title, employee name, or product identifier.

1.4.0 Enforcement

Any employee found to have violated this policy might be subject to disciplinary action, up to and including termination of employment.

1.5.0 Definitions

User Authentication A method by which the user of a wireless system can be verified as a legitimate user independent of the computer or operating system being used.

1.6.0 Revision History

Appendix G

An Insider's Look at a Security Policy and Standards Management System

In Chapter 15 you saw the structure and requirements for a policy manual that's accessible to employees, to help them quickly locate security requirements and determine how to comply with them. There are several commercial products on the market that automate the tasks of policy management to help both executives and those who must live up to these requirements. Notable products in this market space are the Vigilent Policy Center (VPC) from NetIQ (**www.netiq.com**), Polivec (**www.polivec.com**), and the Archer Technologies Management System (**www.archer-tech.com**). We chose to use the Archer Tecnologies system here as an example of automated policy and standards management because of it robustness, ease of use, and comprehensive content library that's linked from regulatory guidance documents all the way through to the procedures that implement the required controls.

This Appendix demonstrates how Archer can be useful to application software developers by quickly extracting system security requirements prior to design and development activities. To do this, we've created the following scenario:

> A programmer is charged with the development of an accounting system for a new medium-sized manufacturing firm. The target development and operating environment is a MS Windows 2003 Server internally called the Corporate Exchange Server. The firm must also meet the compliance requirements of the Sarbanes-Oxley (SOX) Act for corporate accountability.

To begin, it's useful to understand how the Archer Technologies Security Management System organizes policies, standards, and documentation that deal with requirements of compliance. Figure G.1 shows how a policy is used to define a control standard that is tied to one or more industry references. The policy statement, related to Password Expiration, is further refined in the Standard on password expiration that places system requirements on password expiration processes. The Policy and Standard appear in the company library because the management of the firm mandates that IT systems comply with ISO17799 (described in Chapter 15). ISO17799 is the firm's choice for comprehensive controls to comply with the Sarbanes-Oxley Act (SOX) for internal control processes.

Figure G.2 expands upon Figure G.1, showing the internal structure of a Control Standard and its relationship to policies, industry references, and Baseline Standards—which are specific to operating platforms, such as Windows 2003 Server. Baselines include guidance information and procedural instructions on how to implement the control on the target system (in this case how to make sure that passwords expire as prescribed by the standard.)

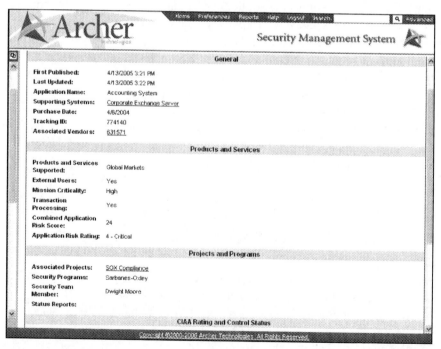

Credit: Archer Technologies

FIGURE G.1 Archer Security Management System control standards data structure.

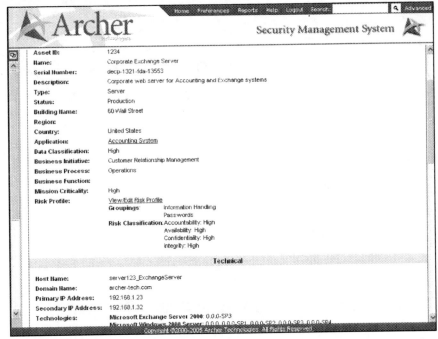

FIGURE G.2 Archer Security Management System policy relationships.

Figure G.3 begins the process that a programmer would see when using the system to set up the project and determine the design, development, and implementation requirements are for the new system. The first step is an "Application Profile" where information about the project is collected to determine the scope of the system (where it will be used, who will use it, and how critical it is to the firm's mission). Following the scope section, any associated projects and programs are indicated. In this scenario, the SOX Compliance program is selected.

Once the Application Profile is completed, information about the target platform is collected, as shown in Figure G.4. Because the Archer system is also an Asset Manager for IT systems, the specific production asset is selected and a risk profile is determined based on the needs for confidentiality, integrity, availability, and accountability of the users. These risk classifications are used to begin determining which Control Standards and Baseline Standards are in effect.

With the basic Risk Profile completed in the Asset Profile, an application-specific risk assessment is performed to determine if financial transactions will be processed and characteristics of the user population (Figure G.5). Since financial transactions are present, the SOX requirements for verification of internal controls are present.

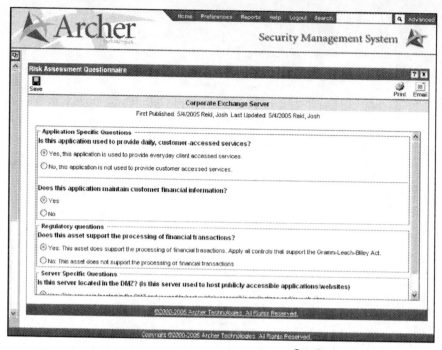

Credit: Archer Technologies

FIGURE G.3 Application profile interface.

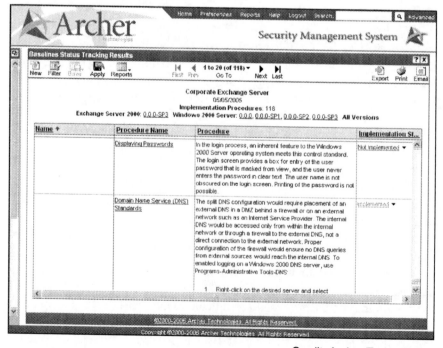

Credit: Archer Technologies

FIGURE G.4 Asset and risk profile interface.

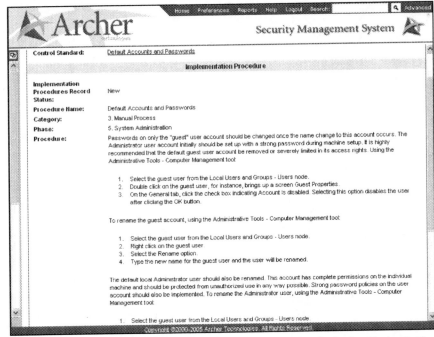

Credit: Archer Technologies

FIGURE G.5 Risk assessment interface.

Upon completion of the Asset and Risk Profiles, the Archer system uses its Policy database to extract the procedures that the system and development must follow in order to be compliant, and permits the operator to indicate if the control has already been implemented or is pending, as shown in Figure G.6.

When the programmer selects the "Default Accounts and Passwords" procedure, a detail screen (Figure G.7) appears. The procedure describes the requirements (as dictated by the standard(s)), and lists the steps the administrator should perform to implement the control using the Administrative Tools console on Windows Server 2003.

Figure G.8 illustrates how the Control Standard (Default Accounts and Passwords) is related internally to one or more policies, sections of other standards, and industry references. A user can click on a hypertext link for additional details.

Now that system development and operational standards are known, it's time to address the Baseline Standards related to the development and operating environment (Windows 2003 Server). Figure G.9 shows the Baseline Standards that are required for a given operating requirement, along with information on whether they are manually implemented, required, or inherent in the system. It also indicates the average time it would take a user to implement the Baseline control.

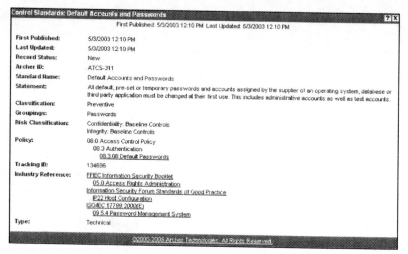

FIGURE G.6 Development and operating requirements based on risk profile.

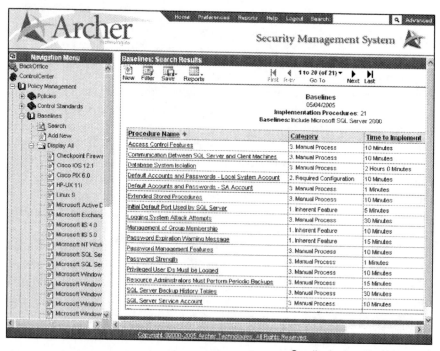

FIGURE G.7 Procedure detail interface.

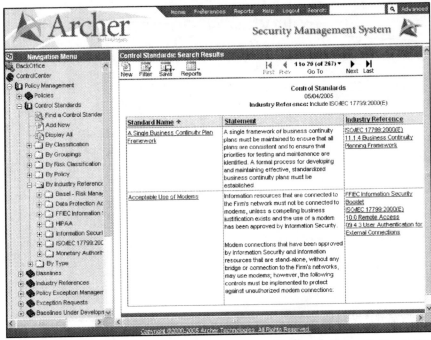

Credit: Archer Technologies

FIGURE G.8 Control standard details.

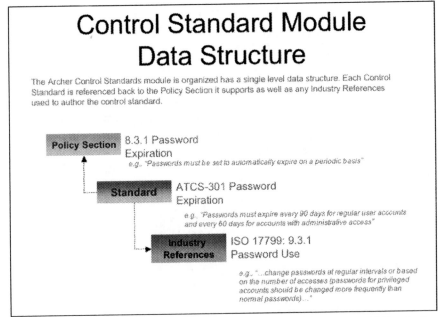

Credit: Archer Technologies

FIGURE G.9 Baseline standards by target platform interface.

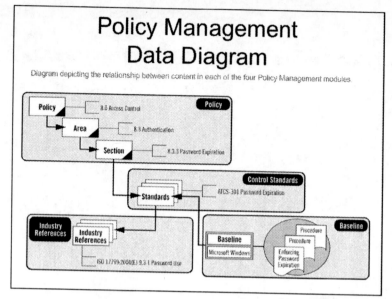

Credit: Archer Technologies

FIGURE G.10 Archer Security Management System Control Standards by industry reference.

Finally, the Archer Security Management System permits the user to determine what Control Standards are required by industry references. Figure G.10 shows an excerpt of the control standards required by ISO/IEC 17799, along with the standard statement and links to additional details (Figure G.8).

With a policy and standards management system like this one, users, developers, managers, associated third parties who perform services for the firm, and auditors can rapidly locate and understand what is expected of them for security compliance and what the current state of security compliance is. It offers greater accuracy and efficiency over paper-based policy manuals.

Appendix **H**

HIPAA Security Rule Standards

As mentioned in Chapter 15, HIPAA is the Health Insurance Portability and Accountability Act. Passed in 1996, HIPAA is designed to protect confidential healthcare information through improved security standards and federal privacy legislation. It defines requirements for storing patient information before, during and after electronic transmission. It also identifies compliance guidelines for critical business tasks such as risk analysis, awareness training, audit trail, disaster recovery plans and information access control and encryption.

HIPAA Security Standards

The proposed HIPAA security regulations establish a minimum framework of standard procedures for ensuring the protection of all individually identifiable health information that is maintained, transmitted or received in electronic form. These standards guard the integrity, confidentiality, and availability of electronic data. The safeguards are intended to protect data from accidental or intentional release to unauthorized persons, and from alteration, destruction or loss. For more information on the proposed HIPAA security standards, visit the US Government Department of Health and Human Services Web site at: **www.dhhs.gov**.

There are 18 information security standards in four areas that must be met to ensure compliance with the *HIPAA Security Rule*. The three areas are:

- Administrative Safeguards: documented policies and procedures for day-to-day operations; managing the conduct of employees with electronic protected health information (EPHI); and managing the selection, development, and use of security controls.

- Physical Safeguards: security measures meant to protect an organization's electronic information systems, as well as related buildings and equipment, from natural hazards, environmental hazards, and unauthorized intrusion.

- Technical Security Services for stored data: security measures that specify how to use technology to protect EPHI while stored.

- Technical Security Mechanisms (particularly controlling access to data and data transmissions).

The Final Rule adopting HIPAA standards for the security of electronic health information was published in the Federal Register on February 20, 2003. This final rule specifies a series of administrative, technical, and physical security procedures for covered entities to use to assure the confidentiality of electronic protected health information. The standards are delineated into either required or addressable implementation specifications.

Administrative Procedures

Policies and procedures must be implemented and documented in each of these twelve areas:

- Training programs in security management and process issues

- Formal data processing protocols

- Formal protocols for controlling access to data

- Internal audit procedures

- Certification of data systems for compliance with DHHS security standards

- Chain of Trust agreements with covered entities with whom we exchange electronic information

- Contingency plan to ensure continuity and preservation of data in the event of an emergency

- Security features for initial clearance of all personnel who have access to health information along with ongoing supervision, training and monitoring of this personnel

- Security configuration management procedures such as virus checking, hardware and software systems review, and documentation

- Specific procedures when personnel terminate employment

- Security management structure that maintains continual risk assessment and sanction policies and procedures

Physical Safeguards

Data and data systems must be physically protected from intrusion and environmental hazards via seven basic elements:

- Designation of a specific person for responsibility of security
- Controlling access to and altering of computer hardware
- Enforcement of "need to know" clearances
- Implementation of work station security activities
- Development of disaster/intrusion response and recovery plans
- Maintenance of security records
- Implementation of identity verification procedures for personnel in order to physically access sites

Technical Security Services

Software control and procedures regarding stored data include these requirements:

- Providing for internal audits and controls within data systems
- Controlling access by users through authentication
- Ensuring that stored data is neither altered nor inappropriately accessed/processed
- Allowing data access to particular privileged classes of personnel, including during crises

Technical Security Mechanisms

These requirements relate to accessed data and the transmission of stored data, to ensure that data cannot easily be accessed, intercepted or interpreted by unauthorized third parties. These proposed procedures include:

- Validation that stored data being transmitted is accurate
- Validation that received data is identical to sent data
- Data transmissions either encrypted or controlled by a dedicated, secure line. If transmissions are not encrypted, DHHS would also require three elements:
- Alarms to signal abnormal communication conditions
- Automatic recording of audit trail information
- A method for authentication of the entity receiving the data

Part 2
Glossary

A

abstract machine Software model that mediates access from any subject to any object.

abstraction Process that defines a specific set of permissible values for an object and the operations that are permissible on that object.

administrative law Legal system in which disputes are resolved before an administrative tribunal and not in a court. Also referred to as natural law, this concept stemmed from the belief that certain legal principles were "natural" or self-evident and did not need to be codified by statute.

assurance requirements Describe how functional requirements should be implemented and tested.

asymmetric key cryptography When different keys are used to encrypt and decrypt messages.

authentication Process of verifying the identity of a person or an application.

B

baseline Specific set of requirements for a technology implementation.

biometrics Methods of identification that work by measuring unique human characteristics as a way to confirm identity.

buffer overflow Intentional overloading of an input area that crashes or disables a program.

business impact analysis Process of assessing risks to a business if critical services are discontinued.

C

Canadian Trusted Computer Product Evaluation Criteria (CTCPEC) Formal computer security testing model published in 1993 as a combination of the ITSEC and TCSEC approaches.

ciphertext   Text that results when a message is passed through an encryption algorithm, or cipher.

closed systems   Use specific operating systems and hardware to perform tasks and generally lack standard interfaces to allow connection to other systems.

Common Body of Knowledge (CBK)   Compilation and distillation of all international security information relevant to security professionals.

Common Criteria   Standardization efforts of formal computer security testing models established in the early 1990s in the United States that supplanted the FC criteria.

common law   Legal system that developed from judicial cases based on precedent and custom. Common law is either unwritten or written as statutes or codes and contains the three primary categories of civil law, criminal law, and regulatory law.

computer forensics   Investigating crimes committed with computers.

confidentiality model   Model intended to preserve the principle of least privilege.

configuration and change management controls   Used for tracking and approving changes to a system by identifying, controlling, and auditing any changes by administrative personnel.

copyright infringement   When a law protecting intellectual property has been broken, such as downloading music from a Web site without paying for it.

cryptanalysis   Science (or art) of breaking a cryptosystem.

cryptography   Science (or art) of designing, building, and using cryptosystems.

cryptology   Study of cryptography and cryptanalysis.

cryptosystem   Disguises messages, allowing only selected people to see through the disguise.

D

data hiding   Mechanism to assure that information available at one processing level is not available in another, regardless of whether it is higher or lower; also called information hiding.

de facto   Accepted practices in the industry.

degaussing   Method to magnetically erase data from magnetic media.

dejure   Official standards passed by international and industry standards committees.

digital envelope   Envelope created when you use a recipient's public key to encrypt both the message and digest, therefore ensuring that no one else can open the envelope.

dual control   Computer security practice borrowed from the military in which two people are required to initiate an action; one person acts as a countermeasure to another.

E

exploit   Program that describes how to take advantage of a specific vulnerability.

F

Federal Criteria for Information Technology Security (FC)   Formal computer security testing model published in early 1993 as an attempt to develop criteria to replace the TCSEC and harmonize North American and European concepts for security evaluation criteria.

finite-state machine   Any device that stores the status or state of something at a given time that can operate based on inputs to change the stored status and/or cause an action or output to take place.

firewall   Insulates a private network from a public network by using carefully established controls on the type of requests that they will route through to the private network for processing and fulfillment.

functional requirements   Describe what a system should do.

H

hardened server   Server whose software has been modified to make it more difficult to attack.

hardware segmentation   Specifically relates to the segmentation of memory into protected segments.

hashing   One-way function that transforms data into distilled forms that are unique to the data.

information storage   Refers to the parts of a computer system that retain a physical state (information) for some interval of time, possibly even after electrical power to the computer is removed.

I

Information Technology Security Evaluation Criteria (ITSEC)   A formal computer security testing model published in 1991 by the European Commission after joint development by France, Germany, the Netherlands, and the United Kingdom.

International Information Systems Security Certifications Consortium (IISSCC or ISC^2)   Organization that administers the most prominent and most demanded information security certifications.

intrusion detection   Detectors and alarms that alert security personnel when an unauthorized person attempts to access a system or building.

K

Kerberos   Network authentication protocol designed to provide authentication for client/server applications by using symmetric-key cryptography.

L

labels   Mechanisms that bind objects to subjects.

layering   Process operation that is divided into layers by function, with each layer dealing with a specific activity.

logical systems   Software that runs on computer hardware.

M

mandatory access control (MAC)   In deciding who may gain access to what information, MAC requires that access control policy decisions are beyond the control of the individual owner of an object, thus requiring the system to make the decisions.

media viability controls   Needed for the proper marking and handling of assets.

Message Authentication Code (MAC) key   Key that is used to generate a keyed hash.

message flow confidentiality   Allows the originating network to conceal the path or route that the message followed on its way to the recipient.

multifactor authentication   Adding more controls and/or devices to the password authentication process.

multiprocessing   Provides for simultaneous execution of two or more programs by a processor (CPU).

multiprogramming system   Allows for the interleaved execution of two or more programs on a processor.

multitasking   Technique used by a system that is capable of running two or more tasks in a concurrent performance or interleaved execution.

N

need-to-know   Defines a minimum set of access rights or privileges needed to perform a specific job description.

O

object   Something within a trusted system that people wish to access or use, such as a program.

open architecture system   Permits different manufacturers to produce systems that can operate with systems from competing manufacturers.

open system   Based on accepted standards and promotes interoperability by employing standard interfaces to allow connections between different systems.

P

packages   Permit the expression of requirements that meet an identifiable subset of security objectives.

packet switching   Division of messages into standard-sized packets for greater efficiency of routing and transport.

patent   Grants an inventor the right to exclude others from producing or using the inventor's discovery or invention for a limited period of time.

personnel security investigation   Meticulous background check for security clearance.

pharming   Network attack that redirects consumers to potentially malicious Web servers.

physical security plan   Developed by executive management, department managers, and physical security site personnel as one of the many policy and standards documents that all effective security programmes require.

physical systems   Computer hardware.

PIN vault   Approach to managing IDs and passwords by using secure methods to locally store IDs and passwords that are protected by a master password that unlocks the vault when it is needed.

plaintext   Message that is passed through an encryption algorithm.

policies   Statements of management intent.

primary storage   Computer's main memory that is directly addressable by the central processing unit. It is a volatile storage medium.

principle of least privilege   Dictates that a process (program) has no more privilege than what it really needs in order to perform its functions.

privileged entity controls   Given to operators and system administrators as special access to computing resources.

process isolation   Design objective in which each process has its own distinct address space for its application code and data.

programme   Ongoing management activity intended to preserve and advance an organization.

protection profiles   Implementation-independent collection of objectives and requirements for any given category of products or systems that must meet similar needs.

protocol data unit   Bundle of data organized for transmission containing control information, the data itself, and error detection and correction bits.

protocol services   Services that define the rules and standards that enable communication between computers over the Internet.

Public Key Infrastructure (PKI)   Public key, known to anyone, and a private key held in secret by a single individual.

R

random memory   Computer's primary working and storage area.

read up, write down   Computer security model in which subjects cannot read objects of lesser integrity and subjects cannot write to objects of higher integrity.

real memory   Refers to when a program has been given a definite storage location in memory and direct access to a peripheral device.

record retention process   Refers to how long transactions and other types of computerized or process records should be retained.

reference monitor   Software model or abstract machine that mediates all access from any subject to any object and cannot be bypassed.

resource protection   Needed to protect company resources and assets such as modem pools, network routers, storage media, and documentation.

ring of trust   Trust in a system moves from the outside to the inside in a unidirectional mode.

role-based access control (RBAC)   Groups users with a common access need.

S

sanitization   Technique of permanently removing information from media.

secondary storage   Nonvolatile storage format in which application and system code plus data can be stored when the system is not in use.

separation of duties   Security practice in which no one person in an organization has the ability to control or close down a security activity.

sequential storage   Computer memory that is accessed sequentially (magnetic tape).

session laws   Laws arranged by subject matter in the order, or session, in which they are enacted.

shared secret cryptography   When the same key is used to both encrypt and decrypt messages; also called symmetric key cryptography.

smart card   Resembles a regular payment (credit) card with the major difference being that it carries a semiconductor chip with logic and nonvolatile memory.

standard   What is needed for a system or process to be considered secure.

subjects   People or other systems that are granted a clearance to access an object within the information system.

substitution   Basic method of disguising messages whereby letters are replaced by other letters and/or symbols.

symmetric key cryptography   When the same key is used to both encrypt and decrypt messages; also called shared secret cryptography.

T

target of evaluation (TOE)   Refers to the product or system under evaluation.

token   Mechanism that generates passwords that change every minute or so.

trade secret   Usually denotes a patent in process or an unofficial and legally unprotected idea.

trademark   Any word, name, symbol, or device or any combination thereof that an individual intends to use commercially and wants to distinguish as coming from a unique source.

Transmission Control Protocol (TCP)   Connection-oriented protocol utilizing the TCP/IP stack to provide reliable, full duplex communication between hosts.

transposition   Basic method of disguising messages whereby letters are rearranged into a different order.

Trusted Computer System Evaluation Criteria (TCSEC)   Formal computer security testing model originated in the United States in the early 1980s.

trusted computing base (TCB)   The totality of protection mechanisms within a computer system including hardware, firmware, and software.

trusted recovery controls   Ensure that security is not breached when a computer system crashes.

V

volatile memory   Complete loss of any stored information when the power is removed.

Part 2
References

Amoroso, Edward. 1994. *Fundamentals of Computer Security Technology.* Upper Saddle River, NJ: Prentice Hall

Anderson, Ross. 2001. *Security Engineering: A Comprehensive Guide to Building Dependable Distributed Systems.* New York: John Wiley & Sons

Anonymous. 1998. *Maximum Security, A Hacker's Guide to Protecting Your Internet Site and Network,* 2nd Edition. Upper Saddle River, NJ: Sams Publishing

Atkins, Derek, Buis, Paul, Hare, Chris, Kelley, Robert, Nachenberg, Carey, Nelson, Anthony B., Phillips, Paul, Ritchey, Tim, and Steen, William. 1996. *Internet Security Professional Reference.* Upper Saddle River, NJ: New Riders Publishing

Bates, Regis J., Gregory, Donald W., and Ranade, J. 1998. *Voice and Data Communications Handbook.* New York: McGraw-Hill

Brenton, Chris. 1999. *Mastering Network Security.* Alameda, CA: Sybex

Cobb, Stephen. 1996. *The NCSA Guide to PC and LAN Security.* New York: McGraw-Hill

Cooper, James Arlin. 1989. *Computer and Communications Security: Strategies for the 1990's.* New York: McGraw-Hill

Daley, Bill. 2005. *Computers Are Your Future.* Upper Saddle River, NJ: Prentice Hall

Dam, Kenneth W., Lin, Herbert S. 1996. *Cryptography's Role in Securing the Information Society.* Washington, DC: National Academy Press

Deborah, Russell, and Gangemi, G. T. 1991. *Computer Security.* Sebastopol, CA: O'Reilly & Associates

Denning, Dorothy. 1998. *Information Warfare and Security.* Boston: Addison-Wesley

Denning, Dorothy, 1997. *Internet Besieged.* Boston: Addison-Wesley

Ermann, M. David, Williams, Mary B., and Shauf, Michele S. 1997. *Computers, Ethics, and Society,* 2nd Edition. Oxford: Oxford University Press

Escamilla, Terry. 1998. *Intrusion Detection, Network Security Beyond the Firewall.* New York: John Wiley & Sons

Fites, Phillip E., and Kratz, Martin P. J. 1996. *Information Systems Security: A Practitioner's Reference.* London: International Thomson Computer Press

Ford, Warwick. 1994. *Computer Communications Security: Principles, Standard Protocols and Techniques.* Upper Saddle River, NJ: Prentice Hall

Garfinkel, Simson, and Spafford, Gene. 1996. *Practical Unix & Internet Security.* Sebastopol, CA: O'Reilly & Associates

Garfinkel, Simson, and Spafford, Gene 1997. *Web Security and Commerce.* Sebastopol, CA: O'Reilly & Associates

Ghosh, Anup. 1998. *E-Commerce Security: Weak Links, Best Defenses.* New York: John Wiley & Sons

Gollmann, Dieter. 1999. *Computer Security.* New York: John Wiley & Sons

Harley, David, Slade, Robert, and Gattiker, Urs. 2001. *Viruses Revealed.* New York: McGraw-Hill

Held, Gilbert. 1994. *Understanding Data Communications,* 4th Edition. Upper Saddle River, NJ: Sams Publishing

Hutt, Arthur E., Bosworth, Seymour, and Hoyt, Douglas B. 1995. *Computer Security Handbook,* Third Edition. New York: John Wiley & Sons

Icove, David, Seger, Karl, and VonStorch, William. 1995. *Computer Crime: A Crime Fighter's Handbook.* Sebastopol, CA: O'Reilly & Associates

Kabay, Michel E. 1996. *The NCSA Guide to Enterprise Security: Protecting Information Assets.* New York: McGraw-Hill

Klarder, Lars. 1997. *Hacker Proof: The Ultimate Guide to Network Security.* Ashburton, Devon, UK: Jamsa Press

Konicek, Joel, and Little, Karen. 1997. *Security, ID Systems and Locks, The Book on Electronic Access Control.* Burlington, MA: Elsevier Butterworth-Heinemann

Kovacich, Gerald L. 1998. *Information Systems Security Officer's Guide, Establishing and Managing an Information Protection Program.* Burlington, MA: Elsevier Butterworth-Heinemann

Krause, Micki, and Tipton, Harold F. 1999. *Information Security Management Handbook, Fifth Edition.* Boca Raton, FL: Auerbach Publications

Krist, Martin A. 1999. *Standard for Auditing Computer Applications.* Boca Raton, FL: Auerbach Publications

Kruegle, Herman. 1995. *CCTV Surveillance, Video Practices and Technology.* Burlington, MA: Elsevier Butterworth-Heinemann

McClure, Stuart, Scambray, Joel, and Kurtz, George. 1999. *Hacking Exposed: Network Security Secrets and Solutions.* New York: Osborne/McGraw-Hill

Merkow, Mark, and Breithaupt, James. 2001. *Complete Guide to Internet Security.* New York: AMACOM Books

Merkow, Mark, and Breithaupt, James. 2004. *Computer Security Assurance Using the Common Criteria.* Clifton Park, NY: Thomson Delmar Learning

Morrison, Perry, and Forester, Tom. 1995. *Computer Ethics,* 2nd Edition. Cambridge, MA: MIT Press

Nichols, Randall K., Ryan, Daniel J., and Ryan, Julie. 2000. *Defending Your Digital Assets Against Hackers, Crackers, Spies, and Thieves.* New York: McGraw-Hill

Nichols, Randall K. 1998. *ICSA Guide to Cryptography.* New York: McGraw-Hill

Northcutt, Stephen. 1999. *Network Intrusion Detection: An Analysis Handbook.* Old Tappan, NJ: New Riders Publishing

Oaks, Scott. 1998. *Java Security.* Sebastopol, CA: O'Reilly & Associates

Parker, Donn B. 1998. *Fighting Computer Crime: A New Framework for Protecting Information.* New York: John Wiley & Sons

Ranum, Marcus. 2003. *The Myth of Homeland Security.* New York: John Wiley & Sons

Rubin, Aviel D., Geer, Daniel, and Ranum, Marcus J. 1997. *Web Security Sourcebook, A Complete Guide to Web Security Threats and Solutions.* New York: John Wiley & Sons

Russell, Deborah, and Gangemi, G. T. 1991. *Computer Security Basics.* Sebastopol, CA: O'Reilly & Associates

Schneier, Bruce. 1995. *Applied Cryptography: Protocols, Algorithms, and Source Code in C, Second Edition.* New York: John Wiley & Sons

Schneier, Bruce. 1995. *E-Mail Security: How to Keep Your Electronic Messages Private.* New York: John Wiley & Sons

Schwartau, Winn. 1999. *Time Based Security.* Seminole, FL: Interpact Press

Scott, Charlie, Wolfe, Paul, and Erwin, Mike. 1999. *Virtual Private Networks, 2nd Edition.* Sebastopol, CA: O'Reilly & Associates

Simonds, Fred. 1996. *Network Security, Data and Voice Communications.* New York: McGraw-Hill.

Singh, Simon. 1999. *The Code Book: The Secret History of Codes & Code-breaking.* London: Fourth Estate Limited

Slade, Robert. 1996. *Computer Viruses: How to Avoid Them, How to Get Rid of Them, and How to Get Help, 2nd Edition.* New York: Springer

Smith, Martin. 1993. *Commonsense Computer Security, Your Practical Guide to Information Protection, 2nd Edition.* New York: McGraw-Hill

Summers, Rita C. 1997. *Secure Computing: Threats and Safeguards.* New York: McGraw-Hill

Tiwana, Amrit. 1999. *Web Security.* Burlington, MA: Elsevier Butter-worth-Heinemann

Umbaugh, Robert E. 1997. *Handbook of IS Management, 5th Edition.* Boca Raton, FL: Auerbach Publications

U.S. Department. of Health, Education and Welfare. 1973. Records, Computers, and the Rights of Citizens, Report of the Secretary's Advisory Committee on Automated Personal Data Systems, p. viii

Walrand, Jean. 1998. *Communications Networks, A First Course, 2nd Edition.* New York: McGraw-Hill

Winkler, Ira. 1999. *Corporate Espionage: What It Is, Why It Is Happening in Your Company, What You Must Do About It.* New York: Prima Publishing

Wood, Charles C. 1999. *Information Security Policies Made Easy.* Houston: Information Shield